America's Asia

America's Asia

RACIAL FORM AND AMERICAN LITERATURE, 1893–1945

Colleen Lye

PRINCETON UNIVERSITY PRESS
PRINCETON AND OXFORD

Library of Congress Cataloging-in-Publication Data

Lye, Colleen, 1967–
    America's Asia : racial form and American literature, 1893–1945 / Colleen Lye.
      p. cm.
    Includes bibliographical references (p.) and index.
    ISBN 0-691-11418-8 (acid-free paper) — ISBN 0-691-11419-6 (pbk. : acid-free paper)
      1. American literature—20th century—History and criticism.   2. American literature—19th century—History and criticism.   3. Asia—Foreign public opinion, American.   4. Asia—Relations—United States.   5. United States—Relations—Asia.   6. Asian Americans in literature.   7. Orientalism—United States.   8. Orientalism in literature.   9. Asia—In literature.   10. Race in literature.   I. Title.

PS159.A85L94   2004
810.9′325—dc22   2004042066

British Library Cataloging-in-Publication Data is available

A portion of chapter 2 was previously published as "American Naturalism and Asiatic Racial Form: Frank Norris's *The Octopus and Moran of the* 'Lady Letty.'" Reprinted from *Representations*, no. 84, by permission of the University of California Press. © 2004 by The Regents of the University of California.

In loving memory of my grandmother,
Chia Guat-Goh

Contents

Acknowledgments   ix

INTRODUCTION
The Minority Which Is Not One   1

CHAPTER ONE
A Genealogy of the "Yellow Peril"   12

Jack London, George Kennan, and the Russo-Japanese War

CHAPTER TWO
Meat versus Rice   47

*Frank Norris, Jack London, and the Critique of
Monopoly Capitalism*

CHAPTER THREE
The End of Asian Exclusion?   96

The Specter of "Cheap Farmers" and Alien Land Law Fiction

CHAPTER FOUR
A New Deal for Asians   141

*John Steinbeck, Carey McWilliams, and the Liberalism of
Japanese-American Internment*

CHAPTER FIVE
One World   204

*Pearl S. Buck, Edgar Snow, and John Steinbeck on Asian
American Character*

Notes   255

Works Cited   301

Index   329

Acknowledgments

THIS BOOK WOULD NOT EXIST were it not for the presence of mentors, colleagues, and friends. Its beginning as a dissertation was overseen by Gayatri Chakravorty Spivak, who demanded, in equal measure, both risk taking and rigor. The late Michael Rogin was a fundamental influence on the book's historical passions. Conversations over many years with Ling-chi Wang animated its political spirit. The critical intelligence of David Palumbo-Liu, Priscilla Wald, Sam Otter, Cathy Gallagher, Chris Connery, and Rob Wilson steered the project to fruition.

As a graduate student, I was deeply fortunate to have met Jean Howard, Joe Cleary, Rebecca McClennan, Sanjay Krishnan, and Donna Jones, who provided formative examples of intellectual and political commitment. Naifei Ding and Kuan-Hsing Chen have sustained my faith in the continuing possibilities of public intellectual life. As a junior faculty member at Berkeley, I received an ongoing education from colleagues Stephen Best, Kevis Goodman, and Chris Nealon who, though diverse in their specializations, share a fierce dedication to their craft. In his example of social engagement, Chris has also nourished my hope for community. Sam Otter set the standard for professional integrity.

In whole or in part, this book has also benefited from the comments of Mitch Breitwieser, Anne Cheng, Marcial Gonzalez, Dori Hale, Abdul JanMohamed, Kerwin Klein, Josephine Park, Michael Rubenstein, Sue Schweik, and Bryan Wagner. Sharon Marcus read repeated drafts and offered valuable encouragement. For their indispensable support at various critical moments, I am grateful to Sunil Agnani, Rakesh Bhandari, Bob Bruman, Judith Butler, Bianca Calabresi, Robby Cohen, Janadas Devan, Melanie Hahn, Geraldine Heng, Ru Hong, Becky Hyman, Qadri Ismail, Shuchi Kapila, David Kazanjian, Song-Nae Kim, Franco Moretti, Meaghan Morris, Janet Roitman, Somini Sengupta, Pat Sieber, Françoise Verges, Milind Wakankar, Tim Watson, Michelle Wolfson, Sau-ling Wong, Paola Zamperini, and Jia Zhen.

My research was aided by an extraordinary group of undergraduate and graduate students. Misa Oyama, Christine Hong, and Paul Stasi were indefatigable archivists and brilliant interlocutors. Joann Virata, Alec MacDonald, Jean Gier, Ruth Jennison, and Hoang Phan provided further assistance. Throughout the publishing process, I have been guided by the savvy intelligence of my editor at Princeton, Mary Murrell. The steadfast support of Jeff Knapp and Janet Adelman, successive chairs of the English department during my time as a junior professor, helped me secure the resources I needed to complete the book.

Funding for my research was generously provided by the Townsend Humanities Center at Berkeley, the Hellman Family Faculty Research Fund, the UC Berkeley Career Development Grant and Humanities Research Fellowship Program, and the Social Science Research Council–MacArthur Program in International Peace and Security. For their help in locating materials, I would like to thank the research librarians at UC Berkeley's Bancroft Library and Giannini Foundation of Agricultural Economics, and the Special Collections and University Archives of the Greene Library at Stanford University.

Diverse opportunities to test my ideas have made this a stronger book. I thank the remarkable student and faculty members of the 2001–2002 Townsend Fellows Group at Berkeley; the faculty associated with the Center for Cultural Studies at UC Santa Cruz, who repeatedly invited me to share my work with them; the participants in the conference on "Borderlands/Bordercrossings" organized by the Asia/Pacific Institute at Duke University, especially Leo Ching and Sucheta Mazumdar; Daniel Monk, who invited me to speak at the conference on "Aesthetic States" at SUNY Stonybrook; Clifton Spargo, who invited me to join a panel at the Modern Languages Association in Chicago; the members of the Bay Area Labor History Workshop, especially Lisa Rubens; the members of the workshop on "Post-Nationalist American Studies" at the Humanities Institute at UC Irvine; and the highly engaged participants in the ninth and tenth annual meetings of the SSRC–MacArthur Program in International Peace and Security, including Susanne Rudolph, Peter Katzenstein, Rob Walker, Achille Mbembe, Julia Dvorkin, and Lynn Eden. I wish to thank my students, too, for the part they've played, knowingly and unknowingly, in stimulating my thinking.

The book is dedicated to my grandmother, who believed in me all of her life. There are others as well for whom no words of gratitude can suffice: Cathy Gallagher, for offering me her warmest friendship as well as her immeasurable wisdom; Randall Alifano, for teaching me some fundamentals I ought to have learned long ago; my parents, for their willingness to wait so long for me to finish; Linda Lye, for being my best friend as well as my sister; and David Pickell, for helping me always remain true to myself.

America's Asia

The Minority Which Is Not One

SOON AFTER I STARTED TEACHING at Berkeley, I was invited to speak in a large student-organized undergraduate English lecture course called "Other Voices," a course that exists primarily to introduce lower-division students to minority faculty on the campus. It was suggested by the course facilitators that I talk about my research interests, but that in preparing my remarks I bear in mind that I would be the only Asian American guest that semester. For the students' reading assignment I chose a short poem by Mitsuye Yamada, "Looking Out":

It must be odd
to be a minority
he was saying.
I looked around
and I didn't see any.
So I said
Yeah
it must be.[1]

I framed my presentation around a reading of the poem, calling attention to the disjuncture between seeing and being seen, to the ambiguity in the speaker's response (registered in the gap between sight and speech) that could indicate either a reluctant acquiescence to social construction or an ironization of the other's perception. I wanted the students to wrestle with the misunderstanding that arises in the poem: is Yamada playing on the gap between external and internal perception or between different kinds of social perception held by the two people in the poem. I wanted the students to reflect on the kind of sociological and psychic construction signified by the term "minority" and its relation to questions of visibility, representation, identification, and subjectification. Yamada's poem helped me to kick off an introductory lecture on a central problematic of Asian American identity: the invention of "Asian American" as a pan-ethnic construction by the yellow power movement of the 1960s, the coalitional character of its structuration, and its limitless tendency toward fragmentation.

Addressing undergraduates on the topic of ethnic identity is always tricky because it involves a double move—one of raising basic historical awareness and, at the same time, of demonstrating the constructedness of that history. In the case of the term "Asian American," this double move (empirical and critical) is particularly complicated by a persistent heterogeneity effect, which generates continual confusion about who Asian American describes or leads to repeated angry notices of "forgotten" Asian Americans.[2] Either the category will not hold or it demands constant supplementation. At the end of my forty-five-minute presentation, an African American student raised his hand and asked the following question: Does the lecturer in fact consider Asian Americans to be a minority group? In his view, Asian Americans are white. At the University of California, where the abolition of affirmative action by state Proposition 209 was just then raising the specter of the resegregation of state higher education for African Americans, Latinos, and Native Americans—but not Asian Americans—there are no politically comfortable responses to this perception, which arises from a sense that the group has somehow been exempt from the historical laws of systemic racial subordination. Even when the existence of historical discrimination is acknowledged, there is a sense that the minority status of Asian Americans is likely to be somehow temporary and that in a world of unfettered competition Asian Americans are likely to rise to the top of the socioeconomic order. Both opponents and critics of Proposition 209 at the time predicted that the law would primarily benefit Asian Americans, whose relative share of the admitted pool of students was bound to increase. Yet to some extent, this pitting of black and brown against yellow was a replay of an admissions scandal in the 1980s in which the university administration had resorted to the (illegal) application of differential criteria for whites and Asian Americans, in the belief that without them Asian Americans were likely to displace whites.

This book explores the history of such perceptions and beliefs. The eccentricity of "Asian American" to the minority discourse of liberal multiculturalism has an origin in the historical identification of an Asian presence in the United States with the social costs of unbridled capitalism. The prominent post-1960s representation of Asian Americans as nonminorities, or as "minorities, yes; but oppressed, no,"[3] forms the kernel of what has come to be called the "model minority" myth—the representation of Asian Americans as capable of upward mobility without the aid of state-engineered correctives. For reasons having to do with the necessarily international context of Asian American racialization, as this book will show, the domestic signification of Asian Americans has its counterpart in the global signification of Asia. While the new visibility of an Asian-American middle class was being used to support a neoconservative-led "retreat from race" in domestic public policy, the expanding economies of the newly industrialized countries of East Asia—the "Asian

Tigers"—were being heralded by free market critics of import-substitution as evidence of the conceptual and political "end of the Third World."[4]

In contrast to the nineteenth-century European object of Edward Said's influential study,[5] the Orient of the American century—at least where it has predominantly tended to mean East Asia rather than the Middle East—has signified an exceptional, rather than paradigmatic, Other. This exceptionalism of America's Asia, resting upon a putatively unusual capacity for economic modernity, extends to moments when the affect of the racial discourse has been hostile ("yellow peril") as well as admiring ("model minority"). Scholars have lately begun to observe the definitional continuities between the "negative" and "positive" stereotypes of Asia and Asian Americans and to question a strictly evolutionary view of the relationship between them.[6] Nevertheless, much work remains to be done in pursuing the historical, theoretical, and rhetorical specificity of American Orientalism.[7] If, as Said has argued, the primitivist relegation of the Other was a crucial aid to European colonial rule, how are we to understand the ambivalent presentation of the economic modernity of America's Asia? When did this discourse arise? Where in American culture is it to be found? What was its social meaning? What can the form taken by America's Asia tell us about the distinctions of American empire from other historical examples of empire? What strategic lessons do the aesthetic properties of the racial form impart for Asian American cultural politics?[8] These are some of the questions this book sets out to answer.

As indicated by the title of a 1993 anthology of recent Asian American writing, *Charlie Chan Is Dead*, the quest for Asian American literary self-expression in the 1990s continued to be premised upon the negation of Oriental stereotypes, even as a new generation of writers and critics sought to break with a confining cultural nationalism.[9] In their introduction to the inaugural anthology of Asian American literature, published in 1974, writers Frank Chin, Shawn Wong, Jeffrey Paul Chan, and Lawson Fusao Inada declared a war on stereotype that engendered a fractious quarrel among Asian American writers themselves about the ubiquitous reach of an internalized Orientalism.[10] Parallels between intra-ethnic attacks on Asian American and black women writers have also exposed the gendered dimensions of the rhetoric of cultural authenticity, though admittedly it has been easier to criticize masculinism than to resist appealing to authenticity, whose legitimating power continues to be felt in our era of post-identity politics through the sanction of a strategically invoked essentialism. Perhaps one way to address our acute anxieties about our inability to represent ourselves without somehow being represented would be to pay more attention to the workings of representation, from which there is no easy escape.

Just as self-representation has not brought freedom from stereotype, empirical rebuttals to media distortions have not succeeded in making the "model minority" go away. The disappointments of trying to dispel myth with reality afford more than a reminder of the general operation of language.[11] They return us to the material conditions of an ideological construct, even as they require us to be cognizant of the fact that there can be no return to historical origins that is not mediated by our present standpoint. A historical approach to racial representation has the advantage of being able to account for the specificities of different marginalized groups, whose stereotypical attributes are located in the shifting dynamics of social relations and social conflicts. A historical approach also helps us to maintain a healthy skepticism toward the "evidence of experience"[12] and toward the temptation to think that the articulation of minority subjectivity can be separated from the history of racialization or can express an independent rejoinder to it. At the risk of ignoring new social history's call to document subaltern experience and agency,[13] this book returns to the study of racism and the power of racialization's effects.

The book's title pays respect to the 1971 collection of essays edited by Edward Friedman and Mark Selden and dedicated to the critical spirit of the Committee of Concerned Asian Scholars, whose call for scholars to "investigate the relationship between knowledge and power, between intellectual creation in America and political destruction in Asia" was occasioned by the crisis of U.S. military involvement in Vietnam.[14] "Asia is America's," Friedman and Selden write,

> . . . in the sense that we impose American categories to describe, evaluate and direct Asian experience. Our cultural chauvinism might mainly provide material for humorous self-analysis were it not for the overwhelming explosion of American economic and military might throughout Asia. For Asia is America's in this second tragic sense that American power has channeled, distorted, and suppressed much that is Asia.
>
> This book explores the dynamic and destructive interaction between American perceptions and American power in the making and unmaking of contemporary Asia. Our focus is at once Asia and America. For the investment of immense intellectual and material resources in American military adventures in Asia does more than deprive us of resources vitally needed at home. It simultaneously strengthens the very repressive tendencies in our society most prone to crush aspirations for freedom, autonomy and equality in America. (vii)

In directing our attention to the relationship between knowledge and power, and the impact of U.S. discourses about Asia on U.S. society, my book shares with its titular predecessor a common political purpose. Departing from the critical strategy of the original, however, this book does not seek to replace racism's projections with the "truth" of Asian or Asian American reality. Instead, taking seriously the difficulties of unthinking Eurocentrism,[15] it attempts a critical intervention through an attentive observation of racism's object, generating a contextualized description that incorporates a strong interpretation of race's social meaning. As such, this book does not aim at a comprehensive account of Asian American representation. It is a genealogy of the surfacing in American history of a particular, paradoxical racial form, with a view toward explaining its predominant ideological usages and mythic persistence into the present.

· · ·

Traditionally, "yellow peril" and "model minority" images have been identified with turn-of-the-century anti-Asian agitation and the civil rights struggles of the 1960s, respectively, and are thought to mark the evolutionary journey of the Asian immigrant from rejection to domesticated acceptance. But yellow peril and model minority are best understood as two aspects of the same, long-running racial form, a form whose most salient feature, whether it has been made the basis for exclusion or assimilation, is the trope of economic efficiency. Long before the stereotype of the hardworking and self-sufficient Asian American came to be the bane of post-1960s activists seeking federal aid for their communities, this figure already manifested itself in the late-nineteenth-century rhetoric of both those who opposed and supported Chinese "cheap labor" immigration.[16] Focusing on American culture in the first half of the twentieth century, during which Asian immigrants were officially classified as "aliens ineligible to citizenship," the book traces present-day attributes of stereotypical Asian American character to the earlier characteristics of Asiatic racial form and examines the historical conditions of their making, the social terrain of their emergence, and the representational material of their composition.

If one goal of the book is to discover a structural pattern to the perplexing shifts in United States–Asian relations over the course of the twentieth century, another is to convey the historicity of the life of social forms. The quest to identify the enduring features of race needs to be qualified by an appreciation of the vast difference between the limitations of post-1960s multiculturalism and the radical informality of Asian immigrant existence in the prewar period. Over the course of the twentieth century, many significant rights have been gained—not least the rights and privileges of U.S. citizenship. Responding to the neglect of Asian American subjects by mainstream U.S. historiography, Asian American studies initially tended to reverse the omission by essentializing U.S. history as the story of racism.[17] In the late 1980s and 1990s, under the influence of Ernesto Laclau and Chantal Mouffe's critique of the concept of totality and an Americanized British cultural studies, the prevailing tendency was to conceive of racial formation as a supplement to class analysis and to make the need to account for race a prime motivation for inaugurating a post-Marxism.[18] Ironically, despite Asian American studies' preoccupation with the category of race, its analytic emergence as a means of explaining—or explaining away—historical causation has in some ways exacerbated its dematerialization and mystification.[19] A strictly culturalist emphasis on the persistent symbolization of the permanent alien obscures the significance of the differences between varying modes of legislated racism. On the other side, our perception of a shift from an era of official Asian exclusion to one of Asian assimilation has been heavily reliant on legal history to supply our sense of racialization's periodization. This may be seen in our inability to decide on a dividing point: 1943 (when the 1882 Chinese Exclusion Act was repealed), 1952 (when the McCarran-Walter Act removed the prohibition on naturalization for other Asian nationalities), or 1965 (when immigration quotas for Asian countries were placed on an equal basis with those of others).[20] We still do not sufficiently understand the conditions of possibility for the legal formalization of the Asian American, (which was not a single event), and the social relations that mediate the cultural persistence of the notion of Asian unassimilability.

What preparations existed for the categorical emergence of the assimilable Asian immigrant in the latter half of the twentieth century? The first part of the book examines the objectifying scenes of the alien's sighting at the turn of the century; the second part of the book turns to the processes of naturalization in the 1930s that helped pave the way for the postwar personification of the alien. In both historical endeavors, developments in American literary naturalism and companion movements of social reform played a major role. Why naturalism? Why social reformism? Historians have demonstrated the extent to which Progressive reform, Populist, and trade union movements in the late nineteenth and early twentieth century helped to effect Asian exclusionism as a national immigration policy.[21] Equally, the decision of Franklin Roosevelt's administration to intern more than 110,000 Americans of Japanese descent is a well-known irony of liberal history, though it is undertheorized as such. From Progressivism to the New Deal, this book traces the logical continuities between liberal reform and U.S. policies on Asia and Asian Americans. By focusing on American literature of the early twentieth century to forge these links, it also stakes a claim for how cultural study enriches historical understanding.

Two unresolved areas within the historiography of Asian exclusion in particular are engaged by this book. The first is the limited ability of a scapegoat theory of racism to explain why it was specifically Asian immigrants who served as the "indispensable enemy" for the organizing of the white, predominantly Irish, working class on the West Coast. Why was it that in calling for the immigration exclusion of Asiatic labor, unionists and reformers imagined that they were striking at monopolists? Here literary reading aims to generate a textured sense of the strength and routes of ideological persuasion. The second has to do with ongoing debates about the causes of Japanese American internment and the relative paucity of material explanations for such a costly and unprecedented order. By attending to internment's discourse of assimilation rather than exclusion, my study invites us to consider the productivity of what we have grown accustomed to seeing as the teleological expression of an earlier era's prejudices. An integration of internment into the context of the social redresses of the New Deal as a whole prevents us from homogenizing different kinds of historical racisms and helps to underscore the darker, disciplinary work involved in Americanization. Here, readings of 1930s cultural texts fill in for what are often considered the lost years of Asian American history.

Film, television, and drama have provided more obvious venues for the study of Asian stereotype in American culture than has literature, where the problem at first appears to be one of absence rather than hyperbole, exclusion rather than caricature.[22] We easily recognize the presence of race in visual media because of its identification with a set of phenotypical traits and a relative absence of interiority. Yet the visuality of Asiatic racial form has a distinctive character insofar as the sense of its deceitfulness or mystery always points to the presence of something not shown. To put it another way, we recognize the Asiatic as a figure for the unrepresentable. Yet how is the unrepresentable to be visualized? Does it have a human body? If not, what shape, as a whole or in part, does it take? These are the kinds of questions that are bypassed if our study of racial figuration begins by supposing the anthropomorphism of Asiatic form. They also happen to be questions that centrally preoccupy American literary naturalism, whose well-known subordination of individual agency to the determinations of force reflects its interest in the effects of commodification at a time of heightened public discussion about the growth of monopoly power. Naturalism provides examples of American literature's most relentless effort at figuring the unseen power of social abstraction. As a cultural discourse, naturalism presents a rich site for the exploration of the representation of class relations.

The literary history of the naturalist novel includes among its essential historical conditions of emergence in the late nineteenth century the rise of mass-circulation dailies, professional muckraking, and various urban reform movements, in particular, Progressivism. American naturalism has been understood to share with the Progressive gaze a documentary interest in exposing the misery of capitalist life while implying its inevitability. My approach to American naturalism follows Georg Lukács's critique of French naturalism as a reflection of the reification of bourgeois existence, exemplified by what Lukács considered to be its inhumanity of subject matter and presentation.[23] I also argue that American naturalism represents a failed critique of capitalism, but that the evidence of this lies in its tendency toward racialization, or the reification of social relations into physiological forms, or types. Readings of racial representation in American naturalism, therefore, do not here serve the purpose of remarking textual attitudes of superiority or exclusion. They provide a way of recovering the trace of the social relations that race marks. Through observations of shifts in naturalism's representation of Asiatic figures to exemplify the promise and peril of free market expansion, my study seeks to reveal one systematic way in which the critical potential for revealing the injustices wrought by globalization in the American context has been short-circuited.

As a nonpsychological brand of realism and for reasons related to its general treatment of character, naturalism provides a significant venue for Asiatic racial form. On the one hand, the literature of naturalism is attracted to representing the socially unrepresented. On the other, naturalism's indifference toward character distinctions reflects a preoccupation with difference at the level of the typical rather than the individual.[24] While an interest in sociological marginality certainly lends naturalism to the representation of race more readily than other modern realisms, its way of engaging difference is particularly pertinent to Asiatic form. A kind of difference that is marked by the lack of difference between individuals, the Asiatic names a paradigmatic social figure in naturalism's taxonomy. Moreover, the deconstruction that naturalism's indistinctions enact—what Walter Benn Michaels has shown to be naturalism's penchant for demonstrating the identity of opposites—describes a logic that distinguishes America's Asia from other sets of race relations.

To the extent that American universality depends upon the possibility of assimilation, there is always also the danger of discovering aliens in our midst, or the wholesale possibility of American takeover by aliens. The undecidable relationship between linked opposites in naturalism— whether human and animal or animal and machine—mirrors the oscillations in the logic of America's Asia between the radically split alternatives of total identity and total conflict. The possibility of a yellow peril takeover is a variant of naturalism's degenerationist imagination, in which hierarchies are always reversible.

It is well recognized that the period associated with naturalist developments in American realism was also the period of the "incorporation of America."[25] What are the implications of this for the literary study of racial representation in that period? In general we tend to think of race as an antebellum legacy—as the evidentiary trace of how class and caste were once equivalent in a slave-owning society. The mode of incorporation of Asian migrant labor into the United States forces us to grapple with the fully industrial modernity of race. Similarly, the rise of U.S. imperialism in the late nineteenth century did not merely entail the extension overseas of an earlier logic of territorial expansion; it was part of a new stage of world capitalism, in which the domination of monopoly finance coincided with the imperial scramble for international markets. The "Asiatic" discloses the ways in which U.S. colonial and race relations are marked by power's more totalizing reach and increasing abstraction in the twentieth century. As Martin Sklar writes of the oft neglected links between U.S. foreign policy in Asia and the "corporate reconstruction of America": "'Missionary' diplomacy was the very essence of rationalism in the strict sense of modernization theory. It was the other side of the same coin occupied by 'dollar diplomacy' and struck in the name of the Open Door and the new capitalist imperialism."[26] The making of Asiatic racial form, therefore, is necessarily a story about the international context in which American race relations take shape.

. . .

Starting from the era when U.S. industrialization began to depend upon the importation of transnational Asian labor and capital expansion into the Asia-Pacific, America's Asia reflected an antinomian character. Its accelerated process of industrial development and labor efficiency at times promised to extend the American frontier—the premier symbol of the putative freedom from class society afforded by the United States—indefinitely into the twentieth century. Alternately, it threatened U.S. social stability with forecasts of declining wages, mass unemployment, and political authoritarianism. The remedy and exacerbation posed by America's Asia to the crisis of the closing of the frontier entwined the emergence of Asiatic racial form with the intensification of commodity relations and capital's global expansion. The legal designation of Asian immigrants as "aliens ineligible to citizenship" reflected the freighting of Asiatic racial form with an abiding tension between U.S. national interests and capital's transnational movement, between the exceptionalist dream of the identity of nation and capital logic and the nightmare of their nonidentity.[27]

The American identification of the Asiatic as the sign of globalization was not arbitrary; it was rooted in the material history of U.S. relations with East Asia.[28] The antinomies of Asiatic racial form reflect the pattern of a modernizing China and Japan changing places as U.S. friend and enemy. At any given point in this history, their opposite status was necessary to the maintenance of U.S. security. Indeed, as my examination of writings from Jack London to Pearl S. Buck will show, the incipient "yellow peril" refers to a particular combinatory kind of anticolonial nationalism, in which the union of Japanese technological advance and Chinese numerical mass confronts Western civilization with a potentially unbeatable force—regardless of whether this specter is meant to encourage a U.S. policy of aggression or accommodation. Before being idiosyncratically generalized to other ethnic Asian groups, the hegemonic construction of Asians—as civilizational threat or as testimony to the universal arrival of American democracy—paradigmatically derived from interlinked Chinese and Japanese examples. China's and Japan's modes of late modernization dually involved trans-Pacific labor migrations and an anomalous inscription into the game of "great power" diplomacy that sought to pit one against the other to neutralize their combined potential. As such, "China" and "Japan" provided examples of a high-civilizational discourse whose intersection with the problematics of late modernization uniquely marked off East Asia from other regions of the non-Western world.

A U.S. "empire without colonies," or what in the post–World War II period came to be generalized as the neocolonial paradigm, was arguably pioneered through U.S. Open Door policies in East Asia, which sought the benefits of "free trade" without the burden of political governance.[29] In the twentieth century, U.S. power was not grounded in the control of limitless territory but primarily around integrated territories of production.[30] Where a European Orientalism had disclosed the discursivity of nineteenth-century, territorial-based colonialism, America's Asia thus reflected the discursivity of a neocolonialism that installed the East as a Western proxy rather than antipode.[31] At the end of the nineteenth century, the ascension of the United States to world power through the expansion of its Asian frontier presented split alternatives between the whole world becoming American and an apocalyptic clash of civilizations. The staging of a Japanese economic miracle formed a crucial element in the extension of U.S. influence, even as its success threatened to exceed U.S. dominance.[32] By the middle of the twentieth century, the cultural production of the Asian American enabled by U.S. political investments in Chinese national independence still indicated the ongoing intimacy between Asiatic racial form and the contradictions of U.S. globalism, if of a different kind. Where the unassimilable alien had emerged as an effect of misdirected resistances to U.S. economic dependency on transnational migrant labor and foreign markets, the cultural production of the Asian American became a feature of U.S. geostrategic necessity: postwar multiculturalism and the hegemony of a Pax Americana went hand in hand.

The story begins at the turn of the century with Jack London's and Frank Norris's exclusionist critiques of monopoly capitalism and ends, at mid-century, with Pearl S. Buck's and John Steinbeck's universalizing remedies to the agricultural crisis of the Great Depression. In a fifty-year period, a vision of California as a post-frontier about to be engulfed by coolie hordes and Oriental despotism is succeeded by premonitions of a Pacific Rim utopia, where the local and the global could be made happily coextensive. Until the literary birth of Buck's and Steinbeck's model economic characters, the Asiatic figures of early-twentieth-century American literature (despot, coolie, mask) referred not to persons but to a host of modernity's dehumanizing effects (laboring conditions, group entities, corporations). Yet these figures were the also ancestors of today's stereotypical Asian American. The initial textual presence of Asiatic racial form as an economic trope helps to explain the primarily economic themes of Asian American racial representation. That a genealogy of Asian American stereotype is discernable in the historical failures of class critique, in the end, I hope, helps shed some light on the painful historical divorce between the homely longings of Asian immigrants and the utopian aspirations of actually existing American liberal reform movements, from Progressivism to affirmative action.

CHAPTER ONE

A Genealogy of the "Yellow Peril"

JACK LONDON, GEORGE KENNAN, AND
THE RUSSO-JAPANESE WAR

THE IDEA OF PACIFIC TRAVEL launched Jack London's literary career, though in his earliest stories Asia itself is never reached. London's first published work, which won a local prize for best descriptive article, is "Story of a Typhoon off the Coast of Japan" (1893), but despite the specificity of the title, this shipboard adventure could have taken place anywhere. A second tale, "The Run Across" (1895), which this time presents the gentle face of nature, is set in the middle of the Pacific, on the passage between San Francisco and Japan; its action ends, however, before the ship reaches its destination. In these early works, "Japan" simply designates the outer horizon of an expansive oceanic world, which is London's stage for adventure. Only the third story in London's Pacific voyage series, "Bonin Islands: An Incident of the Sealing Fleet of '93" (1897), accords Japan an active narrative presence.[1]

These tiny islands, which lie in the open ocean about six hundred miles south of Japan, are described by London as one of the "glorious garden spots of nature" and still almost entirely "unknown" to the (Western) world, even though they have already been twice colonized by Japan (59). With the most recent emigration of several thousand Japanese from "the crowded cities of Yokohama and Tokio," and the "last retreat" of the "savage natives" "before the progressive Japanese," the islands have become a "civilization in miniature that is on par with Japan itself" (60).[2] Except for the biannual arrival of a government steamer from Japan, bearing new emigrants and fresh supplies, the Bonin Islanders live in isolation from the outside world. The story's dramatic action begins with the arrival of a fleet of rough-and-ready American seal hunters. The surprising twist is that it is the seamen, not the islanders, who suffer most in the encounter.

In the seamen's need for food and supplies, the islanders see a golden opportunity. "Prices went up faster than a hot air balloon" (61). After the price of beef reaches absurd heights, the Americans go on a day-long rampage, capped with a "rousing Virginia Reel" held "right in front of the Governor's mansion" (62). Despite this complete breakdown of local authority, however, "the sailors committed no indignities or outrages, and the natives, finding them to be a peaceable, law-abiding people, became reconciled to their presence and were glad that such good customers still remained. Prices soon dropped to their normal level, and complete serenity was restored" (62). All is resolved in the end through the seamen's reasonableness and self-restraint. Some time after the incident, the schooners depart just as suddenly as they had arrived, leaving the islanders to "smack their lips appreciatively over that by-gone event, and jingle the foreigner's gold in their girdle" (62–63).

The narrative encounter between Americans and Japanese in this story marks a moment of uneven development. On the one hand, the Japanese belong to a primitive mindset: they are "easy going, phlegmatic" (61) innocents unused to the sight of foreign sails and prone to weaving history into myth. American arrival serves them a "thorough awakening" (61). The ease with which an entire way of life can be disrupted by a mere handful of maritime renegades, moreover, is a familiar ideologeme of the early colonial encounter. On the other hand, instead of exchanging too much for too little, these "natives" prove to be natural merchants; far from being insensible to the value of gold, they are its irrational hoarders. Not only are the exchange relations of the colonial encounter reversed, they are also accelerated. The Japanese leapfrog from bartering to speculating. American intrusion accidentally launches the islanders into "hitherto unknown channels of commerce" (61), yet this course of development is also portrayed as inevitable. The Japanese come to a realization of "the great possibilities and profits to accrue from their intercourse with strangers" (61) because they "are shrewd speculators—it seems inherent" (61). The story suggests to us how the phenomenon of Japan's rapid modernization complicates turn-of-the-century stagings of the Asia-Pacific scene of "original contact."

The author of widely disseminated portrayals of the Alaskan wilderness, Hawaii, and the high seas at the turn of the twentieth century, Jack London is viewed by critics as a prime example of U.S. colonial discourse in the period of the "closing of the frontier" and America's spectacular ascension to imperial power on the Pacific.[3] London's Yukon provides an untamed and rugged setting for trials of manhood, and his Polynesian paradise offers, among other promises, the recovery of a noble indigenous culture unspoiled by civilization. London's fictionalized journeys into the "remote and internal colonies" of America suggest the renewal afforded by adventuring in the "wilds" of America's newest possessions.[4] London's native inhabitants of the Northland and the Polynesian Pacific are variations upon the noble savage—primitive figures who embody many admirable warrior qualities but who are obviously doomed to extinction by the coming of the "white man."[5] His "Asiatic" marks the reversal and displacement of this primitivist discourse. This can be seen even more clearly in London's dystopian futurist writing.

Partway through London's famous sociofantasy *The Iron Heel* (1908) the apocalyptic struggle between global capitalism and international socialism comes to a temporary halt in a moment of nationalistic insistence. Until this point in the novel, national conflicts have been portrayed as the ideological mystification of class contradiction and the imperialist competition for world markets. Now, however:

> The British Empire was falling apart. England's hands were full. In India revolt was in full swing. The cry in all Asia was "Asia for the Asiatics!" And behind this cry was Japan, ever urging and aiding the yellow and brown races against the white. And while Japan dreamed of continental empire and strove to realize the dream, she suppressed her own proletarian revolution. It was a simple war of the castes, Coolie *versus* Samurai, and the coolie socialists were executed by the tens of thousands. Forty thousand were killed in the street-fighting of Tokio and in the futile assault on the Mikado's palace. Kobe was a shambles; the slaughter of the cotton operatives by machine-guns became classic as the most terrific execution ever achieved by modern war machines. Most savage of all was the Japanese Oligarchy that arose. Japan dominated the East, and took to herself the whole Asiatic portion of the world-market, with the exception of India.
>
> England managed to crush her own proletarian revolution and to hold on to India, though she was brought to the verge of exhaustion. Also she was compelled to let her great colonies slip away from her. So it was that the socialists succeeded in making Australia and New Zealand into cooperative commonwealths. And it was for the same reason that Canada was lost to the mother country. But Canada crushed her own socialist revolution, being aided in this by the Iron Heel. At the same time, the Iron Heel helped Mexico and Cuba to put down revolt. The result was that the Iron Heel was firmly established in the New World. It had welded into a compact mass the whole of North America from the Panama Canal to the Arctic Ocean.
>
> And England, at the sacrifice of her great colonies, had succeeded only in retaining India. But this was no more than temporary. The struggle with Japan and the rest of Asia for India was merely delayed. England was destined shortly to lose India, while behind that event loomed the struggle between a united Asia and the world.[6]

London does not further unfold the outcome of this East-West struggle, but since the presumption of his narrative is that the events being recounted constitute the prehistory of an already achieved socialist utopia, we can only assume that this menace is some time safely put to rest. Why does a world war with Asia—which has all the aura of a civilizational clash—interrupt London's narrative of international class struggle? What is its relevance to London's socialist revolutionary project? And why does London refer to the Japanese oligarchy, among all the advanced capitalist powers, as the "[m]ost savage of all"?

The Iron Heel is London's best-known work of revolutionary socialism, though it was not until after the red scare of 1919 that the novel achieved a belated vogue for having prophesized the ferocity of counterrevolution.[7] At the time of its publication, the electoral legitimacy of American socialism was at its historical peak, and the novel was widely denounced for its endorsement of violence, even by leftist presses.[8] In retrospect, the literary weaknesses of *The Iron Heel* were perhaps symptomatic of London's relationship to his milieu (he was immensely popular among working-class readers, but much less so among socialist intellectuals) and of the theoretical incoherence of the American socialist movement as a whole, which in 1900 split into one Socialist Labor Party and two Socialist Democratic Parties.[9] The Socialist Labor Party of California, to which London belonged, was isolated from the national movement by factionalism within national party headquarters and from local working-class solidarity by its own antipathy to Chinese and Japanese laborers.[10] In general, London scholars who focus on his socialism treat his racist statements as ideologically aberrant, while those who analyze his racial discourse do not take his socialism very seriously or are uninterested in questions of political theory.[11] There is also a biographical tendency in London scholarship that seeks either to reduce his politics to personal hypocrisy or, more recently, to read his fiction in terms of a politics of literary professionalization.[12] I am interested in treating London as a symptomatic figure of American radicalism whose class critiques often took a racializing route. In particular, London's inconsistencies exemplify the contradictory extrication of California socialism in the discourse of Asian exclusion. In writing and in oratory, London was indefatigable on two topics: the certainty of revolution and the coming of the "yellow peril." What was their connection?

References to the "yellow peril" are scattered throughout his works, but two essays are dedicated to the subject: "The Yellow Peril" (1904) and "If Japan Wakens China" (1909). Both reveal the extent to which the turn-of-the-century Asiatic threat rests upon a combinatory notion of Japan and China.[13] Japanese and Chinese civilizations are depicted by London as, in some ways, barbarian, but they share an unusual capacity for sudden development. The examples of Japanese modernization that have "repeatedly surprised the world" (JWC 360) present a wider epistemological challenge—one that potentially recodes a perpetually "petrified" China into a "sleeping giant" about to be awakened. London suspects Japan of a "colossal Napoleonic dream" of conquest (JWC 361) whose untold consequences are magnified by China's sheer numerical abundance:

> The menace to the Western world lies, not in the little brown man [the Japanese], but in the four hundred millions of yellow men [the Chinese] should the little brown man undertake their management. The Chinese is not dead to new ideas; he is an efficient worker; makes a good soldier, and is wealthy in the essential materials of a machine age. Under a capable management he will go far. The Japanese is prepared and fit to undertake this management. Not only has he proved himself an apt imitator of Western material progress, a sturdy worker, and a capable organizer, but he is far more fit to manage the Chinese than are we. (YP 281)

At its core, London's "yellow peril" concerns Japan's inevitable mediation of the modernization of China. Although London appears to agree with Hegel that the potential for historical development is originally Western in spirit, the transmissibility of this potential to Japan (and from Japan directly to others) presents dangerous possibilities for a future non-Western world order: "[W]hat if Japan awakens China—not to our dream, if you please, but to her dream?" (JWC 361).

The binary opposition between "East" and "West" assumed by the "yellow peril" also therefore entails a binary opposition between the key identities that compose the "East." The possibility of a Western exclusion effected by the rise of East Asia rests on the notion that Japan and China are two opposite types of civilization. In London's racial taxonomy, the Japanese are "a race which has always despised commerce and exalted fighting" (YP 279), while the Chinese are a race perfectly suited to industry. No worker "in the world can compare" with the Chinese, and the Chinese merchant is "not to be bullied into lowering his price" (YP 274, 274–75). At a time when American politicians and intellectuals from Theodore Roosevelt and Brooks Adams to Homer Lea were lamenting America's transformation into a "business civilization" at the expense of its "warrior" qualities,[14] the potential combination of a martial Japan and an industrious China appeared to symbolize a magical and maximal merging of what in America were seen to have become polarized tendencies. In Roosevelt's admonishments to the nation to lead a "strenuous life" and London's trials of manhood in the wilderness, a spirit of the frontier—at once uniquely American and essentially Teutonic—presented an antidote to the overgrown corporate trust and ingrown city, both alien to the organic spirit of the nation. The yellow peril fantasy is thus to be located within this constellation of discourses linking decline and industrialization, and a heroic age with the spirit of the frontier, which seized on Asia as both heir and rival to a decaying West.

That a discourse of Western decline was articulated through the opposite and combined categories of "Japan" and "China" seems to me not accidental. In part, "Japan" and "China" represented polarized civilizational tendencies insofar as the very form of U.S. expansion into East Asia appeared to detach "industrialism" from "militarism." The simultaneous appearances of the "yellow peril" and the so-called "warrior critique of business civilization" at the end of the nineteenth century marked the departure of post-frontier economic expansion from the activity of territorial settlement, the heightened abstraction of U.S. colonial form in the era of imperialism, or monopoly finance capitalism.[15] In East Asia, the United States staked a role for itself as a player in world politics through the recognition of states that could be relied upon to serve U.S. economic interests in the liberalization of free trade. In cultivating relationships with China and Japan, U.S. strategy was not direct territorial occupation, but a proxy political relationship.

The "yellow peril" articulates the numerical power of a "Chinese" mass with a miraculous "Japanese" developmental capacity. An expansive logic of racialization would, over the course of the twentieth century, join others (Koreans, Indians, Vietnamese, and Cambodians—but not Filipinos) to the category, but the racial form takes its incipient outlines from U.S. neocolonial relations with China and Japan beginning in the late nineteenth century. The specificity of the mode of East Asia's incorporation into U.S. global modernity situated the temporality of Asiatic discourse differently from other racial discourses. In London's writing, "East" and "West" did not exist in strict, hierarchized relation. In that the "yellow peril" carried the sense that "under a capable management the [Chinese] can be made to do anything" (YP 277), it could operate subjunctively to disturb the indicative order. In showing signs of Orientalized stagnation, a Western progressive spirit suddenly revealed a vulnerability to degeneration. In possessing the potential for a great leap forward, the Asiatic subject was constituted as bearing certain essential qualities that allowed it to awake, fully fledged, into capitalist modernity.

London's article "The Yellow Peril" was written in Manchuria while he was on assignment there in 1904 to cover the Russo-Japanese War for the *San Francisco Examiner*. It was after his return from the Russo-Japanese front that, at a meeting of the Oakland chapter of the Socialist Party, London uttered that famous sentence, "I am first of all a white man and only then a Socialist!"[16] What part did the representational project of U.S. geopolitics play in diminishing the space for leftist dissent from the American Federation of Labor's official position of Asian immigration exclusion? Conversely, why did London's political critique of monopoly finance capitalism, formulated in *The Iron Heel*, become a vehicle for the "yellow peril" lesson he distilled from the coverage of Japan's conflict with Russia? The discursive emergence of one important version of the "yellow peril" from the occasion of the Russo-Japanese War suggests an integral relation between a strangely reversible racial boundary and the contradictory character of U.S. monopoly finance capitalism.[17]

This chapter will examine London's newspaper coverage of the Russo-Japanese War for its significant differences from the consensus of American press coverage. A respected expert on czarist Russia, George Kennan covered the war for *The Outlook* magazine to greater contemporary acclaim and administrative influence. Despite their weaknesses as journalism, however, London's war writings were the source of a racial articulation that proved to have a more enduring cultural legacy. Reading London and Kennan together allows us to see how the Western exemplification of Japan and the dystopian fantasy of an inevitable East-West war were logical antinomies. First, I will provide some historical context for U.S.-East Asian relations in the period. Then I will compare the representations of a war that did not directly involve the United States as a military player, but that was nonetheless crucial to the staging of America's identity as a world power through its brokerage of a new political order in East Asia.[18] In recent years interest in the "cultures of United States imperialism" has importantly directed our gaze to the military events involving U.S. annexation and occupation of Cuba, Puerto Rico, and the Philippines, though in ways that perhaps overestimate the continuities between the imperialism of the late nineteenth century and an earlier mode of continental conquest and colonial occupation.[19] The spectacle of Russian-Japanese conflict, I suggest, entwined allegories of modernization and race in ways particularly illustrative of imperialism in the age of monopoly finance capitalism and the distinctive representational paradoxes of America's Asia. Finally, the chapter will turn to London's socialist fiction and reflect upon its particular hospitality to "yellow peril" fantasy.

The U.S.-Asian Frontier

The "yellow peril" has been part of a Western image of China ever since Genghis Khan's invasion of Europe.[20] However, in the mid-nineteenth century, a historically specific rhetoric of the "yellow peril" entered into transnational circulation with the onset of Asian labor migration to white settler colonies around the Pacific Rim. In numbers estimated to have exceeded those leaving Europe, millions of Indian and Chinese laborers—the vast majority young men—traveled as contract laborers to various destinations in the tropics during the nineteenth century. The gold rushes of the 1850s drew tens of thousands of Chinese to California and Australia, and others were imported to build continental railroads in the United States and Canada. Japanese emigration began in the 1880s, and Indians, mostly Sikhs from Punjab, started arriving in North America after the turn of the century. Asian exclusion leagues were formed soon after the immigrants arrived, and by 1900, the governments of Canada, the United States, New Zealand, and Australia had all enacted legislation to restrict or prevent the entry of non-whites. All of them discriminated against Asians already resident.[21]

One of the major challenges to the British empire as a whole was the Dominion exclusion of the citizens of Japan, which, starting in 1902, was Britain's military ally and the strongest naval power in the Pacific region. The Dominion policy of exclusion "opened the sharpest divergence yet experienced between Britain and the settler societies" and forced Australia and Canada into a foreign policy of their own "in the name of popular sovereignty and nationhood" (Offner, 235–36). On this front, the white settler colonies of the Pacific region looked instead to the United States for leadership. At the height of international tensions between the United States and Japan in 1907 and amid tabloid declarations of imminent war, the route of the "Pacific cruise" traced by the U.S navy around the Pacific, wildly applauded by the residents of California and Australia for "putting Japan in its place," can be seen as the mapping of a new imaginary international space that, in an era of officially promulgated globalization, would eventually come to be known as the "Pacific Rim."[22] A central condition of this space, of which the United States appointed itself custodian, was the refraction of "white republican" virtue through the problematic of Asian exclusion.

As the historian Alexander Saxton has documented, an Asian exclusion movement arose alongside the U.S. labor movement and was very likely foundational to it.[23] Viewed within the regional context of Pacific Rim white settler nationalisms, a discourse of Asian exclusion was also part of the process of U.S. nation-formation. The Asian exclusion question magnifies the centrality of nationalist rhetoric to a strategy of legitimation which sought to make "unionism" synonymous with "Americanism."[24] By 1907 the legislative achievements of the Asian exclusion movement could provide key testimony to the American wage earner's emergence as a subject of national history.[25] Established in 1886, the American Federation of Labor (AFL) upheld its policy of Asian exclusion until the 1930s, which effectively kept Asian workers outside the structure of the mainstream American labor movement for half a century.

Extending Stuart Hall's theorization of the relationship between race and class to the settler societies of the Pacific, we could say that Asian exclusionism was a modality in which white working-class identity was lived in this region.[26] This is not to neglect the fact that Asian exclusionism was also a state policy, a set of official legal practices that accompanied the development of capitalism in the period from 1882 to World War II.[27] Asian exclusionism did not actually keep Asians out; it merely guaranteed a disempowered class of laborers, "aliens ineligible to citizenship," whose ongoing employment in a variety of industries and serial replenishments would suggest its necessity to the mode of accumulation in that period.[28] The basis and consequences of that necessity continue to present a rich area for study.

In his important analysis of how slavery stalled the development of a radical critique of wage labor, David Roediger shows that by the point of black emancipation a sense of whiteness was already too important— politically and culturally—to the white U.S. worker to be dislodged. If in the antebellum period radical labor and proslavery arguments often came together in the use of the term "white slavery"—constituting not an act of solidarity with the slave, but the call to end the inappropriate oppression of whites—then after the war a growing popular sense of whiteness served to hold together a very diverse white working class.[29] Similarly, we might ask, what was the effectivity of labor market segmentation in the postbellum period, which on the West Coast was abetted and enforced by a group of discriminatory laws known collectively as Asian exclusion? It is certainly true that a lexicon of blackness was often the richest available fund from which nativist portrayals of Asians drew and that the Chinese arrived in the 1850s in the midst of, and were inserted into, a race debate already underway.[30] Nevertheless, the fact that transnational migrant labor—of which Asians became emblematic—was seen as a future substitute for a waning system of coercion suggests a different form of racialization. The Asiatic helped constitute whiteness in ways different from, if overlapping with, chattel slavery.[31]

In the case of the Asiatic, racial difference was more strongly entwined with questions of national identity, whose ambiguity reflected the strong influence exerted by U.S. state-to-state relations with China and Japan. The turn toward Asia as a source of imported cheap labor was one dimension of the United States's growing interest in the region as a new frontier of investment, trade, and other economic opportunities. The phenomenon of Asian exclusion was therefore a facet of U.S. expansion, just as the overt engagement of military imperialism in the 1890s marked continuities and discontinuities with earlier principles of New World colonization. The United States in the late nineteenth century may have been one among several regional settler nationalisms securing their borders against an inflow from Asia, but it was also a rising imperial power engaged in the task of prying open the markets and resources of China. Acquisition of the Philippines, in the argument of the pro-annexationists, was often framed as a valuable stepping-stone to China.[32]

Increasingly, as the century drew to a close with the completion of the "scramble for Africa," China acquired a mythic status as the last vast stretch of territory not yet directly colonized. In 1901 Brooks Adams expressed the popular view that "[f]rom the days of Alexander downward, the dream of every dominant Occidental race has been to overrun the East; but with the exception of England, who invaded India from the sea, no Western people have ever established a foothold in the recesses of Asia."[33] Even earlier, China had already been constructed as the determinant of Europe's fate. In an 1853 critique of England's Opium Wars against China, which the British fought to maintain the opium trade, Karl Marx wrote: "It may seem a very strange, and a very paradoxical assertion that the next uprising of the people of Europe, and their next movement for republican freedom and economy of government, may depend more probably on what is now passing in the Celestial Empire,—the very opposite of Europe,—than on any political cause that now exists."[34]

For Marx, the contraction of what had the potential to be the largest market in the world could well accelerate the English industrial crisis. "Under these circumstances, as the greater part of the regular commercial circle has already been run through by British trade," Marx wrote, "it may safely be augured that the Chinese revolution will throw the spark into the overloaded mine of the present industrial system and cause the explosion of the long-prepared general crisis, which, spreading abroad, will be closely followed by political revolutions on the continent."[35] Although writing in 1900 and from a quite different ideological position, the American naval officer and historian Alfred T. Mahan shared with Marx a certain pivotal positioning of Asia. "For the problem of Asia," Mahan concluded, "is a world problem, which has come upon the world in an age when, through the rapidity of communication, it is wide awake and sensible as never before." Its future loomed large because of the "rapid pronounced transfer of the world's ambitions and opportunities to Asia."[36] For the major architect and proponent of American naval power in the Pacific, the "problem of Asia," or "the Asiatic question," was the question of who was to exert the most influence over the "teeming yet stationary" mass on the Asian mainland. Imperialist powers continually accused one another of jeopardizing the balance of world power by signing advantageous deals with the weakened Chinese government.

Viewed by a wide variety of intellectuals and statesmen as the fulcrum upon which Western rivalry turned, China was thus the site for the engineering of what came to be called the Open Door policy, which the United States negotiated not *with* China, but *about* China with other

Western powers.[37] The policy aimed to secure the openness of China to equal opportunity for exploitation among all Western powers and denied the right of monopoly to any one party. Representing the interests of an imperial power entering upon a global terrain already well mined by European rivals, Secretary of State John Hay's "Open Door Notes" declared an American defense of the democratic principles of "free trade" against tyranny by "European monopoly." As a defender of the Chinese nation-state against territorial division by European powers, the United States could portray itself as a friend of the Chinese empire.[38] Using a weakened Chinese state to hold open the door and ostensibly critical of territorial forms of occupation, U.S. policy in China, formalized in 1899 though borrowed from earlier British commercial representatives in China, anticipated the neocolonialism of the post–World War II era. As Mahan explained, American international power offered a new model of nonterritorial economic supremacy—a "painless" economic expansion without the responsibility of colonies.[39]

Western imperial rivalry in Asia was particularly complicated by the participation of Russia, with its ambiguous cultural coding, and by the emergence of an expansionist Japan. Throughout the nineteenth century, British-Russian imperialist rivalry in Asia provided the conditions for Britain's longstanding Orientalist representation of Russia as archaic, irrational, and despotic.[40] Although control of Central Asia was much of the focus of Britian's "Great Game" with Russia, late-nineteenth-century Russian expansion through a "Far Eastern corridor" to Manchuria also came to threaten British interests. With the signing of the Anglo-Japanese alliance in 1902, Britain sought from Japan a check against Russian expansionism in the Far East. Meanwhile, a Russian discourse of the "yellow peril," directed against its East Asian neighbors, began to develop as the regime pursued a policy of eastward expansion, with, for instance, the issuance of a racially discriminatory czarist ordinance of 1882 barring non-Russians (Chinese and Koreans) from acquiring land in Siberia.[41] An 1895 painting commissioned by Kaiser Wilhelm II entitled *The Yellow Peril*, which depicted Confucius astride a dragon menacing the cities of Europe, marked German participation in the rhetoric. The painting was understood to refer to the danger posed to Western civilization by China's large population; however, in the context of the Kaiser's covert backing of Russian interests against British ones, the invocation of a vast Asiatic population was widely interpreted to include Japan in an Asiatic bogey.[42]

Despite the increasing thematization of East-West conflict in world politics, disparate geopolitical interests undermined the certainty of any line that could be drawn between "East" and "West." In the 1904–1905 Russo-Japanese War, contradictory applications of the "yellow peril" were such that while the czarist government tried to bill itself as "the pro-tagonist of the West" in a "battle of the white race," Anglo-American war publicists favored the view of Japan as a modern nation doing battle with an "Oriental Despotic" power. In the Anglo-American version of the "yellow peril," the threat of Russian expansionism in China was fig-ured as a merger of two Oriental despotisms, a combination of Russian bureaucratic corruption and Chinese officialdom, which "likewise lived on bribery and protected itself by lying."[43]

The Western imperialist struggle *for* Asia was therefore itself depicted as a struggle *between* East and West.[44] In the writings of Mahan and the British geographer Halford Mackinder, the British-Russian rivalry sym-bolized a contest between the essential capabilities of "seapower" versus "landpower."[45] For Mahan, Britain and Russia represented principal, an-tipodal influences; however, whereas seapower had historically proved it-self superior to landpower, the great landmass of Asia and its shared land border with Russia potentially limited seapower's influence in this crucial region. Building upon Mahan, Mackinder's theory located a Russian "heartland" within the inner reaches of the Asian continent, a histori-cally repeated source of peril to the European "rimland" nations. Who-ever controlled the heartland, in Mackinder's view, controlled the world.[46] In both Mackinder and Mahan, the "East" was thus to be dis-covered within the inner recesses of Asia's great landmass, which in this sense figured the space furthest from Western Europe. Though both Mackinder and Mahan may have registered alarm over the prospect of Japanese rule over Asia, the geographical imagination they shared pictured Japan as the mirror image of Britain's island empire.[47] Anglo-American magazines and journals at the turn of the century were filled with indignation at the abuses of Russian absolutism and autocracy, while the territorial claims of Japan, often dubbed the "Britain of the East," were rationalized on the basis of Japan's relative modernity.[48]

Although U.S. and British geopolitical interests in East Asia were largely coordinated and allied, American coverage of the Russo-Japanese War registered a separate ambivalence toward Japan that reflected the specificity of the United States's geographical location.[49] Japan's strength afforded a crucial buttress against Russian expansion, which could oth-erwise close the door on free trade in China, but a strong Japan might also rival the United States for dominance in the neighborhood of its frontier. As scholars have shown, the emergence of the United States as a world power was choreographed on the Pacific stage.[50] Though the Japanese-Korean Exclusion League had already formed by 1902, the pe-riod after Japanese military victory over Russia marked the escalation of exclusionist rhetoric against Japanese in the United States, exemplified by the San Francisco school board's move to segregate Japanese from white students and the Japanese-American war scare of 1907.[51] In the warnings issued by prophets of American-Japanese race war like Homer Lea, projections of the "yellow peril" foretold a direct military invasion of America.[52]

The American fantasy of a militarily "Rising Sun" in the aftermath of the Russian war is not, of course, separable from the discourses of "Asiatic invasion" that accompanied the phenomenon of Chinese labor migration from its earliest inception. Just as twentieth-century Asian exclusionism created an expanding pool of Asiatics that included more and more groups of different national origin, the Japanese "yellow peril" of this moment grafted the prospect of military conquest onto a preexisting economic one (Okihiro, *Margins and Mainstreams*, 132). But it was starting in the 1890s that the so-called "Asiatic question" arose to designate an issue of special national import in public debate. The imperialist moment of the "yellow peril" is best distinguished from its earlier incarnations by its intimacy with the dream of America's arrival on a world scale. For the utopian vision of U.S.-Japan relations, George Kennan's writings provide us with a foremost example.

GEORGE KENNAN AND THE RUSSO-JAPANESE WAR

George Kennan was America's leading expert on the Russian empire, who first made his name in the 1880s publicizing the cruel injustices of the Siberian exile system. He was also a member of the national circle of "Republican elite" and a Progressive reformer who crusaded against urban political machines and organized labor. Theodore Roosevelt himself considered Kennan to be one of the most influential journalists of his time; during the Russo-Japanese conflict he used Kennan as a personal courier to the Japanese prime minister Katsura Taro.[53] As a correspondent for *The Outlook*, Kennan wrote articles that ran under the series title "The Story of Port Arthur," which reported on the movements of the Japanese Third Imperial army as it lay siege to the Russian-held position at Port Arthur on Liaotung Peninsula, Manchuria. The events surrounding Port Arthur—beginning with the sinking of the Russian fleet and ending with the fall of the fort to the besieging army—commanded public fascination in the United States and spectacularized Japan's new military formidability. Kennan's coverage of the Port Arthur siege endowed the conflict with even further significance. Paralleling the events of Russia's war in Manchuria with chronicles of internal political suppression, Kennan depicted the conflict between Russia and Japan in terms of an allegorical confrontation between autocratic and democratic forms of government in the Northeast Asian region.

Kennan undercuts the inevitability of Orientalist designations, yet preserves Orientalism's dichotomizing logic. His observation of how the Japanese troops avoid unnecessary risks, for example, pokes at stereotypes of Oriental fatalism: As a matter of fact, [Japanese courage] does not differ in any essential respect from Anglo-Saxon courage. . . . It is no more 'fatalistic' than the courage of the three hundred who rode 'into the mouth of hell' at Balaclava, or of the men who charged up Kettle Hill and the battery-crowned heights of San Juan."[54] Kennan attributes Japanese military success to the mastery of the principles of scientific management and compares Japanese and American organization to the latter's consistent disadvantage. Kennan repeatedly enjoins his American readers to "take notes" on and a "few lessons" from the Japanese army's treatment of the sick and wounded and from their "systematic and efficient methods . . . in the handling, transportation and storage of heterogeneous supplies."[55] The requirements of military victory are the same qualities that guarantee success in business: "[S]obriety, self-control, studious habit and strict attention to duty are among the factors that determine results."[56]

Japan's describability by the abstract principles of scientific modernity works to establish Japanese affinity with the West. Praising the repast served by the Japanese army as entirely "creditable to the chef of a metropolitan club,"[57] Kennan revels in the abundance of "hot veal cutlets, breaded, delicious omelets, fresh bread and butter" (VIII 178) that testify to Japanese cosmopolitanism. Waiting in Dalny for permission to proceed to the front, Kennan observes the contrast between "the large, clean and luxurious staterooms of the Tosa-maru" and a "dirty, abandoned Russian office" (I 527). The Japanese government generously supplies bibles to its soldiers, whereas "[o]ne would not find the local chief of transportation in Russia supplying soldiers with New Testaments. . . . Books have a tendency to 'excite' the mind'" (I 524). The subject of the Japanese state is presented as a modern citizen, whose display of initiative and dependence reflects the difference between modern patriotism and despotic "dependency and submission." The Japanese soldiers act "bravely and intelligently, upon their own initiative"[58] while the Russian soldiers are "less enterprising and self-confident" (VI 995).

Kennan's pro-Japanese war coverage strikes so triumphal a tone overall that his occasional lapses into melancholy bear examining. In "Life in the Japanese Trenches," Kennan is guided to the edge of Japanese-held territory, where from within a trench abutting the southern wall of the Russian fort the Japanese are able to gaze upon Russian territory. Likewise, Russian sharpshooters are "intently watching Japanese lines."[59] Kennan is warned against the risk of taking a direct look at the Russian position through the chinks and loopholes in the sandbag walls but in the end cannot resist doing so:

[T]he first thing I saw was the blood-stained corpse of a handsome young Russian soldier lying on the ground, with his face fully exposed, only fifteen or twenty feet away. In order to lessen the risk of looking through the chinks, the Japanese put up behind them, in particularly dangerous places, light steel shields, pierced with a narrow slit for the eyes; but I noticed that most of the soldiers used, in preference, the larger and more convenient openings left here and there in the wall of sand-bags.

One of the strangest and gloomiest places to which we were taken in front of Sungshushan was a bomb-proof casemate overlooking the moat. The only entrance to it was a rectangular hole in the front parallel, and as I crawled into it on my hands and knees, it looked to me like a low, dark and rather extensive cellar or cave. Its ceiling of massive timbers was only three feet above its earthen floor, so that one could barely sit up in it, and all the light that it received came in through the entrance hole and through a narrow, horizontal slit in the opposite wall. The floor was covered with the bodies of sleeping soldiers, and beyond them, on the side next the fort, stood a machine gun and a box of ammunition. Two soldiers were sitting on their heels at the sides of this gun and were conversing in low tones as they watched the moat through the narrow slit. There was probability of a sortie at that time of day; but the Japanese never relax their vigilance, and these men were prepared to sweep the moat with a hail of bullets if the Russians should attempt to cross it. The gloomy twilight of the low, subterranean chamber; the sleeping soldiers, who did not wake even when we crawled over their bodies; the machine gun with its muzzle opposite the narrow, rectangular embrasure; and the crouching men in loose sand-bag jackets, watching the moat, would have made a dark but striking picture of war. (X 426)

What explains the unusual sense of gloom? What makes this subterranean chamber one of the "darkest" places he visits? There are a number of possible readings, but most striking here is the visual juxtaposition of the handsome young corpse of the Russian and the sleeping Japanese soldiers. Both scenes have an illicit, homoerotic quality—in the one case because of the interdiction against looking, and, in the other, because it involves pushing through a "rectangular hole" into a dark, intimate space. The living Japanese soldiers are corpselike in their sleep, as against the Russian corpse which, despite its blood-stained condition, Kennan finds to be handsome. In contrast to the Russian body lying "fifteen or twenty feet away" that Kennan can look at but not touch, there are so many Japanese bodies in the way that they must be "crawled over." The Russian's face is "fully exposed," but our view of the Japanese is of a mass of bodies covering the floor. Nor are the faces of the two waking soldiers visible, since they are intently watching the moat through a "narrow slit" (the image of the "narrow slit" is repeated three times). Somehow, despite Kennan's greater proximity to the Japanese, he is able to make out detailed Russian features, but where the Japanese face should be there is only a "narrow slit." Kennan's view onto the Japanese body situates him at once (physically) close and (visually) far away. The "narrow slit" is, of course, what the Japanese would look like when viewed through the embankment from the other side. Perhaps it is the unexpected assumption of a Russian perspective that makes the otherwise pro-Japanese writer feel gloomy.

Feelings of discomfort return on other occasions of visual impairment. On looking down from the 229-meter summit upon the field of action, Kennan finds that "of the Japanese I could see nothing whatever. They had put a good many new batteries in position, but if they had any troops massed in the advanced trenches and parallels, I could not discover them, nor could I hear any crackling of rifles to indicate that infantry was engaged."[60] The failure of the correspondent to visualize and represent the Japanese army's offensives curiously parallels the "failure of Russians to discriminate between operations that were really threatening and dangerous and movement that had little if any importance" (XI 624). The reporter himself feels menaced by constant bombardment of long-range missiles whose approach cannot be seen:

> [T]he swelling crescendo of the approaching missile, the impossibility of seeing or avoiding it . . . make an impression upon the imagination that is out of all proportion to the real peril . . . you are conscious that if you try to avoid it by running this way or that, you may throw yourself directly in front it. You therefore await the result with a feeling of blended helplessness and terror. (III 784)

Of the war's technological innovations, Kennan is disappointingly consigned to observing his own internal experience, though he persistently tries to capture an objective visual record.[61] Even though it is Russian shelling that terrorizes, the quality of invisible approach is a military strategy that in the overall account of the war comes to be associated with the Japanese. A comparison of Russian moats and Japanese trenches suggests that "in the art of concealment the Japanese are past-masters" (III 782). In a separate piece outside the Port Arthur series, Kennan concludes from his examination of a captured Russian battleship that the weakness of its design lies in the conning tower's "observation slit," which would allow a single Shimose projectile to enter and "kill or disable every officer in that most important and vital part."[62] Kennan's war account plays upon themes of Russian blindness and Japanese penetration—the ability of the

Japanese to render ineffectual the resources of Russian vision through the art of entering spaces unseen.

Even a text as pro-Japanese as is Kennan's seems to slip between the subject-position of the American correspondent and the military position of the besieged Russians. Such a movement would appear to remap the war through a racial identification against the grain of geopolitical alignment. On one level, Kennan's text might be read as evidence of the subversion of national interest by the parochialism of racial feeling. On another level, we might take the political unconscious of Kennan's account to reflect a quite strategic realpolitik, to disclose the compatibility of an Asian exclusionist imaginary with U.S. geopolitical realism uncertain as to whether the space of Manchuria might not potentially, some day, be "American." His text reveals how the very terms through which Japan is valorized as a necessary U.S. ally also problematize that alliance.

The destabilizing consequences wrought by Kennan's overlaying of the discourse of modernity with the discourse of Orientalism—the inscription of difference into the logic of universalism—become clearer when we examine how difference is figured through spatial organization. The otherness of Russia, for instance, is to be detected in the irrational architectural style of the previously Russian-occupied city of Dalny: "The streets, gutters, and sidewalks were admirably planned and honestly made; but the houses, with their endlessly varied and often eccentric architecture, look as if they had been erected for the purpose of making the utmost possible show" (I 528).

Japanese design, by contrast, is both "practical and imaginative" (III 778). Kennan muses over a simple rock garden Japanese soldiers have constructed at the site of an open army camp, which he interprets as a gesture toward forming "a connecting link—a sort of bridge for the imagination—between themselves and their far distant homes" (III 778). Next to the rock garden is also "an earthen model, or reproduction in high topographical relief, of the hills and forts that formed the eastern sector of the enemy's defense line" (III 778). Whether as a fanciful "bridge for the imagination" or as a practical aid to military strategy, rock garden and topographical model possess a use value discernible to Kennan, a value based upon their instrumentality. The unreadability of Russian architecture places it on the level of pure ornamentality, which makes it exotic. The grandiose construction of Dalny, "which resembles a little the city of Washington" (I 528), displays similitude to and distance from the image of a modern capital city—enough to suggest an architecture of power but one that ultimately veers toward an imperial irrationality.

Japanese space, on the contrary, suggests a different kind of city. The trenches Kennan describes so attentively are a "great system of saps, traverses, gulches and parallels which extends, like an immense maze, from the village of Shuhishi to the moat of the Russian fort" (X 422). Within this labyrinth, the American journalist experiences a feeling of severe disorientation: "[T]he impossibility of seeing out, and the constant zig zagging back and forth, soon deprive you of all sense of direction; and at the end of ten minutes you feel as much bewildered and lost as if you were wandering without a guide, in an unknown part of Canton" (X 422). The trenches, which serve as "kitchens, bathing-places, barber shops, and reading rooms" but which also contain "graveyards, flower gardens and telephones"(X 423), reflect not a suspension of city life but a continuance of it. If the trench permits "the activities of normal life [to be] carried on just as they would have been on a Tokyo street" (X 422), the Asian city, whether Canton or Tokyo, seems to be indissociable from modern urban space as such. Though remote, the Japanese trench is like a world-class city in which the best of all things is to be had: tenderloin steak "broiled and seasoned to perfection" as good as the Tokyo Imperial Hotel's; French fried potatoes "as hot, brown, and crisp as if they had just come from the kitchen of the best restaurant in New York"; "European bread and butter"; "'cookies' from London"; and the most "perfect toast" available in the Far East (X 427).

An association between Asian and urban space is suggested earlier when Kennan invokes New York to convey the density of Chinese quarters in a house in Liukang: "As the whole western half of the house was given up to Mr. Curtis and me, we had plenty of room to move about in . . . but the Chinese half of the building was as densely populated as a sweatshop tenement on the East side" (III 780). The text most historically instrumental in bringing the density and heterogeneity of New York's Lower East Side into public view, Jacob Riis's *How the Other Half Lives* (1890), does just the reverse, making vivid the scene of urban crowding by referencing "China." In an early chapter accounting for the "Genesis of the Tenement," "the tenement house population," Riis writes, "had swelled to half a million souls by that time, and on the East Side, in what is still the most densely populated district in all the world, China not excluded, it was packed at the rate of 290,000 to the square mile, a state of affairs wholly unexamined. The utmost cupidity of other lands and other days has never contrived to herd much more than half the number within the same space."[63] In fin de siècle Progressive writing, Asian spaces and the modern American city seem to be imagined through each other. Kennan's disorientation maps an Asiatic labyrinth through the coordinates of urban modernity, where things are at once "common and familiar" yet "wholly out of place" (X 424). The paradoxical activity of conducting daily life under extraordinarily stimulating and dangerous circumstances becomes a metaphor for the very posture of urban blasé, and against this the foreign journalist plays the part of peasant ingénue who arrives in the big city:

> [The] inhabitants of the gulches paid no more attention to such sounds than they would have paid to the rumble of a street-car or the rattle of a jinkrisha on Ginza. In one place a soldier-barber was cutting a comrade's hair; in another a man was boiling, or re-heating, a ration of rice over a charcoal fire made in a tin biscuit filled with sand . . . with an indifference to shells and shrapnel which fairly made me *ashamed of the quick, excited beating of my own heart.* (X 423; emphasis added)

The incongruity of the situation in which Kennan finds himself partaking of a civilized meal while vigorous shelling proceeds apace reflects the incongruities of modern urban life where luxury and danger exist side by side.

A physical resemblance between the underground trench and the dark and confining qualities of the tenement drives home how Kennan's rhetorical strategy of representing Japanese modernity also pictures American modernity through Asiatic images. "Japan" and "China" appear as the reified images of the progressive and degenerative tendencies of American modernity. For example, during his stay in the Manchurian quarters, Kennan ponders the danger of "lurking seeds of infection" from "two or three generations of more or less unclean Chinese [who] had lived and died in that room" but his fears are offset by a "supply of clean and trustworthy towels . . . brought from Japan."[64] While "China" signifies the squalid aspects of urban density, the Japanese version of modern life manages to achieve a wholesome quality despite the challenge posed by infelicitous conditions. Just as the Japanese manage, through the rock garden, to establish a connecting link between the remote space of wartime Manchuria and home, the warm hospitality and the supreme cleanliness of the narrow trenches most unexpectedly make the Western journalist feel "quite at home" (X 424). In an era in which the tenement encapsulates the modern loss of feeling anywhere "at home,"[65] the ingenious aesthetic of Japanese design, "quick to take advantage of topographical peculiarities of contour" (X 422), seems to offer a potential model for American urban reform. When detailing "Life in the Japanese Trenches," Kennan seems to be implying that, with regard to this way of maximizing efficiency as well, Americans should take notes.

In a sense, Kennan's "China" and "Japan" echo the constructions of London's "The Yellow Peril" by situating China at a remove from both Japan and the West. Indeed, insofar as it serves as a kind of foil for Kennan's task of interpreting the Japanese, China is not in itself a subject of interpretation. The Chinese in Kennan's writing belong to the figure of amusing picturesque. While the Japanese are represented as purposeful, traveling toward their target with teleological certainty, scenes of every-day Chinese life feature circularity and repetitive motion. The Chinese offer a limited entertainment, which depends upon their remaining "queer" and "unknown" (III 777). As Kennan moves on to "the Japa-nese part of the village," he notes that "there were many things which, al-though trivial, perhaps in themselves, were more or less interesting as il-lustrations, or at least indications, of Japanese methods and character" (III 777–78). It is at this point that he goes on to describe the rock garden and the topographical model from which he extrapolates so much of "Japanese methods and character."

The difference between Kennan's reading of Chinese and Japanese de-tails underscores Japanese efficacy to a universal discourse of modernity. If Japanese details are shown to belong within the culture of modernity, it could also be said that modernity depends upon the assimilation of Jap-anese details in order to establish its own position of abstract universal-ity. Yet at the same time the details enabling the move toward universal-ity also stand as illustrations of Japanese national character; and it can be unclear whether, as a work of interpretation whose object is Japanese military superiority, the "Story of Port Arthur" bears witness to the man-ifestation of Japanese particularity or the principles of abstract universal modernity. While Kennan's movement from the Chinese to the Japanese part of the village traces a movement from margin to text, Japanese de-tails themselves can be a matter of interpretive obscurity. The response of helplessness, shock, and terror to the war's pattern of "invisible ap-proaches" may well register a problem of interpretation symptomatic of the ambiguous implications of a Japanese exemplarity as a discourse of Western triumphalism.

In view of the fact that the Japanese military officials are "desirous of showing us everything that was to be seen" (VIII 183), Kennan's repeated problems with seeing in the text may have something to do with the task of recording "a scene utterly unlike anything [he] had ever before wit-nessed" (X 425):

> Taking the whole experience together—the Delmonico lunch, the booming of the siege guns, the familiar ring of the telephone, the whistling and bursting of shells, the blossoming of chrysanthemums in the neighboring trenches, the soldier bringing us slice after slice of hot toast in the gulch, and the artillerymen crouching beside the machine gun in the dark bomb-proof on the edge of the moat—seemed to me the most extraordinary combination that had ever come within the range of my experience. (X 427)

The uncanny quality of the scene has to do with the merging of the everyday (the telephone ring) and the extraordinary (the bursting of shells), the contradictory overlaying of ordinarily separate spaces of dining room, garden, and battlefield.[66] It may also have to do, as I have been suggesting, with the intersection of the spaces of urban modernity and of Asia—whose scenic presence is insinuated by the Oriental motif of blossoming chrysanthemums. The problem Kennan has with seeing properly is perhaps bound up with this peculiar intersection, which posits an exotic experience of Asia as paradigmatic of urban modernity. Ironically, a vision of the "yellow peril" arises in the process of the universalization of the condition of modernity. Insofar as Japan constitutes that universalization, the dissolution of boundaries between Japan and modernity also generates a moment of racialization. Racialization emerges as the representational form of explanation in the midst of interpretive irresolution, in the aporia of "gloomy twilight" when the Western correspondent fails to see. Kennan's thematic peril of Asiatic invisibility can be read as the unintended symbolic resolution of uncertainty generated by proxy representation, in which Western interests are secured by making visible the Other's difference as well as identity.

JACK LONDON GOES TO ASIA

Jack London's war coverage presents a different kind of narrative resolution of the problems of representing Asiatic modernity. Unlike Kennan, London fails to collect many details on Japanese military tactics or to observe much battle action. His reports are preoccupied instead with the matter of the American journalist's harassment by censorious Japanese authorities.[67] His reportage narrates two trips undertaken toward the front line. Almost immediately after his arrival in Japan by steamer, he is detained by local authorities for taking unauthorized photographs and is released from jail only after the U.S. ambassador intervenes. He finds his own way to Korea, and from Seoul to Ping Yang [P'yongyang]—all against government advice—and eventually ends up stuck in Sunan for a month until he is forced back to Seoul. Only after London sets out for the front again, this time with the Japanese army, does he forward any accounts of battle action—some Russian-Japanese skirmishes at the Yalu River viewed from a great distance. Two polemical pieces concluding his correspondence proclaim an end to the genre of war reporting: "Japanese Officers Consider Everything a Military Secret" and "Japan Puts an End to the Usefulness of Correspondents."[68]

London's articles complain that all the journalists have been managed like "a party of Cook's tourists with supervising officers as guides. We saw what we were permitted to see, and the chief duty of the officers looking after us was to keep us from seeing anything" (JPUC 123). Having entered with the "most gorgeous conceptions of what a war correspondent's work in the world must be" and "expecting to get thrills," London experiences continual "indignation and irritation" (JCMS 122). Instead of freedom of movement, war reporting entails extreme claustrophobia. "The correspondent is hedged around by military secrets. He may not move for fear he will pop on to a military secret" (JCMS 119) because practically "everything in the landscape is unspecifically forbidden" (JCMS 120). One skirmish at the Yalu River is humorously entitled "Japanese in Invisible War." There, London writes, "[it] might be a war of ghosts for all that eye or field-glass could discover."[69] The few occasions when London achieves some positional altitude turn out to be just as anticlimactic: "I stood on the summit of Wiju Castle in a sort of summer pavilion and tried to convince myself that I was gazing out upon what Captain Okada was pleased to term 'the theatre of war.' "[70]

Though contemporary developments in warfare technology allowing for increasingly long-range fighting were at least partly responsible for putting things out of sight, London habitually turns to "Asiatic character" for an explanation of the war's visual frustrations. The essential traits of Asiatic character unite an explanation of Japanese military victories and an explanation of the correspondent's problems with seeing how this could have happened. In one dispatch, called "The Monkey Cage," London describes how the Japanese manage to cross the Yalu under the nose of the Russians by the clever use of decoys. Partway through the description of military strategy, we are transported away from current events to the timeless universe of fable:

> Have you ever stood in front of a cage wherein there was a monkey gazing innocently and peaceably into your eyes—so innocent and peaceable the hands grasping the bars and wholly unbelligerent, the eyes bent with friendly interest on yours, and all the while and unbeknown a foot sliding out to surprise your fancied security and set you shrieking with sudden fright? Beware the monkey cage! You have need of more than eyes; and beware the Japanese.[71]

The fable analogizes the Russian predicament in facing a cunning enemy and the American journalist's frustration at the indirection of his Japanese sources. Oriental inscrutability continually produces situations in which "[we correspondents] were more in the dark concerning the Japanese position than the Russians themselves, lying quietly on the opposite bank."[72]

The resistances of London's Russo-Japanese War set up a representational problem that requires some creative solutions. One can be found in an odd piece entitled "Dr. Moffet" (March 13, 1904), which was never actually published by the newspaper.[73] In "Dr. Moffet" London describes himself as leaving the main thoroughfares streaming with Japanese troops and British and American army officers, away from already foreign-occupied spaces, and wandering into an (imaginatively) remote Korean countryside. Pronunciation of the Korean name for a popular resident American missionary, Dr. Moffett, or "Mah-mok-sah," provides access to this other world. This "magic name" functions as "a sympathetic bond capable of connecting [London] with half the Koreans [he] encounter[s]" (DM 83).

In this adventure, London tangles with a corrupt magistrate named Pak-Choon-Song, who is suspected of pocketing the army payments made to the villagers for the delivery of food and supplies. London's involvement is portrayed as a response to an appeal from the locals. Encouraged by the personal enthusiasm of his Korean translator and servant Manyoungi, London seeks restitution from the magistrate on the people's behalf, challenging Oriental indirection with "brutal, point-blank directness" (DM 88). This implied allegorical "overthrow" of "Oriental despotism" by "revolutionary democracy," however, is compromised by the hierarchical necessity of colonial authority. Manyoungi momentarily shows signs of potential agency: "In his head was the ferment of a new idea, the Western idea of the rights of man. In his head were mutiny and revolt. In his head, though dimly perhaps, were the ideas of Revolutionary France" (DM 87). But ultimately the people's reliance on London's intervention imparts the lesson that, for Asiatics, "justice is a characteristic belonging peculiarly to the white man, and that from a white man only is it obtainable" (DM 85). London's Korean interaction, including his confrontation with a petty tyrant, is openly mediated by his reading of colonial travel writing. From the moment that he enters it, Pak's house "was strangely familiar. I had seen it all before—through Mrs. [Isabella Bird] Bishop's eyes" (DM 87).[74] If London's Korean interaction provides for him and his would-be readers an uncommon adventure, the story suggests the compensatory function served by colonial literature in this particular war.

A sense of limited heroism intrudes even into "Dr. Moffett," which ends with an acknowledgment of ineffectiveness: "[S]o far as concerned the return of the seventy-percent squeeze, I knew, and Manyoungi knew, and Pak-Choon-Song knew and we all knew one another knew, that Pak-Choon-Song intended nothing of the sort" (DM 90). London's local power derives from an "invading army" to which he has no secure relation. In 1904 Korea, American missionary presence may have facilitated American tourism, but it was insufficient for establishing overriding political authority without invoking the threat of a Russian or Japanese military. London assumes that he is usually perceived by the locals as Russian. "Shrewdly sheltered in an elbow of the hills I found a tiny village. The children fled at the sight of me, without doubt considering me a Russian, while the elders, after a while, crept timidly forth—a sort of committee of safety, I took it, for anxiety was writ large on their faces and by meek gestures I was invited to leave" (DM 83–84). Yet he takes greater refuge in racial indeterminacy, an acknowledgment of Japan's greater authority in the region since the 1896 Sino-Japanese War. "Who or what I was, or what were my powers, Pak-Choon-Song did not know. He knew only that I was a visitant in the chaos of war, that his authority was not what it once was, and that I was mystery to be feared" (DM 89). The refuge London takes in indeterminacy even in the most colonially conventional of his war writings underscores the defensive nature of the racial Manichaeanism that thematizes his writing overall.

In general, London's reportage distances itself from American journalistic consensus. Not a little begrudgingly, he observes: "Japanese soldiery and equipment seem to command universal admiration. Not one dissenting voice is heard among the European and American residents in Korea. On the contrary, favorable comparison is made with our own troops and the troops of Europe."[75] London himself has praise for Japanese soldiers—for their orderliness, quietness, temperance, endurance, and honesty, and for their undoubted superiority to the inefficient Korean natives.[76] But such compliments are intermixed with polarizing assertions regarding the radical difference between "us" and "them": "the Japanese may be the Britisher of the Orient, but he is still Asiatic."[77] The Japanese's essential Asiatic characteristics can sometimes make for absurd inefficiencies—for example, they wear out their horses sooner than necessary by not caring for them (RSM 47)—which are, however, inextricable from their military successes: "The Japanese are so made that nothing short of annihilation can stop them" (GBRE 103). Thoroughness of purpose explains how "terrifying bravery" can go hand in hand with "cold-blooded precaution" (MC 117), which ensures certain victory in all their endeavors. A Japanese rice diet, for example, means that the average soldier's kit can be twelve and a half pounds lighter than the average American's (APJ 49), allowing the Japanese army to travel greater distances on a given day.

As Jonathan Auerbach has argued, London's exotic locales have "less to do with the primitive wilderness than the discipline required to get yourself into print, to make your mark in public" (16). Yet if the Yukon is figured by a "White Silence" that entwines London's abstract treatment of place with a certain project of race-making, other symbolic regionalisms in London figure race and writing differently. In London's Yukon, "trailing" is an activity through which native Indians and "aliens from a dozen lands" can be molded into a "single sort of man"; Anglo-Saxon supremacy is affirmed by seriously entertaining miscegenation and the primitive origins of communal white manhood (Auerbach, 55–59). In the figurative region of "Asiatic geography," adventure narrative fails under the restrictions imposed by Japanese supervision. The Asiatic may be the opposite of the "white man," but not in the primitive sense. As in Kennan, London's Japanese army exemplifies the systematic conduct of modern warfare compared to the primitive combat of the Zulu, Mongols, and Vikings.[78] However, in contrast to Kennan, for whom Japanese successes are attributable to universal Western signs of modernity, London finds the Japanese formidable on account of their essential Asiatic qualities.

Recent critics who argue for a view of London as an example of the hyper-professionalized writer at the turn of the century are persuasive in reading London's celebratory primitivism to be an effect of market or machine capitalism; his savage figures are recreational exercises, actually functioning to uphold civilization's values and not to present genuine alternatives to them.[79] His "Asiatic geography," by contrast, is the scene of the disablement of such reconciliations.[80] In his writings about Asiatics, London is at his darkest about modernity's degenerationist trajectory. Indeed, London's figure of the "yellow peril" can be understood as the place where his critique of the despotism of modernity is most savage. But the racialization of modernity as Asiatic exacts certain consequences, both political and textual. In the Yukon, the Other's expected primitivism (some of whose tropes recur in London's stolid Koreans) helps regenerate white identity; in Northeast Asia, the tedium of modern warfare accompanies the destabilization of whiteness.

His private letters from Asia written to Charmian Kittredge, his lover at the time and later his second wife, corroborate a link between failed writing and active racial protestation. In a letter dated March 8, 1904, London writes, "How [your] letters have roused me up! Furthermore, they have proved to me, or, rather reassured me, that I am a white man."[81] Reading Charmian's letters secures what his publishing in the *San Francisco Examiner* does not. His letters to her frequently complain of his inability to "think whiteman's thoughts" (March 8), his isolation from "white man's news,"[82] the absence around him of "white man's chow (food)" and "white-man's speech."[83] An April 1 letter pointedly attributes his textual silence to the specific racial character of this war. "I'll never go to a war between Orientals again," he says, "The vexation and delay are too great. . . . Such inactivity, such irritating inactivity, that I cannot even write letters."[84] Whereas Kennan represents an Anglo-American consensus that narrates the Russo-Japanese War as the triumph of Western modernity over Oriental despotism, London's dissenting view of the Japanese as essentially Asiatic leaves him with a "war between Orientals" and nothing to report.

Thus we can say that there are two kinds of competing narrative tendencies in London's correspondence, neither of which can be ideologically sustained. Where London identifies with the Russians as "white men" battling a deceptive, racial enemy, dramatic action is subsumed by fabulous clichés, as in "The Monkey Cage." Where London thinks of the conflict as a "war between Orientals," he must resort to inserting himself as the "white man" at the center of the action, as in the colonial travel narrative, "Dr. Moffett." Neither text, in the end, he knows, properly conforms to the genre of war reporting. "Perfect rot I am turning out," he complains to Charmian, "It's not war correspondence at all, and the Japs are not allowing us to see any war."[85]

In his last letter to Charmian from Asia, London writes:

> Now I don't think it is possible for them to make arrangements for me to go on the Russian side, so, as you read this I may be starting on my way back to the States, to God's country, the Whiteman's Country! Who knows? Who knows? At any rate, believe me, the year in Japan and the Inland Sea is settled and done for. It would take a many times bigger salary than I am receiving to persuade me to put in the year in Japan much less pay for the year out of my own pocket. In the past I have preached the Economic Yellow Peril; henceforth I shall preach the Militant Yellow Peril.[86]

London's "yellow peril" hyperbolizes Japan's contemporary military capability relative to the United States. Curiously, this dystopian projection seems to extend from a textual failure, one resulting in particular from the challenges of narrating an Anglo-Japanese alliance in Asia. London ultimately beats a retreat to "whiteman's country," a terrain increasingly legislated by Asian exclusion, but this retreat means exchanging journalistic credibility for the roomier license of fiction writing.[87] After several months of on-site observation, London concludes, against the consensus of his compatriots and the sway of events, that "I cannot see how Japan can possibly win" (JPUC 125).

JACK LONDON'S "YELLOW PERIL" FICTIONS

In part, George Kennan's and Jack London's alternative representations of turn-of-the-century Japan as a democratic or despotic power can be seen as reflecting the distance between different modes of address to the "incorporation of America"—the difference between the national Progressive movement's fundamental adherence to a "gospel of efficiency" and California socialism's radical othering of the tyrannies of monopoly capitalism.[88] Whereas Kennan found a model of urban reform in the trenches of war, London experienced a loss of freedom in an Asiatic land-scape. Yet the "yellow peril" figures that emerged from both their texts—whether fleeting or persistent, and whether their official positions were pro- or anti-Japanese—point to the general representational contradictions arising from the creation of Japan as an American proxy in Asia, contradictions that constitute the neocoloniality of Asiatic racial form. Kennan's and London's ideological differences regarding appropriate correctives to the abuses of monopoly capitalism are indicated by their quite opposite capacities to believe in Japanese victory. Yet their alternative strategies of representing the war reflect the extent to which the exaltation of Japan as either a model modernity or a "yellow peril" were in fact logical antinomies of each other.

Though London's prediction of the war's outcome turned out to be wrong, the "yellow peril" lesson that emerged from his struggles with the war's representational form anticipated and helped shape immediate postwar expectations of U.S.-Japanese rivalry. Refusing the path of Kennan's exemplification of Japan as an instance of modernity's universality, London's Asian exclusionism is a gesture of spatial containment, one to be repeated in the socialist and apocalyptic writings he published soon after the war. "The Yellow Peril" paints the threat of Japanese expansion into China in terms of superlative corporate management: "Four hundred million indefatigable workers (deft, intelligent, and unafraid to die), aroused and rejuvenescent, managed and guided by forty-five million additional human beings who are splendid fighting animals, scientific and modern, constitute that menace to the Western world which has been well named the 'Yellow Peril'" (YP 347). To London's ear, the contemporary anticolonial slogan "Asia for the Asiatics!" (YP 347) does not resound with the multiple desires of divergent nationalisms but just the single prospect of a continent-wide, pan-Asian combination. London's prophecy of East-West conflict, in contradistinction to Kennan's more comforting allegory of progress, is deeply implicated in his critique of the free market's visible tendencies toward economic monopoly.

As we have seen at the start of the chapter, *The Iron Heel* (1908) features an episode of race war waged between a "united Asia and the world," whose wording is drawn straight out of his article "The Yellow Peril." What is the significance of the Asiatic as that which marks the limits of socialist solidarity? To appreciate the specificity of London's Asian exclusionism, it is important to recognize the extent to which London distances himself from the conventional nativism that suffused the talk of the mainstream labor movement. *The Iron Heel* is narrated by Avis Everhard, whose personal record of events that transpire in the United States between 1912 and 1932 becomes a primary historical document in the archive of a socialist future. Featuring annotations to the narrative written by an editor belonging to this future, *The Iron Heel* plays upon the double perspective afforded by the juxtaposition of two voices issuing from two different time periods and, implicitly, two different sets of cultural values. Avis is celebrated as a revolutionary heroine, but she is also faulted by the socialist editor for holding to a "distinction between being native born and foreign born [that] was sharp and invidious in those days" (338). In the novel's chronicle of world developments, Germany, Italy, and France are among those countries considered to have the strongest socialist movements. London's refusal of an "America first" discourse is consistent with his criticism of contemporary American trade unions for their anti-industrialism and their exclusion of the unskilled working-class majority.

At the same time, mapped out in the episode of East-West war is an imaginative geography of socialist emergence and capitalist reaction tinctured with "white republican" virtue: conforming to the expectations of white settler colonialism in the Pacific, Australia and New Zealand are touted as leading socialist zones; Japan, capitalism's most vicious stronghold. The sense of a racially contested Pacific region frames the stakes of struggle for the world's dominant capitalist power, America. To what extent, then, is London's radical critique of the free market as a system of wage slavery enabled by a brand of whiteness differently constituted from the customary split between "free white" and "black slave"? In London, an uncompromising anticapitalism and an "Asiatic" unfreedom of industrial workers go hand in hand. Two short stories that appeared shortly before *The Iron Heel* are additional evidence of a patterned relation between race war and class struggle in London's socialist fiction. In each case, economic utopia is predicated, centrally or tangentially, upon defeat of the "yellow peril."

London's "Goliah" (1907) imagines the end of capitalism in the United States and elsewhere through the action of an all-powerful character named "Goliah."[89] In the new social order established by this Goliah, the working day shortens, productivity and the standard of living increase (1214), crime disappears, world disarmament succeeds, private property withers away (1217), and no one ever has to do any more housework (1218). Goliah, later revealed to be a twinkly old German American who was an ordinary union man back in 1898, achieves these remarkable results by happening upon a secret weapon called Energon. Energon, reputed to be an undiscovered natural element, lets him destroy anyone who won't obey him. Much of the story's drama centers on people's refusal to take him seriously and the awful fate they meet. The last to be taught this lesson is Japan. "But all the world was not stunned. There was the invariable exception—the Island Empire of Japan. Drunken with the wine of success deep-quaffed, without superstition and without faith in aught but its own ascendant star, laughing at the wreckage of science and mad with pride of race, it went forth upon the way of war" (1209–10).

Unmindful of Goliah's warnings, Japan presses forward with its imperialist ambitions. "America's fleets had been destroyed. . . . The war monsters of Japan were loosed in mighty fleets. The Philippines were gathered in as a child gathers a nosegay. It took longer for the battleships to travel to Hawaii, to Panama, and to the Pacific Coast" (1210). Faced with no other choice, Goliah invites Californians to witness the magical destruction of the Japanese fleet by his yacht, *Energon*, just off the shore of San Francisco. "It was all over in five minutes. Remained upon the wide expanse of sea only the *Energon*, rolling white and toylike on the bar" (1211). The cataclysm met by the entire Japanese fleet convinces most remaining skeptics of Goliah's omnipotence; it is a typical example of London's customary predilection for power displays to effect a narrative turning point.

"Goliah" is not alone in providing us with a spectacle of near-instant Asiatic effacement. London's most notoriously anti-Asian piece of fiction, "The Unparalleled Invasion" (1907) imagines the wholesale genocide of China through a Western-engineered scheme of germ warfare.[90] This time emphasizing the Chinese mass dimension of the "yellow peril," "The Unparalleled Invasion" has Japan fulfill its requisite destiny to awaken China, only to be thrown out by the Chinese when the work of modernization is done. Here the real danger to the West stems not from an Asiatic Napoleonism, but from a passive kind of global expansion engendered by the "fecundity of [China's] loins" (1238). Though isolationist by disposition and even peace loving, China is propelled beyond its traditional borders by rampant population growth into the Western-held colonies of Southeast Asia. Western attempts to contain this spread through invasions of Chinese territory are merely "swallowed up in China's cavernous maw" (1239).

In the story, an American scientist concocts a secret plan that unites all Western nations in a joint mission. As various armies of the West cordon off all routes of human escape, airships bombard the country with plague-bearing germs:

During all the summer and fall of 1976 China was an inferno. There was no eluding the microscopic projectiles that sought out the remotest hiding places. The hundreds of millions of dead remained unburied and the germs multiplied themselves, and, toward the last, millions died daily of starvation. Besides, starvation weakened the victims and destroyed their natural defenses against the plagues. Cannibalism, murder, and madness reigned. And so perished China. (1245)

This extraordinary description of wholesale racial disappearance is followed by coordinated sacking and resettlement of the entire territory by all nationalities according to a "democratic American program" (1245). A renaissance of "splendid mechanical, intellectual, and art output" follows, and, above all, a "vast and happy intermingling of nationalities that settled down in China in 1982" (1245). Whether the strange dependence of interracial harmony upon racial genocide intends a critical irony or confirms an unreflective prejudice,[91] structurally it is significant that utopian arrival and Asiatic disappearance should again be made to coincide.

Situating *The Iron Heel*'s episode of race war within this sustained pattern, one suspects that London's "yellow peril" sequences perform the role of a revolutionary deus ex machina, an easy mechanism for transforming dystopian conditions into utopian ends. Even at the peak of its reputation in the interwar period, *The Iron Heel* was valued more for its vivid imagination of counterrevolution than its capacity to represent revolution.[92] Despite propagating revolutionary class struggle, the novel entertains a contradictorily low opinion of industrial workers, touting its Nietzschean superman, Ernest Everhard, for being exceptional among members of his class. Its characterizations of brutal working-class conditions reproduce Progressive-era stereotypes of workers rendered stupid and deformed by industrial work.[93] The plot is driven by the secret activities of elite underground agents, not by mass action. In a climactic sequence, set in Chicago, the masses are manipulated by counterrevolutionary spies into a premature uprising, which results in wholesale slaughter by the army and a massive political setback.

> It was not a column, but a mob, an awful river that filled the street, the people of the abyss, mad with drink and wrong, up at last and roaring for the blood of their masters. . . . men, women, and children, in rags and tatters, dim ferocious intelligences with all the godlike blotted from their features and all the fiendlike stamped in, apes and tigers, anaemic consumptives and great hairy beasts of burden, wan faces from which vampire society had sucked the juice of life, bloated forms swollen with physical grossness and corruption, withered hags and death's-heads bearded like patriarchs, festering youth and festering age, faces of fiends, crooked, twisted, misshapen monsters blasted with the ravages of disease and all the horrors of chronic innutrition—the refuse and the scum of life, a raging, screaming, screeching, demoniacal horde. (*IH* 535)

Scenes from the Chicago uprising provide the novel's most extended instance of mass agency, but it is instinctual, unintelligent, obscene, and full of gothic horror. In the indictment of one critic, *The Iron Heel* suffers from a serious "blank at the center," which is none other than its "missing revolution."[94] This absent revolution is further reflected in the formal disjuncture between the text and its annotations. The dystopian narrative breaks off without portraying the events that result in utopia, whose eventual achievement is the foregone conclusion of the meta-commentary.

My next chapter will address the convergence between various reform and radical discourses around the "Asiatic question" that help establish the enabling conditions for the representation of what should be a heroic mass as a degenerate mob. Besides Chicago's mob scene, *The Iron Heel* gives us another instance of revolution's flawed substitute, whose comparative brevity in the text should not be taken as the measure of its significance; the imperial consolidation of Asia's populations under Japan's leadership also requires that the challenge of mass uprising be met. The novel therefore establishes a parallel rather than an opposition between the "yellow peril" and the American mass. Its reference to the Japanese oligarchy as global capitalism's "most savage of all" certainly suggests that its subjugation of the Asian working classes and subsequent confrontation by "the world" provide a gratifying and supercharged instance of counterrevolution's defeat. Indeed it is the only such instance in the novel; in the battle for Chicago, it is, after all, oligarchy that wins. Even so, the world's victory over a "united Asia" is not directly represented, only foretold and then assumed, much like the revolution itself. The repeated articulation of East-West war and socialist aspiration in London's corpus provides an avenue for addressing the well-known problem of *The Iron Heel*'s "missing revolution."

The Iron Heel's characterization of Japan as a ruthless despotism was no doubt influenced by the author's nasty experience with its military censors during the Russo-Japanese War. *The Iron Heel* was composed between 1905 and 1907, when London served as president of the Intercollegiate Socialist Society, originally founded by Upton Sinclair. This period of London's most active speaking and writing on behalf of socialism coincides with the years in which his anti-Japanese feeling was reportedly at its peak.[95] Contemporaries hostile to London's political views enjoyed mocking the fact that in the fall of 1905 the author delivered his fiery "Revolution" speech on the national lecture circuit while constantly assisted by a Korean valet who had returned with him from the war.[96] Manyoungi's lingering biographical presence behind the scenes of London's political self-staging is one hint of the intertextual links between the author's war correspondence and his postwar social forecasts.

The unemancipated Asian servant of "Dr. Moffett" may have vanished as a textual character in London's more overtly fictional text, but the dystopian novel can be read as a continuing compensation for the action failures of the Russo-Japanese War reports.[97] For one, the novel offers the satisfactions of violence and suspense that were sorely missing. In Chicago the narrator lives through a military drama in which "every building was a possible ambuscade . . . every street was a canyon, every building a mountain" (*IH* 533). As in the war reports, the Chicago upheaval thematizes the loss of mastery as a primary aspect of visual perception:

> I lived through three days of the Chicago Commune, and the vastness of it and of the slaughter may be imagined when I saw that in all that time I saw practically nothing outside the killing of the people of the abyss and the mid-air fighting between sky-scrapers. I really saw nothing of the heroic work done by the comrades. I could hear the explosions of their mines and bombs, and see the smoke of their conflagrations, and that was all. (*IH* 540)

The Chicago sequence's repeated emphasis on street fighting as a chaotic experience in which the narrator "could make out nothing" (*IH* 538) echoes London's newspaper descriptions of the Russo-Japanese front line and suggests the stylization of the causes for journalistic anticlimax into a naturalist literary effect.

In the retrospective judgment of the novel by one revolutionary reader, London had "absorbed creatively the impetus given by the first Russian revolution . . . [and] courageously thought over again in its light the fate of capitalist society as a whole" (Trotsky, 95). If Trotsky was right to detect a Russian inspiration behind the uncommon radicalism of this American Socialist text, it is arguably the case that London experienced some version of the first Russian Revolution through his East Asian adventure. As much as the Russian concession to the Japanese by 1905 was one result of czarism's overthrow, London's hopes for the victory of revolution over despotism led instead to false predictions of the outcome of the Russo-Japanese War. If London's writing mistakenly translates class struggle into international conflict, or the real enemy of the Russian revolution into Japanese imperial ambition, it is surely in part because the oppressiveness of czarism is for him nowhere felt as deeply as the tyranny of the Japanese censor. Such lopsidedness was, of course, a side effect of the Anglo-Japanese alliance, which sent hundreds of American journalists to the "East" via Japan and not Russia.

We can see in London's stubborn determination to attain that war's front line as much a desire to sight some active Russians as to flee his Japanese handlers. In the end he obtained only a secondhand report on the exchange of fire with some Cossacks on February 28,[98] and in April and May some firsthand views of "black specks of men appearing and disappearing" (*JIW* 108). The only Russians London did manage to see up close were already Japan's prisoners of war:

> And the sight I saw was as a blow in the face to me. On my mind it had all the stunning effect of the sharp impact of a man's fist. There

was a man, a white man, with blue eyes, looking at me. He was dirty
and unkempt. He had been through a fierce battle. But his eyes were
bluer than mine and his skin was as white.

And there were other white men in there with him—many white
men. I caught myself gasping. A choking sensation was in my throat.
These men were my kind. I found myself suddenly and sharply aware
that I was an alien amongst these brown men who peered through the
window with me. And I felt myself strangely at one with those other
men behind the window—felt that my place was there inside with them
in their captivity, rather than outside in freedom amongst aliens.
(GBRE 106)

London's identification with the Russian prisoners helps to elucidate the
insistence on his own inactivity, a fact embarrassing to war journalism
but not if his writing is read instead as a narrative of captivity.

There are parallels, then, between the war reports and the novel, a disparity in both texts between political desire and narrative enactment, a
sense in both of missing agency. The novel makes direct analogies between
the underground's elite corps and Russian revolutionaries. We are told
that Everhard's fighting groups "were modeled somewhat after the Fighting Organization of the Russian Revolution," and that the underground is
aided sometimes by young men of the oligarchy just as "many sons of the
Russian nobility played their parts in the earlier and protracted revolution
in that country" (IH 483, 516). Just as the sight of Russian action constantly eludes the war reporter, the novel's revolutionary agents are always
disguised and somehow ghostly. Just as the reporter is subject to an ever
vigilant foreign censor, the novel entertains a nightmare vision of monopoly capitalism as an omnipresent and alien power in control of congress,
the court, the press, and the university. Just as the reporter is always surrounded by Japanese and no Russians, counterrevolutionary spies are
present everywhere, and the revolution is figurable nowhere. In a sense,
The Iron Heel can be seen to have replayed, to arguably more sustained
effect, the war's allegory of (Russian) revolution versus (Japanese) despotism. Yet from the standpoint of American socialism's transformative aspirations, though the metaphoric Orientalization of corporate oligarchy
may have well served to arouse anticapitalist resentment, uncanny associations between the "yellow peril" and the industrial masses were ultimately disabling for class identification and activation.

Coda

In Jack London's published correspondence from Asia, the term "yellow
peril" is actually used just once, in the course of a reflection that con-

cludes an *Examiner* article entitled "Japanese Supplies Rushed to Front by Man and Beast."[99] "And always one received," London writes, "gazing into the faces of the men who had done these things, an impression of strength. The Yellow Peril became a tangible thing, shaped itself in the intellect, and remained to be pondered, and pondered, and be pondered yet again" (JSRF 95). The piece that amasses the "yellow peril" into a tangible preoccupation contemplates, in its main descriptive body, a scene of Japanese supplies being rushed to the front along a road in Korea. The road

> as far as the eye could see . . . [was] gorged with baggage trains, coming and going in double lines. There were squads of cavalry and detachments of infantry, officers mounted and officers afoot, parties of the Red Cross outfit, bunches of pioneers drifting along and repairing the road, men of the telegraph corps at work on the military wires, coolies, bullock carts, pack bullocks, trains of the little indomitable Korean ponies, tiny braying jack-asses, squealing horses—and down through it all a lone Chinese from Manchuria, looking neither to the right nor left, but heading southward with incurious eyes and expressionless face for a land where peace still smiled. (JSRF 94)

Oriental impenetrability, as symbolized by the visage of the "lone Chinese," emerges as a visual contrast to the scene's disturbing quality. It gives expression to, but does not seem to be itself, what is reiteratively disturbing about the scene. The repeated emphases of the tableau suggest that it is instead the impression of coordinated mass activity that causes disquiet. In the same article London observes that the road "swarmed with white-clad coolies. Their shoulders were stooped forward, their faces bent toward the ground, their backs burdened with rice and fish, soy and saki, and all the food supplies of an Oriental army" (JSRF 93). As thousands of Korean coolies give way to the regular army transport, the line

> thickened instead of ceasing. Hundreds of pushcarts poured down in the midst of the horsecarts. Each pushcart was manned by three soldiers, and they brought the carts down so fast and thick that it was beyond us to count them. And still they poured down from the summit of the pass. . . . Finally in desperation we forced our horses into the living stream, wherever it thinned a trifle, and slowly stemmed it to the summit. It was easier going down against it on the other side, and in the darkness we rode into the large town where we were to spend the night. But the town was filled with soldiers . . . every kitchen was filled with tired soldiers. So we urged our weary horses on into the darkness, and ten li farther along made ourselves lords and masters of a deserted village. (JSRF 94)

In this scene, London repeats a characteristic gesture of competition with the occupying army for mastery over Korean space. Even as the military censor constitutes a genuine nemesis, the writer's discomfort with his host is perhaps most powerfully conveyed by the image of his immersion in an endless human tide. The scene feels disturbing not because of anything identifiable that the people—Japanese troops or Korean coolies—are doing but merely insofar as their indistinguishable bodies fill it up "as far as the eye could see." It is this sense of an elusive Asiatic menace, ambiguously culpable and yet unjustly ubiquitous, that is repeatedly to be found in the literature of naturalism written from the edge of the U.S.-Asian border at the end of the nineteenth century.

A notoriously slippery genre that ranged from the melodramatic to the scientific, the sentimental to the philosophical, American naturalism can perhaps be most usefully regarded as designating a historically specific mode of social representation. In this respect, it was a variant of the larger enterprise of American realism, whose own history of emergence, as compared to the European tradition, did not predate by much the trend toward sensational documentary. Interrogating reality through experimentations of form, realism and naturalism have both been read as registers of disruptive social conditions in the period: in particular, the emergence of mass culture, the social mediation of market relations, commodification, and the presence of class struggle in a nation with an ever increasing and largely immigrant urban proletariat (Howard, 71–77; Kaplan, 8–9). To these might be added the concurrent context of U.S. globalization through Asia. Insofar as turn-of-the-century writing is thought to register the impressions of a world that had become more and more alien, then this alienness might be supplemented by an "Asiatic question." Turning to the U.S.-Asian border on the West Coast, the next chapter will examine the intimacy between Asian exclusionist ideology and the distinctiveness of California naturalism.

CHAPTER TWO

Meat versus Rice

FRANK NORRIS, JACK LONDON, AND THE CRITIQUE OF
MONOPOLY CAPITALISM

BETWEEN MARCH 1894 AND FEBRUARY 1895, several short stories by
Frank Norris appeared in the West Coast magazine *Overland Monthly*
under a series named "Outward and Visible Signs." The title was an allusion to the famous claim by the contemporary Italian criminal anthro-
pologist, Cesare Lombroso, that the bodies of criminals wore the "outward and visible signs of a mysterious process of degeneration."[1] The
term *degeneration* first began to appear in medical dictionaries in the
1850s and was taken to refer to a "morbid change in the structure of
parts consisting in the disintegration of tissue or in a substitution of a
lower for a higher form of structure."[2] Originating in the debates of evolutionary science and the emergent field of criminal anthropology, a
wider fin de siècle discourse of degeneration marked the reversal of earlier progressive expectations of history. While the applications of degeneration should have been reassuring, since atavism was thought to be localized in distinct and immutable individuals, the conceptual possibility
of regression it allowed for led to full-blown anxieties about the decay of
the entire social body. In its characteristic fascination with atavism as a
way of representing the primitive within civilization, literary naturalism
has been viewed as another expressive site for a discourse that predicated
the "survival of the best" upon the exclusion of "bad blood" from the
"national stock."[3] In naturalism and eugenicist social theory both, the
danger of degeneration was closely articulated to the proximity or presence of racial alterity. The stories in Norris's "Outward and Visible
Signs" series illustrate an affinity on the part of degenerationist discourse
for Orientalist tropes in particular.

The first story in the series, "She and the Other Fellow" (March 1894),
concerns the rivalry between two men over a woman, which it resolves
by juxtaposing two kinds of public spectacle—a dogfight, which serves to
distract one suitor from the romance, and a slide show of Parisian monuments, which occasions the reunion of the remaining pair. In the lecture
hall, both the seen and unseen assume a deliberately Oriental aspect. Its
"Egyptian darkness" affords a public yet secret setting for romantic

courtship;[4] on literal display are images of an imposing obelisk "transported from Egypt at the cost of seven million one hundred thousand francs" (244). The decorous lecture audience presents an obvious class contrast to the informal public drawn to the "fierce, brutal noises and the sound of furred bodies striking and rolling upon the ground" (245) in the backstreet alley. At the same time, the pedagogic lesson of French imperial acquisition also ironizes the opposition between civilized bourgeoisie and primitive working class, not least because pillaged Egyptian monuments serve as irrefutable reminders of the mortality of all civilizations. Though the Egyptian obelisk functions to demarcate the suitors' respective worth and taste (the rival goes out to the dogfight because he's bored by the lecture), it also suggests the ambiguous relationship between Orientalism and degeneration in the text. The stately Oriental object is counterposed against a scene of brutish display—reinforcing the distinction between civilization and degradation—but as a dislocated artifact, it also serves to remind us of the impermanence of this dichotomy.

Appearing to strike the most conventional of Orientalist themes, Norris's "After Strange Gods" (October 1894) relates the story of a tragic love affair between a French sailor and a Chinese "flower girl." In Norris's version of the folly of East-West romance, the lovers do manage to beat the odds and stay together, but to achieve this happy ending requires some extreme measures: the woman, disfigured by smallpox, is forced to blind her lover in order to sustain his desire. Lalo Da and Rourevoy eventually make a home in China, "the one distorted by disease and the other blind."[5] Like Pierre Loti's *Madame Chrysanthemum* (1887) or Puccini's opera *Madama Butterfly* (1904), "After Strange Gods" clearly moralizes against miscegenation, but the plot of infection and disability reverses the more familiar "death of Asia"[6] that usually ensues from such "blind" love. "After Strange Gods" associates Chineseness with disease, both in that the flower girl contracts smallpox in a germ-ridden San Francisco Chinatown, and that she is the agent of her lover's infection. The story thus dramatizes the degenerative effects of East-West contact, implying the naive romanticism of an Orientalist vision that may be blind to the barbaric dangers of the "yellow peril."

In the story, the sailor first encounters the flower girl on the Chinese pavilion at the 1893 World's Fair in Chicago, where she is employed. The World's Fair setting for the romance explicitly frames Lalo Da's erotic allure—her resemblance to "starlight amidst the petals of dew-drenched orchids" (ASG 376)—as the most artificial of cultural conventions. Orientalist fantasy is, Norris instructs, at odds with the actual constraints of U.S.-China relations at the time. Lalo Da was "as pretty a little bit of Chinese bric-à-brac as ever evaded the Exclusion Act" (ASG 376). We are informed that "when the great White City should be closed, Lalo Da would return to her little straw village on the Pei Ho, to be mated with a coolie who worked in the tea fields, and who would whip her" (ASG 376). Lalo Da's love affair with the French sailor proposes to disrupt this appropriate course—of the Chicago flower girl's return to the life of a Chinese coolie—until, that is, she contracts smallpox:

> When the small-pox attacks an Oriental it does not always kill him, but it never leaves him until it has set its seal upon him horribly, indelibly. It deforms and puckers the features, and draws in the skin around the eyes and cheekbones, until the face is a thing of horror.
>
> Lalo Da knew that she was doomed, that even if she recovered, her face would be a grinning mask, and that Rourevoy, her "Yee Han," would shudder at it, and never love her any more. (ASG 378)

The notion that smallpox may have a selective deforming effect creates an unusual intimacy between the disease and its privileged victims; the notion identifies smallpox as an Oriental disease, while implying Asiatic racial form to be commonly distorted. Instead of masking the body's normally proportioned features, the disease at a narrative level has the effect of stripping the flower girl costume from the body of the illegal alien. Drawing sharp distinctions between the kinds of East-West relations that are available in the space of the World's Fair (romantic exhibit), in San Francisco's Chinatown (scene of dangerous infection), and in China (degenerate refuge), respectively, the narrative—like those in charge of enforcing the 1882 Chinese Exclusion Act—drives towards exposing the coolie initially masked by Orientalist fantasy. But what is a coolie?

Another story from Norris's magazine series, "Thoroughbred," stages the literal appearance of some coolies. The story involves a competition between two men (Wesley Shotover and Jack Brunt) for the affections of a woman (Barry Vance) who comes from an old-moneyed San Francisco family. Wesley Shotover also boasts a pedigreed ancestry, but his morals are questionable and he is "just saved from effeminacy by certain masculine dints about the nostrils."[7] Jack Brunt, by contrast, is a self-made man of lower-class origins, whose body is a veritable "tower of leathery muscles" (T 197). These initial descriptions have us assume that Brunt will be the preferred romantic candidate, but the curious introduction of an "Asiatic" figure into the action overturns our expectations.

A game of tennis between the rivals at the Vances' mansion is interrupted by the unexpected appearance of a bedraggled and "howling" coolie hotly pursued by "fifty to a hundred" others belonging to a rival clan (T 199). What had begun as an internecine conflict spills out beyond its appropriate boundaries and threatens to turn into a full-fledged racial rebellion, now that the coolies who were chasing the runaway suddenly take it into their minds to ransack the Vances' mansion. A reversal in the romantic stature of the two rivals occurs in a scene of confrontation between Wesley Shotover and the Chinese crowd:

> Shotover faced them, calm and watchful, drawing the lash of the whip slowly through his fingers, and the Hop Sing Tong, recognizing, with a crowd's intuition, a born leader and master of men, felt themselves slipping back into the cowed washmen and opium-drugged half-castes of the previous week, and backed out of reach. (T 200)

The coolie rebellion triggers Shotover's hidden masculinity and exposes Brunt's actual cowardice, as the latter quickly recedes into the house during the racial confrontation and thereafter from the romantic competition.

The appearance of the coolie exposes the fallacy of the democratic argument proudly championed by Brunt that "a dog is a dog, after all" (T 198). The appearance of fearsome coolies who metamorphose back into "cowed washmen" establishes an identity between the coolie and the white man of working-class origins, Brunt, whose ancestors were "leased out to labour contractors to grub and grapple under the whip with the reluctant colonial soil" at a time Shotover's were "framing laws, commanding privateers, and making history generally in the days of the Constitution" (T 197). Thus, if not all dogs are equivalent, by the same token neither are all Americans. The insertion of racial difference into the story is the mechanism by which unseen class difference is made behaviorally visible. Class difference and differences of masculinity between Shotover and Brunt are established through a racializing logic. The Chinese coolie in this scenario functions as the racial form of hereditary servility.

The cultural threat of degeneration, according to Daniel Pick, "involved at once the scenario of racial decline (potentially implicating everyone in society) and an explanation of 'otherness,' securing the identity of, variously, the scientist, (white) man, bourgeoisie against superstition, fiction, darkness, femininity, the masses, effete aristocracy" (Pick, 230). Norris's "Thoroughbred," however, suggests that we not assume the parallelism of alterities—whether of gender and race or of different racial forms. The coolie in "Thoroughbred" is not a counterpart to the woman.[8] It is not a figure that proposes the exchangeability of masculine and imperial desire. Nor does the coolie present the threat of rape. "Barry was a young woman of really virile force of intellect. She merely got upon the veranda and watched the howling wretch with wide-open eyes. She was less frightened than interested. After all, no one is ever afraid of a Chinaman" (T 199). The coolie helps to constitute both Wesley Shotover and Barry Vance as "virile" and Jack Brunt as servile by returning them all to their hereditary class origins. If the coolie can be counted as a kind of atavistic presence, it is primarily so in the effect it has upon other characters, the narrative results of which—taking the last two Norris stories together—are morally ambivalent. Though it seems to be associated with a degenerationist logic, can the coolie be considered one of naturalism's customary brutes? Is the coolie in fact a primitive? To address the question of Asiatic representation more fully, it is necessary to consider examples of racial figuration even when it does not take the shape of a racially identified character.

A trademark of California naturalism was its obsession with the historical obsolescence of Anglo-Saxon physique. Jack London's *The Sea-Wolf* (1904) showcases a physical superman (descended from Vikings) who falls prey to an immobilizing and eventually fatal disease that makes a prison-house of his splendid musculature. Frank Norris's *McTeague* (1899) tells the tale of a dentist whose uncontrolled physical strength ends in his wife's death as well as his own. Making reference to the differences between craft and industrial modes of production, the novel continually directs our gaze to the archaic curiosity of McTeague's oversized, clumsy hands and Trina's tiny, efficient hands, whose fingers are the object of fetishization and assault in the couple's sexual relationship. Many of the better-known works by London and Norris do not deploy a readily noticeable cast of Asian characters or Oriental tropes. Nevertheless, I will argue that the literature's persistent theme of Anglo-Saxon degeneration is necessarily informed by a contemporary history of U.S.-Asia relations, to which its images of bodily besiegement and jeopardy are often an allusion. Through a focus on some of London's and Norris's disparate works—*The Iron Heel* (1908) and *Tales of the Fish Patrol* (1902), *The Octopus* (1901) and *Moran of the* Lady Letty (1898)—I will show how California naturalism's interest in the corporation and the worker as strange new subjects of literary representation engages contemporary contradictions of global market expansion and immigration restriction. If California naturalism articulates a specific variety of Orientalism, this is because the representation of class relations in the era was mediated by the social force of Asian exclusion movements.

The Discourse of Asian Exclusion

Starting in the 1880s, mounting restrictions in federal immigration policy reflected the growing influence of an Anglo-Saxon nativism that drew fundamental distinctions between "new" immigrant groups and America's "original" immigrant stock. By 1924 Congress had passed the National Origins Immigration Act, which vastly restricted immigration from southern and eastern Europe and put an absolute stop to all Asian immigration. From its triumphal rhetoric of Manifest Destiny to its besieged nativist outlook, Anglo-Saxonism as a discourse had undergone a significant tonal change over the course of the nineteenth century.[9] Given the temptations of foundationalist thinking, particularly with regard to the force of racism in U.S. history, it has been easy for us to overlook the fact that Anglo-Saxonism, in its most vociferous period, had recast itself as a minority discourse suspicious of a coming modernity. The encroaching sense of diminishing Americanizable space at the end of the nineteenth century, famously announced by Frederick Jackson Turner in 1893, was partly related to the contradictions of expanding U.S. relations with Asia, which could potentially renew or threaten the perpetuation of the American frontier.[10] Frank Norris's location of "After Strange Gods" at the World's Columbian Exposition, where Turner had first delivered his address just a year before, links the degenerative logic of East-West contact and the epoch of the closing of the frontier.

The prospect that unrestrained Asian immigration would lead to Anglo-Saxon "race suicide" was a notion also propagated by prominent social scientists of the time. In an essay known for having helped attract Theodore Roosevelt's interest in campaigning to boost Anglo-Saxon reproductivity, prominent Progressive Party intellectual and sociologist Edward A. Ross wrote:

> Suppose, for example, Asiatics flock to this country and, enjoying equal opportunities under our laws, learn our methods and compete actively with Americans. They may be able to produce and therefore earn in the ordinary occupations, say three-fourths as much as Americans; but if their standard of life is only half as high, the Asiatic will marry before the American feels able to marry. The Asiatic will rear two children while his competitor feels able to rear but one.[11]

By 1901, when Ross's essay "The Causes of Race Superiority" appeared in the *Annals of the American Academy of Political and Social Science*, advocates of Chinese immigration exclusion had been arguing for several decades that Chinese "cheap labor" threatened to degrade an American standard of living. In adopting the discourse of Asian exclusion, Ross's essay underscores the far-reaching implications of Asian exclusionism's questioning of American powers to eliminate or assimilate the Other. "America is a psychic maelstrom that has sucked in and swallowed up hosts of aliens," Ross writes, but Chinese immigrants are unique in that they "show no disposition, even when scattered sparely among us, to assimilate to us or adopt our standards" (86–87).

The notion of Chinese unassimilability registers something more than an exception to an otherwise confident American advance; the notion of persistent difference, a presence that will neither recede nor accede, marks the new prospect in which the principle of American expansionism could itself be thrown into crisis. According to Ross, Anglo-Saxons may have once found it easy to advance against those "cheaply gotten up manana races" (79) who lack mental reflection, self-reliance, and self-control. But in this new contest with the Asiatic, the Anglo-Saxon is no longer the supreme economic type, but rather a barbarian whose "war-like traits no longer insure race survival and expansion" (Ross, 81). The future, when the "efficiency of average units" (Ross, 81) will trump inventive genius, belongs to the Asiatic.

Ross's essay suggests the close connection between the economic logic of Asian exclusionist discourse and a wider fin de siècle sense of the "decline of the West":[12]

> Henceforth this principle of cosmopolitanism must be reckoned with. Even if the Chinese have not yet vanquished the armies of the West with Mauser rifles supplied from Belgium, there is no reason why that mediocre and intellectually sterile race may not yet defeat us industrially by the aid of machines and processes conceived in the fertile brains of our Edisons and Marconis. Organizing talent, of course—industrial, administrative, military,—each race must, in the long run, produce from its own loins, but in the industrial Armageddon to come it may be that the laurels won by a mediocre type of humanity, equipped with sciences and appliances of the more brilliant and brain-fertile peoples. Not preponderance of genius will be decisive, but more and more the energy, self-reliance, fecundity and acquired skill of the average man; and the nation will do most for itself that knows how best to foster these winning qualities by means of education and wise social institutions. (Ross, 82)

Ross does not distinguish the threat of Chinese immigration to U.S. workers from the potential for China to surpass the United States in terms of industrial development. Though the secret weapon of Chinese "cheap labor" lies at the heart of both perils—the prospect of a Chinese takeover of American manufacturing jobs and China's domination of the world trade in manufactured products—the conflation of two contradictory economic standpoints reflects a widening tension between Anglo-Saxon supremacy and national advancement as a result of capitalism's globalizing tendency.[13] Whereas the first scenario is in fact one of the conditions of the U.S. economy that makes the second scenario improbable, the racial unit of economic competition in Ross's argument suggests that what is at stake is the contested meaning of expansionism in an era when settler colonialism had reached a limit.

The "Asiatic question" marks some of the ways in which postcontinental imperialism reconfigured the American frontier, demanding a reconsideration of twentieth-century U.S. colonial forms.[14] The elusiveness of the U.S.-Asian border involved a host of contradictory trends, including the forging of imperial partnerships with economic competitors, persistent resistances to the development of overseas markets, and the integration of transnational labor forces into the processes of economic accumulation throughout the region.[15] These factors formed a context for a popular rhetoric of decline with respect to Anglo-Saxon-led settler colonialism in the face of emergent and more abstract forms of imperialism. In view of the fact that "with all their energy and their numbers the Anglo-Saxons appear to be physiologically inelastic, and incapable of making Guiana or the Philippines a home such as they have made in New Zealand or Minnesota," Ross warns, the "extraordinary power of accommodation enjoyed by the Mongolians" appears more and more "ominous" (68–69). Ross is ultimately ambiguous as to whether it is physiological adaptability that makes the Chinese a superior colonizer or whether racial stasis somehow makes the Chinese better suited to conditions of economic development that are now post-territorial. However, a theme consistently struck is that, despite the U.S. "opening" of China, "Chinese" is a metonym for the closing of unique American conditions of possibility. The rhetoric of expansion's end and consolidation's onset, shared by writers from Brooks Adams to Jack London, repeatedly articulates the sense of the end of the American frontier with the image of Asia and Asians' new proximity.[16]

In his popular 1894 classification of the Chinese according to twenty-six national characteristics, the American missionary Arthur Smith proposes a theory of Chinese anatomical distinction centered on the "absence of nerves."[17] In the "age of steam and electricity," which has the effect of keeping "Anglo-Saxon" nerves in a "state of constant tension" (Smith, 90), it is precisely this nervelessness that explains why the Chinese are such good workers. For Smith, the Chinese body is the body of the twentieth century. The density of the Chinese empire, as Smith sees it, reflects the reduction of life to "its very lowest terms," the Chinese having "reduced poverty to science" (152). Along similar lines, Adams predicts the growth and spread of Chinese populations as a result of modernity's reduction of everything to the "survival of the cheapest." "Under commercial competition," Adams writes, "that society will survive which works cheapest; but to be undersold is often more fatal to a population than being conquered."[18] By the end of the nineteenth century, a statistical Chinese figure had strangely assumed the place of the "average man."

The coolie is a figural variant of modernity's economic masses; by definition the coolie lacks individuality. "Here they were sure enough," Norris's narrator in "Thoroughbred" announces, "fifty to a hundred of them, and they were evilly minded and meant to do harm. They suddenly boiled in around the corner of the street and in an instant had filled it from end to end. Every yellow throat of them was vibrant and raucous with a droning, oft-repeated monotone: '*Ai Hoang-chow lakh, lakh, lakh*'" (T 199). Norris's boiling insurgents emphasize the salient feature of the coolie figure in filling the scene "from end to end" and as far as the eye can see (T 199). The story's casual introduction of the coolies' dramatic entrance ("here they were sure enough") signals their representational predictability. The narrator does not doubt that following the appearance of the initial lone coolie will be other coolies in mass quantity; his tone implies there can be no such thing as a single coolie. Asiatic racial form is indissociably plural, and its affiliation with the urban multitude at the turn of the century is clearly connected to a contemporary sense of the general foreignness of the city. On the one hand, the Asiatic belonged to a discourse of alien invasion; on the other hand, in embodying the ultimate logic of industrial subjection, the Chinese coolie had paradoxically become a familiar icon of American capitalist modernity. The fact that the "yellow peril" closely followed a degenerationist discourse of modernity allows for a sense of both otherness and exemplarity.

In the first effort to link Asian immigration with a medical discourse on germs, Arthur Stout's sensationalist *Chinese Immigration and the Physiological Causes of the Decay of a Nation* (1862) specifically counterposes the "yellow peril" to more palpable forms of armed invasion:

> Better would it be for our country that the hordes of Genghis Khan should overflow the land, and with armed hostility devastate our vallies [sic] with the sabre and fire-brand, than that these more pernicious hosts, in the garb of friends, should insidiously poison the well-springs of life, and spreading far and wide, gradually undermine and corrode the vitals of our strength and prosperity. In the former instance we might oppose the invasion with sword and rifled cannon; but this destructive intrusion enters by invisible approaches—is aided and fostered in advance by those who forget or never dream of their country's interest, while they seek to advance their private ends.[19]

The invisible mode of its approach suggests how the "yellow peril" denotes a radical dissolution of boundaries between inside and outside, friend and enemy: Asiatics can look just like friends, and enemy aliens have already taken up residence within. As in the threat of degenerationism, the "yellow peril's" alien danger necessarily implies internal decay. When Stout asks: "But against a Coolie who can struggle?" (14), in one sense the coolie is presented as a foe unworthy of "American manhood," and in another sense the menace lies in its prospective undoing of "American manhood." Similarly, the 1902 campaign waged by American Federation of Labor (AFL) president Samuel Gompers in support of a permanent extension of the Chinese Exclusion Act was headlined by the apocalyptic formulation: "Meat versus Rice. American Manhood against

Asiatic Coolieism. Which Shall Survive?"[20] Stout elaborates the consequences of U.S. "coolieism":

> What though the labor of the Coolie be cheaper than that of the stalwart men of our own race? We must nevertheless lose by the exchange. If the former drive back these hardy pioneers, who shall defend the land? Who shall whiten the plains with their homesteads? Who shall form the families of the republic? The vigorous strength of Caucasian labor cannot be nourished with a handful of rice, nor will their intelligence for their own emolument, or their aspirations for their children, accept existence in a state of protracted Coolieism or serfdom. Reduce their wages to the rates of Coolieism and you degrade them, physically and morally, to the state of Coolies. (14)

Just as the discourse of degeneration imagined a "process of pathological decay" that was "at once precisely contained (there were certain identifiable degenerate categories of being . . .) and ubiquitous, affecting whole populations" (Pick, 167–68), the Asiatic does not function as a Self-consolidating Other to Western modernity, but presents the potential for the modern "decline of Western civilization."[21]

As a racial form, however, the Asiatic exhibits a unique temporal assignment, even within the landscape of degenerationism. In positing the possibility of historical regression—and the survival of the unfit—degenerationist discourse generally inverts the expected dominance of civilization over savagery, while tending to leave the racialized dichotomy between them in place. The "yellow peril" discourse of a coming modernity, by contrast, switches the way in which the dichotomy between primitive and modern is typically racialized such that the temporal hierarchization of Self and Other is reversed or abolished. In a sense, the historical emergence of Asiatic racial form can be read as the appearance of the otherness of Western modernity to itself. In the literature of naturalism, the brute is typically a kind of "wild man," desire incarnate loosed from social control, denoting the figure of primitivism within modernity.[22] The coolie signifies a different kind of monstrous presence, not the ambivalent pleasure of the body's libidinal release, but, on the contrary, the prospect of its mechanical abstraction. Its articulation to historical processes of mechanization helps explain the sense of Asiatic labor's inevitability, or what exclusionists saw as "the silent replacement of Americans by Asiatics [which would] go on unopposed until the latter monopolize[d] all industrial occupations" (Ross, 87).

The use of the term "monopolize" in the fantasy of coolie takeover points to particular anxieties concerning the degradation of work as a result of industrialization, a process fully realized when capitalism reaches a monopoly finance form.[23] As suggested by Smith's Chinese body without nerves or by the meager Asiatic diet evoked by Gompers's civilizational clash of "meat versus rice," the coolie also signifies the lowest labor price generated by the increasing transnationalization of labor markets. As the phantasmatically cheapening body capitalism strives to universalize, the coolie represents a biological impossibility and a numerical abstraction, whose social domination means that the robust American body will have disappeared. In this regard, California naturalism's preoccupation with beleaguered Anglo-Saxon physique was one facet of its engagement with the question of monopoly finance capitalism, which for J. A. Hobson and V. I. Lenin—as well as for Frank Norris and Jack London—was also the era of imperialism, when the overproduction of surplus capital stimulated a scramble among Western powers for overseas markets.[24]

American naturalism was a literary development that arose in tandem with muckraking journalism and Progressivism's effort to provide measured correctives to rampant economic injustice. Just as the historical consensus is that Progressivism was ultimately conservative, present-day critics similarly consider naturalism to have failed to transcend a logic of commodification.[25] Rather than debating naturalism's complicity in, or subversion of, capitalism, my own interest lies in developing a reading of naturalism's effort to represent capitalism specifically in its monopoly finance form, in which the domination of the abstract over the concrete seems to have been most intensely thematized by debates regarding the appropriate circulation of goods and bodies across the U.S.-Asian border.[26]

Historical studies of Asian exclusionism highlight the disturbing extent to which, with few exceptions, anti-Asianism pervaded almost every social reform and radical movement in the late nineteenth and early twentieth centuries—organized labor, Populism, Progressivism, and socialism. Somehow, in targeting coolies, many reformers and radicals thought that they were—or at least said they were—curbing corporate excesses. Alexander Saxton has gone the furthest to contextualize the structure of anti-Asian feeling by chronicling the leading role played by trade unions in securing the passage of Asian exclusion legislation and the efficacy of the Asian exclusionist cause in unifying conflicting interest groups.[27] Nevertheless, even in his analysis, anti-Asianism came to be useful to the West Coast labor movement to the extent that anti-Asianism was somehow already there. As a theory of racism, the notion of Asians as an "indispensable enemy" does not fully explain why they rather than some other group might have played such a role, why they did so on certain occasions and not on others, nor why anti-Asianism takes the discriminatory forms that it does. As Moishe Postone writes of anti-Semitism:

The problem should not be posed quantitatively, whether in terms of numbers of people murdered or of degree of suffering. There are too many historical examples of mass murder and of genocide. (Many more Russians than Jews, for example, were killed by the Nazis.) The question is, rather, one of qualitative specificity. Particular aspects of the extermination of European Jewry by the Nazis remain inexplicable so long as anti-Semitism is treated as a specific example of a scapegoat strategy whose victims could very well have been the members of any other group.[28]

Adapting Postone, my purpose is not to explain why Asian exclusionism, whether or not it was an organic ideology of the U.S. working class, came to be promoted by so many of its leaders and allies between the 1870s and the 1930s, but to explore what it was that came to be legitimized as an anti-corporate, and sometimes even anticapitalist, discourse. Attention to the formal specificity of Asian racialization may well be the precondition to a substantive understanding of why Asian exclusionism came to be a leading channel for protest against the growth of monopoly power and class division in American society. The wide range of literary genres that characterizes the oeuvres of Jack London and Frank Norris, who wrote both "light" adventure fiction and "serious" antimonopoly novels, reflects the intimacies of coolie fighting and trust busting that may illuminate some historically well-traveled circuits between racism and utopian energies.

SOCIAL REFORM MOVEMENTS AND ASIATIC RACIAL FORM

Agrarian Populism was the first modern political movement of practical importance to assail the problems created by industrialization, especially the abuses of banking power, railroad monopoly, and the short supply of money.[29] Populism's influence upon contemporary critiques of industrialism was widespread; even urban-based political movements, from Labor to Progressivism, clung to cultural memories of a lost agrarian Eden and a Jeffersonian agrarian worship of the yeoman farmer. In the view of Richard Hofstader, Populism was profoundly limited by dualistic thinking—an apprehension of social conflict as a simple struggle between plutocrats and everyone else, and the apocalyptic expectation that present-day conditions would lead either to "the destruction of civilization, or the establishment of absolute despotism" (67). This dualism reflected a common use of the threat of impending disorder to strengthen the case for social reform. In the fear of violent class conflict shared by varied reformers and conservatives alike, anarchy was often conjured as a dangerous alternative to oligarchy.

In the social reform discourses of the late nineteenth century, the concern for industrialization's victims, many of whom were newly arrived immigrants, was often intertwined with the suggestion of their responsibility for America's cultural degeneration. The Populist Party's Omaha platform of 1892 warned of a nation on the verge of "moral, political and material ruin": "The urban workmen are denied the right to organize for self-protection, imported pauperized labor beats down their wages, a hireling standing army, unrecognized by our laws, is established to shoot them down, and they are rapidly degenerating to European conditions" (Hofstader, 67). In the notion of America's reversion to a "European" feudalism, the ignorance and illiteracy of new immigrants—stereotyped as peasants unschooled in the culture of democracy—were partly to blame for the rise of urban political machines that corrupted the ballot box. Describing the extreme exploitation that explains the competitive edge held by New York's clothing industry, Progressive reformer Jacob Riis wrote: "Every fresh persecution of Russian or Polish Jew on his native soil starts greater hordes hitherward to confound economical problems, and recruit the sweater's phalanx. The curse of bigotry and ignorance reaches half-way around across the world, to sow its bitter seed in fertile soil in the East Side tenements."[30] Riis's account suggests that Jewish self-exploitation on the Lower East Side was a consequence of immigration's transplantation of European social structures onto American soil.

If the increasingly rigid and exploitative class hierarchy of late-nineteenth-century America was somehow a European import, so was industrial modernity's flipside—its sense of teeming chaos and constant flux. Riis's *How the Other Half Lives* (1890) presents a New York that is as multitudinous as it is alien. "The one thing you will ask vainly for in the chief city of America is a distinctively American community," Riis writes; the Americans "are not here. In their place has come this queer conglomerate mass of heterogeneous elements" (Riis 19). The crowd's natural unruliness was often used to symbolize the threat of social conflict in the nineteenth century. Its foreign aspect increasingly remarked by commentators in the 1890s reflects what the historian William Preston has shown to be the common association of aliens and dissenters in the popular and legal imagination of the period.[31] Riis ends his portrait of New York's tenements with a warning of impending social catastrophe. Such may be the solution, he writes, "of the problem of ignorant poverty versus ignorant wealth that has come down to us unsolved, the danger-cry of which we have lately heard in the shout that never should have been raised on American soil—the shout of the 'masses against the classes'—the solution of violence. There is another solution, that of justice. The choice is between the two. Which shall it be?" (207). Within

Riis's teeming masses, the lurking "man with the knife" (207) signifies the potential for violence and anarchism borne by all large assemblies.

Within an urban context perceived as pervasively alien, how does the Asiatic appear? The aesthetic question of Asiatic racial form is necessarily also one of the ideological relationship between Asian exclusionism and anti-European nativism at that historical moment. Less than fifty years ago, it was conceivable for the historian John Higham to take for granted that the history of the United States' Asian exclusion movement was "tangential to the main currents of American nativism," which centered on the "history of the hostilities of American nationalities toward European immigrants" (*Strangers*, 32). Today, it is the notion of Asian immigrants as paradigmatic aliens in U.S. nation-formation that is more likely to attract consensus.[32] On the one hand reflecting the inroads made by Asian American studies into understandings of U.S. history, the national exemplification of Asian exclusion runs the perennial risk, on the other hand, of being overly driven by the logic of academic field legitimation. As Susan Koshy has observed, a weakness of arguments on behalf of Asian American exemplarity is that they depend upon a model of parallel minoritization, occluding understandings of intergroup relations, especially between minorities.[33] Koshy's own research seeks to open up a view of the latter. "The presence of Asians," Koshy writes, "provided a means for 'not-yet-white' groups, such as the Irish, to reinforce the equation between Americanness and whiteness by shifting the debate about Americanness from the question of nativity to the question of race. Both blacks and Asians helped make the liminal European groups white, an identity that would have been less tenable in their absence" (Koshy, 165–66). Partly at stake in Koshy's argument is the demonstration of the psychological compensation of non-blackness for Asians who sought citizenship by proving their whiteness, despite the fact that after 1870 naturalization could also have been claimed by those who were black. Her analysis of the relationship between Asians and blacks boldly illuminates the discomforts of the "productivity of whiteness as law" (Koshy, 167).

My own interest in the career of whiteness in the twentieth century lies in tracing the phenotypical instability that, paradoxically, accompanied the expansion of its legal power. Though some would argue, Koshy among them, that there was a shift during the nineteenth century in the debate about Americanness from the question of nativity to the question of race, it is also the case that early twentieth century nativism had the effect of calling into question the Americanizability of a widening number of groups. However much a discourse of racial delineation between Americans of European and non-European descent may have been solidifying, a vociferous discourse of Anglo-Saxonism, starting in the 1890s, multiplied the possibilities for white aliens. With the negative attention of immigration officials drawn to the geographic shifts in European immigration from the 1890s on, the link between Americanness and nativity was hardly severed. An understanding of the process of Asian American racialization therefore requires situating Asian Americans in relation to the system of slavery, for which they were partly imagined as a postbellum substitute, as well as in relation to the ongoing phenomenon of labor immigration as a whole, whose diverse global sources were integral to the accelerated nature of U.S. industrialization. The prevailing construction of Asian immigrants as "aliens ineligible to citizenship" suggests the presence of a discourse on natives and aliens, as well as a discourse on whites and blacks, in the racialization of Asian Americans.

In historical studies of the intersections between U.S. race and class formation, racism is differently theorized depending on whether black-white relations or immigration is taken to be central. In the influential argument that helped to establish the constitutive role of race in class formation, David Roediger describes a working class that primarily defined its freedom against chattel slavery.[34] In another view, that of Gwendolyn Mink and Alexander Saxton, racial and ethnic discrimination are symptoms of the overall craft bias of the mainstream labor movement and the near synonymity of nationalism and anti-industrialism.[35] Both perspectives understand racism to reflect a failure of class consciousness, if not class radicalism, on the part of the organized leadership of the U.S. working class (and to a certain extent its rank and file) in ways that are linked to the larger question, "Why is there no socialism in the United States?"[36] However, in the first view, whiteness is consolidated through its difference from "preindustrial" labor forms, while in the second it is industrial labor that surfaces as Other. Opposing views of the modernity or antimodernity of whiteness depend on whether whiteness is being primarily considered in relation to black slaves or cheap immigrant labor. In the former case whiteness is inclusive and elastic; in the latter case it has a shrinking tendency and involves making unapparent distinctions between true Anglo-Saxons and other European identities.

What are the implications of whiteness's instability and growing hiddenness for the representation of Asiatic racial form, whose history of emergence betrays the dynamics of both racial oppression and nativist reaction? The extent to which Asian exclusionism and anti-European nativism were both defined against Anglo-Saxonism specifically, rather than whiteness, points to evidence, despite the politically reasoned insistence of today's ethnic studies discussion, of some permeability in the boundary between racial and ethnic difference.[37] There are rich implications, for example, to Saxton's surmise that 1894 may have marked the point at which Gompers's rhetoric against Chinese infiltration could also be analogously applied to selected Europeans.[38] At the same time it is true that although the 1924 immigration law's astonishing enlargement of the pool of all those who counted as undesirable aliens implied some continuity between Asians and non-Anglo-Saxon Europeans, contemporary naturalization case law, such as the 1922 and 1923 Supreme Court decisions of *Takao Ozawa* vs. *United States* and *United States* vs. *Baghat Singh Thind* took for granted that differences between Asians and whites were either scientific or simply commonsensical.[39] What is the place of the Asiatic within a landscape of manifold aliens? What is its figural specificity?

When the coolies make their appearance via the trope of rebellion in "Thoroughbred," Norris is drawing upon a rich set of associations between Asiatic horde and anarchistic mob. Indeed, in shape shifting from insurgent menace back to sluggish docility, the coolie figure in the story traces a movement between the antipodes of anarchy and oligarchy thought to imperil American civilization at the end of the nineteenth century. The policy stance taken by Theodore Roosevelt's newly appointed commissioner-general of immigration, a former leader of the Knights of Labor and with a long record of inveighing against Chinese cheap labor, provides another racial articulation of the dichotomy used to urge reform.

In an article for *Collier's Weekly* entitled "Exclude Anarchist and Chinaman!" (1901), immigration chief Terence Powderly sought to assure the public of the government's security procedures newly installed in the wake of President McKinley's assassination by a U.S.-born citizen of Polish descent. What is the link between the two banned categories of the article's title? Though "the man who killed President McKinley was born, raised, educated and trained in the United States," reassuringly, "the teachings which eventuated in the crime are not indigenous to the soil of America."[40] Similarly, "American and Chinese civilization are antagonistic; they cannot live and thrive and both survive on the same soil. One or the other must perish" (7). While Powderly's reasoning is uniformly circular in justifying their national exclusion on the basis of an assumed foreignness, the paired categories reflect a divergent articulation of ethnicity and politics. Powderly attributes the rise of anarchism in the United States to the southward tilt in European immigration—away from "honest, homeseeking Germans" (5) and toward troublesome Italians.[41] His objection to Chinese immigration, on the other hand, rests on its posing an "appalling menace to American labor" (7). As twinned foreign perils, "anarchist" and "Chinaman" express different crimes against the republic—one political, the other economic. To put it another way, the dependence of industrial profits on the exploitation of cheap immigrant labor was at the time rhetorically diversified into a political disturbance and a racial contamination. It is perhaps not surprising that, in being condensed into political versus economic terms, white ethnics should have gathered a reputation for being undocile workers and that Asians appeared incapable of political action.[42]

Yet, in being jointly named, "anarchist" and "Chinaman" were strangely made to share an apparitional kinship. Powderly's regime marked the vast expansion of immigration policing, and those labeled "anarchists" or "Asiatic" were the primary targets of increased official harassment.[43] These subjects posed a particular visual challenge to border policing. Just as the "alien anarchist who presents himself for admission to our country at an immigration station on the coast or border" (Powderly, 5) was not too readily obvious, a new immigration apparatus of identification and classification began to be deployed on the claim that Chinese individuals were racially difficult to distinguish.[44] Thus, when Powderly defends his measures as the only proper and effectual "guard against the invasion of this stealthy foe to lawfully constituted government and authority" (5), the point could equally well apply to anarchists or Chinese.

The notion of the enemy alien who is ubiquitous and invisible is, on one level, the necessary illusion of any national security discourse and a function of its self-legitimation. On another level, "anarchist" and "Chinaman" are differently invisible: seldom were Chinese and anarchists mistaken for one another. Riis's "man with the knife" remains unseen until his moment of attack, but one can always tell from the outset who is a "Chinaman." The anarchist blends into the "mixed crowd" whose Slavic and Mediterranean character implied a spreading political radicalism.[45] The "Chinaman," on the contrary, presents an obviously identifiable entity. He is not at all concealed in the crowd; his obtrusiveness has to do with the fact that he always comes as a crowd. The anarchist signifies the modern crowd's riot potential; the Asiatic signifies its homogeneity. The Asiatic marks the crowd's outward appearance; the anarchist marks its latent capability.

THE ASIATIC MODE OF PRODUCTION: FROM *CAESAR'S COLUMN* TO *THE IRON HEEL*

On the function of Asiatic racial form, antimonopoly fiction had even more to say. The 1890s witnessed a spate of utopian and dystopian writings credited to the influence of a futuristic bestseller by Populist leader Ignatius Donnelly. His novel *Caesar's Column: A Story of the Twentieth Century* (1891) sold 60,000 copies in the first year of its publication and 260,000 by 1906.[46] A fiction writer, journalist, and Minnesota politician involved in various Granger and Farm-Labor alliance movements in the last three decades of the nineteenth century, Donnelly was instrumental in helping bring the Populist Party into existence in 1892. *Caesar's Col-*

umn was praised by leading members of the Populist movement and by commentators across a wide political spectrum (Hofstader, *Age of Reform*, 67). Frank Norris's portrait of the railroad's stranglehold on farmers in *The Octopus* (1901), and Jack London's apocalyptic depiction of class conflict, *The Iron Heel* (1908), were among those works indebted to Donnelly.

Set in the year 1988, *Caesar's Column* is narrated in a series of letters written by a visitor to New York from a Swiss colony in Uganda, Africa, who reports on life in oligarchic America and the event of its violent overthrow by a secret mass organization called the Brotherhood of Destruction. Neither greedy plutocrats nor brutalized insurgents, however, are fit to rule. In the end, as the country self-destructs, the hero and his friends escape to his home in Africa, where they help to found a utopian republic based upon the economic principles espoused by the Populist Party.

The agrarian basis of the novel's middle-class appeal rejects industrialization but not the institution of private property. The protagonists are themselves direct descendants of America's founding fathers or a rugged Scandinavian yeomanry. The text's vision of agrarian renewal therefore coincides with the project of Anglo-Saxon preservation from a degenerative modernity. The oligarchic America from which they flee is controlled by an evil Jewish financier named Prince Cabano. Indeed, all of Europe has fallen under the sway of a "coterie of bankers, mostly Israelites."[47] On ground level, the dark and swarming cosmopolitanism of the city population reflects an overabundance of travelers "to or from England, Europe, South America, the Pacific Coast, Australia, China, India and Japan" and the complete absorption of public lands by "millions of foreigners" (CC 11–12, 131). Taking an entirely dim view of all cross-border traffic, because "[t]here can be no equitable commerce between two peoples representing two different stages of civilization, and both engaged in producing the same commodities" without the "freest nations" being "constantly pulled down to ruin by the most oppressed" (CC 357–58), the novel insists upon the spatial isolation of its final utopia.

Whereas the anti-Semitic imagination of Populism has already prompted a historiographical reassessment of the movement (Higham, *Send These to Me*, 95–98), Populism's mobilization of Orientalist representations has drawn little scholarly attention. In Donnelly's portrait of the world of monopoly finance capitalism, decadent consumption reflects a specifically Chinese palate. About the menu at the Hotel Darwin, the narrator observes: "The whole world had been ransacked to produce the viands named in it; neither the frozen recesses of the north nor the sweltering regions of the south had been spared: every form of food, animal and vegetable, bird, beast, reptile, fish; the foot of an elephant, the hump of a buffalo, the edible bird-nests of China; snails, spiders, shell-fish, the strange and luscious creatures lately found in the extreme depths of the ocean, and fished for with dynamite" (*CC* 14). While the rich plunder the earth's exotic creatures for their pleasure, the poor must depend on local vermin for survival: "[T]he rats and mice were important articles of diet—just as they had been for centuries in China. The little children, not yet able to work, fished for them in the sewers, with hook and line, precisely as they had done a century ago in Paris, during the great German siege" (*CC* 48). Indeed, the invocation of Chinese cuisine in the dietary instances of both rich and poor—both intended to evoke distaste—suggests the use of the polarized structure of "Oriental society" to figure the radical inequality of advanced capitalism. The anecdote of rodent consumption instructs us that deprivation strikes Europeans on historically specific occasions, but that this condition in China is transhistorical.[48]

The Orientalist taste of New York's oligarchs is used to underscore the cosmopolitanism of modern consumption. *Caesar's Column* describes a world culture that has begun to doubt the genuine superiority of Western civilization and to question the Eurocentric perspective of historiography. The visitor recounts:

> I touched the button for China and read the important news that the republican Congress of that great and highly civilized nation had decreed that English, the universal language of the rest of the globe should be hereafter used in the courts of justice and taught in all the schools. Then came the news that a Manchurian professor, an iconoclast, had written a learned work, in English, to prove that George Washington's genius and moral greatness had been much over-rated by the partiality of his countrymen. He was answered by a learned doctor of Japan, who argued that the greatness of all great men consisted simply in the opportunity, and that for every illustrious name that shone in the pages of history, associated with important events, a hundred abler men had lived and died unknown. The battle was raging hotly, and all China and Japan were diving into contending factions upon this great issue. (*CC* 16–17)

The propagation of cultural relativism in Japan and China is the flip side of a world where English is becoming universal even in isolationist East Asia. Meanwhile, in America, "the multitude seemed . . . to be of all nations commingled—the French, German, Irish, English—Hungarians, Italians, Russians, Jews, Christians, and even Chinese and Japanese; for the slant eyes of many, and their imperfect, Tartar-like features, reminded me that the laws made by the Republic, in the elder and better days, against the invasion of the Mongolian hordes, had long since become a dead letter" (*CC* 44). Asian facial features surface here and there as the physiological sign of a general condition of racial mixing; the relaxation of Asian exclusion law testifies to the spiritual death of the nation. The dystopia of globalization is exemplified by a fantastic merging of Oriental and Western civilizations.

Having had "to contend for the means of life with vile hordes of Mongolian coolies" (CC 111), Donnelly's American mass, like Arthur Stout's, has been degraded to the condition of coolies. The dominant Asiatic semblance of the daily multitude, however, fades during the season of its rebellion. This is led by one Caesar Lomellini, an Italian formerly responsible for a "terrible negro insurrection [which] broke out in the lower Mississippi Valley" (CC 147). The insurgent mass reflects a composite black and ethnic European character, carrying mixed allusions to slave revolt and peasant uprising. The Asiatic, however, is restricted to serving as the support of the oligarchic order:

> When the Great Day comes, and the nation sends forth its call for volunteers, as in the past, that cry will echo in desolate places; or it will ring through the triumphant hearts of savage and desperate men who are hastening to the banquet of destruction. And the wretched, yellow, under-fed coolies, with women's garments over their effeminate limbs, will not have the courage or the desire or the capacity to make soldiers and defend their oppressors. (CC 111)

As Saxton writes of the instrumentality of Asian exclusion to the rise of trade unionism, horizontal class division expressed itself by striking against the Chinese as the tool of monopolists (258). Mere tool, the Asiatic lacks independent agency. The figure's docile qualities are the effect of the physiological rigors imposed by cheapening wages as well as the training of industrial discipline. Of the people of the "Under-World," the narrator comments: "They seemed to me merely automata, in the hands of some ruthless and unrelenting destiny" (CC 44). The automaticity of the urban masses evokes Taylorism's remaking of the human body into a "human motor."[49] Their below ground existence is reminiscent also of Henry George's sinister description of another cityscape. On Jackson Street in San Francisco, George writes, there are

> "many large Chinese manufactories of cigars; while in many fetid dens underground and out of sight the patient Chinaman rolls the fragrant Havanas or cheap 'five-centers' which are to regale the nostrils of the 'Melicans' who despise him. This is the history of other trades in California, and from present appearances will shortly be the history of many more."[50]

Appearing in the *New York Tribune* in 1869, the California socialist's description of an increasingly Chinese-dependent U.S. economy was credited with helping nationalize the sense of alarm crucial to the passage of the Chinese Exclusion Act thirteen years later. George's equation of "Chinatown" with underground space seeks to tap a fear of unseen masses, but what it reinforces is the embeddedness of the Asiatic in the foundations of American industry. "From San Diego to Sitka, and back into Montana, Idaho, Nevada, and Arizona, throughout the enormous stretch of country of which San Francisco is the commercial center, [the Chinese] are everywhere to be found. Every town and hamlet has its 'Chinatown'" (George, 1).

In his study of race and American literary realism, Kenneth Warren reads the "universe of strangers" in which postbellum Americans found themselves in terms of a "black presence [that] was never entirely absent," despite limited African American access to white places.[51] "Because the emancipation of black Americans and the acceleration of capitalist transformation were roughly coincident," Warren writes, "it was also possible to see black America as somehow responsible for undesirable changes" (119–20). But whereas the lurking danger of social integration after the Civil War is constituted through nostalgia for the happy-go-lucky "darky" of the past, the coolie figure—an oxymoronic Chinese figure of modern immanence—collapses the distinction between past and present. As a form of caste labor introduced toward the end of the slavery system and lingering beyond emancipation as an integral component of industrialization, the coolie cannot be seen as a "creature of a pre-industrial life style with a pre-industrial appetite"[52] and is alien to the imaginary pictorial of the preindustrial nation. Replacing a discredited system of forced labor expropriation, coolieism signifies the less tangible forms of domination entailed by the "purely economic" coercion of the market.[53] The International Workingmen's Association (or the First International), for example, may have acknowledged that the Chinese were not the cause of economic depression but nevertheless demanded their territorial removal, "considering their bad moral habits, their low grades of development, their filth, their vices, their race differences from the Caucasian, their *willing status as slaves*."[54] Representing a paradoxical condition of "willing slavery," Asiatic racial form emerged as an historical expression of the actual unfreedom of free wage labor.

Antimonopoly writings of the late nineteenth and early twentieth centuries put into protest's service a vision of Asian exclusion in different ways. Whereas Donnelly's desire for an agrarian Eden sought national seclusion from an Asianized modern world, Jack London's more ambitious and forward-looking program sought to expunge Asian existence from a borderless socialist future. As discussed in the previous chapter, the path to utopia in many of London's writings features an episode of total war with Asia. His "yellow peril" tangents are evidence of the extent to which his economic diagnosis, like Donnelly's, metaphorically Orientalizes the world of monopoly capitalism. London's novel *The Iron Heel* vigorously dissents from *Caesar's Column* in portraying monopoly to be a logical outgrowth of the free market and in ridiculing the folly of small farmers who refuse to recognize the inevitability of their own proletarianization. Yet, as in *Caesar's Column*, the rise of capitalist oligarchy in the U.S. means that the law is now being "twisted and distorted like a Chinese puzzle" to suit the interests of those in power.[55] The co-optation of big unions by big business has led to "the rise of castes" or a labor aristocracy within the working class (*IH* 464). Eventually, stagnant profits require the building of great works. "These great works will be the form their expenditure of surplus will take, and in the same way that the ruling classes of Egypt of long ago expended the surplus they robbed from the people by the building of temples and pyramids" (*IH* 469).

Before London, Henry George, in his 1879 *Progress and Poverty*, which attacked Californian land monopoly, had already warned that the American republic was threatening to devolve not just into constitutional monarchy and then feudalism, but into "imperatorship and anarchy."[56] In the arts and sciences, this process "would not take us toward Bacon, but toward the literati of China" (*PP* 539). Such allusions to China and Egypt reflected the popular use of inherited notions of Oriental despotism by American socialists and agrarian reformers alike to elaborate the decadence of monopoly capitalism. A tradition of European political economy, beginning in the eighteenth century with Montesquieu and culminating with Marx and Engels's theory of an "Asiatic mode of production," sought to identify the traits that distinguished non-European from European forms of precapitalism. Never all present in any single authorial conception, and sometimes radically inconsistent with one another, these traits were: state property in land; lack of judicial restraints; religious substitution for law; absence of hereditary nobility; servile social equality; isolated village communities; agrarian predominance over industry; public hydraulic works; torrid climatic environment; and historical immutability.[57]

Though this alternative form of precapitalism took its name from the paradigmatic failure of "Oriental society" to evolve toward capitalism despite an apparently high level of cultural achievement, in Marx and Engels the Indian and Chinese examples were also generalized to Russia, Mexico, Peru, and the ancient Celts (Anderson, 478). Marx and Engels's distinction between the Asiatic mode of production and European feudalism heavily emphasized the domination of a despotic state machine, which cornered the bulk of the surplus and functioned not merely as the repressive apparatus of the ruling class, but as its principle instrument of economic exploitation (Anderson, 483). In a critique of the concept, Barry Hindess and Paul Hirst argue that the Asiatic mode of production was in fact a theory of a state without classes.[58] For Perry Anderson, the close identity between the ruling class and the state in "Oriental society" meant that "Between the self-reproducing villages 'below' and the hypertrophied state 'above,' dwelt no intermediate forces" (Anderson, 483). The absence of any mediating presence between an external, tributary state and the peasant mass—such as existed in an independent feudal nobility and that could form the basis for bourgeois transition—was central to the explanation of Oriental stagnation.

Both *Caesar's Column* and *The Iron Heel* imagine a condition of advanced industrialization that, as in the Asiatic mode of production, has devolved into two antagonistic groupings—not so much property owners versus wage workers, but oligarchs (and their minions, including artists and company unions) versus everyone else. "Under the oligarchs will flourish, not a priest class, but an artist class. And in place of the merchant class of bourgeoisie will be the labor castes. And beneath will be the abyss, wherein will fester and starve and rot, and ever renew itself, the common people, the great bulk of the population" (*IH* 469). On the one hand, this Orientalist economic vision, fed by a Jeffersonian agrarian belief in the moral guarantees of small property holding, facilitates a crisis scenario of monopoly capitalism, such that the extreme inequality of the present day could be thought to presage the end of History itself. On the other hand, the attribution of Oriental despotism, in resting upon ossification, implies the masses' passivity and an eternally arrested social condition. Historical change within Oriental society would require an alien agency. To an Orientalist representation of American modernity, a naturalist tendency in literary realism in the late nineteenth century was especially friendly.

The more naturalistic the text, the stronger the dystopianism of its social imagination—we might see this encapsulated in the difference between *Caesar's Column*'s happy ending and the inability of the main narrative in *The Iron Heel* to come to a resolution. The chapters recounting the Chicago uprising in *The Iron Heel* are its most stylistically memorable. They are also its most naturalistic, both in their imagistic intensity and sense of disintegrating reality.[59] Written from the perspective of an individual who is part of the mass and trying to escape from it at the same time, these chapters highlight the tensions between the novel's positive revolutionary agenda and its negative preoccupation with sensationalizing the loss of individual autonomy. An incongruous juxtaposition of talking and killing during the mass uprising conveys the paradoxically dissociated nature of experience: "And so we talked, while the killing of the wounded went on. It is all a dream, now, as I look back on it; but at the time it was the most natural thing in the world" (*IH* 540). Minor details take on surreal life:

> Feebly my own limbs were helping me. In front of me I could see the moving back of a man's coat. It had been slit from top to bottom along the centre seam, and it pulsed rhythmically, the slit opening and closing regularly with every leap of the wearer. This phenomenon fascinated me for a time, while my senses were coming back to me. (*IH* 537)

The uncanny involuntarism of independently moving limbs dramatizes what is elsewhere limited to the text's political exposition—the subject's lack of self-mastery in living under a repressive state. Through a convergence of form and content at such moments, naturalism facilitated a more persuasive picture of the social domination of monopoly capitalism than its political overturning.

If London's socialist standpoint enabled him better than Donnelly to grasp the logic of capitalism, it did not, however, lead to the abolition of Asiatic racial form, which remained a primary idiom for representing social abstraction. In contrast to Donnelly's Jewish personification of the interests of monopoly finance capitalism, London's presentation of it importantly lacks anti-Semitism. His plutocracy has a metaphoric physiology: it has a brain and hands (*IH* 425–25), a nervous system (*IH* 522), and a body whose "bulk, like that of some huge monster, blocked our path" (*IH* 463). But it is portrayed as essentially a systemic entity whose invincibility lies in the very impossibility of reducing it to any single personification; it is everywhere and all things at once, including the president of the university, the newspapers, important lawyers, big factory owners, and vigilante mobs. Indeed to vanquish the plutocracy is to try to materialize it so that it might be "brought to earth and lie practically dismembered" (*IH* 523).

Caesar's Column expresses directly nativist objections to the foreign-dominated populace of New York City and sensationalizes its Asiatic miscegenated features. London's masses look different. Paradoxically, *The Iron Heel* reflects both an inclination toward Anglo-Saxon superiority and a celebration of cosmopolitanism in the quest for international working-class solidarity. Like *Caesar's Column*, *The Iron Heel* centers upon a hero who, though born to the working class, boasts an Anglo-Saxon distinction: Ernest Everhard "was a descendent of the old line of Everhards that for over two hundred years had lived in America" (338). Describing in loving detail the protagonist's bulging muscles and forceful mind, the text presents Everhard as a "natural aristocrat . . . *in spite of* the fact that he was in the camp of the non-aristocrats" (*IH* 326; emphasis added). Though the text is careful to observe Everhard's genetic advantages, it deliberately distances itself from the nativist prejudices of its historical moment. The narrator, Avis, is clearly meant to be regarded as a revolutionary heroine, but she is also faulted by the text for taking inordinate pride in her *Mayflower* heritage and making a "distinction between being native born and foreign born [that] was sharp and invidious in those days" (*IH* 338). The *Mayflower*, we are told, was "[o]ne of the first ships that carried colonies to America, after the discovery of the New World. Descendants of these original colonists were for a while inordinately proud of their genealogy; but in time the blood became so widely diffused that it ran in the veins practically of all Americans" (*IH* 437). The happy presence of *Mayflower* blood in the "veins of practically all Americans" might be understood as the obverse of Donnelly's nativist portrayal of an America overwhelmed by foreigners. The inclusiveness of London's international socialism is accompanied by a confidence in the capacity of Anglo-Saxon blood to survive, if not dominate, most racial crossings.

In *The Iron Heel*, the socialist universality of Anglo-Saxonism is mirrored by the flexibility of Asiatic form within the world of monopoly capitalism. Unlike Donnelly, London does not deploy different races to symbolize the different facets of industrial mass existence. The Asiatic can signify the passivity of the masses' absolutely determined condition of existence (as in an Orientalized form of caste society), as well as its potential for insurgency (as in the rise of "Asia for the Asiatics"). London's Asiatic is irreducible to a single class identity, just as "coolie" and "samurai" refer to opposing positions within the social hierarchy. More thoroughly in London's textual universe than anywhere else, the Asiatic metaphorizes the totality of capitalist modernity. London's recognition of the ultimate impossibility of any nationally enforceable policy of Asian exclusion, given capitalism's global dimensions, explains why the fight against the "yellow peril" is waged internationally and apocalyptically, why the defeat of the "yellow peril" carries a condensed symbolic importance in excess of its literal narrative utility.

If London's internationalism generates an instance of Asiatic militancy rarely found among his more reform-oriented contemporaries, his naturalistic emphasis on lost autonomy heightens the alien effect of the masses. The episode of an obliterating war with Asia finds an echo in the Chicago uprising, when, paradoxically, the most visible battles are not those fought between the police and the insurgents, but between the revolution's elite and the uncontrolled masses they are supposed to lead:

Half a mile of the mob had swept by when we were discovered. A woman in fantastic rags, with cheeks cavernously hollow and with narrow black eyes like burning gimlets, caught a glimpse of Hartman and me. She let out a shrill shriek and bore in upon us. A section of the mob tore itself loose and surged in after her. I can see her now, as I write these lines, a leap in advance, her gray hair flying in thin tangled strings, the blood dripping down her forehead from some wound in the scalp, in her right hand a hatchet, her left hand, lean and wrinkled, a yellow talon, gripping the air convulsively. (*IH* 536)

The scene is reminiscent of standard episodes from "yellow peril" pulp fiction in which the Anglo-Saxon protagonist encounters a mob of coolies fronted by a Chinese "hatchet man." We have already seen one example in Norris's "Thoroughbred"; more from London's and Norris's adventure fiction will be drawn below. *The Iron Heel* paints a portrait of mass degradation for which London's journalistic documentation of British East Enders was already known. *The Iron Heel* does *The People of the Abyss* (1903) one better, though, in showing that wasted workers can suddenly metamorphose into a fearsome, running horde. The earlier version of "the people of the abyss" embeds its attack on industrial civilization's falling standard of living in a patriotic comparison of egalitarian American frontier conditions with a British empire doomed to self-destruction.[60] With the coming of the "people of the abyss" to the United States, *The Iron Heel* provides yet another allegory of the closing of the American frontier. That the "last of the frontier writers" might also have been the "first of the proletarian school"[61] signals some literary evidence of the connection between the emergence of mass form and the history of U.S.-Asian relations.

THE FORCE OF ASIATIC HUNGER: *THE OCTOPUS*

By the spring of 1899, when Frank Norris began writing a trilogy of novels about the production, distribution, and consumption of American wheat, he had already gained recognition for two novels and was working for *McClure's Magazine*, a key outlet for the publications of leading Progressives such as Ida Tarbell and Lincoln Steffens. However, it was *The Octopus: A Story of California* (1901),[62] the first volume of "The Epic of Wheat," that brought Norris to widespread public attention, selling a remarkable 30,000 copies.[63] Based partly on an actual historical incident at Mussel Slough in the San Joaquin Valley in 1880 involving a bloody shoot-out between ranchers and representatives of the Southern Pacific Railroad, *The Octopus* centers its portrait of monopoly capitalism on the travails of the large-scale wheat farmer. Norris's wheat farmer is a figure who is being squeezed out of existence by forces beyond his control—the punishingly high transportation costs extracted by rail monopoly and low wheat prices, a product of the new and highly competitive world commodity market. Though the predicament of the wheat farmer is pathos filled, the text resists the easy sentimentalization of his suffering. In many respects resembling the railroad they battle, the farmers of Bonneville conduct themselves like speculators, gambling with the land and failing to husband it. In eschewing an idealized portrait of the farmers' agrarian virtue, *The Octopus* acknowledges the historical antagonism between the California wheat economy and the small family farm, which large wheat farmers opposed for fear of the increase in property values and taxes that would ostensibly have followed population growth. The 1890s demise of California wheat farming was due to declining per-acre yields, increasing land values, and the availability of cheaper credit, which made the high costs of specialty agriculture cropping more viable.[64]

The text conveys contradictory perspectives on the corporation, which is sometimes portrayed as an avaricious monster and other times presented as the servant to a greater good—the social value of worldwide wheat delivery. The text's concluding celebration of "wheat power" has long puzzled critics.[65] In the 1960s and 1970s, critics read the novel's ending as evidence of *The Octopus*'s ultimate preoccupation with nature over the concerns of society.[66] More recent critics have viewed the novel as a "corporate fiction," in which the monstrosity of the corporation is the monstrosity of personhood (Michaels, 206); as a radical emptying of the category of production by the collateral reassertion of the middleman (Seltzer, *Bodies*, 26); as Progressivism's evasion of the representation of class relations by its exclusion of farmworkers (Howard, 122–23); and as California rural realism's affirmation of a bourgeois sublime in which capital circulation is an end in itself (Henderson, *Fictions of Capital*, 140). Despite differences of opinion regarding the viability of ideological reading (and whether critics think they are performing one or not), the critical consensus is that the novel reflects or animates the logic of capitalism. Here a central focus on the racial discourses in *The Octopus* may contribute an added complexity to our understanding of the text's political economy.

Critics have long noted that Norris's dramatization of monopoly's stranglehold relies heavily upon the vehicles of nativism and anti-Semitism to make its case.[67] In Norris's San Joaquin Valley, as elsewhere in his fiction, blood and class converge. The action of large wheat farmers, who are Anglo-Saxon, is set against a background of small farmers, farm tenants, workers, and the dissolute unemployed, who are ethnically Portuguese and Latino. In one notorious passage, Norris describes a rabbit drive—the community mounts an organized extermination—in which racial types are explicitly character types: "The Anglo-Saxon spectators round about drew back in disgust, but the hot, degenerated blood of Portuguese, Mexican, and mixed Spaniard boiled up in excitement at this wholesale slaughter" (*TO* 502). The productive wheat-farming town of Bonneville is juxtaposed to the neighboring town of Guadalajara, whose picturesque sleepiness stands for a superseded Spanish mission-based economy.[68] The text merges the figures of California's colonial past (lazy Indians, Mexicans, mixed Spaniards) with new immigrants (drunk Portuguese tenants and gang workers) into a general Latino palate that provides dashes of local color. Here and there, on festive occasions, we see a "swarming family of Spanish-Mexicans, gorgeous in red and yellow colours" (*TO* 233). For the most part, the major characters are Anglo-Saxon, and the minor characters are Latino, with the exception of one German farm tenant, Hooven, whose absurdity and foreignness are intertwined in his obtrusively accented and broken English.

What we might call a nativist aesthetics, however, serves as more than just comic diversion or a scenic means of differentiating novelistic foreground and background. It also actively codes what is good and evil in the epic conflict itself. In the story, the leader of the farmers' defense league, Magnus Derrick, is betrayed by his own son Lyman, who sits on the railroad commission and whose gubernatorial ambitions lead him to oppose the reduction of San Joaquin Valley freight rates. Harran, the good son, inherits his father's Duke-of-Wellington nose and blond hair; Lyman has black hair and protruding eyes that give him an unusual "foreign expression" (*TO* 286). In one climactic scene of confrontation with the farmers he betrays, Lyman is told to take his "dago face" out of there by one of his father's friends (*TO* 286). That the farmers of the valley on the whole turn out to be difficult to organize politically is partly attributed to the presence of a few too many "ignorant Portuguese and foreigners" (*TO* 458) among the league's membership, who are lacking in loyalty to Derrick.

Meanwhile, the railroad's corporate chief and local agent are both Jewish. When we are finally introduced to the hidden figure behind all the company's far reaching actions, we are shown a man wearing "a silk skullcap, pushed to one side and a little awry, a frock coat of broadcloth with long sleeves, and a waistcoat from the lower buttons of which the cloth was worn, and upon the edges, rubbed away, showing the metal underneath" (*TO* 572). Shelgrim's "enormous breadth of shoulders" and massive frame (*TO* 571) symbolize the gigantism of corporate power and wealth, but still, the text hints, a certain cheapness shows through in the frayed edges of his buttons. "At the top," the description continues, "this waistcoat was unbuttoned, and in the shirt front disclosed were two pearl studs" (*TO* 572). The pearl studs, or a lesser version of them, recur in the dress of Bonneville's banker and real estate agent, S. Behrman, who is the railroad's most visible human representative and the farmers' villainous nemesis. S. Behrman is a "large, fat man with a great stomach," neck moist with perspiration, wearing a heavy black moustache and "vest buttons of imitation mother-of-pearl" (*TO* 66). The corporate chief's commanding and controlled massiveness contrasts sharply with the soft and wheezing corpulence of his local agent, yet their affiliation is established through a shared sartorial motif of blended cheapness and luxury. Following Donnelly's *Caesar's Column*, Norris's Anglo-Saxon farmer is situated in a middle position, oppressed from above by Jewish villainy and threatened by degenerate "new immigrants" from below.[69] Yet the wheat farmers' ongoing implication in global commerce reflects this text's rather complex relationship to things foreign. The ambiguous status of the alien can be seen especially, I suggest, in the text's less obvious figuration of the Asiatic—less obvious because there are no Asian characters with speaking parts and not even a significant background demographic, as there is with the area's Latino residents.[70]

In the midst of his travails, Magnus Derrick encounters a manufacturer called Cedarquist who, though he is himself a wealthy capitalist and a member of the San Francisco social elite, personally identifies with the wheat farmer's struggle against the railroad. "We are well met, indeed, the farmer and the manufacturer," Cedarquist says to Derrick, "both in the same grist between the two millstones of the lethargy of the Public and the aggression of the Trust, the two great evils of modern America" (*TO* 305). Cedarquist's own bitterness stems from the failure of his plant, but fortunately for him, unlike the farmer, he owns a diversified investment portfolio. "The building of ships—steel sailing ships—has been an ambition of mine,—for this purpose, Mr. Derrick, to carry American wheat" (*TO* 305). In a novel about the predicament of the farmer who is captive to the railroad to move his wheat, transportation industries trump other kinds of productive enterprise. In Cedarquist's business ventures, there is a parallel between what can or cannot be done with iron and where consumers are to be found. Steel ships provide the means beyond an American public whose political "lethargy" and feeble consumption mirror each other. That most of San Joaquin Valley wheat is destined for Europe, binding the California farmer to the vicissitudes of a global market, hints at this limiting condition.

Cedarquist launches into a speech that captures Derrick's imagination:

At present, all our California wheat goes to Liverpool, and from that port is distributed over the world. But a change is coming. I am sure of it. . . . Our century is about done. The great word of this nineteenth century has been Production. The great word of the twentieth century will be—listen to me, you youngsters—Markets. As a market for our Production—or let me take a concrete example—as a market for our Wheat, Europe is played out. Population in Europe is not increasing fast enough to keep up with the rapidity of our production. In some cases, as in France, the population is stationary. We, however, have gone on producing wheat at a tremendous rate. The result is overproduction. We supply more than Europe can eat, and down go the prices. The remedy is not in the curtailing of our wheat areas, but in this, we must have new markets, greater markets. For years we have been sending our wheat from East to West, from California to Europe. But the time will come when we must send it from West to East. We must march with the course of empire, not against it. I mean, we must look to China. Rice in China is losing its nutritive quality. The Asiatics, though, must be fed; if not on rice, then on wheat. Why, Mr. Derrick, if only one-half the population of China ate a half ounce of flour per man per day all the wheat areas in California could not feed them. . . . Send your wheat to China; handle it yourselves; do away with the middleman; break up the Chicago wheat pits and elevator rings and mixing houses. When in feeding China you have decreased the European shipments, the effect is instantaneous. Prices go up in Europe without having the least effect upon the prices in China. We hold the key, we have the wheat,—infinitely more than we ourselves can eat. Asia and Europe must look to America to be fed. What fatuous neglect of opportunity to continue to deluge Europe with our surplus food when the East trembles upon the verge of starvation! (*TO* 305–6)

Cedarquist's grand vision catches fire with Derrick, who immediately begins to fantasize about a new era in which farmers can emancipate themselves from speculators by "organizing into one gigantic trust, themselves, sending their agents to all the entry ports of China" (*TO* 319–20). The mass market afforded by a limitless China provides the imaginative means by which farmers could achieve a scale of power equivalent to the monopoly form by which they are now oppressed. Norris of course means for us to view Derrick's dream of escape through repetition with a measure of irony, in the same way that we know that Derrick the gambler is just another kind of speculator. As it turns out, Derrick's fantasy of being economically rescued by a China market soon collapses "like a pyramid of cards" (*TO* 322), with receipt of the latest news of another adverse court decision. In the end, Derrick is financially and psychologically destroyed, but the novel closes with Cedarquist successfully "organizing a line of clipper wheat ships for Pacific and Oriental trade" (*TO* 647). Having appropriated Derrick's bonanza crop, the nefarious Behrman meets his memorable end when he tumbles into the cargo hold of the *Swanhilda* and is buried alive by the wheat he's just sold to Mrs. Cedarquist and other charitable San Francisco women for famine relief in India. Undiscovered, Behrman's corpse sails out with the wheat bound for Asia. On board ship is also Presley the poet, for whom a trip to India will be a restorative vacation from too much immersion in the farmers' miseries.

What are we to make of this U.S.-to-Asia export as the novel's closing gesture? What is the status of the fantasy of an Asian "fix" for the California farmers' problems? Anticipating by many years William Appleman Williams's diagnosis of the roots of twentieth-century American empire, *The Octopus* locates expansionism in a marketplace conception of reality held by the subjects of commercial agriculture in the late nineteenth century.[71] The sailing of the *Swanhilda* for India occurs without regard for the ruined farmers, however, so that the feeding of Asiatic bodies presents an ironic epilogue to the story of monopoly capital's draining of the lifeblood of the American commonwealth. From this perspective, the novel seems to be questioning rather than endorsing a turn-of-the-century rhetoric of expansion that, in Derrick's momentarily excited words, saw "the whole East . . . opening, disintegrating before the Anglo-Saxon" (*TO* 319).[72] Norris's essay "The Frontier Gone At Last" (1902) would confirm this sense of skepticism. In it, Norris shifts the significant moment in Frederick Jackson Turner's narrative from the disappearance of available homestead land to the date of U.S. arrival in China. "Suddenly we have found that there is no longer any Frontier," Norris writes, "Until the day when the first United States marine landed in China we had always imagined that out yonder somewhere in the West was the border land where civilization disintegrated and merged into the untamed."[73] The inhospitablity of a Chinese ground for U.S. military occupation requires Americans to reverse the course and form of colonial conquest: " 'Eastward the course of commerce takes its way,' and we must look for the lost battle-line not towards the sunset, but toward the East," Norris writes, meaning England, Europe, and beyond (FGL 1187). The "great word of our century is no longer War but Trade" (FGL 1185).

Despite the fact that Norris intended his novelistic trilogy to chronicle just this trade movement—with the first novel concerning production in California, the second the commodity market in Chicago (*The Pit*), and the third consumption in Europe (never completed)—*The Octopus* nevertheless ends by moving spatially in the opposite direction.[74] Whatever the limitations of the farmers' rescue by Asia, the wheat does exact a final revenge against the railroad's representative. The shipping of Behrman's corpse across the Pacific forms an integral part of the narrative movement toward the realization of market inevitability, the recognition that wheat is all-powerful and, moreover, that its power is good:

But the Wheat remained. Untouched, unassailable, undefiled, that mighty world-force, that nourisher of nations, wrapped in Nirvanic calm, indifferent to the human swarm, gigantic, resistless, moved onward in its appointed grooves. Through the welter of blood at the irrigation ditch, through the sham charity and shallow philanthropy of famine relief committees, the great harvest of Los Muertos rolled like a flood from the Sierras to the Himalayas to feed thousands of starving scarecrows on the barren plains of India.

Falseness dies; injustice and oppression in the end of everything fade and vanish away. Greed, cruelty, selfishness, and inhumanity are short-lived; the individual suffers, but the race goes on. Annixter dies, but in a far distant corner of the world a thousand lives are saved. The larger view always and through all shams, all wickedness, discovers the Truth that will, in the end, prevail, and all things, surely, inevitably, resistlessly work together for good. (*TO* 651–52)

Where the tragedy of the farmers' deaths arouses a political critique of injustice, this ending suggests a final acquiescence to market forces—not just an impersonal representation of limited human agency, but a moral justification of determination in the name of a Oriental fatalism ("Nirvanic calm"). Norris's fixation on the wheat, in particular, as the symbol of that "mighty world-force" which spreads everywhere regardless of human resistances, seems to mystify the circulation of commodities as unmediated movement. Recalling Cedarquist's speech, the seduction of a China market lies in the fantasy of removing the middleman—the idea that the farmer can sell direct to his consumer in a world of increasingly globalized marketplaces that has meant ever reduced agency for the producer. The ranchers "no longer felt their individuality. The ranch became merely the part of an enormous whole, a unit in the vast agglomeration of wheat land the whole world round, feeling the effects of causes thousands of miles distant—a drought on the prairies of Dakota, a rain on the plains of India, a frost on the Russian steppes, a hot wind on the llanos of the Argentine" (*TO* 54). What interests me is the way in which the magnetic figure of insatiable Asian hunger works in tandem with the naturalizing tendencies in the text's representation of commodity exchange: the wheat functions as an abstract symbol of nonhuman force, but it is also the concrete substance that is supposed to answer embodied human need. The figure of Asian hunger is integral to the positing of a circuit of supply and demand whose natural inevitability is confirmed by the narrative's spatial destination.

The novel is certainly all about food. The focus on a staple grain whose distribution is captive to a monopolized mode of transport enlarges the sense of injustice that would be more attenuated in the case of selling, say, vacuum cleaners. About this distinction, the novel reflects a deliberate canniness. It does not, in fact, conflate the distinction between shipping wheat for free to India and selling wheat for profit in China. Cedarquist is banking his future on the latter, though the only wheat shipment to Asia by the close of the novel is motivated by his wife's international charity. Mrs. Cedarquist's exaggerated sympathy for starving Indians is consistent with her frivolous sponsorship of decadent arts and exotic charlatans in her salon. About her "Million-Dollar Fair" intended to promote artistic renaissance on the West Coast, for which she successfully solicits a large contribution from her cousin, the railroad chief himself, Norris writes, "Money to the extent of hundreds of thousands was set in motion" (*TO* 315). Mrs. Cedarquist presides over a subeconomy of the "Fake" (*TO* 314), which is subsidized by the oligarchy that lives off the valley's farmers. Originating as her pet project, the *Swanhilda* voyage is simply another exotic indulgence on the part of the wealthy do-gooders who close their eyes to the real suffering of their immediate neighbors. Mrs. Cedarquist's husband, however, knows very well the difference between the real and the fake. For him, the *Swanhilda* voyage may be a write-off, but the vessel is also the "mother of the fleet" that will start shipping to Asia for profit: "the keel of her sister ship will be laid by the time she discharges at Calcutta. We'll carry our wheat into Asia yet" (*TO* 647). "My respects to the hungry Hindoo," Cedarquist continues, "Tell him 'we're coming, Father Abraham, a hundred thousand more.' Tell the men of the East to look out for the men of the West. The irrepressible Yank is knocking at the doors of their temples and he will want to sell 'em carpet-sweepers for their harems and electric light plants for their temple shrines" (*TO* 648). The good public relations of sending wheat to Asia aside, Cedarquist knows that expansionism is ultimately about creating consumer demand for items previously unimagined.

The novel's focus on wheat affords a way of naturalizing commodity production, literally. Once sown, the wheat grows itself: "the Wheat, wrapped in Nirvanic calm, grew steadily under the night, alone with the stars and with God" (*TO* 448). No human presence seems to be involved in this product manufacture. The supreme autonomy of the wheat is certainly the view that serves the railroad chief, Shelgrim, and given the way the narrative unfolds, it seems also to be the one embraced by the novel. The focus on wheat, moreover, naturalizes consumption: just as wheat will grow in abundance, people always need to eat. But here is where we can begin to see that for Norris, the problem with monopoly capitalism is not just that the "iron-hearted monster of steel and steam" lies between the "fecund San Joaquin, reeking with fruitfulness, and the millions of Asia crowding toward the verge of starvation" (*TO* 322), but that consumption must keep pace with production.[75] The fecundity of the valley is paralleled by myriad examples of troubled consumption, extremes of gluttony and fasting. Behrman's protruberant stomach no doubt symbolizes the trust's greed: ". . . was S. Behrman to swallow [Derrick's ranch] Los Muertos? S. Behrman! Presley saw him plainly, huge rotund, white; his jowl tremulous and obese, the roll of fat over his collar sprinkled with sparse hairs, the great stomach with its brown linen vest . . ." (*TO* 542). Behrman is all digestive tract (jaw or jowl and stomach); his oversized stomach so crowds out his lungs that one can always hear his "difficult breathing" (*TO* 66).

Annixter, a friend of Derrick's, and another wheat farmer, is in many respects the novel's true martyr, the man whose murder by railroad agents is especially poignant since he has just been personally transformed as a result of falling in love. Besides irascibility, Annixter's main trait seems to be finicky eating habits. We first encounter him fasting on dried prunes because his "stomach was out of whack" from "terrific colics all the preceding night" (*TO* 24); apparently he once returned early from a European trip because he couldn't tolerate European cooking. As an emotional character, the man is utterly unself-reflective—his "only reflection upon his interior economy was a morbid concern in the vagaries of his stomach" (*TO* 27). Though Annixter and Behrman are representative antagonists in the narrative conflict between the farmer and the railroad, they share the characteristic of being predominantly defined by their stomachs. One peculiar episode involving Annixter dining at the Derricks' ranch calls attention to the symbolic significance of Annixter's difficult eating:

> The Chinaman had made a certain kind of plum pudding for dessert, and Annixter, who remembered other dinners at the Derricks', had been saving himself for this, and had meditated upon it all through the meal. No doubt it would restore all his good humor, and he believed his stomach was so far recovered as to be able to stand it.
>
> But unfortunately the pudding was served with a sauce that he abhorred—a thick, gruel-like, colorless mixture, made from plain water and sugar. Before he could interfere, the Chinaman had poured a quantity of it upon his plate.
>
> "Faugh!" exclaimed Annixter. "It makes me sick. Such—such sloop. Take it away. I'll have mine straight, if you don't mind."
>
> "That's good for your stomach, Buck," observed young Osterman. "Makes it go down kind of sort of slick; don't you see? Sloop, hey? That's a good name."
>
> "Look here, don't call me Buck. You don't seem to have any sense, and besides it isn't good for my stomach. I know better. What do you know about my stomach, anyhow? Just looking at sloop like that makes me sick." (*TO* 102)

Later Osterman, another guest at the ranch and a personality known for his tricks, places the syrup in Annixter's bed as a joke, sending Annixter into a disgusted fury in the middle of the night. "'Ah yes, in my bed, sloop, aha! I know the man who put it there," he went on, glaring at Osterman, "and that man is a pip. Sloop! Slimy, disgusting stuff; you heard me say I didn't like it when the Chink passed it to me at dinner—and just for that reason you put it in my bed" (*TO* 121). Antipathy to viscous (semenlike) fluid has been read in terms of the text's misogynistic displacement of generative power away from women and biology toward a "resolutely abstract account of force" (Seltzer, "Naturalist Machine," 28, 32). The misplaced syrup's provocation of a racial slur in the text suggests that the substance carries racial, as well as sexual, meanings. In Annixter, we have an Anglo-Saxon whose defeat does not deservedly follow from a process of internal degeneration, as is the case with the Derrick family. The novel draws a parallel between Annixter's aversion to the syrup and his exceptional moral protest against the bribery scheme entertained by the farmers' league that evening: "It runs in my family to hate anything sticky. It's—it's—it's heredity. How would you like to get into bed at two in the morning and jam your feet down into a slimy mess like that? . . . And you mark my words . . . this business we talked over tonight—I'm *out* of it. It's yellow. It's too *cursed* dishonest" (*TO* 123). Annixter's metaphor for what's objectionable about manipulating a political process elaborates upon something formless by giving it more color.

By the end, we have been prepared by the Indian associations of Annixter's hair, which stands "defiantly erect as an Apache's scalp lock" (*TO* 227), to view his demise as a tragedy of the noble savage. In this story of the vanishing American, the "Chinaman" has a metonymic agency. Annixter's phobic reaction to Chinese "sloop" is part of the text's extensive discourse on food and feeding. The syrup episode can be read against other moments of feasting when Chinese cooks are serving something more palatable:

> The half-hundred men of the gang threw themselves upon the supper the Chinese cooks had set out in the shed of the eating house . . . The plowmen rinsed their throats with great drafts of wine, and their elbows wide, their foreheads flushed resumed the attack upon beef and bread, eating as though they would never have enough. All up and down the long table, where the kerosene lamps reflected themselves deep in the oilcloth cover, one heard the incessant sounds of mastication and saw the uninterrupted movement of great jaws. At every moment one or another of the men demanded a fresh portion of beef, another pint of wine, another half loaf of bread. For upwards of an hour

the gang ate. It was no longer a supper. It was a veritable barbecue, a crude and primitive feasting, barbaric, Homeric. (*TO* 132)

More than other occasions, barbeques promise to awaken the community's Homeric potential. Hearty eating of beef and bread is the key sign of the people's continuing epic vitality. Moreover, such eating is properly Anglo-Saxon. "An epic simplicity and directness, an honest Anglo-Saxon mirth and innocence, commended it" (*TO* 505).

A centerpiece of the American Federation of Labor's campaign on behalf of the renewal of the Chinese Exclusion Act, Gompers's contemporary pamphlet *Some Reasons for Chinese Exclusion. Meat vs. Rice: American Manhood versus Asiatic Coolieism. Which Shall Survive?* (1902) memorably defined the Asiatic threat to the American social body in terms of the physiological capacity of Asiatics to survive on a lower standard of living; protecting the American worker from falling wages was couched as a matter of the right to meat. Norris's and London's reputation as founders of the "red-blooded school of American literature"[76] may be worth reconsidering in light of their protagonists' dietary vulnerabilities as well as their exceptional muscular definition. If eating meat returns Americans to their Anglo-Saxon origins, so does American contact with China. In "The Frontier Gone At Last," Norris writes:

[A]s the first boat bearing its contingent of American marines took ground on the Asian shore, the Frontier—at least after so many centuries, after so many marches, after so much fighting, so much spilled blood, so much spent treasure, dwindled down and vanished; for the Anglo-Saxon in his course of empire had circled the globe and had brought the new civilization to the old civilization, had reached the starting point of history, the place from which the migrations began. So soon as the marines landed there was no longer any West, and the equation of the horizon, the problem of the centuries for the Anglo-Saxon was solved. (FGL 1184–85)

Norris's essay identifies "Asia" as the mythic origin point of an Anglo-Saxon identity based on westward expansion, which is why the arrival of the Western frontier in Asia eliminates a ground for the "West" itself. In Gompers and Norris both, Anglo-Saxon epic identity is defined, and potentially undefined, by an Asiatic origin and destiny.

The Octopus thematizes the thwarting of many an individual's epic aspiration. A key figure for this is the beset masculine body. Norris's novel contains many instances of the image of men everywhere caught within a vortex of forces or immobilized by an intractable foe. In the case of Dyke's submission to relentless, swarming bounty hunters, in Presley's engulfment by the surging crowd, and in the image of the final, ironic drowning of S. Behrman in the cargo hold of wheat, a "dreadful substance that was neither solid nor fluid" (644), *The Octopus* is replete with individuals struggling against "an enemy that could not be gripped, toiling in a sea that could not be stayed" (645). Robert Wiebe writes, "[w]hen writers first adapted naturalism to America . . . they turned automatically to the huge and vast. . . . Crane, Norris and Dreiser were giving singular form to the perplexity of a nation. As the network of relations affecting men's lives each year became more tangled and more distended, Americans in a basic sense no longer knew who or where they were. The setting had altered beyond their power to understand it, and within an alien context they had lost themselves."[77]

In portraying the grip of monopoly power, the novel suggests a correspondence between the wheat and the corporation, whose invisibility and ubiquity give it its special quality. Thus "the League was clamorous, ubiquitous, its objects known to every urchin on the streets, but the trust was silent, its ways inscrutable; the public only saw results. It worked in the dark—calm, disciplined, irresistible" (*TO* 346). The corporation's elusive representability partly explains the mixed metaphors that clutter Norris's melodramatic evocation of the railroad:

> [A]bruptly Presley saw again, in his imagination, the galloping monster, the terror of steel and steam, with its single eye, cyclopean, red, shooting from horizon to horizon; but saw it now as the symbol of a vast power, huge, terrible, flinging the echo of its thunder over all the reaches of the valley, leaving blood and destruction in its path; the leviathan, with tentacles of steel clutching into the soil, the soulless Force, the iron-hearted Power, the monster, the Colossus, the Octopus. (*TO* 51)

Norris's description intermittently veers off into abstraction, with the train disappearing into what it symbolizes ("vast power" or "soulless Force"). Where the description stays concrete, a taxonomic disorder—where the mechanical, mythological, and animal collide—makes it difficult to visualize whether the entity is moving or embedding itself, whether swiftness, largeness, or tenacity takes priority.[78] It is true that sometimes we see a victim of the trust "caught and choked by one of those million tentacles suddenly reaching up from below, from out the dark beneath his feet, coiling around his throat, throttling him, strangling him, sucking his blood" (*TO* 352–53). However, one cannot help noticing how relatively little the text works with its titular metaphor. Veering between abstract and concrete—sometimes signifying nothingness, as in endless fields of monoculture, and sometimes signifying life's pure substance itself, as in the germinating seed—the wheat more richly conveys the specificity of *The Octopus*'s representation of monopoly capitalism.

Perhaps even worse than the suspicion of corporate parasitism or centralized conspiracy is the horror of the wheat's formlessness, the erasure of all spatial boundaries that suggest capital's totalizing reach and blanketing homogenization. This may be why, in the grand confrontation of railroad and wheat, finally only "*the* WHEAT *remained*" (*TO* 651).

The equivalence between various kinds of inescapable substances associates an Asiatic presence with capitalist modernity's assault upon individual autonomy. Parallel themes—crowd, wheat, and syrup—help to explain the powerful allure of empty Asiatic bellies to the increasingly dependent entrepreneur, who dreams of a figure of unfulfillable consumption able to forestall the dangers of overproduction. The racial figure deftly condenses capitalism's mass dimension with its tendencies toward global expansion—hence *The Octopus*'s detour across the Asia-Pacific despite the trilogy's intended geographical trajectory and the historical facts of the California wheat export economy.[79] Approaching the American Asiatic Association as a "historical bloc" during the McKinley and Roosevelt administrations, John Eperjesi attributes to the trade group an appreciable effectiveness in instituting the Asia-Pacific as a regional entity whose geographical inclusions and exclusions were defined by capital's sphere of circulation (Eperjesi, 198–204). Though *The Octopus* certainly toys with the Asiatic as a romanticized figure for unfettered circulation, its ambivalent status alludes to the conflict between business and labor lobbies on the appropriate openness of the U.S.-Asian border at the turn of the century. Clamoring Asiatic hunger reverses a racial economy in which too-easy Asian satiation, in the Asian exclusionist rhetoric of the period, popularly portends American starvation. The question of Asian consumption levels could well refer to the pressures placed upon American workers by transnationalizing labor markets or to the predicament faced by American businesses, whose drive to lower domestic wages and need for overseas markets went hand in hand.

Maintaining the average rate of profit may require searching for new ways to lower the cost of labor reproduction, but there is still no overcoming the tendency toward overproduction without stimulating more consumption—somewhere. The figure of perpetual Asian hunger reflects *The Octopus*'s borrowing of an Orientalist fantasy to recharge a classless frontier vision of noncontradictory and endless American growth. But the silent presence of Chinese cooks in the household economy of the California ranches, who exist to prepare and serve food they do not eat, and the disturbing connections between eating and dying in the text are dark reminders of the destruction wrought by global expansion. We suspect that what really kills Annixter is eating Chinese food. Despite *The Octopus*'s attraction to the idea that everyone might well benefit from Asia's economic development, the ominousness of the text's consumer problems registers a grave skepticism about the free market's promise of universal emancipation.

After 1898, at a time when half of an unskilled worker's income was spent on food, public discussions of farmers and their markets increasingly revolved around potential wheat shortages, rather than chronic surpluses, and the issue of the cost of living.[80] Cedarquist's proposed notion of elevating Asiatic dietary standards from rice to wheat addresses the fear that food prices may be both too low for American farmers and too high for American workers. Actually, the text makes clear that, in contrast to public discussions that may have construed the conditions of labor reproduction to be determined chiefly by natural swings in crop surpluses and shortfalls, industrial overproduction and declining relative wages go hand in hand. The text knows that what fills the cargohold of the *Swanhilda* is not really food. It is more than Behrman can eat, and it is also not going to fatten up Presley:

> "Get fat yourself while you're about it, Presley" [Cedarquist] observed, as the two stood up and shook hands.
> "There shouldn't be a lack of food on a wheat ship. Bread enough surely."
> "Little monotonous though. 'Man cannot live by bread alone.'" (*TO* 648)

The wheat cannot be eaten because human need is mediated by commodity relations: the monotony of wheat signals exchange value's domination over use value. The wheat is a social relation, not a thing. Though the *Swanhilda* carries a portion of the bonanza crop from San Joaquin Valley, its uncertain nutritious quality (not just for Presley and Behrman, but for the vegetarian recipients of that contaminated cargo) forces us to recognize that what is being represented there is not the exported excess of California's natural bounty, but the movement of U.S. capital.

Though commodities represent the abstraction of social relations, their sensuous existence manifests the materiality of capitalist abstraction. The wheat is capable of literal force: "It filled the pockets of the coat, it crept up the sleeves and trouser legs, it covered the great, protruberant stomach, it ran at last in rivulets into the distended, gasping mouth" (*TO* 646). The insatiable and invincible Behrman finally can only be conquered through force-feeding. If it is suggested that the decadent feasting at a railroad magnate's home—at the very same moment when displaced farm tenants are starving as a result of the railroad's brutality—is a kind of cannibalism of "dog eat dog" (*TO* 608), the corpse buried within the wheat intended for famine relief certainly de-romanticizes consumption. As a final gesture, the filling of Asiatic bellies with the body of the trust's representative presents a macabre solution to the crisis of overproduction by staging another version of "meat versus rice." In the same way that the wheat oscillates between the abstract and the concrete, the Asiatic helps figure both utopian and dystopian narratives of monopoly capitalism. Evoking a myth of endless creation and recreation, a "Nirvanic" mysticism helps propagate a universal vision of industrialized wheat production. As part of the theme of troubled consumption, chronic Asiatic need alludes to the darker social consequences of global expansion and the crises brought on by capital's falling average rate of profit.

ADVENTURES ON THE COASTAL FRONTIER

Antimonopoly novels were also racial polemics—narratives of Anglo-Saxons imperiled by aliens. In Norris's *The Octopus* and Donnelly's *Caesar's Column*, corporate oligarchies are controlled by Jews, and the social landscape teems with new immigrants. London's *The Iron Heel* differs from these in its unusual lack of anti-Semitism and by investing the Asiatic with villainous agency. Despite such variations, all of these works presented monopoly capitalism as a world of Orientalized social relations. They issued pessimistic verdicts on the future by drawing resemblances between the prospective decline of the West and the permanent stagnation of Oriental civilizations. In *The Octopus*, the Asiatic is a metonymic figure for the loss of autonomy experienced by individuals caught in the web of globalizing markets, whereas in the other novels the American masses have themselves begun to grow Asiatic visages. In naturalism's degenerationist emplotment of history, the Jew is the personification of monopoly capital, but the Asiatic refers to a condition of extreme economic determination. This is why the Asiatic is a ubiquitous but not necessarily manifest presence in naturalism. Anti-Semitic anticapitalism strikes at Jewish bodies, affording the satisfaction of transforming an abstracted power into something tangible: Donnelly's Prince Cabano and Norris's Behrman are made to suffer lingering, painful deaths.[81] By contrast, the final solution of the Asiatic question tends in the opposite direction, toward instantaneous evisceration rather than materialization. This can be seen especially in the genocidal fantasies London entertains toward Chinese and Japanese populations in his socialist science fiction.[82] That the Asiatic embodies but does not usually personify a logic of capitalism requires that we switch genres to view naturalism's staging of Asiatic character.

To the extent that it is distinguishable from realism in the American context, naturalism more relentlessly interrogates the autonomy of the subject, devising characters who behave more like animals or machines than human beings.[83] Writing of the European novel, Georg Lukács reads in naturalism a reflection of the declining ability of bourgeois realism to represent history over the course of the nineteenth century. Lukács's assessment of the critical failure of naturalism, despite its sincere protests against the sordid realities of capitalist life, can be understood as a literary extension of his philosophical theory of reification. For him, the tendency of writers in the later nineteenth century to portray history as an inorganic compound of inner modernity and outward exoticism, with Flaubert being an early example of this, reflects commodity fetishism's growing divorce of subject and object in everyday life.[84] In suggesting that *Madame Bovary*'s psychological explorations and *Salammbô*'s frozen archeological grandeur form two sides of a single development, Lukács's dialectical account of apparently disparate genres may help us contend with the taxonomic slipperiness of California writers whose naturalism was more often clothed in romantic and exotic formulas than in the trappings of the social urban novel.

A number of California adventure tales feature iconic scenes of Anglo-Saxon warriors in martial face-off with coolies. In Jack London's "The Plague Ship" (1897), mutinying sailors clash with rioting Chinese after the outbreak of typhus aboard ship. One of the engineers

> was evidently suffering the tortures of delirium tremens: his eyes were set and dilated; his gigantic body convulsed with nervous spasms; his mouth a mass of froth and blood. Throwing himself into the doorway, armed with nothing but a huge battle-axe (some curio of his), he held the fiends at bay. The fleeing passengers blocked the other exit while those that remained, beheld a wondrous struggle. Among the Chinese were some of the most redoubtable highbinders and hatchet-men of the coast—mercenary and trained fighters for the societies to which they owed their allegiance. Unlike the average Chinese, they were not cowardly: murder and bloodshed was their profession.[85]

The leader steps forward from among the group of Chinese, apparently to finish the fight one-on-one. "It seemed as though David had come forward to face Goliah. His appearance belied his reputation as the wonderful Ah Sen, the fiercest of all the hatchet-men: slender and effeminate of form, his delicate face seemed more that of a smooth-faced boy or woman, than that of a notorious desperado" (PS 90). Though the combatants are starkly mismatched in size, their qualitatively different strengths are cause for suspense, until Ah Sen sinks to the floor, "his neck wrung like a chicken's" (PS 90). In the next moment, however, he is joined by his antagonist who is "literally hacked to pieces by a score of knives and hatchets" (PS 90). The victor of the duel is simply overrun by the mass backing his opponent.

Here, London's "David" and "Goliath" symbolize two destructive forces manipulated into fighting each other by the first-class passengers, with whom our sympathies are meant to lie (PS 89). More often, the giant who falls prey to a lesser yet formidable opponent is the martyred hero, the individual caught in the vortex. The scene from *The Octopus* in which a hops farmer, driven into crime by ruinous freight prices, is captured by a railroad posse suggests a shared aesthetic between representations of the corporation's reach and the coolie swarm above:

> They swarmed upon him from all sides, gripping at his legs, at his arms, his throat, his head, striking, clutching, kicking, falling to the ground, rolling over and over, now under, now above, now staggering forward, now toppling.
>
> Still Dyke fought. Through that scrambling, struggling group, through that maze of twisted bodies, twining arms, straining legs, S. Behrman saw him moment to moment, his face flaming, his eyes bloodshot, his hair matted with sweat. Now he was down, pinned under, two men across his legs, and now halfway up again, struggling to one knee. Then upright again, with half his enemies hanging on his back. His colossal strength seemed doubled; when his arms were held, he fought bull-like with his head. . . . Yet, however Dyke might throw off the clutches and fettering embraces that encircled him, however he might disintegrate and scatter the bands of foes that heaped themselves upon him, however he might gain one instant of comparative liberty, some one of his assailants always hung, doggedly, blindly to an arm, a leg, or a foot, and the others, drawing a second's breath, close in again, implacable, unconquerable, ferocious, like hounds upon a wolf. . . . But he could no longer protect himself from attacks from behind, and the riata was finally passed around his body, pinioning his arms to his sides. After this it was useless to resist. (*TO* 485)

The description of Dyke's ensnarement by the tentacles of the corporation might well be the companion piece to Gompers's *Meat versus Rice*, which carried an illustration of American labor pictured in the shape of a prone Gulliver (see fig. 1). The torso and limbs of this American Gulliver are pinioned by fetters that bear the words, "starvation wages," "heathen competition," and "cheap labor." Swarming over this body are hordes of Chinese who flow in inexhaustible supply from across the ocean, greeted by the welcoming sign "Lapse of the Chinese Exclusion Law, May 5th, 1902." At the bottom, the accompanying caption reads, "The American Gulliver and Chinese Lilliputians—shall the last spike be driven?"[86] Such images commonly evoked the increasing sway of, in Hofstader's formulation, combination over competition in the renaissance of American social thought in the period from the 1890s to the First World War.[87] In the contemporary discourses of naturalism and Asian exclu-

THE AMERICAN GULLIVER AND CHINESE LILLIPUTIANS—SHALL THE LAST SPIKE BE DRIVEN?

[From the Philadelphia North American.]

Figure 1. From Samuel Gompers's *Meat versus Rice*.

sionism, cheap immigrant labor was also cast as a kind of monopoly tendency that paralleled the swelling of corporate titans.

Norris's earlier novel *Moran of the* Lady Letty (1898) explicitly racializes the confrontation between competition and combination as an adventure story. Here again is the Anglo-Saxon facing the coolie:

> Wilbur caught his breath as the two stood there facing each other, so sharp was the contrast. The man, the Mongolian, small, weazened, leather-colored, secretive—a strange, complex creature, steeped in all the obscure mystery of the east, nervous, ill at ease; and the girl, the Anglo-Saxon, daughter of the Northmen, huge, blond, big-boned, frank, outspoken, simple of composition, open as the day, bareheaded, her great ropes of sandy hair, falling over her breast and almost to the top of her knee boots. As he looked at the two, Wilbur asked himself where else but in California could such abrupt contrasts occur.[88]

Just as "yellow peril" discourse routinely installs both men and women as Anglo-Saxon representatives, the coolie is a figure that is neither fully male nor female. In this explicit instance of cross-dressing, the Anglo-Saxon's feminine identity accords a heightened melodrama to the message of civilizational endangerment while a masculine exteriority reiterates the bodily dilemma of "American manhood" confronted by Asiatic coolieism. In actual pitched battle, this opposition is no contest, but the Mongolian eventually carries the day through an underhanded murder of the Anglo-Saxon. *Moran of the* Lady Letty recounts the "passing of the great race"[89] in a California overrun with coolies, just as in "Thorough-bred," Barry Vance represents pedigreed San Franciscans who are being edged out of home by a Mongolization of cityscape: the events of "Thor-oughbred" are narrated from a point in time when, despite the heroic as-sertion of Anglo-Saxon authority in the story, "the place is practically surrounded by Chinatown . . . and the Vances have moved out into the Western addition. The homestead is cut up and honeycombed to lodge some hundred Chinamen" (T 198).

Repeating the scenic confrontation of Anglo-Saxon and coolie we first glimpsed in "Thoroughbred," *Moran of the* Lady Letty extends the short story's racial articulation of the contradictions of Californian political economy. "The only theme, when all is said and done, that keeps its seri-ousness for these California novelists," wrote Edmund Wilson, "is the theme of class war. . . . The labor cause has been dramatized with more impact by these writers than it has been on the whole in the East. . . . This tradition [of radical writing] dates from Henry George, who saw the swallowing of the whole state by capital accomplished in record time during the sixties and seventies of the last century."[90] If Wilson is right that California literature engages questions of class in a manner distinct from other regional literatures, in what way is Wilbur's reflection on the California-specificity of the visual contrast between Anglo-Saxon and coolie a key example?

The Octopus and *McTeague* may be Norris's most well-known explo-rations of the problems of the corporation and of money, but we can see that his earlier, explicit interest in coolies already formulates some of the same concerns with the elusive forms of monopoly finance capitalism that are to be reiterated throughout his work.[91] Despite the rapid growth of cor-porations in American life beginning with the railroad industry in 1850, Alan Trachtenberg writes, at the turn of the twentieth century, the " 'face-less' corporation and the 'organization man' had not yet arrived as public perceptions."[92] Norris's range of economic writings suggests that Asiatic racial form in this era may have been an overlooked yet major site where corporate life was registered but not fully recognized, to use Trachtenberg's words, except in the already outmoded language of individualism.

Moran of the Lady Letty tells the story of a San Francisco society dandy named Ross Wilbur, who is kidnapped and pressed into service aboard a Chinese-operated fishing vessel. In the course of a voyage down the California coast to Magdelena Bay in Baja, the vessel rescues a tough female Anglo-Saxon seafarer named Moran from a floating wreck, of which she is the sole survivor. Wilbur and Moran develop a sympathy;

they gain mastery over the Chinese crew members, who are more easily cowed by nature's tempests, combat Chinese pirates over a valuable piece of ambergris, and return triumphant to San Francisco. Wilbur and Moran make plans to continue a buccaneering life on the high seas, "filibustering" in Cuba, but the defeated pirate leader Hoang, despite having pledged his service, treacherously murders Moran and escapes unpunished to Chinatown.

Hoang's easy camouflage in an urban scene in which "no one even noticed . . . his passage to the station" (*MLL* 250) and Moran's striking outlandishness together certainly imply a racial allegory of modernization, in which, in London's concurring words, those of "Saxon" lineage are "the last of the Mohegans."[93] As the last in a family of Viking explorers, Moran's continued means of livelihood was, before her death, already subject to question. Employees of the Chinese Six Companies, the Chinese of the *Bertha Millner* are engaged in the harvesting of shark-liver oil; their operation is dually illicit, because Chinese operators must engage a "dummy white" captain for the ship's permit and because they plan to market the shark-liver oil as cod-liver oil. In one sense, Moran and the Chinese are alike in belonging to the informal fringes of American economic modernity. In another sense, Moran and the Chinese signify opposite forms of economic organization. Moran is a (marine) pioneer without visible ties. Despite the fact that the pirates are obviously independent entrepreneurs, and that the seamen on the *Bertha Millner* have a financial stake in the operation's profits, the text uniformly refers to them both as coolies. The racial opposition between the Anglo-Saxon and the coolie, therefore, also erects a dichotomy between independence and dependence, between individual and corporate models of economic existence.

The only actual "coolie" in the text is Wilbur, who is involuntarily indentured by the Chinese Six Companies—until, that is, he internalizes his servitude as an adventure.[94] Having to "work this boat 'long with the coolies," the dandy is transformed as soon as he dons "oil skins and a sou'wester" (*MLL* 152, 144). "It was Wilbur, and yet not Wilbur. In two minutes he had been, in a way, born again" (*MLL* 144). Later, his resemblance to his Chinese shipmates is even more complete when the heat impels him to trade his pocketknife for a "suit of jeans and wicker sandals, such as the coolies wore" (*MLL* 154). His startling reappearance in society after a long absence "dressed in a Chinaman's blouse and jeans" (*MLL* 236) advertises the changes his experience has wrought. *Moran* can be read as a kind of bildungsroman, in which the pampered dandy is toughened into a buccaneer, who by the end is eager to volunteer to "liberate" Cuba from the Spanish. Besides functioning to cultivate an imperialist masculinity suitable for the late 1890s (gained through an experiment with fighting and killing Chinese), the adventure of Magdelena Bay explores the tension in Asian-American relations between the principles of free will and external imposition, competition and combination. As the novel's center of consciousness, Wilbur can shape-shift between Anglo-Saxon manhood and Asiatic coolieism, just as morally we see him negotiating between the rule of violence and the rule of law.

For all his infatuation with Moran and adventure, Wilbur has his moments of doubts about the ethics of piratical behavior. Their conflict with the Chinese beachcombers arises over the proper ownership of ambergris in a whale that the contracting parties have agreed to cooperate in stripping. The text emphasizes Chinese observance of agreements: "The three principals came to a settlement with unprecedented directness. Like all Chinamen, Hoang was true to his promises and he had already set apart three and a half barrels of spermaceti, ten barrels of oil, and some twenty pounds of bone as the schooner's share in the transaction. There was no discussion over the matter. He called their attention to the discharge of his obligations, and hurried away to summon his men aboard and get the junk under way again" (*MLL* 194–95). Trouble arises when Moran notices the existence of ambergris after the division of spoils has already been agreed to and hopes to appropriate all of it. It occurs to Wilbur that "it was quite possible that at least two-thirds of the ambergris did belong to the beachcombers by right of discovery" (*MLL* 198), but Moran's claim sets them on a collision course. Wilbur is eventually convinced by Moran's assertion that "the stuff belongs to the strongest of us" (*MLL* 211), but the accession to the rule of violence, leading to Moran's ruthless torture of Hoang, suggests the poetic justice of Hoang's ultimate revenge. On California's post-frontier, it is Moran who represents an outdated rule of force and the coolies who adhere to contracts.

The narrative is propelled by a series of unstable Asian-American business partnerships, reluctantly entered into by both sides and easily abandoned or compromised: we witness this in the "white dummy" captain's employment by the Chinese Six Companies and the ready betrayal of his post; Moran and Wilbur's agreement to work with the crew of the *Bertha Millner* in Captain Kitchell's place until the Chinese abandon ship out of fear of the oceanic unknown; Moran and Wilbur's joint whaling project with the Chinese pirates; and Moran's final deal with the original crew to fight the pirates (she gets the ambergris, worth $150,000, and promises $1,000 to $1,500 to each of the men). The instability of Asian-American partnerships is registered in the text's continual puzzlement over what is voluntarily undertaken and what is forced. Moran and Wilbur's debate over the fatal injury dealt to one of the Chinese on their side during the fight reflects the text's concern with the question of free will that arises in the case of coolie subjectivity. Can a coolie undertake a contract freely?

Despite having earlier asserted the irrelevance of agreements made with Chinese in their deal with Hoang, Moran now worries that they may have been wrong to bring Charlie into the quarrel, "only to have him killed" (*MLL* 226). Wilbur attempts to absolve his guilt in the death by insisting on the fullness of Charlie's personhood: "I didn't force him to anything. I—we, that is—took the same chances" (*MLL* 226).

The power relationship between Americans and Asians in this joint venture to Mexico is prone to sudden reversal: Wilbur is abducted to supply extra muscle, yet soon his Chinese captors recognize his superior navigational skills and ask him and Moran to captain their ship. The relational instability is reflected in coolie character: coolies can be coercive and menacing, yet they are also easily abused into servility by tough-talking Anglo-Saxons. Charlie's face reflects this flux, oscillating rapidly between gravity and hysteria on an instant (*MLL* 187). In a sense, the coolies are less like human characters than a kind of unmotivated movement, hence their swarming tendency. From Moran's perspective, they are a kind of vermin: "Huh! More Chinamen; the thing is alive with coolies; she's a junk" (*MLL* 191). Coolies resemble one of nature's obstacles in that they might generate narrative conflict at one moment and turn out to be mere scenery at another. Despite the fact that Moran and Wilbur are aboard a ship full of Chinese, the two are described as being "left alone on the open Pacific" (*MLL* 173); as in "Thoroughbred," Chinese tong warfare provides an enabling background for Anglo-Saxon romantic union. Though the novel appears to confront its protagonists with the challenge of primitive survival, nature's threats are only half-hearted. *Moran of the* Lady Letty self-consciously parodies the epic possibilities of Pacific adventure. Its short-distance voyage to Baja California and mild bay setting reflect the banal circumscriptions of "late imperial romance."[95] The decayed whale carcass available for easy looting marks a considerable distance from the original force of Melville's leviathan. In the contrast between Moran's passion for the sea and the coolies' discomfiture on stormy waters, it is the Anglo-Saxon who is at home in nature, which is shown to be fast vanishing.

Like Norris's coastal adventure tale, Jack London's semiautobiographical stories of his stint with the San Francisco Bay fish patrol also associate Asiatics with the disenchantment of nature.[96] In these adventures, coolie-fighting does not entail the conquest of nature but instead its necessary protection from those who threaten its preservation as a recreational area. London's symbolic wilderness has predominantly been thought to fall into four categories: the Yukon "White Silence," where "man" is improved through a contest with "nature"; a "Melanesian Hell," where "man" is degraded through that contest; a Polynesian Paradise Lost, where "nature" is despoiled by American colonialism; and a

California "Valley of the Moon," where an agrarian vision can be per-fected.[97] However, this account is complete only if we disregard the dif-ference between London's Pacific islanders (both noble Polynesians and savage Melanesians) and his Asiatics, who exist as a third term through-out many of his writings and function to situate the American subject be-tween a native primitivism and a coming modern. As seen through the lens of Asiatic discourse, London's California is part of the greater sym-bolic wilderness of an Asia-Pacific in which nature's despoilation is at-tributed to Asiatic agency.[98]

London's 1902 stories of environmental protection, later collected under the title *Tales of the Fish Patrol*, dramatize the law's fight against the dangers of overfishing—especially Chinese shrimpers who persist in using fine-mesh nets that wastefully entrap other fish. London and his pa-trol mates also pursue other ethnic immigrants who are in violation: Greeks who won't stop fishing on Sundays, Mexican oyster pirates, and generally impudent Italians. Nevertheless, within this general landscape of ethnic illegality, the Chinese shrimpers are London's most vicious enemy; they are not convertible through a shared code of honor as are, for example, the Greeks, and they very nearly kill him through some foul play on his final tour. Furthermore, the Greeks and Italians themselves are culpable for fishing sturgeon with a "Chinese line." A "Chinese line," London explains, in "King of the Greeks," is "a cunning device invented by the people whose name it bears."[99] "By a simple system of floats, weights and anchors, thousands of hooks, each on a separate leader, are suspended at a distance of from six inches to a foot above the bottom. . . . Because no sturgeon can pass through a Chinese line, the device is called a trap in the fish laws; and because it bids fair to exterminate the stur-geon, it is branded by the fish laws as illegal" (KG 825).

As with the fine-mesh shrimp nets, the total efficiency of the "Chinese line" threatens, much like capitalism's monopoly tendency, to eliminate the future of all competition. In various episodes, the under-equipped pa-trolmen have to deploy old-fashioned American imagination and will against the enemy's superior technological power.[100] London, like Norris, consistently refers to self-employed Chinese persons as coolies. The term indicates less a formal, indentured labor status than the totalizing po-tential of capitalist rationalization. The shrimpers travel in an exotic-looking "junk," which is equipped with an "antiquated tiller" and a "strange outlandish sail," yet this colorful appearance is coupled with un-usual speed.[101] A combination of exotic appearance and superlative tech-nical efficiency suggests that the Asiatic is modernization rendered visible, the alienating effects of whose process is worn on a surface exterior.

Imagistic juxtapositions of heroic warriors and diminutive coolies in California adventure fiction reflect naturalism's generally typological rather than developmental, descriptive rather than narrative, mode of representing difference. While realist progression is developmental, naturalist degeneration is metamorphic. The scenic confrontation between Anglo-Saxon and coolie at Magdelena Bay communicates the snapshot possibility of American degeneration into coolieism: it is the racially imaged equivalent of narratives of individuals sucked into vortices. Despite the apparent visual clarity of contrast between Anglo-Saxon and coolie bodies, at a narrative level these literary texts insinuate the unreliability of identities. With a mere change of clothing, Wilbur can start to look like a coolie. Disguise is so important to subversive operations in *The Iron Heel* that Avis Everhard can make herself unrecognizable even to her husband simply through adjustments in bodily manner and speech. Despite, or perhaps because of, the extent to which naturalism encodes exteriors with truthful meaning, appearances are radically changeable. In London's only text to center on a coolie protagonist, "The Chinago" (1908), an internal Oriental fatalism merges with an unjust, colonial penal system in the South Pacific to distinguish coolie character by the fact of Asiatics' individual indistinction.[102] Perhaps, in the end, coolies have no less developed interiors than most characters in naturalism, a literature whose impulse toward representing the socially marginal is rivaled only by its lack of differentiation between characters. But as archetypally nonindividual agencies, indeed, as entities without independent agency, coolies are specifically useful to naturalism's representation of modernity's dehumanization of character. That this is true is simply more physiologically visible in Norris's and London's exotic genres than in their more overt contentions with the determining force of monopoly capitalism.

CHAPTER THREE

The End of Asian Exclusion?

THE SPECTER OF "CHEAP FARMERS" AND ALIEN LAND LAW FICTION

SHORTLY AFTER THE BOMBING of Pearl Harbor, the western halves of the three Pacific Coast states and the southern third of Arizona were declared a military zone, from which all persons of Japanese descent were to be removed.[1] The sequence of events, proceeding from Executive Order 9066 on February 19, 1942, to the wholesale evacuation and incarceration by the end of the year of more than 110,000 Americans of Japanese ancestry, 70,000 of whom were United States citizens, presented an extraordinary diversion of military and civilian governmental resources at a time when the country was under the immediate wartime imperatives of labor mobilization and increased production. Support for the decision came from across the political spectrum, with just a few notable exceptions.[2] Forty years later, the judgment delivered by the Congressional Commission on Wartime Relocation and Internment of Civilians that a "grave injustice was done to American citizens and resident aliens of Japanese ancestry"[3] expressed an equally broad consensus. In light of the disparate wartime treatment of Americans of enemy alien descent (German Americans and Italian Americans were not interned as a group), the event of Japanese American internment has become almost impossible to narrate without recourse to the explanatory factor of anti-Asian racism.

According to the official governmental reasoning of 1942, total removal of the West Coast Japanese population was necessitated by the military threat that enemy subversion, both actual and potential, posed to national security in that area. In a February 14, 1942, recommendation to Secretary Henry L. Stimson for exclusion, chief of the U.S. Army's Western Defense Command, Lt. General John L. DeWitt cited "hundreds of reports nightly of signal lights visible from the coast, and of intercepts of unidentified radio transmissions" and the discovery of "60,000 rounds of ammunition and many rifles, shotguns and maps of all kinds" by FBI raids of premises occupied by Japanese nationals.[4] Moreover, sharing the stance of California State Attorney General Earl Warren, Dewitt held that "the very fact that no sabotage has taken place to date is disturbing and confirming indication that such action will be taken" (DeWitt, 34).

As the historical record subsequently revealed, not a single documented act of espionage or sabotage was in fact committed by an American citizen of Japanese ancestry or by a resident Japanese alien on the West Coast (*PJD* 3). What we now know of Japan's intelligence activities at the time is that its operatives tended to be naval officers attached to various Japanese consulates in the United States, or they were white Americans; the Gunreibu (the naval General Staff that directed and coordinated general intelligence) apparently avoided recruiting overseas Japanese, in part to avoid a local backlash against them and in part because it was felt that westernized Japanese could not be trusted.[5]

Nevertheless, in the days and weeks following the Pearl Harbor bombing, rumors were rife in the U.S. media that the attack in Hawaii had been aided by local Japanese American saboteurs and that the Japanese fliers shot down were wearing class rings of the University of Hawaii and Honolulu High School.[6] The public's identification of Japanese Americans with enemy Japanese—and of enemy Japanese with American institutions whose schooling they had "infiltrated" and betrayed—were strongly encouraged by allegations of fifth column activities made by an official committee of inquiry on Pearl Harbor headed by Supreme Court Justice Owen J. Roberts and press statements from Secretary of the Navy Frank Knox, despite the fact that U.S. intelligence agencies knew these to be unfounded.[7] Beginning as early as 1932, the West Coast and Hawaii Japanese communities had attracted the scrutiny of government intelligence agencies, the result of which was the acknowledgment, laid down in an FBI memo in November 1941, that "although surveillance, spot checks, and a thorough and logical investigation of individuals reported to be engaged in espionage activities has been conducted, no evidence has been obtained indicating that any have been guilty of violating any federal statutes for which prosecution would lie" (Kumamoto, 70). Furthermore, the report of special investigator Curtis B. Munson, dispatched in October 1941 by Roosevelt to investigate the loyalty of Hawaii and West Coast residents of Japanese descent, had also reached the conclusion that they were likely to be no less loyal to the United States than any other racial group. Though Munson's findings were known to top officials in the State, War, and Navy Departments by November 1941, his report was withheld from public knowledge until after the war.

The nonevidentiary reasoning that dominated the allegations of Japanese American sabotage was openly justified by stated expectations of race-determined behavior. "The Japanese race is an enemy race,'" De-Witt wrote, "and while many second and third generation Japanese born on United States soil, possessed of United States citizenship, have become 'Americanized,' the racial strains are undiluted. . . . That Japan is allied with Germany and Italy in this struggle is no ground for assuming that any Japanese, barred from assimilation by convention as he is, though born and raised in the United States, will not turn against this nation when the final test of loyalty comes" (Dewitt, 34). It is no wonder that the foremost historian of Japanese American internment, Roger Daniels, should assert that the internment decision was at root a reflection of what he considered to be American history's most central theme, white supremacy.[8] Daniels represents a paradigmatic post-1970s historiography that contextualizes internment by a prior history of Asian exclusionism. "The evacuation of 1942 did not occur in a vacuum," Daniels writes, "but was based on almost a century of anti-Oriental fear, prejudice, and misunderstanding" (Daniels, *Concentration Camps,* 2). Author of the pioneering study *Years of Infamy* (1976), Michi Weglyn similarly blames ingrained anti-Asianism for fueling the "incredible governmental hoax" of a fifth column peril that sent "some 110,000 men, women and children to concentration camps": "Behind it all was a half century of focusing anti-Asian hates on the Japanese minority by West Coast pressure groups resentful of them as being hyperefficient competitors. An inordinate amount of regional anxiety had also accompanied Japan's rapid rise to power" (35). Where scholars have narrowed their investigations to the culpability of particular decision makers—whether in the case of Lane Hirabayashi and James Hirabayashi's emphasis on the military interest in Japanese American removal that preexisted the appearance of public demand for it, or in the case of Greg Robinson's more recent study of Roosevelt's role, which shows that the president had made up his mind even before receiving DeWitt's recommendation—the behaviors of these actors are fundamentally attributed to anti-Japanese prejudice.[9]

The project of historicizing internment has largely entailed situating it at the endpoint of a chronological sequence of Asian exclusionist acts, a narrative of Asian exclusionism whose periodizations are ordered by the manifest ebb and flow of anti-Asian racism. In historical narratives of Asian exclusionism, the reliance on racism to explain historical causation often leads to a dehistoricization of racism. The result is that while we are well aware of the presence of racial dynamics in U.S. policy making, we are none too clear on the conditions of their operationality. What is anti-Asian racism? Are there ideological distinctions between the various governmental acts that go by the name of Asian exclusionism—including official restrictions on immigration and naturalization, legislated economic discrimination, spatial segregation, and population removal and internment? How might greater attention to the various concurrent contexts of these different acts further illuminate the evolving historical relationship between them? Beyond moral interpretations of internment as an essential aberration from or a reflection of American history, how might we grasp both the racial logic of internment *and* its historical specificity?[10]

One aspect of internment's historical obscurity is the signal neglect of its material theorization.[11] Just a handful of studies exist that attempt an economic account of internment. Among the most important, one effort by Morton Grodzins and another by Gary Okihiro and David Drummond take divergent approaches to the relationship between race and economics; despite their value, both have theoretical limitations. *Americans Betrayed* (1949) by Grodzins was the first postwar analysis to indict the government's actions and in so doing emphasized the influence of economic pressure groups, in particular western growers, who stood to gain from the elimination of competition from Japanese American farmers.[12] Not long after the publication of Grodzins's findings, a group of University of California professors, who, like Grodzins, had been involved in the anthropological fieldwork conducted in the internment camps under the auspices of the Japanese American Evacuation and Resettlement Project *(JERS)*, came out with their own study that questioned the primacy of "economic motives" behind the government's actions.[13]

The authors of *Prejudice, War, and the Constitution* (1954) challenged Grodzins on a series of key facts, arguing that only a minority of West Coast agricultural associations actually publicized pro-evacuation opinions (190); that the pressure prior to the date of DeWitt's recommendation to the president was "trifling" and not directed at DeWitt himself (191); that there was no evidence to show that a December visit to Washington by a representative of the Grower-Shipper Association had any effect on congressional or administrative policy (191); that military decisions were made before the activities of pressure groups commenced (187–89); and finally, that the agricultural and food associations themselves failed to present a united front, since two Washington groups went on record against mass evacuation, asserting that it would be an "economic waste and a stupid error" (191–92). Jacobus tenBroek and his coauthors proposed the alternative causality of "multiple agents," in which the people, the military, the president, and the Supreme Court were all to blame. *Prejudice, War, and the Constitution* may have been, as the authors claimed, "less a study of the Japanese Americans in particular than of Americans in general" (vi), and it may have been motivated by a quietist desire to counteract the most incendiary aspects of Grodzins's study,[14] but its rejection of an "economically reductionist" view of internment was to be reiterated by a politicized post-1970s historiography whose intent has been to expose the U.S. government's systematic oppression of people of color.

Internment scholars Lane Hirayabashi and James Hirabayashi, for example, also de-emphasize the instrumentality of business lobby groups and direct attention instead to the shared racism of various historical actors—the civilian and military branches of the government as well as the private sector (Hirabayashi and Hirabayashi, 94). Their analysis moves away from a positivist approach to the study of interest group politics toward a theorization of racial dynamics that accommodates broader questions of structure and culture. However, their positing of Grodzins's "pressure group theory" as the primary stand-in for an "economic" explanation of historical events has been part of a pattern in the scholarly literature on internment that is inclined to pit "racism" against "economics." Western historian Richard Drinnon, too, joins in this critical chorus against Grodzins's work for containing "much useful data, but exaggerat[ing] the responsibility of economic pressure groups," and concludes that, in the end, "a racist ideology was much more important than economics."[15]

Despite a surface resemblance to Alexander Saxton's analysis of nineteenth-century Chinese immigrants as the "indispensable enemy" of trade unions and other groups, the standard account of Japanese exclusionism, even when evoked as an "ideology," explicitly thematizes its peculiar lack of social location. According to Roger Daniels's *The Politics of Prejudice* (1973), by the time of the Second World War, anti-Japanese racism had become a near autonomic "reflex" of the "American psyche" or a "sleeping lion" that could easily be awakened at any time.[16] In framing the events of 1942 as the recurrence or fulfillment of a popular regional prejudice, Daniels's account of internment's causes bears a strong similarity to the argument of tenBroek and his coauthors that the event was traceable to "those opinions and attitudes which gradually congealed in the public mind to form the Japanese stereotype—that special blend of fabrication, myth, and half-truth on the basis of which, in large part, the wartime evacuation of the Japanese Americans was authorized, executed, and approved" (22).

In fact, the notion of anti-Japanese racism as a transhistorical psychology is present in Grodzins's study itself, which was theoretically restricted in that it conceived of "racism" and "economics" as opposing, independent variables. *Americans Betrayed* maintains that, prior to the war, economic self-interest overrode racial animosity, such that some white Californians were willing to subordinate prejudice in favor of profit, renting land and doing business with Japanese American farmers. The outbreak of war had the effect of heightening prejudice, which had been "pounded into the political and social structure of the region" (Grodzins, 15), at the same time that general prosperity made profits less dependent on Japanese industry. Ultimately, internment occurred, Grodzins argues, because war conditions had weakened the vested interests responsible for maintaining Japanese American farmers on the land, aligning for the first time the forces of economic self-interest and racial prejudice (175–76). We can see that despite a disagreement on the primary causation for internment,

Grodzins and his critics are united by a similar conception of "racism" and "economics" as opposing—irrational and rational—behavioral factors.

A contrasting effort to establish racism's rationality can be found in an analysis by Gary Okihiro and David Drummond, which conceives of the state as a prime agent of a racial capitalist order. Following a neo-Marxist direction, established in Asian American studies in the early 1980s by Lucie Cheng and Edna Bonacich with their framing of immigration history by global capitalist development,[17] Okihiro and Drummond describe Asian exclusionism as an integral mode of exploitation in which the importation of aliens deemed permanently ineligible to citizenship was a systematic means by which the United States could gain cheap, vulnerable, and reliable workers without having to bear the costs of labor reproduction.[18] The authors emplot Japanese American history in two stages: an initial period of "labor migrancy" from 1900 to 1924, and a second period of "internal colonialism" from 1924 to 1942. Ending with the Immigration Act of 1924, the first period is characterized by the extraction of surplus value from labor exploitation, and the second period by value extraction from a racial rent premium (Okihiro and Drummond, 170–71). Okihiro and Drummond depict evacuation and internment as fully economic transactions, detailing: the government-managed transfer of thousands of agricultural businesses from Japanese American farmers to the control of corporate growers and shippers; the systematic means by which substitute operators cheated the internees of their rightful profits; and the extent of authorities' failure to protect Japanese American property rights. No less than at other phases of Japanese American history, the events of 1942 involved, in their view, the collusion of state and capital (specifically large landholders and corporate growers) in profiting at the expense of Japanese Americans.

Okihiro and Drummond avoid confronting the executive order's final cause by taking for granted that "there is very little question that many [of the agricultural groups] stood to gain from their elimination" (171). They provide compelling evidence to suggest that discrimination always pays. In describing the serial domination of different techniques of racialized exploitation, however, their analysis does not offer reasons for the transition between them—why in 1942 a new mode of exploitation, the direct expropriation of Japanese American property, might have emerged and why the arrangements of internal colonialism came to an end. "Pearl Harbor," Okihiro and Drummond write, "sparked a return to [pre-1924] exclusionism and offered an opportunity for immediate profit and the expulsion of the Japanese from the level of farm operators"; evacuation and the pursuit of escheat actions to deprive Japanese Americans of property in the 1940s reveal the "genuine exclusionist intent of the removal and confinement of the Japanese" (174).[19] But if mass removal and internal colonialism both share the principal aim of economic gain, what explains the priority of "quick profits" over the long-term attractions of systemic dependency at one moment compared to another? When it comes to the question of historical change, Grodzins's hypothesis that the new agricultural boom instigated by World War II diminished the advantages of the racial rent premium at least attempts some kind of explanation.

The underdevelopment of a materialist historiography of internment stands in curious contrast to the fact that the Japanese peril and anti-Japaneseness have primarily found expression through an economic modality. In this, even the historiography most skeptical of the primacy of "economic causation" for Japanese exclusionism tends to agree. "Whatever its cause," Daniels writes, "the spectacular economic achievement of the Issei generation—especially within agriculture—was an important causal component of the animosity it generated" (Daniels, *Concentration Camps,* 7). It may well be that the prevalence of "anti-economism" in Japanese American studies is itself a symptom of the economism of Asiatic racial form—a form in which economic interests are not masked but are the primary medium of race's historical expression. As Keith Aoki's revisitation of prewar anti-Japanese legislation has it, "The denial of civil rights to Asian immigrants 'ineligible to citizenship' under Alien Land Laws paved the way for the denial of civil rights to Japanese American citizens under Executive Order 9066 only two decades later."[20] Aoki's linkage of California's earlier Alien Land Laws (which had twice before sought to limit Japanese American agricultural operations) with internment's purposes entertains, but unfortunately does not pursue, the possible significance of their shared attack on the rights of property ownership.

Indeed the 1942 discourse on Japanese American sabotage and the earlier Alien Land Laws can be seen to belong to a discursive history of the specter of the Asiatic farmer, a history that this chapter will trace. In concert with those who have linked internment to earlier anti-Japanese acts, this chapter picks up on the primacy of the economic as a medium of anti-Japanese feeling, but so as to question the assumed teleology of Japanese exclusionist history. First, we will turn to the economic aspects of the 1942 discourse of Japanese American sabotage that supply a texture to the perceived urgency of ridding U.S. territory of one kind of enemy alien and not others. Then, a survey of the empirical knowledge we have of prewar Japanese American agriculture and its limits will allow for a reflection on the specific modalities of Asiatic racial form. Finally, a look at two best-selling novels associated with a burst of anti-Japanese legislative activity twenty years earlier will help us appreciate the distinction between regional demands for Asian exclusion and the federal orchestration of mass removal.

The Specter of the Japanese Farmer: Agriculture and National Security

It is certainly possible to view the wholesale removal of the Japanese American population in 1942 as the latest episode in the history of California's agricultural development. Let us return to Lt. General DeWitt taking stock of the military situation in February 1942. The general recommended "[t]hat the Secretary of War procure from the President direction and authority to designate military areas in the combat zone of the Western Theater of Operations (if necessary to include the entire combat zone), from which, in his direction, he may exclude all Japanese, all alien enemies, and all other persons suspected for any reason by the administering military authorities of being actual or potential saboteurs, espionage agents, or fifth columnists" (appendix to chapter 3, *Final Report*, 36). "The continued presence of a large, unassimilated, tightly knit racial group, bound to an enemy nation by strong ties of race, culture, custom and religion along a frontier vulnerable to attack constituted a menace which had to be dealt with" (*Final Report*, vii).

A significant aspect of the evacuation order was the military classification of the West Coast as belonging to the "Western Theater of Operations." At least since the U.S.-Japanese war scare of 1907, the scenario of war with Japan had been entertained by pulp fiction writers as well as military strategic experts. During the 1907 war scare, Theodore Roosevelt received, and dismissed, a recommendation from the Joint Army and Navy Board to fortify West Coast ports and outlying territories. Military strategists mostly considered a sustained Japanese invasion of the U.S. mainland to be beyond Japan's military capability. How far into the Pacific the Western Hemisphere was held to extend tended to shift over time: by 1941 some naval planners argued that it reached a thousand miles west beyond the International Dateline to include Wake Island. But pragmatic leaders calculated that Japan would not be able to take and hold U.S. Pacific islands against an U.S. counteroffensive.[21]

In contrast to military calculations, many popular novels projected a Japanese sweep of an unfortified West Coast, or the suicide bombing of the Panama Canal by an explosive-laden Japanese merchant ship.[22] After the outbreak of actual war, fantastic fiction appears to have provided an advance script for the U.S. government's warfare psychology. Ironically, though the clearly strategically important base of Hawaii escaped the imposition of mass detention orders, the continental coastline from Alaska and Canada to Latin America (from which people of Japanese descent were kidnapped and dispatched to U.S. Department of Justice internment camps) was literally turned into a militarized national border, where persons of even partial Japanese racial descent, regardless of citizenship, became suspect. Spatially the racial war in the Pacific was comprised of two fronts: a military front between armed combatants in the southwestern Pacific, and a home front waged against thousands of civilians, whose equally Manichaean flair would strongly suggest a replay of nineteenth-century frontier war.[23]

The insistence that the West was the location of vital military and strategic installations in need of protection against sabotage was obviously inconsistent, since not only were there major defense industries outside this area but throughout 1942 German submarines regularly torpedoed American ships along the Atlantic coast (Yang Murray, 5). The "Western Defense Command Area" DeWitt was charged with defending extended thousands of miles inland, to include Arizona, Utah, and Montana, in addition to the states actually bordering the Pacific coast. A hard-to-fix abstraction, the U.S.-Asian boundary was arguably the Second World War's most anxiously defended national border. Its physical contours, as they came to be defined through administration, reflected the historical determinations of Japanese American demography.

Here is the commanding officer's summary of the dangerous situation obtaining in California:

The Japanese population in California aggregates approximately 93,500 people. Its disposition is so widespread and so well known that little would be gained by setting it forth in detail here. *They live in great numbers along the coastal strip, in and around San Francisco and the Bay Area, the Salinas Valley, Los Angeles and San Diego. Their truck farms are contiguous to the vital aircraft industry concentration in and around Los Angeles.* They live in large numbers in and about San Francisco, now a vast staging area for the war in the Pacific, a point at which the nation's lines of communication and supply coverage converge. Inland they are disposed in Sacramento, San Joaquin and Imperial Valleys. They are engaged in the production of approximately 38% of the vegetable produce in and along the water fronts at San Francisco and Los Angeles. Of the 93,500 in California, about 25,000 reside inland in the mentioned valleys where they are largely engaged in vegetable production cited above, and 54,600 reside along the coastal strip, that is to say, a strip of coast line varying from eight miles in the north to twenty miles in width in and around the San Francisco bay area, including San Francisco, in Los Angeles and its environs, and in San Diego. Approximately 13,900 are dispersed throughout the remaining portion of the state. In Los Angeles City the disposition of vital aircraft industrial plants covers the entire city. Large numbers of Japanese live and operate markets and truck farms adjacent to or near these installations. (DeWitt, 35)

A prima facie problem is presented through a relationship established between two things: Japanese production and defense-related installations. Though the report places heavy emphasis upon a contiguity between them, the absence of numerical data supporting the definition of physical proximity suggests that persuasion lies in mere rhetorical coupling. It is precisely through the coupling of two things strikingly unlike, farmers and war industries, that the description successfully generates suspicion. "It could not be established, of course, that the location of thousands of Japanese adjacent to strategic points verified the existence of some vast conspiracy to which all of them were parties. Some of them doubtless resided there through mere coincidence. It seemed equally beyond doubt, however, that the presence of others was not mere coincidence" (DeWitt, 9).

That the "distribution of the Japanese population appeared to manifest something more than coincidence" (DeWitt, 10) rests specifically on the nature of the lands occupied:

Throughout the Santa Maria Valley . . . every utility, air field, bridge, telephone and power line or other facility of importance was flanked by Japanese. They even surrounded the oil fields in this area. Only a few miles south, however, in the Santa Ynez Valley, lay an area equally as productive agriculturally as the Santa Maria Valley and with lands equally available for purchase and lease, but without any strategic installations whatever. (DeWitt, 9)

The report continues along this line of reasoning: "There were no Japanese on the equally attractive lands between these points" (9–10). Given the wide range of things classified as a "facility of importance"—including telephone or power lines, bridges or highways, and not merely, for example, aircraft industrial plants—one cannot help but suspect that it is Japanese population location that determines what is to be defined as a war-related installation. Of particular concern to the report was the "productive" and "attractive" nature of Japanese settled lands. In fact the official maps used by government officials to indicate the existence of suspicious proximity were originally drawn up for the purpose of marking areas that could be subject to alien land lawsuits. Although such data would have been necessary to establish a provable pattern, the maps did not include information on the many "strategic installations" where there were no Japanese nearby, nor did they show the nonrural land-holding Japanese population. That the weight placed upon Japanese agri-cultural holdings was disproportionate is underscored by the fact that only 44 percent of the Japanese residents of California were rural resi-dents, and of these a large number either lived on nonfarm areas or on land that was not Japanese-operated (Grodzins, 156–57).

How is it that farmers could have been mistaken for spies and soldiers? Rumors about Japanese sabotage in public circulation in the months be-tween Pearl Harbor and evacuation imparted a specifically agrarian qual-ity to subversive activity. There were stories of secret signs intended for enemy pilots that were cut into wheat fields, or tomatoes planted in the shape of an arrow pointing to a nearby airfield (Grodzins, 136; tenBroek, 70). The "surprise attack" at Pearl Harbor was thought to have been fa-cilitated by cane farmers communicating with the bombers through meaningful patterning of their fields. Given the predominant occupations of the Japanese population in the United States, the notion that food might function as a means of sabotage had earlier antecedents.

In 1935 an anti-Japanese group in Los Angeles calling itself the Com-mittee of One Thousand published a newsletter, the *American Defender,* that focused on the dangers of eating Japanese-grown vegetables due to unhygienic farming methods, including the use of human excrement as fertilizer (McWilliams, *P* 70). By early 1941 the FBI had generated a list of over 2,000 suspects divided into three categories of relative danger-ousness. In Group A, the most dangerous category, were fishermen, pro-duce distributors, Shinto and Buddhist priests, farmers, influential busi-nessmen, and members of the Japanese Consulate. In Los Angeles, every prominent Japanese grower and distributor fell into Group A (Ku-mamoto, 58, 61). *The Spectre of Sabotage,* a 1941 novel by Blayney Matthews, reveals the linkage between the concept of sabotage and the sexualization of the bogey of racial integration: "The [American] house-wife might become the object of a saboteur's attack just as readily as an armament plant. The vegetables, meats, groceries, and milk she pur-chases may be contaminated just as the water supply of the community in which she lives may be polluted. . . . What is to prevent Japanese spies, in their fanatical zeal, from striking a blow for their Emperor by excessively dusting vegetables with arsenic?"[24]

Directly after the First World War, although Japan had been an ally, concerns raised about the control of important foods by enemy aliens were directed at Japanese fishermen.[25] A significant aspect of the debate about whether or not to "evacuate" the Japanese population in the months after Pearl Harbor involved not just the quantity of crops grown by Japanese farmers but also the kinds. With the launching of the "Food for Freedom" program, which prevailed upon all farmers to increase production for the sake of patriotism, the reservation that evacuation would dangerously disrupt food production was met with assurances that "we might be short of radishes, green onions, and a few odds and ends for a short time but there would be no hardship."[26] Since war needs prioritized staple foods, some argued, the fact that the Japanese were engaged in growing mainly specialty crops, such as artichoke, asparagus, and strawberries, meant that the shortage of such "luxury" foods would be incidental. As the Bureau of Agricultural Economics reported to Congress, "Reduction in the supplies of some crops in which Japanese have specialized will be felt more at the middle class dinner table than in the Food for Freedom program."[27]

Almost all the tales of sabotage were set in broad daylight and out in the open. They situated danger in settings of everyday life, directing suspicion at the mundane. The necessity for total evacuation—the inadequacy of selectively arresting dangerous persons—was based on the argument that in the case of the Japanese Americans, it was impossible to distinguish between loyal and disloyal. In the discourse of evacuation's military necessity, character faded before phenotype. In the words of a contemporary observer, the "essential problem" of the West Coast Japanese was that "his physical characteristics make his position at present almost unbearable. No matter what he does he is regarded with suspicion."[28] Internment dramatized the power of appearance over legal status in the disparate treatment of U.S. citizens. Weirdly, though, Asiatic appearance was something that was at once obvious and not obvious. In this racial discourse, appearance was determining, and yet precisely so because of its surface indeterminacy.

Following a cautionary statement by California state government officials in the wake of Pearl Harbor that 40 percent of California vegetables were Japanese-grown, the California State Department of Agriculture was bombarded by letters from grower associations protesting that this figure was grotesquely inflated and was bound to trigger a national boycott of Californian produce because of its general association with Japanese industry. In the correspondence, Japaneseness is treated as paradoxically self-evident and undetectable. The author of one letter writes that "it is not far-fetched or beyond the realm of possibility that at least 25,000 of these Japanese, in the event of invasion, by exchanging civilian clothing for uniforms are full fledged members of the Japanese armed forces." The letter worries that Japanese "are allowed to go about and conduct their business as loyal American citizens." The focus on clothing suggests the clear external difference between Japanese soldier and American citizen, but also just the opposite—that a switch could occur at any moment, as easily as clothing can be changed. Thus despite what should have been the obvious distinction between "yellow termites," as the president of the Western Growers Protective Association called the Japanese, and "red-blooded American citizens," the sense of emergency derived precisely from the ease of its collapse. The letters were at pains to prove that what looked Japanese (California vegetables) was really American, and what looked American could be, at core, Japanese (citizens).[29]

The paradox of Asiatic appearance encapsulates the irony of how a group so visibly marked in Jim Crow America could have been prime suspects of espionage when spy operations would presumably depend on the ability to blend in and go undercover. The conflationary logic that lumped together Japanese and Japanese Americans cannot help but strike us as an unimpeachable example of Orientalism dictating U.S. policy. But besides reflecting the familiar dictum that "all Orientals look alike," the episode more interestingly suggests an uncertainty as to what Orientals always look like. What are the bodily implications of the expectations of "Oriental mystery," a theme we think we already know so well? Imaginative fiction written in support of the passage of anti-Japanese legislation presents the most detailed archive of the "yellow peril" 's aesthetic properties. But for an appreciation of the particular spectrality of the Japanese farmer, a survey of what we know and don't know about prewar Japanese Californian agriculture is first in order.

JAPANESE FARMERS IN CALIFORNIA: A HISTORICAL MYSTERY

Originally figured as a threat to the American working man, the Asiatic question only grew more confounding over time. As compared to the drive to close Chinese immigration in the late nineteenth century, anti-Japanese legislation during the 1910s gathered mass popularity despite the fact that, by disabling Japanese farm proprietorship, it would have had the effect of creating more Asiatic labor competition, not less. Each rhetorical eruption on the occasion of a discriminatory measure issued from so wide a cross section of social groups as to reinforce the appearance of a classless popular sentiment. They included farm bureaus, business associations, labor unions, and the usual series of patriotic organizations, such as Native Sons of the Golden West and the American Legion. Looking back upon the passage of the Alien Land Act of 1920 from the standpoint of the 1940s, Carey McWilliams wrote: "It would be extremely difficult to determine precisely what groups profited by the passage of this act, the agitation for which has jarred two continents and nearly precipitated war. . . . Landowners certainly did not profit, for they were forced (at least momentarily) to accept lower rentals. Agricultural workers did not profit, for their wages declined to an all-time low by 1933. . . . The competitive position of the California farmer was not improved. The general public did not benefit; on the contrary, it paid the bill."[30] Support for the 1920 Alien Land Law across contradictory constituencies has led scholars to conclude that "[p]atently, organized labor's anti-Orientalism was an inherited position and was no longer dictated by economic interest" (Daniels, *Politics*, 87).

If the popular desire for Chinese exclusion could have been attributed in part to the "false consciousness" of the American worker, who, in the face of falling wages, turned to racial barriers instead of international solidarity, as an ideology Asian exclusionism nevertheless once had a discernible class content.[31] Even as the "wages of whiteness" afforded certain material advantages to working-class subjects,[32] the division of the working class along racial lines fundamentally benefited employers, since it helped to enforce a segmented labor market and politically disorganize the union movement.[33] In the case of the Japanese peril, the class interests of Asian exclusionism were far murkier. Anti-coolie alarm bells had sounded from union organs and city sandlots; now warnings against the Japanese "yellow peril" were issuing from the farmland. What were the implications of the lexical slide in Asian exclusionist discourse from Chinese "cheap labor" to Japanese "cheap farmers"?[34]

Entering in significant numbers during the 1890s, Japanese immigrants throughout the western states were first employed in various occupations, including railroads, lumber, mining, canneries, and domestic service. By 1910, agriculture had eclipsed other occupations as the leading enterprise of the Japanese. Between 1900 and 1913, Japanese workers composed the majority of California's field labor.[35] The U.S. Immigration Commission estimated that some 30,000 Japanese were employed in California agriculture in the summer of 1909—according to Japanese sources, about two-thirds of the total number of Japanese in the state.[36] Among the factors at work, historians have cited the agricultural background of the immigrants themselves, obstacles to entering urban manufacturing industries, and the fact that steady rural-to-urban migration opened up new farming opportunities.[37] During World War I especially, when the labor demands of defense industries exerted an increased pull on the rural population, Japanese regional migration flowed in the reverse direction, from urban to rural sectors. By 1920 the vast majority of Japanese were working on farms either for themselves or as employees of other Japanese. All told, by the end of World War I Japanese farmers claimed 10 percent of the market price of all California crop (Daniels, *Politics*, 87).

Until the passage of the 1924 National Origins Act by the federal government put an end to Japanese immigration, anti-Japanese measures undertaken at the state and local levels targeted the agricultural sector. Starting in 1909, various bills designed to restrict Japanese agricultural economic activity were proposed on the floor of the California state legislature but failed to gain passage until 1913, when the Webb-Heney Alien Land Law prohibited aliens ineligible to citizenship from owning agricultural property and restricted the leasing of such property to a maximum of three years. In 1920 a second alien land law passed by popular initiative sought to close the loopholes of the earlier legislation. The initiative prohibited any leasing of land to aliens ineligible to citizenship, extended the power of the attorney general to institute escheat proceedings to the district attorney at the county level, prohibited corporations in which Japanese aliens held a majority of stock from leasing or purchasing land, prohibited Japanese parents who were noncitizens from serving as guardians of property for their minor children, and further stated that any Japanese alien who furnished the funds for the purchase of land held in the name of another person would be presumed guilty of the intent to avoid the Alien Land Law and would be subject to escheat proceedings by the state.[38] With the exception of the section affecting a minor's right to own property and the right of a father to serve as the guardian of his own minor child regardless of nationality, all sections of the 1920 law withstood legal challenges until it was deemed unconstitutional in the landmark case of *Oyama* vs. *California* in 1948 (Chuman, 80–87). By 1925, seven states followed California's lead in denying aliens ineligible to citizenship the right to acquire any interest in land for agricultural purposes, with variation on some minor points: Arizona (1917), Louisiana (1921), New Mexico (1922), Idaho (1923), Montana (1923), Oregon (1923), and Kansas (1925).[39]

The historiography is largely in agreement that the California Alien Land Laws of 1913 and 1920 stemmed from a reaction to Japanese agricultural upward mobility, but there is no agreement on what the laws were intended to accomplish.[40] By 1910 large numbers of Japanese had risen to share tenantry, cash tenantry, and even ownership; indeed, by 1920 Japanese ceased to be an appreciable source of farm labor.[41] In one influential view, alien land legislation came about when the entrepreneurial tendency of the new aliens, notable as early as 1907, began to erode big business's support for Japanese immigration, which had been a crucial buttress against the hostility of small farmers and labor to Asiatic competition.[42] According to McWilliams, who was the first to make this argument, consequential anti-Japanese feeling dates from the moment large numbers of Japanese started to become small-scale owners, joining large shipper-growers—whose enduring interest lay in maintaining large units of production and a cheap labor supply—to the cause of small farmers who resented the fact that Japanese agriculturalists tended to increase land values, to bid more for leases, and to pay more than their competitors for land (*FF* 111). This view does not, though, account for working-class support for the Alien Land Law by 1920, since the dispossession of the Issei of their landholdings and their reduction from farm operators to wage workers would actually have swelled the pool of labor competition: by that time no significant number of Californian Japanese were competing with organized labor, the Issei being mainly small farmers and business people. In the end, there is none too clear a consensus on the laws' social basis. More recently, Yuji Ichioka interprets the laws to have represented the triumph of small farmer populism over the vested interests of large landowners, who he contends opposed the measures.[43] Okihiro and Drummond, by contrast, think the laws were a subtle strategy developed by large landowners to force Japanese farmers into informal, disadvantageous arrangements, allowing for the extraction of higher rents and more land improvements (169). Okihiro and Drummond's theory of a racial rent premium proposes that the Alien Land Laws—like the calls for eliminating Chinese labor, which helped reinforce a split labor market—functioned not to kick Japanese farmers out of California agriculture but to stabilize a split rental market within it. Unlike McWilliams, Okihiro and Drummond thus view Japanese small farming as compatible with, not antagonistic to, the state's dominant pattern of land monopoly.

If the attack on Japanese farmers does not, in retrospect, constitute a distinct class subject, this is related to the fact that the actual impact of the Alien Land Laws on Japanese farmers remains a matter of dispute. Between 1910 and 1920 Japanese farm acreage more than doubled, raising questions as to whether the inefficacy of the 1913 legislation had in fact been intentional; while 1920 represents a peak in Japanese farm acreage for the state, with reports of a decline of over 40 percent between 1920 and 1925, it is very difficult to discern what portion of the reported decline represents an evasion of the 1920 law.[44] Citing the drop in Japanese farm acreage and in Japanese farmers' percentage of the total state farm economy over the course of the 1920s, Masakazu Iwata holds that Japanese agricultural development in California was checked in the period 1924–1941 (Iwata, 31). Robert Higgs maintains just the opposite, that "Japanese immigrants substantially improved their tenure status in California agriculture during the two decades after the passage of the harsh initiative act of 1920."[45] Higgs acknowledges the acreage reduction in the early 1920s but points to other influential factors—the general collapse of farm prices after World War I and the cessation of immigration, causing a disproportionate decline of Japanese adult males (221–23). Iwata and Higgs both agree with the finding that by 1940 the number of Japanese American farms had made a comeback to 1920 levels.[46] But whereas Higgs claims that between 1932 and 1940 owned acreage considerably increased in proportion to rented acreage, Iwata finds a stagnant rate of tenancy from 1910 to 1940, with 70 to 85 percent trapped

in the tenant category (Higgs, 222; Iwata, 32). Iwata is thus led to the opposite conclusion of an "unstable tenure pattern among the Issei agriculturalists with the associated undesirable features inherent in short-term
leasing, insecurity of land occupancy, and high tenant mobility" (32).
Higgs minimizes evidence of the drop in Japanese farm acreage between
1920 and 1930 by pointing to the likelihood that an increased number of
tenant operators listed themselves as "managers" in official data due to
the necessity of legal evasion (221). Ichioka challenges Higgs on precisely
this speculative point, writing that "since many (the exact number is unverifiable) were actual managers, [Higgs's] interpretation must be modi-
fied" (Ichioka, 178).

The historiography presents an inconclusive picture of pre–World War
II Japanese American agricultural trends, and highlights the difficulty of
relying upon sources of economic data from the prewar era. For example,
the U.S. census indicates Japanese farm holdings between 1900 and 1910
to have increased from 37 to 1,816 farms, and from 4,674 acres to
99,524 acres, but the figures recorded by the Japanese Association are
much higher, showing the 1910 acreage to be 194,742 (Ichioka, 158). In
1920 the Japanese Association once again reported vastly different figures on Japanese land holdings from those collected by the U.S. census
that year (Bloom and Riemer, 70). The unreliability of the data is at least
partly the result of conditions of economic informality characterizing
Japanese farm operation that, with the passage of the 1920 Alien Land
Initiative, were only exacerbated. In the interwar period, the number of
Japanese farm operators in existence supplied a topic of fanciful speculation and political partisanship, even when generated under the guise of
academic undertaking. In 1935 the University of California sponsored a
study entitled *The Story of Japanese Farming* that continued to blame
the state's agricultural woes on expanding Japanese incursions into the
best farmlands, a trend it purported to be ubiquitous even if ultimately
unverifiable.[47]

Insofar as it is difficult to separate the economic facts from the discursive effects of debates about the pros and cons of Asian immigration, the
research of Japanese American economic history constantly comes up
against the ideological nature of its archival sources. To this extent, even
our contemporary academic anxiety about reducing race to class runs the
danger, in the case of Asian American history, of rehearsing a particular
racial discourse attached to the notion of the Asiatic's exceptional escape
from the laws of class fixity. As we have seen, the superlative industry
of the "cheap farmer"—in contrast to that of the exploited "cheap
coolie"—is not only not demystified by our present-day understanding of
prewar history, but confirmed by it. Even as it seems to restore Asian
American agency to the historical narrative of Asian exclusionism, the

apparent miracle of upward mobility achieved by the "cheap farmer"—
the narration of Japanese Americans as Horatio Algers in the otherwise
caste-bound world of California agriculture—comports with the persistent identification of the Asian as an eternal economic superpower, whose
flipside, for the yellow perilists, was a super-problem.

Despite its empirical indeterminacy, the economic status of prewar Japanese agriculture is a high-stakes question. It was central to the 1980s redress movement's efforts to calculate the economic losses suffered by the
Japanese as a result of relocation.[48] While the value of Japanese American
property, business, and income loss is likely to remain forever unknown,
the place of Japanese farmers within the state's agricultural economy on
the eve of World War II is directly relevant to the question of the material
conditions of internment. An emphasis on their economic centrality lends
support to the thesis that evacuation was driven by business competition,
underscoring the conflict between private gain and national interest in
the disruption of wartime agricultural production. At the time, Fisher
and Nielsen reported the value of Japanese truck crops in California to be
somewhere between $30 million and $35 million, or as much as 30 to 35
percent of the value of California truck crops as a whole (2). Even so, to
what extent the interests of large growers lay in the elimination of Japanese agriculturalists, who were essentially small farmers, remains unclear.
Morton Grodzins attempts to account for this by arguing that though
Japanese farmers made comparatively slight inroads into large-scale agriculture, there were some acreages in Imperial Valley and Salinas in direct
competition with the Western Growers Association (Grodzins, 22). On
the one hand, Grodzins insists, West Coast Japanese were evacuated because their share of business was substantial; on the other hand, he implies, they were evacuated because, in contrast to Hawaiian Japanese
(who were not evacuated), they must not have been economically central
enough (168–69). In 1942, as in the era of the Alien Land Laws, the difficulty of establishing the economic causation for anti-Japanese measures
once again suggests an epistemological effect of the economism of Asiatic
racial form.

As to the periodization of Asian exclusionism, mass evacuation reads
as an epilogue to a racial drama whose ending was reached already in
1924, when exclusionist momentum—fueled by the successes of the
Alien Land Laws—effected an immigration law that conclusively ended
Japanese immigration and, with it, for a time, vociferous anti-Japanese
agitation. In the narrative history of Asian exclusion, the period between
1924 and 1941 marks an archival silence on the "Asiatic problem" and,
correlatively, the relative submergence of knowledge about Japanese
American history—all the more reason that evacuation appears as a lingering reflex, as the psychic residue of a separate past. We are tempted to

see it as a belated fantasy, a furious response to nothing real, except possibly a set of outdated social conditions. Grodzins characteristically describes the "economic basis of the antipathy held toward resident Japanese" to have been demonstrably "chimerical" (14). He is speaking of the immediate post–World War I era, but the most spectacular chimera is, of course, the fifth column perceived by authorities to have been gathering after Pearl Harbor amid West Coast Japanese communities. What social necessity produced the coastal mirage of flashing signals and radio transmissions that members of the public claimed to have witnessed? In what ways does internment represent a continuity and a discontinuity with earlier expressive forms of Asian exclusion?

At the height of the public debate over the Alien Land Initiative of 1920, Toyoji Chiba, the managing director of the Japanese Agricultural Association of California, sought to defend Japanese immigrant farmers against charges of unfair competition by evoking agriculture's putatively level playing field. Agriculture, Chiba writes, "differs from mercantile and manufacturing industries, where plans and processes are worked out in secret, in the factory or at the table. In agriculture, which is carried out in the public view under the open sky, there is absolutely no room for secrets."[49] Pre–World War II discourse on Japanese immigrant farmers articulates a racial convention with a historically specific problematic of California agriculture. "Nature with her sunshine, wind, rain, heat and cold," Chiba continues, "metes out no discriminatory treatment. . . . Anyone can immediately learn and imitate the superior methods of another farmer. If only he has correct ideas and operates properly, he should by no means be defeated by competition" (220). Chiba's remarks point to the double oddity of the discourse on Asiatic competition in the years from 1913 to 1920. First, it places the specter of alien invasion in a setting that diverges from its customary city location.[50] Second, by discovering the "yellow peril" in western rural territory, the discourse on "cheap farmers" involves a particularly dystopian version of agrarianist declamations against monopoly's ruination of the frontier. The eccentricity of agriculture to industry in agrarianist ideology can be related to the shock effect of spotting alien masses in the country scene. The era of most extensive Japanese involvement in farming (1900–1941) coincided with and facilitated the rise of industrialized agriculture in California (Matsumoto, 23).

Dating from patterns of land monopoly in the heyday of the Southern Pacific Railroad, large-scale operations predominated in California from agriculture's inception, but the extensive nature of class stratification on the farmland did not attract full public notice until the Wheatland hop pickers' strike of 1913. That same year witnessed the creation of the California Commission of Immigration and Housing (CCIH) by the state legislature, envisioned as a social welfare agency whose purpose was to facilitate the assimilation of immigrants into mainstream social and economic life.[51] The commission was created as part of a host of Progressive reform initiatives following upon the 1910 gubernatorial election of Hiram Johnson, including: the creation of a state conservation commission, the appointment of a commissioner of corporations to examine all public securities for fraudulent practices, the creation of an irrigation and rural credits commission, the extension of the state civil service, the licensing of real estate dealers, and other administration-sponsored legislation. As historian of Progressivism George Mowry argues, Progressivism sought to aid the underprivileged individual but opposed the rise of labor as a collective bargaining group; it attacked corporate control of government, but also often combined with conservatives in order to defeat the labor movement in municipal elections, helping to keep Los Angeles an open-shop town.[52] If the Webb-Heney Alien Land Law was also one of the fruits of the California Progressive agenda in the legislative session of 1913, what relation might the concern to limit "Mongolian ownership of soil to a space four feet by six"[53] bear to liberal techniques of social justice sought in the context of accentuated class struggle?[54] The sensational appearance of racial peril and the ideological invisibility of class relations in American agriculture may turn out to be mutually explanatory.

In California, agricultural class struggle, or indeed the very existence of a rural proletariat, was largely invisible until the emergence of the radical Industrial Workers of the World (IWW, or Wobblies) in 1905. Around the same time, the American Federation of Labor (AFL), whose craft bias had long led it to look askance at unskilled or semiskilled labor as a threat to its own organizational power, also began to take an official interest in hired farm laborers. Even so, between 1903, when the California State Federation of Labor began adopting annual resolutions favoring farm labor organization, and 1916, when this policy was officially abandoned, the AFL leadership's reluctance to antagonize farm employers was obvious in the halfhearted nature of the labor-organizing campaigns (Daniel, 77–81). By contrast, starting in 1909 the IWW seriously undertook the organizing of casual farm laborers. Anticipating the antiracist program pursued by the Congress of Industrial Organizations (CIO) during the 1930s and '40s, the IWW was unique among early-twentieth-century labor and radical groups in striving to appeal to workers across racial lines and, during periods of anti-Japanese agitation, editorialized against racism and praised Japanese farm workers for their class consciousness.[55] In its actual ability to recruit Japanese members, the IWW is considered to have been less than successful, though more and more scholars are interested in revisiting this question.[56]

In the historiography of pre-1920 California agriculture, the subject of racial subordination and the subject of working-class struggle tend to be split off from each other. In contrast to the topic of nineteenth-century cheap labor in which racial hierarchy and class subordination are aligned, the history of Californian Japanese agriculturalists tends to be told as the story of a "traditionally petit bourgeois ethnic group."[57] Even the radical effort to document the multiracial aspirations of the IWW, for example, by demystifying mainstream labor's anti-Asianism as an inheritance of American middle-class fears of future competition with immigrant businessmen, ends up reinforcing this sociological impression.[58] Though there are some celebrated instances of friendly cooperation between Japanese farmworkers and the Wobblies, by and large the historical consensus perceives ethnicity and class to have functioned as competing forms of collective identification. Cletus Daniel, for example, writes that "[b]eyond the fact that they had nothing to gain in terms of greater economic strength by joining the IWW, most Japanese farm laborers appear to have been in fundamental disagreement with the Wobblies' revolutional objectives. While Wobblies sought to destroy capitalism in America, the Japanese aspired to better their relative economic position within the existing capitalist system" (Daniel, 83). In class-conscious accounts of California agricultural history the Asiatic often appears as an antiradical figure,[59] while histories of Japanese Americans have painted a picture of a vertically integrated "ethnic economy" in which "the entire ethnic community often played a crucial role in the pursuit of collective economic goals sought by the petit bourgeoisie" (O'Brien and Fugita, 524). Investigating Japanese American presence in California agriculture presents the challenge of confronting conventional assumptions regarding the apparent whiteness of class and the apparent classlessness of race.[60]

In a recent article on the Walnut Grove Japanese community in the interwar years, Eiichiro Azuma writes:

> The historical impact of the 1913 and 1920 California Alien Land Laws on Japanese immigrant farmers has been a much debated issue. Some scholars argue that, because of numerous loopholes, the laws had little or no adverse effect on Japanese farmers. Others insist that the laws served as a serious deterrent to Japanese immigrants in agriculture and in fact undermined their economic foundation. To support this latter contention, a careful analysis of Japanese immigrant sources recently demonstrated the oppressiveness of the laws from a Japanese perspective. Still the question of whether the laws adversely affected all Japanese farming communities in the same way, or whether they had a distinct impact on each, remains open. To answer this question, more studies of specific farming communities will have to be undertaken,

with special attention to local economic conditions that influenced Japanese immigrants.[61]

Such local research, including the documentation of statistics and oral history, is absolutely crucial to building knowledge about Asian American subjects and to the increased historicization of anti-Asian racism. Despite Asian American studies' early sense of the need to move away from an exclusionism-directed history toward an experience-based one,[62] the premises of this book are that the two are closely interlinked. The best research into Japanese American community history complicates our theoretical understanding of how racialization affected racial formation.[63] Working from the other side, I hope to contribute to an understanding of Asian American history by pursuing an acquaintance with the hostile sources of "yellow peril" fiction. In the absence of an empirically settled consensus on the effectivity and purpose of Japanese exclusionism, the literary reading that follows will seek to venture a historical hypothesis about the difference between the prominence of dangerous Japanese farmers in the pre-1924 period and their discursive recurrence during World War II.

First serialized in 1920 in widely circulated national periodicals, *Pride of Palomar* (1921) by Peter Kyne and *Seed of the Sun* (1921) by Wallace Irwin are often cited by historians as part of the post–World War I psychological context for the popularity of the Alien Land Initiative that year.[64] Kyne and Irwin were journalists and best-selling writers, each of more than twenty novels and stories that appeared in national newspapers and magazines.[65] While *Pride of Palomar* was the only work of Kyne's to have centered on "the Japanese problem" in California, Irwin also authored the vastly popular *Letters of a Japanese Schoolboy,* first serialized in *Collier's* in 1907.[66] Both *Pride of Palomar* and *Seed of the Sun* strike the twenty-first-century reader as blatantly jingoistic and of little artistic merit, though at the time of publication Irwin's novel was actually praised by reviewers for racial objectivity and literary accomplishment in the *New York Times,* the *Times* of London, and other influential news organs outside the U.S. West Coast. These two novels about Japanese land-grabs in California have often been mentioned by historians as a key barometer of popular anti-Asianism, but from critics of the Asian stereotype in American culture they have received scant scrutiny.

Alien Land Law Fiction I: The Question of Value

In *Pride of Palomar,* a veteran of the First World War returns to California only to find his father dead and his childhood home, a large ranch property, in jeopardy of bank foreclosure. The banker himself, accompanied by wife and daughter, has arrived to take possession of the estate, which he plans on acquiring as his personal residence, but he is persuaded to give the war hero a final chance to repay the loan. Over the course of several weeks, the family members, who have decided to stay on at the ranch as guests, find themselves succumbing to the place's, and the owner's, romantic charm. Through a combination of wisdom and panache—and, not least, a secret loan from the banker's daughter—the protagonist wins back his ranch, now updated into a financially viable business, and marries the girl. This is the main plot. A subplot provides atmosphere. From the start, a parallel set of unpleasant circumstances greets our returning war hero: the creeping acquisition of land in the region by Japanese farmers. Nearby an entire valley has already been settled by a Japanese colony. His own ranch is threatened with Japanese ownership because the banker's partner is a wealthy Japanese businessman who wishes to develop the land for the settlement of his compatriots. This Japanese businessman reveals himself to be unscrupulous in his methods, which include an assassination attempt on the rancher. However, the plot is defeated, the Japanese businessman is run out of town, and in the course of events the undiscriminating banker is converted to the rancher's racial views.

The text is part romance and part political treatise, intermixing plot action with extended dialogue between the banker and the rancher on the virtues and evils of Japanese settlement. Parker, the banker, speaks from the purported impartiality of market principles. The Japanese, he admits, are "impossible socially, but they do know how to make things grow. They are not afraid of hard work. Perhaps that is why they have supplanted the white farmer."[67] Voicing the authorial point of view, the rancher, Miguel Farrel, challenges Parker on the social value of Asiatic work habits, which entail the exploitation of family labor (in particular, female labor), and single-minded accumulation without "building a decent home or laying out a flower garden" (*POP* 125, 313).[68] The ranch Farrel inherits from his father showcases a charming but indolent world of genteel country living. The debate thus begins by pitting a pleasureless life of work against a financially unsustainable life of enjoyment. Since we can as well expect whites to prevail against Japanese competition as "water to run uphill," denunciations of "industry, with its peonage, its horrible, unsanitary factory conditions, its hopelessness" (*POP* 312, 125–26) at first seem to ensue from a novelistic position of romantic anticapitalism, whose only rejoinder to the inevitable domination of economic logic is the aesthetic superiority of premarket social arrangements and values. "[If] this be progress as we view progress," says Farrel, "if this be desirable industrial or agricultural evolution, then I'm out of tune with my world and my times, and as soon as I am certain of it I'll blow my brains out" (*POP* 316).

The uncontrolled tendency the novel fears is the growing division of classes. It is, after all, different types of work ethic, not the material conditions of work, that are the novel's central concern. The hierarchical social relations of the traditional ranch world are heavily sentimentalized— in particular, the bond between benevolent master and loyal servant. In a sense, the Japanese incursion can be read as the affront to a landed gentry posed by a nouveau riche, since "the class of Japs who have a stranglehold on California are not gentlemen but coolies" (*POP* 40–41). The point of the whole plot exercise may be to show us who is a real "feudal baron" and who is "just a coolie dressed up" as the "potato baron of California" (*POP* 25, 40–41). Okada's flamboyant clothing and brutish manners reveal him to be not the gentleman he pretends to be.[69] Implied contrasts between a noble but dying feudalism and strange new productive subjects suggest that the text is spurred by questions of transition in California's political economy. Interestingly, the crisis of change is represented by the arrival of an Asiatic figure.

The "Japanese question" assumes specific focus through the subject of land, for which the Japanese are portrayed as insatiably greedy. Whereas a Japanese looks at land simply in terms of its productive capabilities, the native son feels an emotional attachment that is extra-economic. The descriptive passages of landscape are the novel's most overwrought, sentimental (and patriarchal). For instance: "There had fallen upon the land that atmosphere of serenity, of peace, that is the peculiar property of California's foothill valleys in the late afternoon; the world seemed very distant and not at all desirable; and to Kay there came a sudden, keen realization of how this man beside her must love this darkling valley with the hills above presenting their flower-clad breasts to the long spears of light from the dying day. . . ." (*POP* 217). Elsewhere, we are brought to a commanding elevation, and shown a beautiful view:

> The car had climbed out of the San Gregoria and was mounting swiftly along the route to La Questa, affording to the Parkers a panorama of mountain, hill, valley and sea so startling in its vastness and its rugged beauty that Don Mike realized his guests had been silenced as much by awe as by their desire to avoid a painful and unprofitable conversation.
>
> Suddenly they swung wide around a turn and saw, two thousand feet below them, La Questa valley. The chauffeur parked the car on the outside of the turn to give his passengers a long, unobstructed view.
>
> "Looks like a green checker-board with tiny squares," Parker remarked presently.

"Little Japanese farms."

"There must be a thousand of them, Farrel."

"That means not less than five thousand Japanese, Mr. Parker. It means that literally a slice of Japan has been transplanted in La Questa Valley, perhaps the fairest and most fruitful valley in the fairest and most fruitful state in the fairest and most fruitful country God ever made. And it is lost to white men!" (*POP* 311)

The passage juxtaposes a natural sublime with a scene of human cultivation in which the homogeneity of a "green checker-board" and the horror of racial clustering are interchangeable. An old buddy of Farrel's points to a sign bearing the words "No more Japs wanted here," and updates the returning war veteran on recent developments: "This is entirely an agricultural section. . . . There are no labor unions here. But . . . you could throw a stone in the air and be moderately safe on the small end of a bet that the stone would land on a Jap farmer" (*POP* 5). The proud agrarian setting of the anti-Japanese sign authenticates the autonomy of Asian exclusionist sentiment from a potentially contaminated association with labor unions. At the same time, if the anti-Japanese sign's rural location implies its social legitimation, it also conveys the shock of an agricultural life jeopardized by the arrival of elements associated with the "Asiatic question." The use of the Asiatic as a figure of mass crowding— "Jap farmers" a stone throw's away—contrasts a traditional spaciousness of the country (where nothing should be a stone-throw's away) and a new population density. An agrarian discourse of Asian exclusionism could therefore be read as an antidevelopment impulse as such.

Yet the ideological perspective of the novel is ultimately not nostalgic. The narrative's familial union of banker and rancher projects an ideal wedding of modernity and tradition. Narrative suspense centers on provable demonstrations of Farrel's possession of economic rationality. Of mixed Spanish-Irish heritage, Farrel is described as "the first of an ancient lineage who had ever dreamed of progress" and having "progressed . . . he could never, by any possibilities, afford to retrograde" (*POP* 52). Whereas indolence is responsible for having doomed the old Californios to extinction, Farrel himself combines feudal virtue with commercial sense. Through Parker's unsparing lectures, the novel takes a measure of satisfaction in observing that the native sons of California would do well to "imbibe a few lessons in industry and economy from their Japanese neighbors" (*POP* 64). The old Mexican Californios and the new Japanese are made to stand in for two extremes, which the contemporary Californian must moderate in order to achieve economic development without cultural dislocation. As always, the Asiatic is a coming menace, the racial form of the dark side of change. The hero says, "we ought to have Jim Crow cars for these cocksure sons of Nippon . . . We'll come to it yet if something isn't done about them. They breed so fast they'll have us crowded into the back seats in another decade" (*POP* 27).

Farrel achieves solvency by capitalizing upon a water source located on his property. He sells dam and watershed riparian rights to the power company in exchange for the use of the water for irrigation. It is on this question of land use and development potential that the form of racial peril and the problematic of economic change specifically intersect. Farrel's main task of raising revenue rests upon the assessed value of his land. As grazing land, his property is worth a great deal less than if proper irrigation allows him to put it to agricultural use. The deal he brokers at the end with the power company reflects the idea of water as a resource of multiple use originated by hydrographers of the U.S. Geological Survey. Fundamentally, *Pride of Palomar* concerns the harnessing of water and its application to arid Californian land, converting it from cattle range to irrigated cropland.

Starting in the late 1880s, the federal government embarked upon water resource investigations throughout the West, with the idea that the planning of irrigation works represented a solution to the dilemmas of declining farm population, land shortage, and the surplus of arid land. However, federal planning efforts were often thwarted by frontier characteristics of rising land values, quick profits, and rapid change.[70] The history of western irrigation involved issues of conflict between states' rights and federal power, and between the interests of private development and the ideology of public planning. Though federal land laws were undertaken in the name of benefiting the individual homesteader, federal reclamation instead created more opportunities for speculation, as a result of the massive escalation in land values it effected. The history of western land development presents a drama of speculators posing as homesteaders and government efforts to prevent these abuses. A good part of these efforts rested upon the ability to determine the exact quantity and quality of resources on the land and to classify it according to its true value. In short, western land had the characteristic of indeterminate and flexible value, the key to which was water availability.

"Give me the water," Farrel says to his friend Bill Conway who, at this point in the novel, has been contracted to build a dam, ". . . give me the water that will make my valley bloom in the August heat, and then, with the tremendous increase in the value of the land, I'll find somebody, some place, who will trust me for three hundred thousand paltry dollars to give this man and save my ranch. This is a white man's country, and John Parker is striving, for a handful of silver, to betray us and make it a yellow paradise" (*POP* 211). What is the significance of the linkage between water resource development and the "yellow peril" as alternative futures for California? The historical transition of the state from one kind of land-based economy to another, from grazing to agriculture, is figured by a crisis of Asiatic invasion. Okada's deceptive appearance, the coolie disguised as a gentleman, suggests the class transgression of the bourgeois arriviste, but also perhaps the aesthetics of the California speculative land economy in general. The extension of market principles to landed property, in the context of rampant speculation, presents the mystery of the abstract housed in the shell of the concrete. One can never be sure that the land—whose value depends upon what might be discovered in, or added to, it—is what it seems.

After all, the dramatic conflict is occasioned by an encounter between two representative forms of wealth, which projects a potential exchange between a financier looking for some land to settle on and a landowner who is capital-poor. While the financier's wealth exerts the power of universal equivalence, the landowner must convert land into money in order to escape total liquidation. The invocation of "traditional values" in the face of threatened bank repossession describes the struggle between relative value and the general equivalent, coded as the polarization of use value and exchange value. No wonder then that the text should be so preoccupied with survey excursions, contrasting price assessment with aesthetic appreciation. The story of the banker and the landowner, in a sense, allegorizes the diachronic progression from one value-form to another. A continuation of the problematic taken up by *The Octopus*, Peter Kyne's novel actively embraces the accommodations of agriculture necessary to the possibility of farming upon arid western lands. *Pride of Palomar* resolves the conflict between farmers and monopoly capitalism so that agriculture is now happily wed to finance. A solution is provided by the conceptual ingenuity of nature's multiple use: the water that is harnessed by the power company is still available, after flowing through the dam, for irrigating and revaluing Farrel's land.

Narrative resolution also depends upon a technique of Asian exclusion, through which the homogenizing evils of monopoly are entirely displaced onto sinister Japanese characters. The personification of the bank by the benevolently paternal Mr. Parker—adopted as the rancher's father (in-law)—enables the splitting of corporate-financial power into a cross-racial partnership. Okada, Parker's other half, is the residue of the representational recuperation of monopoly capital in these late Progressive texts. His automatic villainy allows the economic character of Farrel and the moral character of Parker to be subjects of suspenseful narrative unfolding. Mrs. Parker observes of Okada to her husband, "Your little playmate's quite like a mechanical toy" (*POP* 73). Though the Asiatic assumes the shape of a character in this novel, it is weakly personified. A limited set of identifying features and gestures comprises the crudely anthropomorphized logic named Okada.[71]

The open artifice of Asiatic humanity helps explain the recurring scenes of gratuitous physical humiliation. In one episode, Farrel's faithful Indian manservant, Pablo, discovers Okada's residency in the master bedroom and gives him a good thrashing for his presumption. In another, Pablo locks up the Parkers' Japanese cook, who had been stationed by his employers in the kitchen. Later Okada is again beaten by Pablo for his part in a dishonest scheme to steal Farrel's livestock. The text strategically expresses its racial violence through the physical agency of the Indian, a "relic" of the period of Spanish missions in California history. The Indian's instinctual dislike authenticates anti-Japaneseness as an indigenous reaction. The sanctioned violence of the original "vanishing American" articulates the imaginary social reversal in which now vulnerable whites may have to "take the back seats."

What else, however, besides the pleasures of sadistic expression, do these displays of violence permit? Other allies of the California rancher also indulge in acts of anti-Asian violence. In one scene, Farrel's Irish friend, Bill Conway

> seized the Japanese by the throat and commenced to choke him with neatness and dispatch. When the man's face was turning purple and his eyes rolling wildly, Conway released his death-grip and his victim fell back on the mattress, whereupon Bill Conway sat down on the edge of the bed and watched life surge back into the little brown man . . . (*POP* 268)

Through this physical contact, Conway sends Okada the message that he needs to leave El Toro. He is also torturing him for information:

> A faint nervous twitch of the chin and the eyelids—then absolute immobility. The potato baron had assumed the "poker face" of all Orientals—upon which Bill Conway knew the man was on his guard and would admit nothing. (*POP* 269–70)

The facial impassivity concluding the scene strikes an extraordinary contrast to the spasmodic responses of a moment earlier—the nervous twitch, the wildly rolling eyes, surging life, purple face. On the brink of death, the Asiatic betrays an animal truth. Otherwise, the Asiatic reverts to its unyielding, inanimate posture.

Only the absolute defeat of the Asiatic seems to bring sure knowledge of its biological, organismic identity. In one scene, Pablo nabs an anonymous Japanese agent who has been dispatched to assassinate Farrel. Cowboy-style, Pablo lassos the would-be assassin and drags him to death by horse. Viewing the corpse, Parker protests: "The rope—take it off!

... It's cutting him in two. He looks like a link of sausage! Ugh! A Jap! Horrible!" (*POP* 256). Here, finally, the Asiatic body is turned into meat, a "dusty, bloody, shapeless bundle" (*POP* 256–57). The defeat of the novel's villains bears witness to the successful transmutation of matter (from inorganic to organic), regardless of bodily lineament or shape (it has none). The name for those remains—the "THING,"[72] as Pablo thinks of it—alludes to a problematic of racial representation structured by an antinomy between the abstract and the concrete, or in the chosen metaphors of the novel, the mask and the sausage. On the one hand, we have the inflated threat of finance capital, which is intangibly abstract; on the other hand, we have the reduced thingliness of the defeated Japanese.[73] Perhaps any ambivalence to land speculation, the endlessness of revaluation, is to be found here, where a compensatory movement in the opposite direction from the abstract to the concrete occurs. An advancing, inanimate peril is halted by being literally beaten and dragged into organic materiality, into a motionless corpse.

Alien Land Law Fiction II: The Mask of Asia

Wallace Irwin's *Seed of the Sun* is more concerned with the social relations internal to the agricultural world and with developing an adequate metaphor for their unassuaged alienation. This time, the protagonist is a woman, the widow of an officer killed in the First World War. Left without the income to maintain her accustomed lifestyle in New York, Anna Bly moves with her small son, her younger sister, and a female servant to a small rural Californian town, where she takes charge of a plum orchard of which her family has been a longtime absentee owner. Since she has little acquaintance with agriculture, she retains the existing tenant as a business partner to help in working the estate. Unknown to her, a large corporation that has already absorbed most of the nearby farms has designs on her land. The corporation extorts the cooperation of her tenant in engineering a work stoppage just when the fruit is ready. Since her continued viability is dependent upon a profitable harvest that year, Bly is financially ruined. Dispirited by so many obstacles, she unwittingly sells the property to the very party responsible for her predicament. Bags packed and on the verge of returning to the East Coast, she is prevented from departure at the last moment by a marriage proposal from a neighboring gentleman farmer, with whom she has been in love all along.

This contest between family farm and agribusiness is in part a morality tale that cautions against the folly of female independence. If sexual merger with a neighboring competitor at first strikes us as poor compensation for business absorption by another, this is consistent with a novel that throughout is uncertain about the distinction between feelings of romantic love and economic valuation—Anna Bly is swept off her feet from the beginning by the sheer efficiency of Dunc Leacy's farm operation. *Seed of the Sun* reverses the pedagogic structure of *Pride of Palomar,* this time by making the protagonist the target of the text's ideological conversion; but as in *Pride of Palomar,* female domesticity and subordination to masculine experience are a vehicle for the parallel reassertion of proper racial hierarchy. Bly discovers upon arrival that her orchard is located in a district farmed almost entirely by Japanese, who include her tenant.[74] The corporation that conspires against her turns out to be Japanese-owned. The protagonist begins with a highly favorable opinion of Japanese people as a whole, even numbering among her oldest family friends a wealthy and cosmopolitan Japanese gentleman. Her gradual exposure to the farm town's sinister atmosphere, and the deliberate sabotage of her crop, however, serve to disabuse her of her naive regard for the Japanese. Bly discovers that her own friend, Baron Tzumi, is in fact the secret head of the corporation that ruins her and that the corporation in turn is an instrument of Japan to conquer the United States. Beside national loyalty, Tzumi's motives include a personal interest in making Bly his wife, which explicitly sexualizes the threat of colonial conquest. Bly's eventual marriage to a suitor possessed of an "Anglo-Saxon look of health and well-being" thus symbolizes both a sexual and racial rescue.[75]

The "human bundle" of Asiatic remains with which *Pride of Palomar* climaxes also surfaces in this novel, when Bly comes upon the hanging body of Mrs. Shimba, the tenant's badly treated wife, who has committed suicide in the barn: "And still the human bundle hung there, perfectly still, as though it had always been a part of the place" (*SS* 126). Here it is the ironic continuity between life and death that is emphasized by the Asiatic body's motionlessness and permanence. Absence of gesture and immobile expression, signifying actively concealed intent, dominate *Seed of the Sun*'s obsession with the Asiatic as a mask. The treacherous tenant Shimba always wears one: "Rather gracelessly he wore the mask of Asia, and through the slitlike eyeholes living fires glittered constantly, fed forever by his restless thoughts" (*SS* 57). One Mrs. Matsu is no less unmasked by the agony of childbirth. Even during its throes, we see that her "head, braced against a notched block of wood, was still as a mask of wax. Dull coals burned behind the slitlike eyeholes" (*SS* 112). The Japanese residents of the town move around mechanically and in aggregation. At the schoolhouse, "little girls from six to twelve, impish-eyed, flat-faced, docile, stood in line marking time mechanically at the teacher's command" (*SS* 109). In the children's parade, "their flat faces [were] impassive, their blossoms waving mechanically, they advanced like a snow-white army. . . ." (*SS* 163). In work, as in play:

They gave the appearance of men worked until everything but a lust
for work had been driven from their characters—men born of tired
parents to a heritage of hard ambition. They smiled mechanically, they
bowed mechanically. Behind them stood the invisible slave driver,
goading them on to reclaim their souls from an age-old bondage. (*SS*
327)

The "batwinged, barbaric" kites flying over the town, "violent of face
and spiteful of movement" (*SS* 279), also present the uncanniness of motion without self-volition, announcing the menace that the masks ostensibly veil. Heralded by face-bearing kites and reduced to expressionless
masks, the Japanese body is an artificial prosthesis being manipulated
from elsewhere. In Irwin's story, the entire population of immigrant
farmers is an instrument of Japan's national ambitions to create a "yellow belt" in the United States.

This tropology, in which everything is concealed and everything is connected, merges Japanese takeover of American agriculture with corporate
takeover. Anna Bly's education involves traveling, socially and geograph-
ically, from the position of the East Coast urban elite—then viewed as
pragmatically favoring friendly relations with Japan—to a world of prin-
cipled rural virtue. Japanese nonpersonhood converges with the artificial
personhood of the corporation at the site of "K. Sato," the nominal head
of the Natural Energy Fruit and Land Company. "But why shouldn't he
be merely an idea, the consensus of opinion of all the stockholders in the
Natural Energy Company?" (*SS* 170). The grotesquerie of a human face
that resembles a mask reverses the chief horror of what a familiar face
may belie. The agent working on behalf of the company, though ostensibly white, is actually a "Jap under his skin—just one of those poor spec-
imens willing and anxious to sell out his country on a commission basis"
(*SS* 194).

After the passage of the 1913 Webb-Heney Act, prohibition of agricultural property ownership by aliens ineligible to citizenship was often
evaded through the creation of corporations in which the majority of
stockholders were American citizens. In contemporary rhetoric, the
American stockholders of such corporations were referred to as "white
dummy directors."[76] Prohibiting alien ownership of land, the Alien Land
Laws sought a limit upon market alienability. Refusing the notion of land
as infinitely exchangeable property, they insisted upon a territorial definition of land as national soil. In this period, representations of agricultural
corporatization and representations of the Japanese in agriculture overlap. Were the Alien Land Laws a popular idea because Japanese farmers
were being mistaken for speculators or because speculators were perceived to be agents of Japanese? In *Seed of the Sun,* a displaced farmer

gives voice to a strange racial indeterminacy: ". . . see them land speculators—callin' 'emselves white! Look at me, lady! For twenty years I
farmed a nice strip down by the delta—sparrow-grass down by the river
and fruit above. What happens there? So-called white man comes along,
refuses to renew my lease on the good ground, send me up to the skinny
orchards if I want to rent—otherwise I git out. So out I got, and here I
am" (99). Who are these "so-called white men" and what do they look
like? In the context of possible Japanese-white business partnerships, it is
whiteness that has become a mask.[77] Writing in 1935, McWilliams observes in retrospect that the effect of the Alien Land Laws was "to solid-
ify Japanese American relations . . . [since] it has forced Japanese and
Americans into a conspiracy to violate the law."[78] Since the majority of
Japanese farm enterprises were transacted in the name of a corporation
owned in majority by American stockholders, "it would be difficult,
therefore, to single out one industry or business in California owned exclusively by Japanese. To strike at the Japanese today means to strike at
American capital" (McWilliams, "Yellow Peril," 736). The omnipresent
"mask of Asia" alludes not to the artifice of Japanese presence in California's natural surroundings, but rather the erosion of whiteness as a reliable phenotype, the paranoid prospect of aliens masked as whites.

On the West Coast whiteness was constituted through an ongoing
problematic of Asian exclusion. Percy Edwards confesses in *Overland
Monthly* in the year when the first alien land law was passed:

> What we mean by this term 'white man' is a trifle hard to determine.
> It is not color or character. By consent of those most concerned, in
> these parts, the term is not confined to citizens of this country. . . . In
> this part of our common country the negro is called a 'white man' and
> the Mexican is not. And there you have it. And there now seems to be
> forming an opinion on this coast that everybody is a 'white man' but
> the Jap.[79]

Edwards is writing in 1913, and by 1922 in *Ozawa* vs. *United States* the
Supreme Court would conclude that Japanese immigrants were not eligible for citizenship on the authority of anthropological science that they
were Mongolian and not white. How were they to be physically distinguished? Alien land law fiction underscores the disarticulation of whiteness from stable attributes of external appearance. *Pride of Palomar* has
the banker scrutinizing the ancestry of his prospective son-in-law, affirming his daughter's choice on the basis that "Farrel is clean-strain Caucasian, Kate. He's a white man—inside and out" (150). In light of the fact
that Farrel is descended of mixed Spanish-Irish blood, the novel opens
the eligibility of mongrel European ethnicities to white certification, reinforcing Percy Edwards's claim that "on this coast . . . everybody is a

'white man' but the Jap."[80] Attention to alien land law fiction also illuminates the extent to which California racial discourse was conducted on the terrain of agriculture's industrial transformation.[81] In the context of farming increasingly alienated to large-scale corporate undertaking, a landscape devoid of human farm operators is pictured to be teeming with Japanese.

Advocating Japanese land removal in the name of small-farming interests, a 1920 report prepared by the California State Board of Control was sent with a cover endorsement by the governor to the U.S. secretary of state. *California and the Oriental* (1920) purports to be an examination of the status of Japanese, Chinese, and Hindus, but focuses chiefly on the Japanese in sections broken down into categories such as "land," "fishing industry," "labor," and "corporations." The section on labor clearly identifies the constituency on whose behalf the report as a whole is presented as speaking. "The most serious injury done by Oriental laborers," the report states, "is to the American small farmer" (*CO* 101). Who counts as a "small farmer"? The text at first proposes a strict definition—one "who actually farms his own land"—but soon loosens it to include all those "who perform the larger part of their own work" (*CO* 101, 103). Castigated are those "land speculators or developers who do not farm their own lands but lease them upon some crop basis to Orientals" (*CO* 101). In a move by now familiar to us, the text of Japanese exclusion presents the individual small farmer confronting an evil partnership of Asiatics and speculative capital, both presumed alien to the agricultural scene. On a rhetorical level, the imaginative and documentary literature of the Japanese yellow peril seem to be in agreement.

Upon consideration, however, the novels do not depict any ideal examples of those who manage to farm their own land or even "perform the larger part of the work." Farrel's estate stretches thousands of acres, and Leacy, the exemplary farmer whom Bly weds, owns a large-scale operation employing hundreds of workers. The fictional narratives of Japanese landgrabs disclose more fully than do the government documents the extent to which California farming is big business. The novels further expose the antagonism between farmers and workers hidden by the populist consensus forged by Asian exclusion. Paralleling *Pride of Palomar*'s hostility to trade unions, *Seed of the Sun* depicts its farmer as threatened by uncooperative workers as well as corporate greed. Far more than utopian/dystopian literature at the fin de siècle,[82] these novels openly assume a managerial identification; they are an example of what George Henderson has called "California rural realism," a literary mode of bourgeois discourse that flourished from the turn of the century until 1930 (*Fictions of Capital*, 119, 217). IWW workers make a minor appearance as "dangerous men, with cruel, weak and criminal faces" (*SS* 254), and the shortage of good workers in general can be attributed to the fact that "American labor has been joy-riding between radical meetings" (*SS* 334). Bly's maidservant is praised for going about her work "without a thought of union hours or overtime charges" (*SS* 306).

Irwin even implies a causal relation between the threat posed by organizing farm workers and the "Japanese problem." "It was no fault of [Anna Bly's], surely, that none but the Japanese worked on her farm. The machinations of the I.W.W., she was informed, had made white labor well nigh impossible" (*SS* 119). Japanese sabotage and the absence of reliable labor combined result in Bly's ruin. In fact, the real problem seems to be that nowhere in the novel are real workers of any sort to be found: white workers have devolved into degenerate and weak criminals, and those Japanese who resemble workers "picking and hoeing away in all the fields" are beneath the surface "a lot of calculating little businessmen temporarily embarrassed for capital" (*SS* 136). Concurring with *Seed of the Sun*, *Pride of Palomar*'s complaint that "there is no such thing as a Japanese laborer in this country" (136) reveals that the masking metaphor partly alludes to the frustrations of a nondocile labor force. The simultaneous crescendos of nativism and labor repression in the years immediately following the First World War—which in the West found their targets in Japanese "cheap farmers" and the IWW, respectively—suggests more than an analogy between red-baiting and yellow perilism. As tactical instruments of class domination, they were historically coincident and politically coterminous.[83]

Evoking doubleness, the Asiatic figure provides the imaginative possibility of combining employees and employer into a single conspiratorial entity. In part, the Asiatic presence evoked by alien land law discourse functions to mask the classed nature of agrarian life. In *Pride of Palomar* we have in Okada a coolie dressed up as a businessman, and in *Seed of the Sun* we are presented with fields full of businessmen pretending to be coolies. When we are looking at Japanese, we can never be sure whether we are seeing businessmen or coolies. This socially indeterminate appearance signified by the Asiatic also points to the development over the 1910s of a vertically integrated "ethnic economy," which threatened to monopolize grower competition. Shima's treachery at harvest time reflects growers' fear that racial solidarity between Japanese farmers and Japanese workers would give Japanese farmers an unbeatable edge. As the prominent Progressive intellectual Lincoln Steffens commented at the time: "The Japanese business man does not oppose the organization of Jap labor; he promotes, he requires it. . . . Most of our business men fight the unions! and the walking delegate! Well, it's precisely the walking delegate that the Jap employer takes in, and at the rate he was going in California [but for the 1913 Webb-Heney Act] he would soon have had monopolistic control of many of the most profitable agricultural, and possibly other, industries in the West."[84]

In an era of accentuated class struggle and relentless corporatization, the myth of Jeffersonian agrarianism produced a racial figure on the California farmland horizon. No doubt this is why the Japanese menace played to the heart of Populism, which aspired to universal farm ownership. The remarkable mystery of Japanese upward mobility and relentless land acquisition marked, by inversion, an acknowledgment of the more common pattern of class fixity in an agricultural system dominated by large-scale, specialized commercial enterprise and seasonal labor. At the same time, the alienating conditions imposed upon California farm labor were naturalized as innately alien characteristics, an Asiatic suitability to long work hours, low wages, and substandard housing.

The intersection of the Asian exclusionist project and agrarian nationalism comprises an important chapter in an intellectual history of American exceptionalism that has long celebrated the U.S. as a classless society. In renewing the yeoman's mythic life, alien land law discourse sought to preserve the human body from the deforming effects of industrial mechanization. The inorganic quality of the Asiatic body in the fictional narratives is one symptom of this effort. However, in contrast to the earlier discourse of "cheap labor," the discourse of "cheap farmers" should not be read as the fantasy of a more socially just arrangement sidetracked by ambivalence toward modernization. It represents a way of resolving a crisis of economic development by providing assurances of realizable utopia. In the next section, I will examine a sample of additional documents occasioned by the 1920 Alien Land Initiative and return to a final aspect of the novels.

MODERNIZING AGRARIANISM

One of the more intriguing endorsements of the 1920 Alien Land Initiative was issued by Elwood Mead, then chair of the California State Land Settlement Board, an irrigation engineer and a prominent national advocate of the back-to-the-land movement.[85] Though it was written to support the prohibition of "alien land ownership," Mead's letter dwells mainly on the evils of "alien labor" because its elimination was "the most direct and effective way of mitigating if not ending the menace of alien land ownership . . ." (CO 123). Prolonged dependency on cheap foreign labor would result in a stratified society and destroy the moral basis of the United States as an agrarian democracy. Contemporary environmental conditions also cautioned against the continuation of "the pioneer methods of development which worked well so long as land and water were both cheap" (CO 123). Mead's letter argues for Asian exclusion in the interests of conservationism as an ideology appropriate to post-frontier scarcity. Drawing an association between the underlying assumptions of "cheap labor" and wasteful use of land and water, Mead's letter points to twentieth-century labor as also a limited resource. "No labor is or should be looked upon as humiliating if it is done well, and this is especially true of anything that requires the intelligence, industry and skill of work on the farm" (CO 123). In Mead's proposal, the elevation of the status of farm labor means the literal substitution of alien workers with the "best kind of citizens" (CO 123).

Much of Mead's letter is devoted to promoting the activities of the Land Settlement Board in making more land available for private settlers through government-subsidized expenditures on land purchase, irrigation, and reclamation. Mead was a proponent of replacing the West's predominantly large estates with small, privately owned subdivisions, to be interconnected by the formation of cooperative communities. As an emergent technology of reclamation and settlement at the turn of the century, irrigation permitted smaller acreages to be economically sustainable in places where, due to prevailing aridity, they once had not been. What interests me is the intersection between Progressive social reform—specifically, the Progressive pursuit of a cooperative agrarian vision—and support for the Alien Land Laws. At the 1922 conference "Colonization and Rural Development in California," held at the University of California's College of Agriculture, Mead continued to air his worries about the lack of land available for private settlement in California. His speech touted some concrete solutions and general principles: expanding state responsibility for encouraging land settlement through the provision of credit, increasing opportunities for tenants and laborers to own their own homes, applying scientific technology to agriculture, recognizing the virtue of small farming and increased settlement. All of these, he said, were in the interest of ensuring that "rural California is to continue American."[86]

R. L. Adams, a professor at the University of California's College of Agriculture, was another expert witness who rallied to the 1920 initiative.[87] Speaking as a recognized authority on farm management and the writer of one of the earliest textbooks on the subject, Adams wrote a letter to the State Board of Control that portrayed California's agricultural system to be at an urgent historical crossroads. If it is to continue with the system as organized, Adams writes, then the state "must continue to constantly recruit a supply of labor able and willing to do the hand work necessary to the harvest of many fruits, the growing and harvesting of many field crops. . . ." (CO 126). Any reduction in the labor supply would necessitate a "reorganization in our scheme of production" (CO

126). The state economy's reliance on "cheap foreign labor" is presented as a conundrum framed by opposing considerations of public interest and financial gain. The author makes it quite clear that his sympathies lie with the former. It is interesting that here, too, the text is fixated on the problem of "foreign labor" when the referendum that occasions it proposes to ban alien land ownership. In contrast to Mead's letter, however, the relation between alien labor and alien land ownership remains inexplicit. For the next two decades, Adams's monographs and the graduate research projects under his direction at the University of California would reflect a continuing preoccupation with the issue of Japanese agricultural presence. At the same 1922 conference on land colonization, Adams delivered a lecture on the capital requirements for settling in California. Such interest in renewing the homesteading opportunities of a bygone era in the West can be seen as an offshoot of Progressive reform efforts nationwide in response to urban crowding. In California the campaign to encourage the westward migration of eastern city dwellers was also a disavowal of western economic dependence on transnational labor migration.

In studies submitted in the 1930s to the state's Soil Conservation and Domestic Allotment Administration, an agency created under the New Deal, research supervised by Adams at the university emphasized the environmental aspects of tenancy. Research into the ways of increasing the "crop producing power of California lands" posited an association between the failure of farmers to practice soil conservation and the predominance of tenancy. Many farmlands in California, the studies concluded, were characterized by excessive rental prices and high tenant mobility, which resulted in constant production and discouraged crop rotation or cover cropping. Bad environmental practices were especially associated with Japanese farmers, who were concentrated in truck farming, and who, as a result of the Alien Land Laws, tended to be tenants rather than owners. For example:

> The Japanese due to their unceasing industry, large families, and low standard of living are able to pay more rent than the average white man, so control most of the choice land that is available to tenants. While they fertilize heavily and obtain excellent crops they concentrate on vegetable crops and so do not have a diversified rotation program. A white man must follow the same program, in order to compete for the land. Such programs are mining the land and will eventually run the natural fertility down and increase the disease problems of the crop used most often.[88]

The author, Adams's student William Salvage, expressed the hope that people would recognize "that it is or soon will be necessary to start definite conservation programs" (29). The study enumerates some ideal conservationist practices, but apart from a general reference to the need for more public education, it doesn't explain how they might be widely encouraged or implemented. When Salvage states that "no effort is being made at present to solve the tenancy problem" (15), it is not clear what alternatives he has in mind. Nevertheless, the study does make a series of linkages between the need for conservationist practice, a critique of farm tenancy, and the existence of a "Japanese problem."

The association of a Japanese presence with a host of social and environmental issues establishes a pattern of correspondences between Japanese characteristics and the effects of a highly capitalized agricultural system in California. This pattern provides evidence of a displacement that contained the potential for radical social critique. Propounding a doctrine of limited growth in the interest of future preservation, conservationism enabled agrarianism to strike a chord more persuasive than one of pure nostalgia.[89] Alien land law discourse provided a choice not between an idealized past and future dystopia but between two futures, in which modernization without alienation could be a happy possibility. In *Pride of Palomar,* we have already witnessed an allegorical marriage between tradition and modernity, allowing for the preservation of the country's "historical character" in the midst of accelerating change. The narrative technique of Asian exclusion on which such a union depends scatters a trail of barely anthropomorphized Asiatic figures—economic forces and their evacuated residue, moving mechanisms and inert bundles.

In both *Pride of Palomar* and *Seed of the Sun* the idealized farmer is no rustic. He is an accomplished student of agricultural science. A graduate of UC Davis's agricultural college, Farrel is "sharp on pure-bred beef cattle, pure-bred swine and irrigation" (*POP* 33). Even more impressively, Leacy trained as an engineer at Cornell and "devoted his time to problems of river dredging and drainage canals" before assuming his father's farm in the Sacramento Delta region (*SS* 133). His farm is a model of rational planning that applies the latest technology to the control of nature. "He mortgaged his future for traction plows and gas-driven harrows. A little later he invented an ingenious device by which a gas-driven caterpillar can pile up the peat ridges in clumsy toil. He set up a laboratory on his ranch and studied the chemical eccentricities of peat until he found the sun-born acid that destroys crops; and that he learned to wash away by a system of drainage ditches" (*SS* 134). *Seed of the Sun* registers more than a pang of regret for the days when "cheap Chinese gang labor" was abundantly available for direction under a firm hand: "But just think of it! Eleven thousand Chinks at forty cents a day! With a gang like that in these times we could build a system of safety locks across the whole mouth of the Sacramento . . ." (*SS* 132). But the novel doesn't just define the present-day predicament of cheap farmers against a past utopia of abundant cheap labor. *Seed of the Sun* depicts the present-day farmer confronting a choice between two types of farm labor arrangements: one involves a cropping agreement with a Japanese tenant farmer who doubles as a labor contractor; the other is based on the owner who possesses the know-how to manage his own multiracial workforce. Readers of *Seed of the Sun* are treated to a glowing tour of Leacy's model farm:

> Over the broad plantation all the dark-skinned tribes of men labored in the sunny wind. Japanese mechanics drove caterpillar tractors up and down, drawing harrows and the ingenious ridge-making machines of Dunc's invention. Muscular Chinamen pushed hand cars laden with the new-cut asparagus into washing sheds, where other swarthy people kept count of the day's gathering. Out of an irrigation ditch a square-built man, dark as a negro but with fine Caucasian features, rose and smiled. (*SS* 151)

Exclusionism is in fact a misleading term for the novel's attitude to California Japanese, since Asiatic labor is a crucial part of its ideal vision—as long as the Anglo-Saxon farm owner remains "master of the place" (*SS* 151). A Progressive gospel of efficiency had manifold uses for racial taxonomy, assigning racial groups to tasks according to reputed natural ability. Anna Bly falls victim to corporate conspiracy precisely because of organizational weaknesses in her operation: undependable and unruly labor, together with old-fashioned, rusting machinery. Shimba led "Anna to the tool house and displayed piles of broken wood and rusty iron which resembled nothing so much as a collection of wreckage gathered from some ancient battlefield . . . 'Bursted!' was his favorite expression as he picked up split hoe handles, blunted plowshares and fragments torn from spring harrows" (*SS* 105). In contrast, Leacy "cast away the slow hand devices with which slavish coolies had grubbed among the asparagus ridges" (*SS* 134) and wisely updated his technology.

Japanese mechanicalness in this novel does not, ultimately, signify the threat of industrial automation as such. Somewhat backward, the Japanese contract labor system is represented as in the midst of being superseded by a more efficient means of production. Resembling the machine, the Japanese body does not symbolize the mechanization of agriculture but its negative substitute, not its logical end but an alternative incompletion. While the Japanese represent a labor-intensive mode of industrial modernity, Leacy's technological investments belong to the world of increasingly capital-intensive farming. The novel's pointed ridicule of Japanese drudgery alludes to mechanization's promise of universal freedom from labor. According to a contemporary observer, "The great land question in California is whether to encourage these intensive industries mainly unsuited to American standards of living, promote other crops perhaps less profitable to the land areas, or let the land lie fallow; whether to continue using the Oriental (if possible) or some other race, such as the Mexican or Filipino—fresh importations are apparently needed in any case—or to supplant them through the introduction of machinery. . . . For some crops the most efficient substitute that could possibly be made for the Japanese seems to be the use of machinery."[90] Notably dismissed by Eliot Mears is the use of white farm workers, because "[i]t is doubtful whether we care to have Americans do this kind of work, even assuming that they could compete economically." Objections to farm work include the fact that it entails "squatting, hard work, monotony and drudgery" (Henderson, *Fictions of Capital,* 203). As we have seen in the writings that promote land settlement initiatives, the Americanization of the agricultural terrain in California entails the ultimate fantasy of eliminating work itself and the creation of universal opportunities for labor's graduation to ownership. In the meantime, alien and machine manifestations of the agricultural worker reflect the categorical inhumanity of California farm labor conditions.[91]

The immediate post–World War I years bore witness to the crisis of an industry squeezed by a massive depression in farm prices, diminished labor supply, and class warfare. But if mechanization seemed to offer an ideal solution to labor problems, many specialized crops could not be machine-harvested and continued to require hand labor. These included orchard fruits; field crops such as rice, cotton, sugar beets, and beans; all truck crops in the Sacramento delta; and cantaloupes and lettuce in the Imperial Valley. The ability to grow these specialized crops, enabled by the vast extension of irrigation, accounted for the high average value of California acreage compared to that of other states. Describing the industry's postwar predicament in 1920, R. L. Adams warned, "[r]eliance upon labor as now available without future augmentation, greater use of machinery, or similar recommendations, will result in a change from many specialized crops of high acreage value to general crops of low acreage values, if no other relief is forthcoming" (CO 126).

A combination of primitiveness and mechanicalness in Japanese morphology expresses the paradox of a globally competitive production system in which labor could not be fully mechanized or, because of its seasonal structure, regularized. Japanese bodies move simply and repetitively, and seem naturally proportioned for field work: "Their short, crooked legs seemed to carry them so close to the ground that they had scarcely to bend over" (SS 123). In these Progressive representations, racial form directly follows economic function: "We demand a man with two qualities: he shall be a hibernating man and a squatting man. The Japanese fulfills both conditions. He exists somehow, without bothering us, during the season of no work, and he can do as much work squatting as he can standing up."[92] Repressing the nightmare of corporate owner-ship and an intensive mode of labor, *Seed of the Sun* proposes retooling the yeoman pioneer as an entrepreneur through the miracles of farm management science.

The passage of the 1920 Alien Land Initiative did not necessarily rep-resent the political achievement of a social class, though it was clearly the symptom of a growing crisis in agriculture, compounded by high land values and low farm prices. Adding to the indeterminacy of the rural landscape was federal reclamation activity promising to make vast tracts of arable land newly available. Though irrigation promised to renew the frontier by making the acquisition of land affordable for individuals, the effect of reclamation was in fact to exacerbate a frenzy of speculation. Under these conditions, alien sightings may well provide the only con-crete explanation as to why the conduct of something so mundane as farming had become a mysterious enterprise, owned by beings who could not be seen: absentee landlords, corporations, developers, and specula-tors. The phantasmatic nature of the thing being masked by the alien figment means that the two historical subjects constituted by Asian exclusionism—the American worker and the independent farmer—are two quite different kinds of fictions. Helping to give flesh to an emerging body of organized labor in the nineteenth century, Asian exclusionism could be considered at first a tragic rhetoric of mass ideology. Later, ani-mating something that was a purely illusory, Asian exclusionism becomes more and more of a historical mystery.

A survey of the newsletter of the Western Growers and Shippers Asso-ciation from February to December 1942 shows that though the associa-tion may not have taken an official stand on evacuation, it did repeatedly insist that the Japanese were a negligible factor in the California produce business.[93] The Japanese operated only a small percentage of the total number of farms in the state, newsletter editorials argued, and their im-portance as labor was also minor. Moreover, though labor was in short supply at the time, this was scarcely a result of Japanese removal, since Japanese farmers themselves had relied upon Mexican labor ("Western Growers," 10, 11–12). In an October 1942 interview, Chester Moore, the secretary manager and lobbyist for the association, claimed that the grower members faced "practically no competition from the Japanese . . . We represent large growers and shippers. The competitive factor was exceedingly small."[94] Moore's statement, delivered months after Japanese American evacuation was underway, disavowed any commercial interest the association may have had in the elimination of Japanese American farmers, and since then historians and social scientists have held oppos-ing views on the sincerity of this denial. Though we can not settle this question empirically, we are now in a position to appreciate the significance of the rhetorical difference between 1942 and twenty years earlier, when those on both sides of the alien land law issue hyperbolized the extent of Japanese agriculture.

This is not to say that the rhetorical reversal during World War II was universal. An interesting fracas broke out in January 1942 when officials of the California State Department of Agriculture issued a public statement to the effect that any stop to Japanese agricultural production would be grossly harmful to national interest because 40 percent of California vegetables was Japanese-grown. The department director, William Cecil, received a host of letters from growers protesting the accuracy of this assessment. One letter, written by the president of the Grower-Shipper Vegetable Association and the operator of Holme and Seifert California Vegetables in Salinas, claimed that if the Japanese were removed, it would take five months at most for the industry to adjust. The letters worried about the national perception that most California vegetables were Japanese-grown and that this might result in a general boycott of the industry.[95] In industry publications, articles took great pains to argue that the Japanese contribution to California agriculture was insignificant to wartime consumption.[96] Articles in general periodicals did not reflect uniformity on the question, and there were certainly strong public arguments that economic necessity ruled against military security. In an article for the *Nation* entitled "Cool Heads or Martial Law," for example, Robert Bendiner found it easier to brush aside Constitutional objections to evacuation than economic ones: "From 30 to 40 per cent of California's truck gardening is in Japanese hands, and in some parts of the state the raising of green vegetables is virtually a Japanese monopoly, with stores and markets wholly dependent on their production. Important at any time, the yield of the Japanese truck farms is vital with the sudden quartering of something like half a million troops in California. Nor is it possible to supplant these Japanese farmers in a hurry" (Bendiner, 81). The evacuation year thus witnessed a spectacle of contending representations. But the fact that, in the end, the view of Japanese economic inconsequence held sway signals the ebb of a more familiar fiction.

Despite first impressions, therefore, the public demand for Japanese removal during World War II was not of a piece with the public demand for it in 1920. Instead of representing the fulfillment of a fantasy long-held, the event marks, rather, the dissipation of a particular fiction's ideological necessity. The extent of the historical difference between the two moments is distilled by Chester Moore's remark that "we represent large growers and shippers. The Japanese are small growers and shippers" ("Interview"). In Moore's simple statement, Japanese farmers suddenly look to be vastly different. In the past, Japanese visibility signified the absence of independent farming in the California countryside. Now Japanese farmers finally appear as what they had been all along—small farmers dwarfed by surrounding corporate giants. Ironically, while their identification with monopoly tendencies was a peculiar feature of their perpetuation by the Alien Land Laws, the perception of their smallness was a condition of their forced removal. The president of a grower association outlined his upbeat view of the 1942 crisis: not only would the industry be able to adjust quickly for the dip in production levels as a result of Japanese elimination from the industry, but also the long-term impact would be "more goods and generally speaking as far as vegetables are concerned, better goods" (Siefert, 1). The improvement of farming methods accompanying their replacement by other operators would "completely revolutionize the operation of ranches that are now farmed by Japanese . . ." (Siefert, 2).

During the evacuation process, several federal agencies were charged with responsibility for the handling of evacuee property—including the roughly six thousand Japanese farms for which non-Japanese operators had to be found. The Farm Security Administration (FSA), the New Deal agency that was assigned the task of overseeing the farm transfer, was handed the twin objectives of ensuring equity and preventing "serious interruption of agricultural production."[97] The outcome, as we now know, was the wholesale transfer of Japanese farms to the control of a few fruit companies, which received risk-free government loans to subsidize their operations and cheated the evacuees of their rightful profit share (Okihiro and Drummond, 172–73). Though the FSA tried to find human individuals to replace the evacuees, thousands of individually operated farms were largely consolidated into the hands of a few major corporations. The FSA's *Final Report* had to acknowledge: "Frequently the prevailing size and highly specialized character of Japanese farm enterprise made successful operation by individual substitute operators impractical and uneconomical, and consequently some consolidation of the operation of these small farms was found to be necessary" (FSA 18). In northern California, for example, nine farm corporations assumed 196 Japanese farms totaling 5,772 acres (Okihiro and Drummond, 173). Evacuation removed some of California's last small farmers, the last few exceptions to the West Coast's agribusiness norm.[98] The actual cleansing of the landscape of its alien figments suggests that lost opportunities for independent farming by then no longer needed permanent explanation. Why? The next chapter will address the forging of a New Deal consensus around federal interventions into market relations that came about with wider recognition of California agriculture's large scale. Through the cultural interventions of 1930s academic experts, governmental policy makers and fiction writers, the classed nature of California agricultural society became more openly visible than ever before. So too was the status of permanent aliens affected.

EPILOGUE: CALIFORNIA AS *CHINATOWN*

In his testimony before the Tolan Committee investigating Japanese evacuation in 1942, California State Attorney General Earl Warren defined what he considered to be the "points of strategic importance" to which Japanese lands seemed to be in suspicious proximity: "landing beach, air field, railroad, highway, powerhouse, power line, gas storage tank, gas pipe line, oil field, water reservoir or pumping plant, water conduit, telephone transmission line, radio station." His list named just about every conceivable signpost of economic infrastructure. In the *Final Report* by the U.S. Army, we have seen how the "attractiveness" of the land settled by Japanese was itself probable cause for treason. In the arid soil and climate of the western states, the best lands are irrigated lands. The 1920 report *California and the Oriental* observes that, though it is true that "Orientals" occupy only 16 percent of total irrigated land in the state, all lands occupied by "Orientals" are irrigated. "The very nature of the crops raised by Orientals necessitates irrigation" (50).

Historically, nativist outcry against Japanese agricultural advancement and Progressive intervention against monopoly power sometimes found common cause.[99] In the western region, monopoly enjoyed a natural host in the countryside. The climate west of the Rockies required of agricultural undertaking high capital output and government-sponsored land improvements, which were negative conditions for the settlement of small family farms. In this environment, articulations of agrarian virtue must have been especially fragile. Advertising hyperbole of California's natural fertility—its frequent characterization as a "smiling paradise"—suggests that environmental artifice was displaced onto deceitful Asians. Perhaps this is why the Japanese faces in alien land law narratives recur as unfathomably smiling.[100]

Before land and water fell back under the control of concentrated economic power in the 1910s and 1920s, the early phase of irrigation was accompanied by some degree of democratization of land ownership, including the movement of Asian farmers into farm-owner or operator status (Henderson, *Fictions of Capital,* 116). Asiatic racial form offers belated palimpsests of the contradictory and uneven effects of irrigation's history. From Raymond Chandler to Roman Polanski's film *Chinatown* (1974), the political economy of the "Cadillac desert" has been a potent subject of the mystery genre, whose regional variation reflects the use of Orientalist tropes that are far from arbitrary metaphors for the hidden secrets of California's prosperity.[101] In critical studies of western development, scholars have even found Karl Wittfogel's improbable theory of Oriental despotism to be uniquely pertinent to the Far Western frontier whose inequality and unfreedom constitute the true, organic conditions for a theory Wittfogel mistakenly named for China.[102] The 1942 *Final Report*'s justifications for the tragic evacuation of 110,000 people may also be seen to belong to this California genre of Orientalized economic mystery.

Far from grabbing the best land, Japanese tenant farmers, and the Chinese before them, historically were left with poorer plots discarded by white farmers and were responsible for improving them. Overcoming the challenges of Bermuda grass, swamps, aridity, and heat, Chinese and Japanese tenant farmers in fact extended the arable acreage of the state. "In the enhancement of land values alone Japanese farmers have added millions to the total wealth of the state. . . ."[103] Putting Asian immigrants to work on the land, like bringing water to the desert, was a fetishized technique of creating land value. Turning to the racial work performed by New Deal fiction, the next chapter will explore a shifting ideology of conservation that highlights the liberal aspects of wartime internment.

CHAPTER FOUR

A New Deal for Asians

JOHN STEINBECK, CAREY MCWILLIAMS, AND THE LIBERALISM OF JAPANESE-AMERICAN INTERNMENT

LOOKING BACK upon Japanese American internment in 1971, William Petersen, a conservative pundit who began promoting postwar Japanese American success and self-reliance in the 1960s, observed: "This was an era dominated by liberals, among who one counts virtually every civilian significantly involved in the action against Japanese Americans."[1] Petersen's polemic, repeated and made more explicit in an article for the *National Review* the next year, attacked liberalism for its "support—partial or total, knowing or innocent—of totalitarianism."[2] Disregarding whatever shifts within liberal outlooks on race may have occurred between the 1940s and the 1960s, Petersen sought to cast suspicion on the civil rights measures of his day by excavating liberalism's dirty heritage. While the ideological nature of his interest in a model minority is only barely concealed, Petersen did have plenty of ammunition to use against Roosevelt's left-liberal coalition. Among its members who failed to object to the government's violation of civil liberties were the national leadership of the American Civil Liberties Union, Walter Lippman (then the country's most influential liberal commentator), California Attorney General Earl Warren, and the Communist Party (then backing the Popular Front), with Norman Thomas of the Socialist Party forming a notable exception.[3] Liberal complicity in internment is also a common note of Asian American studies scholars, despite the fact they sit on the opposite side of the aisle from Petersen on the need for federal remedies to injustice and that for them it is government's latent racism rather than its totalitarianism that always threatens to subvert American democracy.[4]

We have been aware for some time now that "the men who ran America's concentration camps were liberals of the genus New Deal" (Drinnon, 4), but we are only just beginning to take serious account of this fact.[5] What does it mean for how we think about both New Deal liberalism and anti-Asian racism that the War Relocation Authority (WRA), or the civilian agency created by Roosevelt to run the ten camps, was, in the words of Dorothy Swaine Thomas, a "typical, New Deal, idealistic agency?"[6] By positing either the hypocrisy of liberalism or its lack of influence, we have customarily evaded the uncomfortable tie between internment and the New Deal, which demands wrestling with racism's heterogeneity.[7] As we have seen in the previous chapter, the historicization of internment has tended to situate the event within a diachronic context of Asian exclusionism, divorced from its contiguous social milieu. On the other side, standard studies of the New Deal—either for reasons of partisanship or because the onset of World War II is typically taken to mark the foreshortening of Roosevelt's domestic agenda—do not cover the events of internment. To integrate the Roosevelt administration's treatment of Japanese Americans into its forging of the welfare state means opening up a more general line of inquiry regarding a most obscure topic, the question of the relationship between American political culture of the 1930s and Asian Americans.

To date, just a few scholarly works have focused on the black subject of the New Deal, and none on the Asian American.[8] The invisibility of Asian Americans in New Deal history is partly attributable to the fact that only a minuscule number of Asian Americans were served by New Deal relief efforts and none were appointed to high-level administrative or agency positions.[9] Until the Roosevelt administration assigned the management of 110,000 incarcerated West Coast Japanese and Japanese Americans to an agency it created specially for that purpose—a process that generated unprecedented levels of documentation (demographic, statistical, anthropological, narrative) about any Asian American group—Asian Americans were not constituted by the federal government as a significant subject of social inquiry. To the contrary, the paradigmatic subject of New Deal culture is all too obviously white. The Great Depression's most famous icon is the white southern or midwestern sharecropper or farm tenant, as memorialized by such documentary and fictional texts as James Agee and Walker Evans's *Let Us Now Praise Famous Men* (1941), Dorothea Lange and Paul Taylor's *An American Exodus: A Record of Human Erosion* (1941), Erskine Caldwell and Margaret Bourke-White's *You Have Seen Their Faces* (1937), and John Steinbeck's *The Grapes of Wrath* (1939). The whiteness of the fallen yeomen who are the protagonists of these texts does not bespeak the racial transparency of universal subjecthood, however, but rather something actively, historically constructed.[10] In the southern context traceable to the social formations of Reconstruction and its aftermath,[11] this chapter will show how the "poor white," framed by the environs of a 1930s California migrant labor camp, is a figure constituted by another racial genealogy.

If the entry of the Dust Bowl refugee into California's industrial army of migrant labor would appear to have been central to the very possibility of the political and cultural emergence of a "rich choral symphony of migrant voices"[12] by the early 1940s, the racial significance of this entire episode was by no means straightforward. Though two earlier works by Steinbeck on the exploitation of white Californian farmworkers had been well received, it was his invention of the Joad family that definitively established the reality of the migrant worker's suffering.[13] Shortly after the publication of *The Grapes of Wrath*, journalists and politicians began discussing the Joads as if they were real people. In his testimony during the Tolan Committee hearings on rural migrancy, the editor of the newspaper of Salislaw, Oklahoma, where the Joad family came from, saw fit to contest Steinbeck's depiction point by point; President Roosevelt himself, during one of his Fireside Chats, referred to the Joads when raising the topic of federal housing projects (Starr, *Dreams,* 257–59). In considering what the Joads contributed to the New Deal farm program, we will see that it was not simply that an added whiteness made the existence of migratory labor more visible. The resignification of whiteness was itself a condition of migrant representability. In the Joads' difference from their white proletarian predecessors Lenny and George in *Of Mice and Men* (1937) and the striking apple pickers of *In Dubious Battle* (1936), we will see how the Asiatic is present in a way that is constitutively central.

The insertion of interstate migrants from Oklahoma, Arkansas, and the Southwest into the socioeconomic position of the California migrant farmworker necessarily situated the representation of Okies in relation to a prior California discourse on unassimilable aliens.[14] Responding to the public storm over the arrival of thousands of migrants from other states—more than three hundred thousand between 1930 and 1934 alone—in May 1935 the California legislature passed a bill to prohibit all "indigent persons or persons liable to become public charges" from moving into the state.[15] The Los Angeles chamber of commerce recommended that a hard-labor concentration camp for vagrants be established to discourage other unemployed transients from coming, and the Los Angeles police department was dispatched to seal off the borders of the state against Los Angeles-bound migrants (Starr, *Dreams,* 227). Recognizing the link between contemporary white migrants and their foreign predecessors, University of California economist Paul S. Taylor observed at the time: "In the spirit of the legislature which sought unconstitutionally to debar Chinese immigrants from California in the 50's, the present session is asked to exclude American 'immigrants' without money."[16] James Gregory, the historian of Okie culture, writes that anti-Okie prejudice was largely a measure of the Central Valley's "caste-like social structure" (Gregory, 102). "Though they were whites," Gregory argues, "the migrants inherited many of the social disabilities previously associated with the nonwhite farm labor force—much of this was simply the price of farm labor in California" (Gregory, 102).

What does it mean for interstate migrants to have "inherited many of the social disabilities" of their transnational predecessors? What is the relation between the social identity conferred by labor price and physiological distinction? As Don Mitchell writes, "Malnourished and unkempt, Dust Bowl migrants forced an even greater visibility to the rural conditions of the state. Growers, both rejoiced at the influx of desperate workers seeking any kind of work at all, and feared it. Perhaps the new migrants were *too* hungry" (179). I will show how a fundamental condition of that visibility was a discursive engagement with Asiatic racial form. Though Asian immigrants were not of manifest concern to 1930s culture, I will argue that the representation of the interstate migrant necessarily intersected with a prior discourse on Asiatic unassimilability. The effect of this intersection was the undoing of a constitutive opposition between American and alien that was to presage the growing Americanization of the postwar international order. In the late 1930s, at the height of the Californian New Deal, a prime result of this intersection, as is fairly well known, was the Farm Security Administration's building of a "government camp program . . . designed specifically for white workers" (Don Mitchell, 178). As to the social impact on Asian Americans, its effects were palpable slightly later, with the wartime building of government camps specifically for Japanese Americans. In order to understand the liberalism of Japanese American internment, this chapter will examine the War Relocation Authority's extension of a discourse of rural rehabilitation, the grounds for which are traceable to the racial dimensions of New Deal diagnoses of California's economic maladjustments. In the documentation of this, the historical archive served by Steinbeck's fiction will help to illuminate the imaginative extravagances of governmental practice and social scientific thinking.

The Asiatic Descent of Migrant Visibility

According to the historian Cletus Daniel, the years from 1890 to 1930 in California agriculture were punctuated by labor challenges that were only sporadic and unorganized. Progressivism relied to a large extent on the political support of farmers, and therefore reforms sought not to increase the political power of labor but to curb the extremities of employer abuse.[17] The state legislature responded to the 1913 Wheatland hop pickers' strike by creating the California Commission of Immigration and Housing (CCIH), which sought to facilitate the assimilation of immigrants into social-economic life. Investigations into the poor housing and sanitation conditions endured by farm workers usually concluded that a low standard of living was natural to the numerous foreigners among them. In 1920 the commission's chief sanitary engineer testified that Japanese farm laborers lived in shack houses "not fit for human habitation," and this was used to argue in support of the Alien Land Initiative.[18] The conventional agrarian wisdom that a permanent class of farmworkers had no rightful place in the American republic often found a solution in the permanent exclusion of cheap laborers themselves.[19]

The heterogeneity of California's farm labor supply notwithstanding, the radically unassimilable alien, however, was paradigmatically designated by the Asiatic, otherwise known as the alien ineligible to citizenship. The reform of housing conditions for Mexican migrant workers constituted part of the Progressive effort to "stabilize" the supply of farm labor, while outside the prospect of "Americanization" schemes altogether were Chinese and Japanese workers whose use in the same period Progressives simply sought to stop (Don Mitchell, 99). In the post–World War I era inaugurated by the dual crackdown on the Industrial Workers of the World (IWW, or Wobblies) and on Japanese agriculturalists—two prime signifiers of agricultural labor's intractability—California farming was characterized by further corporate consolidation and relative worker quiescence (Daniel, 87, 100–105). By the mid-1920s, Mexico emerged as the new source of migrant labor, ideal in that this source was nearby and abundant enough to meet the cyclical needs of seasonal harvests without delay and without social consequences: during the off-season, workers could simply be shipped back across the border (Daniel, 68). With the sealing of the U.S.-Asian border by the 1924 National Origins Act, Filipinos also composed an important, alternative source of labor, since under the terms of the United States's annexation of the Philippines Filipinos counted as U.S., not Asian, nationals.[20]

The 1930s represented a radical departure in the history of California agriculture. Whereas most American farmers had been struggling since the end of World War I due to the shrinking of European markets, the decade represented the first real contraction in the profits of the California fruit and produce industry. Furthermore, ostensible support of the New Deal for the rights of labor helped to fuel labor militancy among farmworkers who, starting in 1928, were once again beginning to demand social recognition as workers. A significant arena of Communist Party organizing and the scene of a series of nationally prominent strikes—particularly during the "great upheaval" of 1933—California agriculture suddenly became an emblematic site of social conflict and crisis. The decade reflected related changes in the demographic composition of the state's agricultural workforce. Rising farmworker militancy is a known factor in the Immigration and Naturalization Service's forced repatriation of Mexican workers—nearly 150,000 by 1937—and the passage of the Tydings-McDuffie Act (1934), which, by phasing in independence to the Philippines, aimed at cutting off the unrestricted flow of Filipino immigration.[21] In the same period, 683,000 migrants from the south-central states of Oklahoma, Texas, Missouri, and Arkansas arrived in California to take their places (Starr, *Dreams, 223–25*). As California historian Kevin Starr succinctly put it, "The actors in the drama of farm labor in California in the first half of the 1930s had been Spanish-speaking and brown-skinned. In the second half of the decade, they became white, English-speaking, of the oldest Anglo-American stock" (Starr, *Dreams, 225*).

John Steinbeck's most famous depictions of agricultural class conflict would certainly seem to confirm the necessity of whiteness to the project of constructing literary protagonists out of migrant workers. In *The Grapes of Wrath* (1939), the Joads encounter no non-whites on any of their peregrinations. In the novel *In Dubious Battle,* based on a composite of labor actions including a peach strike at the Tagus Ranch in Tulare County in August 1933, where Mexicans formed the majority of the workers,[22] the characters reflect instead a range of white ethnicities.[23] Indeed, where Mexicans do feature in Steinbeck's writing, like his Indians, they are noble savages who exist in a world outside time and money.[24] Except for his first published story—"Fingers of Cloud" (1924), which concerns an interracial relationship between a Filipino gang boss and a white, mentally disabled young woman—Steinbeck did not write about Filipinos.[25] By comparison, the manifest absence of Chinese and Japanese from Steinbeck's portrait of the agricultural workforce, in light of post-1924 demographic trends, would seem to imply less of an active omission. What does it mean for us to raise the question of Asiatic cultural representation at a historical moment when Chinese and Japanese Americans were not, by all accounts, the central actors of social struggle?[26] As my approach to the recovery of Asiatic racial form in the New Deal seeks to show, during an era when absolute Asian immigration exclusion was the ideological dominant (1924–1943), a historicist reading of racial representation need not be restricted to judging fiction for its empirical fidelity or distortions.

According to Don Mitchell, federal efforts to ameliorate the lives of California's migratory workers were the result of both Mexican and Filipino radicalism and the fact that more and more white workers were entering the migratory labor stream. The temporal coincidence of the two developments makes the factors of racialization and class struggle in producing worker visibility difficult to disentangle. While no doubt the relative increase in white migratory workers contributed to the building public sense that labor conditions were insupportable, the terms of their social legibility were themselves contingent upon the reworking of the racialized figure of rural inequality. Even as the demographic statistics would indicate a substitution that proceeded along a different set of racial axes, textual narratives of California's agricultural crisis suggested the necessity of the New Deal's ideological displacement of the discourse of Asian exclusion. In the field of agricultural economics, the 1930s reflected an increasing recognition of the industrial nature of California farming and, with it, institutional prescriptions for the alleviation of conflict that departed from Progressivism's panacea of Asian exclusion.

In seminal studies of the farm labor crisis conducted by Paul Taylor in the 1930s, the legitimation of farmworker demands coincided with a regional and structural, rather than a biological, explanation for a low standard of living among agricultural workers. Taylor began writing about migratory labor for academic journals and magazines in the late 1920s, and by the 1930s, when he served as a part-time consultant for the Division of Rural Rehabilitation of the State Emergency Relief Administration (SERA), he had earned a national reputation as an expert on rural poverty and migration. Taylor's portrait of rural California depicted a class-divided scene that exploded existing myths of egalitarian opportunities for upward mobility and farm ownership. Instead of evoking a singular sense of the "American farmer," his analysis apprehended a social field broken down into owners, tenants, managers, and laborers, with laborers accounting for more than half of the total and constituting the largest rural wage-earning class nationwide.[27] If in Taylor's writing California's rural proletariat looked to be "partly of alien race, propertyless, and without ties, protective or otherwise, to the soil which it tills" (CBCL 408), these traits were a reflection of the state's historical reliance upon poorer regions throughout the world for labor supply. Moreover, with the drought of 1934 adding refugees from other states to a California migrant labor pool already comprising a "long line of immigrant nationalities," the southwestern United States had now joined Asia and Mexico as one of the "areas of the world with a low standard of living."[28] There were no more comforting divisions to be drawn between a necessarily higher American standard of living and living standards elsewhere. In Taylor's view, given growers' shortsightedness and recalcitrance, the only alternative to a future of unending class conflict was federal intervention.

The legitimation of worker demands meant substituting images of an uncomplaining body with evocations of a body in distress. As we have seen in chapter 3, functionalist representations of labor's form depended heavily upon its racialization. "Work of a stooping nature, such as sugar beet thinning or pulling and topping, thinning of lettuce, weeding of carrots, transplanting of celery," R. L. Adams counseled the California State Chamber of Commerce, "call[s] for a build and stamina that can perform under conditions difficult for most Americans because of their lack of 'a hinge in the back' . . ."[29] (FL 4–5). In particular, the efficiency requirements of agricultural work were thought to be unusually well met by Asiatic anatomy. Even the secret of Japanese American rural upward mobility was attributed to a morphology suited to agricultural labor. Speaking of the rise of famed "potato baron" George Shima from modest origins, a University of California report held that "Owing to his shorter legs, [Shima] could worker faster than [his fellow workmen] and showed his form especially during the periodical potato-picking contests."[30]

Taylor's 1930s California farmworkers, by contrast, "would as soon be shot as starve to death working."[31] His characterization of the 1930s workforce—politically vocal *and* "largely Mexican and Oriental, but including southern poor whites and Negroes"(UF 19)—underscores the extent to which labor protest and the entry of drought refugees dually informed the metamorphosis of the willing coolie into the suffering migrant. The figural convergence between Okies and California migrant workers threw into question a longstanding dichotomy between Americans and aliens. At the moment when the bearers of "classic" American features entered an economic existence thought to be physiologically deforming, how did the California migrant worker appear? Counter to our initial assumptions, the morphology of the California Dust Bowl refugee is no simple matter. Might the racial puzzle it presented help to explain the obsessive propagation of images of Dust Bowl migrants, as if the question of their bodily form were not easily satisfied? Might their elevation to the status of the quintessential emblem of the times have bespoken not their automatic identity with the nation but in fact the extent to which their Americanness required active assertion and reassertion?

Paul Taylor's various efforts to explain the farm labor turmoil reveal something of the racial impact of Okie arrival upon labor's representation. One article coauthored with Clark Kerr, "Uprising on the Farms" (1935), begins with the nineteenth-century establishment of an agricultural workforce "numerous and racially alien" and concludes with a contemporary snapshot of a demographic still "largely alien, but inclu[ding] 'whites' and Negroes" (UF 20). The quotation marks around whiteness convey a definitional hesitation, a sense of the term's uncertain application given the predominance of racial discourse by Asian exclusion, or the perception that, as Percy Edwards had put it, "on this coast . . . everybody is a 'white man' but the Jap."[32] Appearing in *Survey Graphic* that same year, a different piece by Taylor, "Again the Covered Wagon" (1935), begins the narrative of California's agricultural crisis outside the state, on the Great Plains, with the story of drought victims who will eventually end up "part of the under-employed labor army—white Americans, Mexicans, Negroes, Filipinos."[33] Here, where Dust Bowl migration supplies a major theme, there are no quotation marks around whiteness. Their absence suggests how the Okie figure accords an ethnic specificity to the term

"white" (as one group among others, including "Mexicans, Negroes, Filipinos"), undoing its exclusive synonymity with national identity, as part
of a process in which the capacity for alienation had become recognizably
universal—had become no longer, by definition, un-American.

"Them goddamn Okies got no sense and no feeling," says a bigoted
character in *The Grapes of Wrath,* "They ain't human. A human being
couldn't live like they do. A human being couldn't stand it to be so dirty
and miserable. They ain't a whole hell of a lot better than gorillas."[34]
When people see Okies, they stereotypically see "[t]hree hundred thousand in California and more coming. And in California the roads full of
frantic people running like ants to pull, to push, to lift, to work. For every
manload to lift, five pairs of arms extended to lift it; for every stomachful
of food available, five mouths open" (*GW* 324). Instead of ants and gorillas, when we rest our eyes upon Okies what would the novel have us
see? The text dwells at length on physical descriptions of the Joads, investing in the power of the visual to counteract the determinations of
blind prejudice:

> He wore a black, dirty slouch hat and a blue work shirt over which
> was a buttonless vest; his jeans were held up by a wide harness-leather
> belt with a big square brass buckle, leather and metal polished from
> years of wearing; and his shoes were cracked and the soles swollen and
> boat-shaped from years of sun and wet and dust. The sleeves of his
> shirt were tight on his forearms, held down by the bulging powerful
> muscles. Stomach and hips were lean, and legs, short, heavy and
> strong. His face, squared by a bristling pepper and salt beard, was all
> drawn down to the forceful chin, a chin thrust out and built out by the
> stubble beard which was not so grayed on the chin, and gave weight
> and force to its thrust. Over old Tom's unwhiskered cheekbones the
> skin was as brown as meerschaum, and wrinkled in rays around his
> eye-corners from squinting. His eyes were brown, black-coffee brown,
> and he thrust his head forward when he looked at a thing, for his
> bright dark eyes were failing. His lips, from which the big nails pro-
> truded, were thin and red. (*GW* 96)

In the novel, Steinbeck repeatedly brings narrative movement to a stand-
still with such detailed descriptions. We are brought close enough to the
subject to see his wrinkles and stubble, but kept distant enough to appreciate the overall proportions of his anatomically correct figure. Perhaps it
seems strange to stress the text's purposefulness in distinguishing *Homo
sapiens'* physique from that of the gorilla or the ant, in light of the critical perception of Steinbeck's failure at portraying human beings on the
basis that he tends to assimilate them to animals (Benson, 64). Steinbeck's
fundamentally animal view of human beings places him within a tradi-

tion of literary naturalism, even as the divergent currents within his work—between his social concerns and his romanticism, between his fatalism and "phalanx" theories and his individualism—raise questions as to the appropriateness of this classification.[35] Like earlier naturalists, Steinbeck maps the social onto the natural, but his view of nature is holistic rather than Darwinian. Where turn-of-the-century naturalists explored the animal (or mechanical) quality of the human in order to emphasize its degeneracy, Steinbeck's animalization moves in the opposite direction—toward the "non-teleological" acceptance of the universe's myriad biological life forms.[36] As to the limitations of Steinbeck's Okie representation, critics have had much to say about the cultural condescension and the political reductions of sentimentalism.[37] What interests me, however, is not his characters' lack of complex interiority but the form of their exteriority.

In a 1936 article for the *Nation*, "Dubious Battle in California," his earliest publication on Dust Bowl refugees, Steinbeck describes the proud traits of a people who, "having gone through the horrors of the drought and with immense effort having escaped from it, . . . cannot be herded, attacked, starved or frightened as all the others were."[38] Thus, "[t]he men will organize," he predicts, "It is understood that they are being attacked not because they want higher wages, not because they are Communists, but simply because they want to organize" (DBC 304). What's different about these new migrants is that they are "undeniably American" (DBC 303). What does the term "American" here mean? Americanness seems to be constituted by an opposition to two kinds of aliens—rightless transnational migrant groups and "outside agitators." In both instances, the guarantees of moral fiber and legal standing are closely intertwined.

The double meaning of the Americanness of recognized labor is also present in Steinbeck's novel about white, but not specifically Okie, agricultural workers, also published in 1936 and bearing a similar title: *In Dubious Battle*. Here is a conversation between a strike leader and the president of the Fruit Growers' Association in that novel:

> "Mr Bolter," he said, "Like Mac says, I guess we ain't American workin' men. You wanted cards laid down, and then you laid yours down backs up. . . . Your God damn apples got to be picked and we ain't picking 'em without our raise. . . ."
>
> At least the smile had faded from Bolter's face. He said gravely, "The American nation has become great because everybody pitched in and helped. American labor is the best labor in the world, and the highest paid."
>
> London broke in angrily, "S'pose a Chink does get half a cent a day,

if he can eat on it? What the hell do we care how much we get, if we got to go hungry?"

Bolter put on his smile again. "I have a home and children," he said, "I've worked hard. You think I'm different from you. I want you to look on me as a working man, too. I've worked for everything I've got. Now we've heard that radicals are working among you. I don't believe it. I don't believe American men, with American ideals, will listen to radicals."[39]

In this exchange between representatives of labor and capital, Americanism can be used to insinuate the unpatriotic implications of labor organizing, or it can be used to portray labor exploitation as the nation's racial betrayal. In Steinbeck's novel about Communist organizers in the San Joaquin, the Asiatic emerges momentarily as the familiar mark of American labor's subminimal standard for reproduction.

Steinbeck's Okie-related writing, however, inflects the coolie's political relation to organized labor in a decisively different way:

The completion of the transcontinental railroads left in the country many thousands of Chinese and some Hindus who had been imported for the work. At about the same time the increase of fruit crops, with their heavy seasonal need for pickers, created a demand for this mass of cheap labor. These people, however, did not long remain on the land. They migrated to the cities, rented small plots of land there, and worst of all, organized in the so-called 'tongs,' which were able to direct their efforts as a group. Soon the whites were inflamed to race hatred, riots broke out against the Chinese, and repressive activities were undertaken all over the state, until these people, who had been a tractable and cheap source of labor, were driven from the fields.

To take the place of the Chinese, the Japanese were encouraged to come into California; and they, even more than the Chinese, showed an ability not only to obtain land for their subsistence but to organize. The 'Yellow Peril' agitation was the result. Then, soon after the turn of the century Mexicans were imported in great numbers. For a while they were industrious workers, until the process of importing twice as many as were needed in order to depress wages made their earnings drop below any conceivable living standard. In such conditions they did what the others had done; they began to organize. The large growers immediately opened fire on them. The newspapers were full of the radicalism of the Mexican unions. Riots become common in the Imperial Valley and in the grape country in and adjacent to Kern County. Another wave of importations was arranged, from the Philippine Islands, and the cycle was repeated—wage depression due to abundant labor, organization, and the inevitable race hatred and riots.

This brings us almost to the present. The drought in the Middle West has very recently made available an enormous amount of cheap labor. Workers have been coming to California in nondescript cars from Oklahoma, Nebraska, Texas, and other states, parts of which have been rendered uninhabitable by drought. Poverty-stricken after the destruction of their farms, their last reserves used up in making the trip, they have arrived so beaten and destitute that they have been willing at first to work under any conditions and for any wages offered. This migration started on a considerable scale about two years ago and is increasing all the time.

For a time it looked as though the present cycle would be identical with the earlier ones, but there are several factors in this influx which differentiate it from the others. In the first place, the migrants are undeniably American and not deportable. In the second place, they were not lured to California by a promise of good wages, but are refugees as surely as though they had fled from destruction by an invader. In the third place, they are not drawn from a peon class, but have either owned small farmers or been farm hands in the early American sense, in which the "hand" is a member of the employing family. They have one fixed idea, and that is to acquire land and settle on it. Probably the most important difference is that they are not easily intimidated. (DBC 303)

Rather than reiterating the stereotype of the Asiatic as labor's "indispensable enemy," Steinbeck's account of California agricultural history here exposes "yellow peril" discourse to be a strategic means of labor suppression in the face of worker resistance. This background piece on Dust Bowl refugees unfixes a low standard of living from certain races, and rewrites the willing coolie as a starvation victim. A revolution wrought by the arrival of American migrants promises to end California history's cyclical pattern of labor importation, resistance, and suppression. Their Americanness resides in the legal protections afforded by citizenship, and also the virtues ensuing from a familiar Jeffersonian agrarian discourse. If the article would seem to validate collective forms of organized action, a mixed idiom of yeoman self-sufficiency and family values also permeates the text's sense of political optimism. A similar ambiguity also structures *The Grapes of Wrath,* where the possibility of broader counterhegemonic forms of social identification is opened by a subplot involving the labor-organizing trajectories of the ex-preacher Casey and the political flight of Tom Joad, within the main plot's focus on the travails of the biological family. The fictional treatment follows the investigative article in supplying a history of California's industrialized agriculture that forms the background to Okie migrancy, beginning with the cynical importation of "Chinese, Japanese, Mexicans, Filipinos" who "the businessmen said . . . don't need much" (*GW* 316). In *The Grapes of Wrath,* too, a historical approach to the humanization of the Okie begins with a necessary demystification of the "yellow peril."

Reiterations of the Okies' Americanness suggest a specific engagement with an Asiatic question in Steinbeck's making, or maturation, of the California agricultural working class. Steinbeck's fictional work participates in a wider field of discourse on agricultural crisis that proliferates in the wake of the 1933–1934 labor unrest that helped to make the migrant worker visible in a domain particularly obfuscated by agrarianist ideology. In the Dust Bowl migration narrative, the Okie is a complex figure, defined by resemblance *and* opposition to the Asiatic. In Steinbeck's epic narrative, the Joads may come face-to-face with no live Asians, but upon crossing state lines they are suddenly made into descendants, and potential avengers, of a prior Asiatic ancestor. To this extent, the cultural production of the poor white subject in the 1930s is also the re-presentation of Asian-American relations. "Dubious Battle in California" ends with an explicit gesture toward a new cross-racial solidarity: "It is fervently to be hoped that the great group of migrant workers so necessary to the harvesting of California's crops may be given the right to live decently, that they may not be so badgered, tormented, and hurt that in the end they become avengers of the hundreds of thousands who have been tortured and starved before them" (DBC 304). In New Deal reformist texts such as these, public recognition of migrant worker alienation means that the alien is being, in some sense, humanized, but the paradoxical conditions for interracial class solidarity make it difficult to evaluate the historicization of Asiatic racial formation, now that the Asiatic is ancestrally, rather than competitively, constitutive of the organized worker. In universalizing alienation, Steinbeck's Okie texts install the Asiatic as a founding figure of California's agricultural working class and one that is, simultaneously, relegated to pre-history. For the far-reaching consequences for Asian Americans of the New Deal's assimilationist strategy, we need to turn to the record of the Roosevelt administration's wartime handling of Japanese Americans.

Japanese American Internment and Rural Reform

"As part of their accommodation to Communism," William Petersen wrote, "most liberals accepted or half-accepted the Party's line on Japanese Americans" (Petersen, *Japanese Americans,* 75). Among them, Carey McWilliams particularly drew Petersen's fire as an "important locus of Communist influence" (Petersen, *Japanese Americans,* 75) and as a direct example of, in Petersen's terms, totalitarian-infiltrated liberalism. A member of a prominent circle of literary radicals in Los Angeles in the 1920s, a labor lawyer, a public intellectual whose book reviews, literary essays, and political analyses appeared in national periodicals, and an editor of the *Nation,* Carey McWilliams was a leading example of California's left intellectuals who became involved in the New Deal. McWilliams was also one of the leading antiracist voices of his time, authoring numerous articles and books on Mexican immigrants, anti-Semitism, Japanese Americans, and the multiracial history of California.[40] With the gubernatorial election of Culbert Olsen in 1938, McWilliams was appointed to head the Division of Immigration and Housing (the successor to the California Commission of Immigration and Housing) and became the top state official responsible for the welfare of migrants, a job in which he took so active a role as to be quickly named enemy number one by the Associated Farmers. While it is not true that McWilliams was an "active proponent" of Japanese American evacuation, as Petersen claims, it is the case that over the course of 1942, as evacuation kicked into gear, McWilliams's public statements suggest an increasing reconciliation with the government's removal policy. In March, McWilliams was strongly urging against "any wholesale evacuation of the Japanese."[41] In September, however, when evacuation had become a *fait accompli,* he credited the army for having accomplished "this largest mass evacuation in American history . . . on time, without mishap, and with virtually no friction" and, without "attempting to rationalize what has been done," presented the government's case for evacuation's necessity.[42] Two years later, in a book entitled *Prejudice: Japanese-Americans, Symbol of Racial Intolerance* (1944), McWilliams had become certain of evacuation's military nonnecessity and quite vocal about the injustice of disparate treatment. "What was accomplished, in terms of the war effort, by the removal of the Japanese," he wrote, "was the elimination of a wholly theoretical hazard to the detriment of nearly every other aspect of the war."[43] As for the unprecedented nature of a group of U.S. citizens being systematically singled out solely on the basis of race or ancestry, McWilliams lamented that "[t]here was virtually no realization, among the generality of citizens, that they were witnessing a unique departure from American tradition" (*P* 134). His analysis of the conditions of incarceration was also highly critical: "No one has starved in these centers and no one has frozen to death; everyone has shelter and sustenance," he wrote, "But this is about as much as can be said in defense of the centers as housing projects" (*P* 156–57). More intriguing than the suspicion of political hypocrisy or cravenness attaching to McWilliams's public shifts is the suggestion of an unfolding disillusionment. Is it possible to understand the perspective from which internment might have been, however fleetingly, an occasion for liberal hope?

In the article in question, "Moving the West-Coast Japanese," which appeared in *Harper's* magazine in September 1942, McWilliams lauds the mechanics of evacuation as a "miracle of effective organization" on the part of the army; questions the impact any self-seeking groups might have had on the government's decision; plays down the agricultural disruption posed by the removal of Japanese American farmers; and speculates that, in the long run, "the Japanese will probably profit by this painful and distressing experience"(MWJ 359–69). McWilliams only gingerly touches on the government's violation of citizens' civil rights: "The curtailment of the rights and privileges of the American-born Japanese citizens of this country will furnish one of the gravest tests of democratic institutions in our history" (MWJ 364). His tone is that of a sympathizer with federal decision makers who had to weigh "considerations, many of which are quite persuasive, which led [them] to believe that the measure was necessary" (MWJ 364). In hindsight, what makes this article so strange, coming from McWilliams (a leading antiracist writer), is not just its lack of skepticism toward government assertions that Japanese American–operated hotels along the Seattle front "provided an almost impenetrable screen for espionage activities" (MWJ 365) or that "[n]o one has doubted, and least of all the *Nisei* themselves, that there were disloyal elements among the Japanese" (MWJ 366).[44] Harder to accept is McWilliams's representation of evacuation as a potentially positive social opportunity for Japanese Americans themselves. McWilliams speculates that the break-up of West Coast Japanese communities may well place them in "a far more satisfactory position in American life" after the war, since it is clearly not "desirable that the Japanese should be concentrated in localized areas as they were prior to December 7th" (MWJ 369).

McWilliams's vision of assimilation reflected an ethnocentric conceptualization of racial equality predicated upon the cultural disappearance of minorities themselves. However, in envisioning the assimilation of Asian subjects at all, McWilliams also represented a major departure from the exclusionist assumptions of earlier Progressive liberals. It is perhaps nearly impossible for our present-day reconstructions of a way of life destroyed by evacuation and internment to be entirely free of nostalgia, though the tight-knit Japanese American communities that existed before the war were in part a product of a Jim Crow order. As Roger Daniels writes, "Throughout the 1930s all but a very few of the second generation adults were confined, economically and socially, within Japanese America. The first Japanese American to graduate from the University of Oregon Law School, for example, could find professional employment only with a consulate general of Japan."[45] The coercion involved in the dismantling of a racial community seemed to be justified, in McWilliams's mind, by the social violence of entrenched segregation.

Perhaps even more strange to us now than envisioning evacuation as the prelude to a federally managed process of racial integration was imagining, alternatively, that the internment camps themselves might develop into potentially permanent sites of voluntary colonization:

> Vast improvements are being made in the relocation projects: land is being reclaimed, towns are being constructed, new communities are being laid out, small-scale industries are being planned. These improvements, by their very nature, are permanent in character. The Japanese, moreover, are going to have a strong equitable interest in the product of their labor and their industry; and it is at least foreseeable that the government will eventually work out some scheme by which they can acquire ownership of these projects. As free American citizens, the Nisei can of course go wherever they wish after the war; but my point is that they will probably refer to remain where they are rather than go through the dislocations occasioned by a second resettlement. (MWJ 369)

The genuine confusion of mandatory detention with experiments in co-operative living seems nearly implausible, unless we situate McWilliams within a genealogy of California writing in which perceptions of rural inequality and fears of Asiatic concentration have repeatedly converged. In this vexing genealogy, the farm system's disposal toward tyranny often found expression in an Oriental metaphor, while archeological excavations of anti-Asianism have, on occasion, yielded earnest intentions of social reform.[46] The two-decade-long government career of Elwood Mead points to continuities between the Progressive-era idea of government-aided land settlement and the subsistence homesteads and resettlement programs of the New Deal.[47] The array of concerns, in particular, reflected by Mead—a leading irrigation authority, rural colonization proponent, and alien land law sympathizer—testifies to the presence of a link between rural utopianism and an Asiatic question. Within this context, we will see how the liberal discourse of internment reflected neither an idiosyncratic vision of social change nor a racial politics homogenizable with Progressivism.[48]

As we saw in chapter 3, starting in the 1910s Asian exclusionism found an expressive home in various discourses of land reform, including populist critiques of land monopoly and speculation, the promotion of scientific farming methods and irrigation, and back-to-the-land experiments that sought to resurrect the small family farm. Even into the late 1930s, scientific research projects at the University of California's College of Agriculture continued to highlight a correlation between the state's prevailing system of high land values—which led to high rents, making constant production necessary—and poor soil conservation practices by tenants, who could not afford to practice crop rotation. Under the directorship of R. L. Adams, a series of agricultural studies concluded that there was a systematic correlation between Japanese farmers and soil exhaustion: since almost all Japanese farmers were tenants, Japanese farms were those in the greatest environmental danger.[49] Another, more anecdotal, study in 1937, by Emil Bunje, excoriated the Japanese "potato king" George Shima for reclaiming Sacramento delta marshlands, which "should have been left untouched and preserved for future generations of Americans" (*SJF* 43). The notion of Japanese soil damage established a simple parallel between disinherited American persons and sapped American land. Japanese "soil mining"—like gold mining, bonanza wheat farming, oil drilling, and the real estate industry,—presented yet another instance of the irresponsible nature of California economic development, favored quick profits and speculative practices over long-term husbanding of resources. Acting like financial speculators, Japanese farmers were accused of an exploitative, temporary relation to the land.

Not only were these accusations, to a great extent, simply false, but the correctives offered basically made things worse. Targeting the Japanese for their short-term approaches to soil use, the Alien Land Laws exacerbated the problem of transience by restricting Japanese land tenure. Whereas Japanese holdings supposedly consisted of the best lands in the state, in actuality Japanese tenants were forced to take up marginal lands that were unwanted by others. Whereas Japanese farmers were accused of reducing soil fertility, the improvements they made increased the value of the lands they occupied. Even the *San Francisco Chronicle* admitted that "the most striking feature of Japanese farming in California has been the development of successful orchards, vineyards, or gardens on lands that were either completely out of use or employed for far less profitable enterprises."[50] These included cut-over timberlands of the Northwest, and delta lands in California, that were converted into valuable farmland. Thus news of Japanese soil exhaustion appeared alongside reports of Japanese farmers' positive agricultural contributions and specialized skill in intensive land use, purportedly derived from centuries-old knowledge of feeding a large population on the small islands of Japan. In Wallace Irwin's *Seed of the Sun* (1921), Japanese imperial expansionism derives not just from Malthusian population pressure, but from an essential, primeval "land hunger," a "passionate devotion to the land" as such.[51] Notions of Japanese as physiologically robust and capable of surviving physical conditions that whites could not were consonant with the discourse on Japanese farm labor that featured the Japanese body as particularly suited to the work required by intensive farming, the ability to eke out a living in desiccated or swampy areas most people found intolerable.[52]

The terms of the debate on Japanese farming came from the conservationist movement which, beginning in the 1890s, grew out of a concern with the problems of western economic growth and, more precisely, water development. As part of the scientific movement to promote efficient development through rational planning, conservationism during the Progressive era emphasized expansion, not retrenchment, even though it was predicated on the fear of diminishing resources.[53] Arising at the same time, the debate over Japanese farming practices mirrors these contradictions. The discourse on the Japanese and the discourse of conservationism both concern questions of land use at a moment when the disappearance of cheap land was at the forefront of public consciousness. Both discourses involve theories of productive efficiency and attempts to innovate new models of economic growth in the post-frontier era. The shift from extensive to intensive farming in that period represents part of the movement toward greater efficiency of land use, as irrigation changed the kinds of crops that could be grown and made smaller acreages economically practical. Yet the viability of smaller acreages did not necessarily make farming more affordable, because more efficient land use simply boosted land values even further. In this national trend toward agricultural intensification, California led the way.

Progressive conservation proposed a post-expansionist model of growth through an improved economy of internal management; and the Asiatic signified, above all, a miracle economy. In his alarmist report on the expansionist tendencies of Japanese agriculture in the state, *The Story of Japanese Farming*, Bunje wrote: "Living on next to nothing, and hoarding practically all of his wages, Shima soon had enough capital to set himself up as a labor boss" (*SJF* 39). The Asiatic figure, with its extraordinarily favorable ratio of output to input, epitomized the productive powers of capital accumulation. On the flip side, the Asiatic could also signify accumulation's reverse image, a false alchemy that produced something less than what is invested—not the production of value but the wasting of raw materials. In the interest of safeguarding future productivity, certain acts of conservation sought to privilege the concrete over the abstract. For in limiting the extent of the land's market alienability, the Alien Land Laws' literalist apprehension of landed property sought to arrest the fluidity implied by exchange, to protect the land's real value (essentialized as fertility) from the dissipating effects of price inflation. In a sense, the Alien Land Laws were an expression of the extreme crisis scenario of unsustainable development.

Was it an accident that during World War II governmental evacuation of West Coast Japanese Americans should have chosen to present itself as an act of conservation? In the year that it disbanded, the War Relocation Authority (WRA) published a report of its wartime activities under the title *A Story of Human Conservation* (1946).[54] The government's decision to portray mass incarceration as a conservationist act discloses more than an arbitrary use of euphemism. At the level of institutional history, there were various examples of material overlap between the conservationist undertakings and the internment operated by the Roosevelt administration. The first appointee to direct the WRA, Milton Eisenhower, formerly headed the Office of Land-Use Coordination and was credited in particular for having negotiated the Mount Weather Agreement, which was intended to end the conflict between land-grant colleges and the Farm Security Administration (Drinnon, *Keeper,* 19). His replacement, Dillon Myer, had held the position of acting administrator of the Agricultural Conservation and Adjustment Administration, a division of the Soil Conservation Service (SCS), just prior to his appointment as WRA director. In 1933 Myer served as a state supervisor of the Agricultural Adjustment Administration within the U.S. Department of Agriculture, later moving on to the SCS. As a result, the WRA staff, many of whom accompanied Myer from his previous office, consisted equally of former members of the Bureau of Indian Affairs (BIA), the SCS, and other agricultural agencies (Drinnon, *Keeper,* 39). Speaking of those WRA administrators, Richard Drinnon writes that "[g]iven their careers in agriculture, they would have been more at home in the Farm Security Administration and more qualified for resettling subsistence farmers on productive lands" (*Keeper,* 5). Drinnon's assessment is that "for the public servants who went from land conservation to people keeping, administration was administration" (*Keeper,* 5), but our analysis will mark instead the particularity of administrative practices.

Besides the continuity of personnel, there were also programmatic links between land-use related agencies and the WRA. Established by Executive Order 9106 on March 18, 1942, the WRA was authorized to "formulate and effectuate a program for the removal, from the areas designated . . . of the persons or classes of persons designated under such Executive Order, and for their relocation, maintenance, and supervision."[55] However, the WRA was actually created as an afterthought to the evacuation order. Only after the voluntary migration of some West Coast families into the interior states began meeting with intense local hostility did the federal government assume responsibility for "resettlement."[56] For quite a while, just what this responsibility entailed remained internally vague and contentious. Eventually, the term relocation evolved to include both the notion of "constructive custody" during wartime and the promotion of Japanese American "assimilation into normal life" afterward. Beginning with the initial release of a small number of Japanese Americans in 1942, a comprehensive policy was developed permitting indefinite leave on work furloughs outside the excluded area for those who could pass an FBI security check and a loyalty test. By the end of 1944, when the evacuation order was revoked, over 35,000 mainly young, single Nisei men had availed themselves of this policy; in August 1945, 44,000 remained in the camps, mostly middle-aged or elderly Issei, or first-generation immigrants.[57] Thus throughout the war years, the WRA could represent itself as an agency created simultaneously to "encourage the movement of evacuees from the relocation centers back into private life" and to maintain the centers "as a place of refuge for the evacuated people as long as they were denied the privilege of returning to their former homes" (*SHC* 141–43).

Throughout the deliberative period of 1942, the planning of "relocation" was extensively framed by land policy issues, beginning with the question of where the camps were to be located. An April 7, 1942, address by Milton Eisenhower to an audience of western local and state officials projected the camps' "wide geographic distribution"—not just to assuage his listeners' fears of racial concentration, but also to emphasize the camps' projected connection to "useful public work."[58] In the end, the camps were built on "undeveloped portions of Federal reclamation projects," lands purchased by the Farm Security Administration originally for the "rehabilitation" of low-income farm families, unused parts of Indian reservations, a mix of public domain land and private tracts that had reverted to the county for nonpayment of taxes, army land, and "land controlled by the City of Los Angeles as protection for the municipal water supply and which was taken over by military authorities" for evacuee processing in March 1942 (*SHC* 20–22). As a civilian agency, WRA operations were the provenance of agencies and departments presiding over federal land policy, in some cases those created specifically for economic and ecological reconstruction purposes in response to the Depression. The exchange of correspondence between government agencies in the initial planning period reveals the modeling of the WRA program after the Civilian Conservation Corps and the Works Progress Administration, with the idea that the internees could be applied to land improvement projects that had been interrupted by the war. Among the ideas pitched to the WRA were clearing and irrigating land on Indian reservations, participation in the Wheeler-Case (water conservation and utilization) program of constructing irrigation projects "essential to the rehabilitation of distressed farm families," engaging in soil erosion control programs, and farm drainage (*FIR* 209–20). As Thomas James observes, panoramic photos in the National Archives reveal strong similarities in the Japanese American internment camps and the more permanent camps established by the Civilian Conservation Corps (34). That the ten sites selected "were almost without exception in desolate, nonproductive locations of the mountainous West"[59] and yet were expected to become, through the efforts of the internees, economically self-sustaining further suggests the informing presence of grandiose visions of western land reclamation and frontier settlement.

The articulation of internment and conservation was, no doubt, double sided. The captive population could figure as replacements for the volunteers and employees of New Deal domestic programs—now overshadowed by war conditions, including labor shortage, and opposed by an increasingly powerful congressional bloc. A "latecomer among social programs launched by the New Deal administration" and a "wartime mutant of earlier efforts to ameliorate the nation's miseries during the Great Depression" (James, 97), the WRA could be considered one of its last projects to be dissolved. As famed agriculturalists, Japanese Americans were thought to be able to work miracles of reclamation, having historically converted the most unpromising of "wastelands" throughout California into arable fields. Though no more than 25 percent of the total prewar Japanese American population actually fell into agricultural occupation categories, internal WRA memoranda disclose that "agriculture bulked large in the initial plans of the War Relocation Authority."[60] Ironically, the construction of the internees as ideal agents of land reclamation required the WRA to engage in rebutting accusations of soil damage caused by Japanese agriculturalists. Myer drew upon his years of experience in the Department of Agriculture to attest that "I personally know something about soil conservation and I know these people bought as much fertilizer as the average California farmer."[61] A 1945 WRA public relations pamphlet, entitled *Myths and Facts about Japanese Americans,* emphasized how Japanese American farmers had never displaced whites and did not leach the soil.[62]

Thus the perception of Japanese Americans as environmentally damaging—and damaged—pointed to another sense in which they would figure as the WRA's targets of reform, not the agents of its mission. This was the most manifest implication of the report whose title, after all, showcased the human, rather than environmental, aspect of conservation. In *A Story of Human Conservation,* the WRA acknowledged that in the protection of evacuee property, also charged to its responsibility, it had been less than successful; but it consoled itself that the camps could offer Japanese Americans protection from the "racial terrorism" of unreasoning West Coast leaders and many of their constituents (130). The closing report pointed to the horror of vigilante mobs who had awaited the internees' return and the "unreasoning prejudice" (*SHC* 109) of leaders such as Idaho Governor Chase Clark, who famously declared that "A good solution to the Jap problem in Idaho—and the nation—would be to send them all back to Japan, then sink the island."[63] The justification of internment as a form of protective custody meant that the WRA's subjects were being saved from "human degradation" (*SHC* 15), even as confinement threatened to cause a loss of "initiative and self-reliance" that might lead to future disaffection and maladjustment (*SHC* 184). In one sense, then, the act of "human conservation" implied the federal preservation of a species threatened with extinction by a hostile local environment.

At another level, the act of "human conservation" connoted something actively transformative—"the desirable redistribution of the Japanese American people" who had once been "formerly congregated in a strip of land about 200 miles along the western coast line" and "are now spread out across the remainder of the country" (*SHC* 192). A major goal of "relocation"—in the way the WRA sought to direct and structure postwar settlement—was to undo the previous tendency of the Japanese to "gather much more in some areas than in others" (*SHC* 192). In the interest of promoting assimilation and preempting racial conflict, its target was the prevention of Japanese Americans from exceeding a "projected ratio of one-tenth of one percent" (*SHC* 192) in any one region. In 1946 the WRA congratulated itself above all for having achieved "one of the most rapid population readjustments in American history" (*SHC* 192).[64] The horticultural rhetoric of the WRA's social engineering—what the report described as the uprooting, clearing, and replanting of a population, or nurturing the seeds of interracial understanding[65]—tapped familiar New Deal themes of environmental adjustment. In publicized feats of heroism in the '30s, the Civilian Conservation Corps had thinned forests, stocked fish, built wildlife shelters, dug diversion ditches and canals, and fought insect infestations and forest fires.[66] In *A Story of Human Conservation*, evacuation was symbolized as a natural disaster—as if by lightning, "the Nisei community . . . was hit as it had never been hit before in its history" (*SHC* 6)—which allowed the WRA both to distance itself morally from the event and to avoid assigning decision-making responsibility to anyone. More importantly, the metaphor actively constructed an analogy between the mandate of the WRA, as an agency born out of the emergency of mass dislocation, and the Resettlement Administration (RA) and its successor, the Farm Security Administration (FSA)—agencies created during the 1930s to aid farm families displaced by drought and depression. Indeed, the link between Japanese American relocation and rural rehabilitation went beyond analogy. The wartime retooling of the FSA itself—and its direct involvement in addressing the danger of an agricultural labor shortage—point to elements of a material relationship between the two federal undertakings. For a fuller appreciation of the ideological contradictions of "Japanese American conservation," it is necessary that we now turn to the broader context of New Deal agricultural reform to which the Farm Security Administration belongs.

A NEW CONSERVATIONISM

Major tensions within the New Deal farm program were to be seen in the original commitments made by Roosevelt's 1932 election platform, which promised to remember those at the bottom, while actually incorporating a businessman's program for agricultural reform: efficiency in production, higher and more stable prices, improved markets at home and abroad, and the avoidance of surpluses.[67] The term "agricultural equality," in its 1930s campaign usage, carried two different meanings: it could refer to the inequality *within* the agricultural world, but more commonly it referred to the disadvantaged position of commercial farmers *in relation to* the rest of the economy (Baldwin, 32).[68] The Agricultural Adjustment Act (AAA), which passed in 1933, included provisions for a processing tax, administrative decentralization, and formal contracts between the federal government and the producer. However, its key item was the adoption of a "domestic allotment plan," designed by several economists, which sought to raise farm prices by restricting crop acreage and paying benefits to farmers who agreed to limit production (Leuchtenburg, 48–49). From its inception, the AAA reflected compromises between those who wanted it to serve as the means for raising farm commodity prices and those who hoped it would reform social inequality in agriculture (Baldwin, 52). As it turned out, the AAA program exacerbated the condition of rural displacement and resulted in the eviction of more than 100,000 sharecroppers and tenants from land that owners found more profitable to retire from production. The efforts of administration liberals to put the teeth in provisions for the equal sharing of AAA benefits between landlords and tenants were undermined by pressures to enlist the support of landlords in what was a voluntary program. As a whole, the AAA tended to benefit the largest farm businesses. In California, for example, where less than 10 percent of cotton farmers controlled half the acreage, 2.34 percent of all cotton farmers received 33 percent of AAA payments.[69]

The establishment of the Resettlement Administration (RA) by executive order in 1935 represented the main alternative approach to farm security. The RA's chief activities were land reform and "rural rehabilitation," which included the acquisition of twenty-five land projects providing for the resettlement of 20,000 farm families. The RA promoted indi-

vidual farms and cooperative communities, dabbled in suburban resettlement, classified land and water resources, and increased government reg-
ulation of private exploitation of land resources (Baldwin, 105–6). In
1937 the Bankhead-Jones Farm Tenant Act was passed, and soon after-
wards Roosevelt established the Farm Security Administration (FSA) to
replace the Resettlement Administration. The Bureau of Agricultural
Economics (BAE) now supervised the land programs, and the FSA assumed the duties of the RA concerned with people. In 1937 the Presidential Committee on Farm Tenancy defined farm security as "the protection
against economic, political, social and personal forces which had con-
spired to place chronically impoverished people in disadvantaged positions." Rather than focusing only on reducing tenancy, the mission of
rural reform was broadened to combat poverty regardless of the cause.
This new agenda reflected increased skepticism that farm ownership was
a panacea and argued that without government intervention the agricultural ladder was a fiction (Baldwin, 163, 170). Officially in existence
until 1946, but weakened by congressional attacks and a campaign
waged by the Farm Bureau in its latter years, the FSA attempted to make
strategic use of agrarian symbolism, while promoting controversial programs oriented to collective organization such as cooperative enterprises
and loans to pool resources. However, of the thirty-eight resettlement
projects completed, in the end almost all were based on the family farm
model, which received mainstream acceptance. Geared toward providing
emergency subsistence to the desperately poor, the FSA confronted the
paradox of rural rehabilitation efforts in the midst of national trends toward commercialization and mechanization. Thus the program increasingly found itself caught between restoring an unsatisfactory status quo
and removing land-use maladjustments, which would have meant facili-
tating the movement of marginal farmers into nonagricultural enterprises
(Baldwin, 220–21).

From the creation of the Federal Emergency Relief Administration
(FERA) in 1933 to the FSA of the later years, the New Deal relief agenda
reflected the renewal of interest in the back-to-the-land movement conditioned by the Depression's removal of an urban outlet for rural population surplus (Baldwin, 64–65). On the one hand, a rural rehabilitation
program sought to make it possible for destitute persons to achieve a
state of self-sufficiency, and on the other, a movement to reform the land
itself sought to improve land use by retiring submarginal land from production and conserving fertility and resources. Among the main objectives established by the National Program of Rural Rehabilitation in
1934 was the "promotion of self-support among destitute families on a
plane consistent with 'American standards'" (Baldwin, 62). The rejuve-
nation of chronically depressed rural areas was thus conceived as a kind

of nationalizing work. Efforts to improve agricultural living conditions extended beyond poor tenant farmers and sharecroppers to include migrant workers. By the end of 1942 the FSA had built ninety-five migrant labor camps, ten of them in California, which housed a total of 75,000 people (Baldwin, 222). Upon U.S. entry into the Second World War, rural rehabilitation became even more explicitly patriotic. The FSA's work was celebrated by then Vice President Henry Wallace as "the first line of defense for hundreds of needy farm families which are suffering most severely from the economic dislocation of the war" (Baldwin, 329). At that point, the FSA took on the role of stabilizing farm labor in support of the Food-for-Freedom program, relocating families displaced by defense activities, and establishing relocation corporations for the purchase and development of 256,062 acres of land (Baldwin, 226). Two other wartime assignments involved the agency in the direct reshaping of the social relations of California agriculture.

With the labor shortage jeopardizing food production, the United States signed an agreement with Mexico allowing for the recruitment and transportation of temporary, migratory farm laborers with the stipulation that they would be provided transportation, housing, and subsistence, and that they would not replace other workers. The FSA was placed in charge of the Mexican operation and by the end of 1942 had transported more than 4,000 contract workers (Baldwin, 223–25), which marked the introduction of the Bracero program.[70] Another major new responsibility assigned to the FSA was to oversee the transfer of Japanese American farms to new operators in the months and weeks before evacuation was completed. As set forth in a letter from Lieutenant General John L. DeWitt to the western regional director of the FSA, Laurence Hewes, the FSA's twin objectives with regard to Japanese American farm transfer were, first, "to insure continuance of the proper use of agricultural lands evacuated by enemy aliens and other persons designated," and, second, "to insure fair and equitable arrangements between the evacuees, their creditors and the substitute operators of their property."[71]

The Mexican guest worker program and the supervision of Japanese American farm transfer were crucial aspects of the FSA's overall wartime responsibility for maintaining the continuity of agricultural production in the western region. The FSA's role in enforcing a labor standard that, on the one hand, established minimal living conditions for the migrant workers and, on the other, guarded against the displacement of American workers by alien workers exemplifies the Roosevelt administration's ambivalent negotiation of the problematic of transnational labor. The FSA's involvement in Japanese American farm transfer points to yet another contradictory aspect of the administration's social reform agenda. Within a two-month period from March to May, the evacuation of roughly

6,000 Japanese American farmers suddenly made available, in the words of an FSA press release, "227,000 acres of rich vegetable land in coastal military areas."[72] Working a variety of mass communications channels, the FSA urgently advertised for persons, corporate or individual, who might be interested in assuming the newly available land. A radio interview ended with the pitch from the announcer: "If you are interested in operating this land that will be vacated, then be sure you check with the Farm Security agent. This isn't just our request—it's an *Army* request! Let's keep this Food for Victory growing and be sure that it's grown and harvested, along with the other food that we're counting on to *win the war* and write the peace."[73] For those lacking the financial means, the FSA had a variety of loans and subsidies to offer as incentive. To quote the FSA's West Coast regional director, speaking in a radio interview: "Ken, the big job is to keep these vital crops in production. Often a day's delay will mean a crop loss. So we'll loan money to almost anyone who can farm the land properly" (KPJF 3).

The previous chapter ended by reflecting upon the irony of the fact that evacuee farms were taken over mainly by large corporations. What was the significance of the fact that this process was facilitated by the New Deal's most redistributive agency, which now applied its machinery of rural rehabilitation to the newly assigned task of expropriating Japanese American property? The FSA press release acknowledged that "[m]ost of the farms were taken over by individual farmers who expanded their present acreage and by corporations created to manage groups of holdings on a scientific basis."[74] However, the press release also stressed the existence of counterexamples of "new farmers who went 'back to the land' in states where the farming frontier disappeared a generation ago."[75] A rhetorically compelling narrative of the transfer operation—if not an empirically dominant aspect of it—was the agrarian reestablishment of the Dust Bowl refugee:

> A few migratory workers went back to the land after lean years of wandering and seasonal work. Near Bakersfield Doil Ash, whose Oklahoma "dust bowl" living blew away in 1935, leased a 26-acre farm from Hido Miwa. If any questions arise, Miwa said, Ash can always write to him.[76]

In such cases, farm transfer could not be expected to lead to an increase, or to even to the maintenance, of productive efficiency. As an editor at the *Nation*, Robert Bendiner, observed: "Trained in a tradition of intensive cultivation, [Japanese farmers] have learned to make their few acres yield down to the last square foot. As a rule, moreover, an entire family works a farm, so that even on a strictly numerical basis it would take more than one Okie to replace a Japanese farmer."[77] The competing narratives of evacuee farm transfer as the acceleration of corporate consolidation and as the recreation of small farming opportunities reflect, in a sense, the broader contradictions between the modernizing and nostalgic—as well as the rationalizing and redistributive—tendencies in the New Deal's overall farm program.

Furthermore, the FSA's showcase anecdote of Miwa and Ash points to an unlikely intersection between the Okie and the evacuee, a symbolic relationship that was complexly opposite *and* parallel. The anecdote allegorizes a point of contact between the New Deal's modes of address to agricultural crisis and wartime evacuation policy, between Dorothea Lange and Paul Taylor's emblematic diagnosis of rural displacement, *An American Exodus: A Record of Human Erosion* (1941) and the social remedies proposed by the WRA's *A Story of Human Conservation* (1945). In the figural intersection between Okie and evacuee, was it the perpetual migrant, then, who was the ultimate imaginary subject of wartime human conservation? We are reminded of McWilliams's excitement at evacuation's potential for leading to permanent rural communities that seemed oddly blind to the fact that the West Coast Japanese were already settled. Spatially, the orchestrated movement of 110,000 people east provided an inverse image—both directionally and in style—to the chaotic displacement of hundreds of thousands west over the previous decade. The transportation of an entire population over the matter of a few months was, as McWilliams's sense of marvel communicated, more efficient an exercise of governmental machinery than had been witnessed in earlier 1930s examples of planned resettlement.

Assumptions that such a strategy for addressing the broader Depression-era theme of "human erosion" was also in the interest of Californian soil conservation, however, could not be taken for granted, given the doubtful reputation of the lands' new occupants, whose agricultural know-how—as even the FSA press release acknowledged—was clearly subordinate to the Japanese farmer's. Though the farm transaction may have been partly evocative of a comforting agrarian solution to the state of perpetual migrancy, installing the Okie as an antidote to the Asiatic, Asiatic and Okie were unavoidably united by a shared association with the predicament of soil erosion. In the 1930s, the disasters incurred by soil erosion throughout the United States, but particularly in Oklahoma and Arkansas, had become emblematic of the need for federal rescue of a crisis-ridden market system; in this context, an agrarian myth no longer offered the same ideological consolation. Though the prevalence of environmental metaphors can certainly be read as a depoliticizing reduction of social struggle—one in which, as Denning writes, "the villain's role is often taken by 'the sun and the wind,' the hero's part is often taken by the New Deal itself" (266)—the very naturalness of nature in the 1930s was more questionable than usual.

The Grapes of Wrath illustrates just this tension between the familiar comforts of a Jeffersonian agrarian discourse and a new consciousness of its contemporary inadequacy. Locating the specific experiences of the Joad family within an epochal trend, the novel's fifth chapter provides a memorable, mythic depiction of rural eviction. We learn that the profit-driven principles of the bank, the land's legal owner, whose own survival has been endangered by contemporary conditions of economic depression, motivate the eviction. We are shown the vivid replacement of farmers with tractors, whose relentless movement across the country "in straight lines" and "through fences, through dooryards" (*GW* 47) dramatizes the dehumanization of the agrarian landscape and the inevitability of mechanization. Marshalling heavy-handed imagery of the tractor driver who, "gloved, goggled, rubber dust mask over nose and mouth, . . . was a part of the monster" (*GW* 48), the novel would appear to establish a simple dichotomy between the impersonal, deadening touch of the machine and traditional methods of cultivation involving direct contact with the living earth that the farmer daily "sift[s] past his fingertips" (*GW* 49). Yet countervailing representations of men and machines elsewhere in the text undo their apparent antagonism. As the Joads make their journey west in an "overloaded Hudson," Al Joad is at "one with his engine" and "had become the soul of the car" (*GW* 167). Here a spiritualized cyborg image of the automobile driver replaces the unfeeling "robot in the seat" (*GW* 48) description of the tractor driver and implies a far less antimodern attitude toward the machine.[78]

The evicted farmers themselves, from the very moment they are introduced, defy our expectations of meeting a yeoman ideal:

> The tenant men squatted down on their hams again to mark the dust with a stick, to figure, to wonder. Their sunburned faces were dark, and their sun-whipped eyes were light. (*GW* 46)

We do not come upon our protagonists sifting earth through their fingers but "squatt[ing] on their hams" and tracing their "fingers in the dust" (*GW* 42–43). Their squatting reminds us of their illegitimate legal status, the lifeless dust of a vanished topsoil. Instead of plowing, these ex-farmers are left to "mark the dust with a stick, to figure, to wonder" (*GW* 46). This emblematic activity—which the text's repetitions insist that we notice—foregrounds the absence of work (the unemployed "handplow lying in the shed" [*GW* 47]), as well as the illiteracy and lack of education that keep the tenant men "perplexed and figuring" (*GW* 47). Producing no answers, mathematical or otherwise, to the nonviability of their economic continuance, the marking evokes, and falls short of, humanity's unique potential for abstract figuration; instead of representing writing, the marking indicates an absence of civilization. This primitivist image of men with implements that are neither plows nor pens is more ignominious than noble. Their ways are complicit with an industrial mode of cotton farming that has made the land poorer and "suck[ed] all the blood out of it" (GW 43). They themselves acknowledge that if "they could only rotate the crops they might pump blood back into the land" (GW 43). Even before the invasion of the tractors—and the mass tenant evictions that the Agricultural Adjustment Act triggered—the land as tended by farm families such as the Joads is shown to be already dead. Measured against the yeoman ideal, the tenant sharecropper is a far fallen figure.

Within the context of California's tradition of post-frontier fiction, including works centering on land monopoly, speculation, and railroads, the narrative of the Dust Bowl refugee represents a continuity and a discontinuity. Like the antimonopoly fiction that preceded it, such as Wallace Irwin's *Seed of the Sun* (1921), the westward travelers to California threaten to end in homelessness, not on a happy homestead; as in Peter Kyne's *Pride of Palomar* (1921), instead of free and open spaces they are faced with gridded regimentation.[79] However, in the narrative of the Dust Bowl refugee, the tragic movement toward California proletarianization originates with an exilic condition of rural modernity and crisis; it begins with the absence of the yeoman anywhere in America, even in places we thought we might find the nineteenth century frontier.[80] The Dust Bowl migration narrative therefore shares with earlier alien land law fiction populist declamations against California's domination by absentee, corporate farming, but it also demystifies small farming as a viable or extant alternative. In general, the chronic failure of the market during the 1930s opened up sharper perceptions of the extent to which industrial capitalism constituted a totalizing system.

In a speech that sketched the road to recovery during the election campaign in 1932, Franklin Roosevelt voiced the impact that the persistent downturn had begun to exercise on economic thinking: "Our task is not discovery or exploitation of natural resources, or necessarily producing more goods. . . . It is the soberer, less dramatic business of administering resources and plants already in hand, of seeking to reestablish foreign markets for our surplus production, of meeting the problem of underconsumption, of adjusting production to consumption. . . ." (Lowitt, 6). Efficient use of resources now rested on the adjustment of relations, and balance, rather than productivity, came to be the defining term after the crash of 1929. Though decrying waste and spurred by a growing recognition of limited natural resources, Progressive conservationism had been committed to maximizing productivity. Insofar as increased efficiency served to compensate for a diminishing nature, Progressive conservationism was fascinated by the allure of endless economic growth. During the Depression, in a marketplace afflicted by an unfavorable ratio of production to consumption, the puzzle confronting New Dealers instead was the problem of an undisposable surplus. In the initial desperation of 1934–1935, the AAA's zeal in preventing surplus goods from reaching the market was such that it even ordered the destruction of certain bumper crops: to the horror of the American public in the midst of the worst economic disaster of the century, 10 million acres of cotton were plowed under, and 6.2 million hogs were slaughtered (Leuchtenburg, 72–73). Later, the AAA managed to restrict yields in a less scandalous fashion, paying farmers to curtail production in advance. In general, despite a strong faction favoring export-dumping as a way to dispose of surpluses, and the resistance posed by the culture of farming itself, the method of bolstering farm prices by limiting production remained dominant at the AAA.[81]

As a conservationist project, the WRA's economic administration of internment also enacted this latest turn away from maximizing efficiency to standardized adjustment. In its earliest stages, the agency's leadership envisioned that the centers would produce food both for its own consumption and for sale. Women and children who could not leave the center for seasonal labor could be employed in reducing the cost of operating the centers and, in addition, helping feed the army; centers were to be located at points where there would be opportunity for evacuee employment in government-sponsored manufacturing, such as camouflage net factories, as well as in private enterprises, which would be encouraged to take advantage of an otherwise idle workforce (Wallinger, 65). Pondering the limitless potential for private industry-government partnerships, Milton Eisenhower proposed:

> [W]e could get a contract to produce camouflage nets for the Army, involving a great deal of hand labor, involving the kind of skills that the Japanese have a great aptitude for, and one thing that the fishermen pulled off the sea with no place to fish might be particularly good at doing. Such work as this involving a maximum of hand labor and a minimum of machinery will not only be good for the country but it will be very good for the Japanese who want, many of them, to show their loyalty to this country. (*CEEA* 18–19)

Looking back upon the agency's agricultural program, WRA agricultural section head Ernest Reed acknowledged that because the evacuees "had the reputation of being very industrious," it had been expected at the outset that "the amount of work accomplished per worker on relocation centers would at least equal, and probably greatly exceed, that of the average worker on the outside" (PAP 2). As it turned out, the shift toward prioritizing immediate relocation outside of the camps and a work-leave policy under Dillon Myer meant a reduced number of workers at the relocation centers available to carry out large-scale commercial ventures. Moreover, when put to work on the internment farms, Japanese Americans were found to lack experience in growing a wide variety of crops and in working with soil and climatic conditions different from those on the West Coast. In many cases, such as at Topaz, where the majority of the internees were urbanites, the internees were found to have "no previous experience in agriculture" at all (PAP 22).[82]

Perhaps it was only inevitable that the federal expropriation of Japanese American labor power should have resulted, to some degree, in the demystification of Asiatic labor's mythic efficiency. Nevertheless, it was clear that the most hyperbolic of productionist fantasies were structurally constrained by a governmental obligation to the protection of social welfare. This tension was evident in an early draft of an agricultural report, dated May 31, 1943, written by Reed: "It was expected that considerable quantities of fresh vegetables might be produced for consumption by the civilian population. . . . In marketing these vegetables, it was the wish of the Authority to compete as little as possible with established farmers."[83] The agency's concerns were not simply with how to avoid exacerbating American farm bankruptcy or displacing "normal labor" (CEEA 19). The consideration that the "people will have in the relocation centers to work at prevailing wages" (CEEA 19) tempered the earliest prospectus for governmental capitalization upon internee labor. If the WRA can therefore be viewed as having operated a prison-industrial complex of a sort, the federal assumption of Japanese American exploitation exerted untold contradictory effects. Even as a familiar yellow perilism fed the government's projections of a formidable Asiatic competition, the project of universalizing an "American standard of living," under these auspices, effected not the reification of Asiatic cheap labor but in fact its deinstitutionalization.

This is not to say that the WRA actually enforced fair employment practices. Only a few of the "many promising connections . . . , notably some war industries and Farm Security Administration camps for seasonal agricultural labor, led to large movements of Japanese American workers into jobs, and most of these jobs turned out to be temporary" (James, 41). Private employers were supposed to pay prevailing wages, but enforcement provisions were sorely lacking, and the WRA work-leave policy essentially enabled American farmers to utilize Japanese American workers at very low wages even at a time when war mobilization and higher-paying war industries had created a farm labor shortage (Sandra Taylor,

114–15). Within the camps, some 75 percent of the able-bodied residents were employed in administrative operations, services, and farms, earning $16 a month for a 44-hour week, as compared to most Americans who made $150–$200 a month. A ceiling on evacuee pay was set through comparisons to army salaries, which paid soldiers $21 a month; however, when army pay was later raised to $50, evacuee wages remained unchanged (Sandra Taylor, 158). There is no question that for Japanese Americans internment was impoverishing, even as there continues to be an uncertainty concerning their total losses—from lost property as a result of evacuation to lost income during incarceration. But even if the economic exploitation of Japanese Americans is one measure of internment's profitability to other groups and entities—including, without doubt, the western sugar beet industry—internment's articulation of a common standard for Asiatic labor price and American labor price contributed to the dissolution of a traditional West Coast "ethnic economy."[84]

Instead of overdriven factories, the camp desert cities turned out to be more like bureaucracies staffed by lethargic civil servants who, it was feared, sought "duration care, at public expense, without responsibility."[85] Having once "lived quietly apart, relatively untouched by the social programs and public assistance" (James, 18) in the Depression's worst years, Japanese Americans had been turned into total subjects of social welfare.[86] As the WRA stepped up its campaign to resettle the internees outside the camps, its spokespersons increasingly fretted out loud about the negative impact of incarceration upon Japanese Americans' native sense of self-reliance and initiative that would make them ideal members of any American community. Paradoxically, the case for the safe return of these "enemy aliens" to the outside world—the proof of their assimilability and their humanness—was made at least partly on the grounds of their having lost, or having the potential to have lost, their virtuous efficiency. Indeed, in the WRA's paradoxical praise of the internees for having persevered in the face of the low economic incentives it had itself imposed on them we can mark the first beginnings of the postwar discourse of the "model minority."[87]

In terms of their actual productive capacity, the camps not only did not generate agricultural surpluses, most fell short of achieving their own self-maintenance. Food had to be supplied, prompting the *New York Times* to complain on January 9, 1943, that "huge shipments of scarce foods" were being supplied to the camps (Wallinger, 114). That year, House Committee on Un-American Activities chair Martin Dies appointed a subcommittee to investigate so-called WRA pampering, which charged that the internees were "Among the Best-Fed Civilians in the World" (Wallinger, 139). Rumors circulated in the press of vast quantities of meat, potatoes, coffee, and marmalade ordered for Manzanar Center; of evacuees hiding bread in the desert for Japanese invasion; and, at, Heart Mountain Center, of food hoarded in "secret pantries reached by sliding doors" and of shocking luxuries, such as bananas, everywhere in abundance (Wallinger, 131, 146). Was it just further testimony to the flexible economic superiority of Asiatic racial form that, with the dethroning of a Progressive "gospel of efficiency" during the Depression, the Asiatic figure of the moment was now a specter of overconsumption?

Or is it that the peculiar, mixed economy of the internment camps conveys something of the reconstructive intention of a New Deal reformist imagination? Here and there, WRA practices reenacted the Agricultural Adjustment Act's limits upon production and echoed the Farm Security Administration's vision of rural subsistence communities as a practical alternative to chronic urban unemployment. On appearance fantastic or hypocritical, McWilliams's hopes of "Japanese American rural settlements" taking root in the desert correlated quite closely with the leadership's original preference for setting up self-supporting cooperative communities. Poston Center director Wade Head, in particular, had adopted Eisenhower's vision in his welcome address to his new charges in the summer of 1942. Poston was to be a "community run by the people and for the people," Head expressed, "a community which will set an example for the entire world to follow" (Wallinger, 89). At that time, Head was quite convinced that many would "want to stay here and raise crops after the war is over, perhaps to stay here for five, ten, fifteen years and operate on their own" (Wallinger, 90).

The anti-industrial, at times even anticapitalist, elements in the rhetoric of internment hints at the existence of some kind of articulation between the "conservation of Japanese Americans" and New Deal modes of address to economic crisis. In the relative absence of Japanese Americans from the national record until the occurrence of the disciplinary event that occasioned their scrupulous documentation, we can only speculate as to the full context for the willful degradation of Japanese American productive power when the government decided to jeopardize the harvests of 6,000 farm operations despite the war's increased demand for food production.[88] Let us turn now to imaginative sources of historical knowledge about California's social relations. From these we will not learn directly about the experiences of Asian Americans, but we may glean something of the power of racialization that affected them. In the rest of this chapter, I will explore the prehistory of the construction of the Japanese American as a subject of rural rehabilitation in the Orientalization of the rural subject of California during the 1930s. The writing that created the most public sympathy for farm labor—Steinbeck's fiction— was a key part of this process.

STEINBECK'S 1930S AGRICULTURAL FICTION

Any consideration of California Orientalism must take into account the proliferation of Asian characters and Oriental themes in works written by Steinbeck after *The Grapes of Wrath;* in these, an ecological perspective is explicitly associated with Taoist philosophy.[89] The Chinese grocer Lee Chong in *Cannery Row* (1945) plays a significant role in the coastal community that is the novel's subject, and in *East of Eden* (1952) the servant Lee figures centrally as an authorial alter ego. In Steinbeck criticism, the period "after *The Grapes of Wrath*" usually designates an artistic decline that coincides with a retreat from the engagé quality that made his reputation in the late '30s. Inflecting this periodization of an authorial trajectory in terms of our concerns, and taking the consecutive publication of *The Grapes of Wrath* and *Cannery Row* as representative evidence, the image of a conflict-ridden California without Asians yields to a socially harmonious scene that is heavily Orientalized. What accounts for this transition? Chapter 5 will examine the global context of the 1930s and '40s for the postwar emergence of Asian American literary character. Here we will investigate its hidden, domestic antecedents in the New Deal's cultural work of humanizing California agricultural labor. Even as its Americanness seemed to be the operative condition by which the migrant figure could accrue public sympathy, the attribution of a national character to the condition of migrancy effected a signal rearticulation of Asian-American relations from one of Manichaean opposition to potential political solidarity. In this realignment, the Asiatic had to disappear. We will be in a better position to appreciate the racial significance of the event of Okie representation if we first turn to the presence of the Asiatic in Steinbeck's earlier portrayals of rural California, when there were as yet no redemptive solutions to labor alienation.

Of Mice and Men (1937) centers on two itinerant farmhands, George Milton and Lenny Small, who nurse unfulfillable hopes of owning a "little house and a coupla acres"[90] and who are forced to live a life of agricultural migrancy. "We'd jus' live there," muses George at one point to Lenny, filling in the imaginary details of their dream home, "We'd belong there. There' wouldn't be no more runnin' round the country and gettin' fed by a Jap cook. No sir, we'd have our own place where we belonged and not sleep in no bunk house" (*MM* 839). Eating food prepared by a "Jap cook" represents the stark alternative to living in a state of natural abundance—or in the myth of Jeffersonian agrarianism, on a small farm—where it would be possible just to "live offa the fatta the lan'" (*MM* 839). The "Jap cook" signifies a postlapsarian relation to the land and the text's use of a racialized means of representing labor alienation through the tragedy of lowered consumption.

The text references a familiar yellow peril idiom, but it is not reducible, in my view, to a piece of Asian exclusionist propaganda: the text's recognition of the ontological constitutiveness of the Asiatic to working-class identity is such that narrative sympathy cannot help but be racially vagrant. The story's drama involves Lennie's accidental killing of the wife of the son of an employer. Lennie is mentally underdeveloped but physically powerful and has survived until now through the help of his friend George. This time, however, George cannot save him, and must shoot Lenny to spare him from death by lynching. Lennie's mental disability and powerful physique exemplify Steinbeck's recurrent interest in manifesting social marginality through physiological deviance. Reminiscent of Norris's title character of *McTeague* (1899)—another simple giant who lacks self-control—Lennie's end reflects the themes of degeneration and social Darwinism familiar to literary naturalism. In the problematic of Lennie's physique, as in McTeague's, California naturalism registers the historical dependency of the state's mode of production on foreign labor.[91]

Like McTeague, Lennie's problem lies with the clumsy strength of his hands. He chokes a puppy with tender caresses and breaks a woman's neck with a mere shake. His hands get him in trouble even earlier when he crushes the hand of the owner's son, Curley, in a fight. "Curley was white and shrunken by now, and his struggling had become weak. He stood crying, his fist lost in Lennie's paw" (*MM* 844). The leader of the workmen threatens Curley with publicizing his physical humiliation if he doesn't pretend that he had got his "han' caught in a machine" (*MM* 845). The excuse echoes an actual workplace injury sustained four years earlier by Candy, whose wrist now ends in a stump. In situating Lennie and farm equipment as parallel sources of injury to workers' hands, the text deliberately juxtaposes animal paws and machines. Curley's wife, disbelieving the excuse for her husband's broken hand, jokes to Lennie, "O.K., Machine. I'll talk to you later. I like machines" (856). In one sense, Lennie's unintentional violence symbolizes that of the machine. In another sense, Lennie is also the victim of a relentless evolutionary process bound to eliminate the unfit. His execution is foreshadowed by the euthanasia of Candy's aged dog, considered "no good" to anyone or to himself. A shared set of physical features link Lennie and this "drag-footed sheep dog, gray of muzzle, . . . with pale, blind old eyes" (*MM* 814). Here are Lennie and George as they are first introduced by the text:

They had walked in single file down the path, and even in the open one stayed behind the other. Both were dressed in denim trousers and in denim coats with brass buttons. Both wore black, shapeless hats and both carried tight blanket rolls slung over their shoulders. The first man was small and quick, dark of face, with restless eyes and sharp, strong features. Every part of him was defined: small, strong hands, slender arms, a thin and bony nose. Behind him walked his opposite, a huge man, shapeless of face, with large, pale eyes, with wide, sloping shoulders; and he walked heavily, dragging his feet a little, the way a bear drags his paws. His arms did not swing at his sides, but hung loosely. (*MM* 798)

Resembling a bear in appearance, size, and movement, and yet serving the social function of the machine, Lennie seems to be inhuman in two opposite ways. These contradictory forms of inhumanity play upon the historical process of substitution of machines for farm hands and farm hands for machines.[92] Possessing matchless strength that is capable of flexible application under precise instruction, Lennie embodies the qualities of machine labor.[93] However, his brutish clumsiness also calls to mind antiquated means of production that have been technologically superseded. Lennie's hands lack a crucial requirement of intensive farming—more specifically, a "quickness of fingers where nimbleness is essential (as in cotton picking or bunching and tying carrots), carefulness, thoroughness, and spacing sense . . ." (*FL* 5). George, Lennie's physically opposite partner, has precisely such "small, strong hands." In a sense, George's reluctant execution of Lennie can be read to allegorize the involuntary passage from one labor form to another. George's manual dexterity may well imply the racially alien labor that, as "the introduction of irrigation encroached upon grain production . . . overshadowed the typical farm hand" (*HBCL* 282). Is it a pure coincidence that George's "restless eyes," in contrast with the "large, pale eyes" that mark the doomed creatures, should repeat as well a prime motif of the expansionist Japanese farmers in Wallace Irwin's *Seed of the Sun?* Echoes of *Mice and Men* in Steinbeck's short story "Johnny Bear" help to establish the specifically Asiatic inflection of Steinbeck's representation of agricultural social relations.

In "Johnny Bear" (1938) sexual miscegenation is a metaphor for the historical contradictions of white-Asian contact—rural social relations that are structurally entwined yet culturally repressed. The story concerns an implied liaison between a reputable single white woman, Amy Hawkins, and one of her Chinese sharecroppers, which ends tragically in her pregnancy and suicide. Their affair scandalously couples two figures situated at opposite ends of the town's social hierarchy, one who is an unassimilable alien and the other who is a member of the town's landowning "aristocrats, its family above reproach."[94] Yet just as oligarchic and mass threats have tended to be conspiratorially linked in an agrarian populist imagination,[95] here the woman and the Chinese sharecropper are similarly linked in their marginality to the narrative's field of vision. This nameless tenant sharecropper belongs to an undifferentiated and socially invisible population:

> I thought a heard a soft moaning in the Hawkins yard behind the hedge, and once when I came suddenly out of the fog I saw a dark figure hurrying along in the field, and I knew from the dragging footsteps that it was one of the Chinese field hands walking in sandals. The Chinese eat a great many things that have to be caught at night. (JB 106)

No better delineated than a "dark figure," the Chinese tenant sharecropper surfaces only at times when we suspect we might be catching him in places he shouldn't be. His abode and his landlord's present impassive surfaces to the inquisitive gaze of the town's denizens and are contiguously associated by being located on the same piece of property. When she is not immured within her house, Amy Hawkins, too, we only glimpse once, and just briefly. By telling the story of a white woman penalized for her expression of interracial desire, Steinbeck links and criticizes the joint racism and patriarchy of rural Californian society.

Though the Chinese sharecropper has no name, the short story creates an indirect way for us to hear his voice. The short story's title refers to the text's unusual narrative vehicle, a physically and mentally disabled character with a strange genius for mimicry. Possessed of a recorder-like ability to duplicate the conversations he surreptitiously overhears, Johnny Bear makes use of his talent to win drinks from listeners at the local bar. It is through Johnny Bear's repetition of the Hawkins' conversations that the bar audience learns of Amy Hawkins's secret pregnancy and suicide. Conclusions as to the father's true identity, however, are drawn only by the narrator and his friend, Alex, who quickly acts to silence the messenger to protect Amy's reputation. Hints of the identity of her lover lie in Johnny Bear's repetition of a pedagogical exchange in which the white woman is apparently learning to speak Chinese. "I heard the sing-song nasal language that sounded like Chinese," the narrator reports, ". . . and then the other voice, slow hesitant, repeating the words without the nasal quality" (JB 109).

In contrast to the unseen figures, we are given a detailed accounting of Johnny Bear's body:

> He looked like a great, stupid smiling bear. His black matted head bobbed forward and his long arms hung out as though he should have been on all fours and was only standing upright as a trick. His legs were short and bowed, ending with strange, square feet. He was dressed in dark, blue denim, but his feet were bare; they didn't seem to be crippled or deformed in any way, but they were square, just as wide as they were long. He stood in the doorway, swinging his arms jerkily

the way half-wits do. On his face there was a foolish happy smile. He moved forward and for all his bulk and clumsiness, he seemed to creep. He didn't move like a man, but like some prowling night animal. (JB 95)

The description suggests a series of correspondences between the half-wit and the Chinese. Both are outsiders to the town's community. Johnny Bear's movements resemble "some prowling night animal"; the Chinese sharecropper surprises the narrator by creeping around in the night. Johnny Bear's body is bulky, but formless: "He looked twisted and shapeless, and yet he moved with complete lack of effort" (JB 98); so too does the Chinese "dark figure" lack definition and shape. Both represent deformations of human anatomy and yet are unaccountably mobile and potentially everywhere. Signaled by "soft moaning" or "dragging footsteps," the Chinese in fact exerts more of an aural than a visual presence. Through Johnny Bear, we approach a greater intimacy with him, enough to hear his sing-song, nasal voice. As the sharecropper's aural mimesis, Johnny Bear represents the fullest character actualization we have of the Chinese Californian in Steinbeck's prewar writing.

The ironically named Lennie Small, of course, closely resembles Johnny Bear, not only in his physical bearlike qualities but in his fondness for oral mimicry, a trait which emphasizes a noncognitive relationship to language. Indeed, insofar as he is described as "walk[ing] heavily, dragging his feet a little, the way a bear drags his paws" (*MM* 798), he explicitly combines the characteristics of both Johnny Bear and the Chinese sharecropper. In Lennie's abnormality, at once idiot and marvelous, we could read either the example of the monstrous alien or the evolutionarily displaced native. Given the contradictory Asiatic associations of both Lennie and George, George's reluctant execution of Lennie does not, I think, allegorize a simple tale of racial conflict and substitution. The complexity of racial identification at work in the opposite morphologies of this working-class pair emphasizes the relational modality of Asiatic presence, rather than its embodiment as a fixed identity. Asiatic racial form shows up in the naturalist grotesque of Steinbeck's migrant farm laborers, whose bodies register the traces of California's industrial history.

As a variety of racial discourse, the animalistic Chinese immediately calls to mind European Orientalism's customary reliance on primitivist strategies of racial Othering. In the specific context of California Orientalism, however, Steinbeck's use of primitivism marks a new intervention: it has the effect of indigenizing rather than distancing the alien. Before Steinbeck turned his attention to the sensational topic of farm labor exploitation, his early work was concerned with creating a regional "literature of place" that celebrated the incomparability of California's scenic beauty as well as undermined Edenic myths about the state. As the place where continent meets ocean, Steinbeck's California repeatedly thematizes the exertion of environmental limits upon national expansion—limits set by nature's uncanny force, not its human exhaustion. In Steinbeck's early 1930s texts, human resourcefulness often bows before nature's potency, and yet even in the more romantic and mystical of his texts it is possible to recover a social commentary. *Pastures of Heaven* (1932), for example, is composed of disparate stories centered on different individuals, which form a coherent pattern only through the implied influence of a superstitious agency. Freaks of nature bordering on the magical abound in this world; even more unrealistically, the dominant economic mode of Carmel Valley, which is the text's setting, is portrayed as the small family farm. But it is precisely this institution that is at the center of the text's critical inspection. As we will see, the textual perspective that troubles agrarian ideology is one that recognizes the alien diversity of California's native ecology.

Most critics agree that *Pastures of Heaven* depicts a fallen Eden, the failure of the American dream, and a world governed by illusion.[96] The setting is introduced to us as a place where people "lived prosperously and at peace. Their land was rich and easy to work. The fruits of their gardens were the finest produced in central California."[97] Through seeming coincidence, a newly arrived family, the Munroes, are associated with a series of tragic events in which various of their neighbors end up going to jail, are institutionalized, commit murder, suffer unrequited love, lose their homes and other beloved possessions, and are forced to leave the valley. The Munroes' responsibility for these events is more or less accidental, forming an interpretable pattern only through the extrapolation of a legend about the farm property's haunted reputation. Despite having been a consistent failure in his other endeavors, Bert Munroe ironically succeeds in breaking the land's curse by being the first of its occupants to farm it without harm to himself. Someone in a bar makes a prophetic joke, "Maybe your curse and the farm's curse have mated and gone into a gopher hole like a pair of rattlesnakes. Maybe there'll be a lot of baby curses crawling around the Pastures the first thing we know" (PH 10).

Pastures of Heaven depicts the normalizing violence of a "meretricious morality" or, alternatively, the inevitable collapse of illusion—depending on whether one romanticizes the Munroes' victims as symbols of an endangered nature or criticizes them for seeking in nature an artificial refuge from their problems.[98] The text lends itself to both readings. Its sympathy lies with the victims of displacement, but it also shows them to have previously displaced others and questions the authenticity of any claim to true nativity. In the last chapter, travelers on a tour bus gaze down on the valley and see:

The land below them was plotted in squares of green orchard trees and in squares of yellow grain and in squares of violet earth. From the sturdy farmhouses, set in their gardens, the smoke of the evening fires drifted upward until the hill breeze swept it cleanly off. Cowbells were softly clashing in the valley; a dog barked so far away that the sound rose up to the travelers in sharp little whispers. Directly below the ridge a band of sheep had gathered under an oak tree against the night. (PH 167)

Though beckoningly rustic, the scene is perhaps already too geometrically regimented. It appears to us from the perspective of a suburbanizing gaze, as both an investment property and a space of leisure, a place where "Rich men will live . . . men that are tired of working away in town, men that have made their pile and want a quiet place to settle down to rest and enjoy themselves" (PH 167). Someone comments, "If I had any money, I'd buy the whole thing. I'd hold on to it, and sometime I'd subdivide it" (PH 167).

Pastures of Heaven narrates a process of the transformation of place into real estate, the inevitable eviction of nonmaterialistically oriented individuals. The story of Shark Wicks, whose famed business acumen is exposed as a lie, corroborates the contemporary urgency of distinguishing between real and symbolic wealth. Yet there is also an implication that subdivision merely extends a process of social division instituted long ago by the rise of private property, when "a few families of squatters moved into the Pastures of Heaven and built fences and planted fruit trees. Since no one owned the land, they squabbled a great deal over its possession. After a hundred years there were twenty families on twenty little farms . . ." (PH 4). At the origin of the yeoman republic is possession based on theft. The valley is first named by a Spanish corporal out on a mission to recapture Indian slaves whose escape "crippled the work in the clay pits where adobe bricks were being moulded" (PH 3). Stumbling by accident upon the place, "The disciplinarian corporal felt weak in the face of so serene a beauty. He who had whipped brown backs to tatters, he whose rapacious manhood was building a new race for California, this bearded, savage bearer of civilization slipped from his saddle and took off his steel hat" (PH 3–4). That the appearance of the place on a European map of consciousness serves as an allegory of colonial nationalism is made explicit by the fact that the event occurs "some time around 1776" (PH 3).

The Munroe family's displacement of the valley's eccentric and marginal personalities therefore continues a much older process. Among the valley's disappearing types are its traditional farmers, though our mourning for them can only be ambivalent, given the text's portrayal of Pat Humbert's parents, who may have been "good workmen with the soil"

but who were "spiteful" (*PH* 125–26), or the fact that an internal steril-
ity is responsible for the decline of the Whitesides' rural heritage. At the
center of the text's troubled representation of agrarian life is the land purchased by the Munroes with its gruesome and mysterious history. We
learn that the son of the original owners had been killed by a snake on the
property, and its last family of owners simply disappeared one day. They
"had paid cash for the farm, and in going away had left no trace. No one
saw them go, and no one ever saw them again" (*PH* 9). Their disappearance remains an unsolved mystery, though there are hints of a historical
context that may explain it:

> In 1921 the Mustrovics took possession of the Battle farm. Their
> coming was sudden and mysterious. One morning they were there, an
> old man and his old wife, skeleton people with tight yellow skin
> stretched and shiny over their high cheek bones. Neither of them spoke
> English. Communication with the valley was carried on by their son, a
> tall man with the same high cheek bones, with coarse-cropped black
> hair growing half way down his forehead, and with soft, sullen black
> eyes. He spoke English with an accent, and he only spoke his wants.
> (*PH* 8)

That the Mustrovics disappear two years after arriving in 1921 dates the
episode to the the passage of the Alien Land Initiative barring agricultural operation by aliens ineligible to citizenship and the National Origins Act, which reduced eastern and southern European immigration and
prohibited Asian immigration altogether. Though Slavs were not techni-
cally aliens ineligible to citizenship, (they were restricted but not excluded by the 1924 immigration law), the "old Mustrovics who were
rarely seen" (*PH* 8) and speak no English are treated as outsiders by the
community. The "tight yellow skin stretched and shiny over . . . high
cheek bones" endows these aliens with an Asiatic phenotype. Their explicit foreignness has the effect of foregrounding the outsider status common to all the farm's occupants, except for Bert Munroe, who "within
three months . . . had become a part of the valley, a solid man, a neighbor" (*PH* 15). The text's point, of course, is the ironic contrast between
this ostensibly seamless integration and his actually disruptive presence.
Whether one wants to interpret the text as cautioning against dangerous
aliens who appear harmless or as regretting the homogenizing effects of
modernization, *Pastures of Heaven* entertains some serious reservations
about the intrinsic value of cultural assimilation.

The ambivalence of cultural assimilation is embedded in a juxtaposition between different techniques of farming. The striking peculiarity of
the farm property in question, of course, is that it represents a section of
the best soil, and yet no one wants it. It produces great vegetables and re-

sponds well to human care. Under George Battle, "[t]he vegetables grew crisp and green in their line-straight rows" (*PH* 6). The land that had lain fallow for so long, Under the hand of the Mustrovics' son, soon "began to grow beautiful again" (*PH* 9). The problem is that, on this piece of property, "[o]nly the fruit trees and the fresh green rows of vegetables were vital" (*PH* 7). The Battles and the Mustrovics share a singular devotion to farming, to the exclusion of sociability or even respectable upkeep of the farmhouse. "For two years . . . [Mustrovic] slaved on the soil" and "[a]t any hour he could be seen working feverishly" (*PH* 8–9). George Battle "went on with the work, yearly bending his body lower over his earth . . . His hands were permanently hooked, had become sockets into which the handles of tools fitted tightly" (*PH* 7). While the farm's previous owners were one with the land, Bert Munroe strikes a far less traditional figure. A failure at an assortment of business endeavors, he turned to professional farming only as a last resort for some "rest and security" (*PH* 14). His first actions are to renovate the house so that it is "made to look like a hundred thousand other country houses in the west" (*PH* 11). Besides the advice of popular magazines, Munroe does not hesitate to make use of employee labor: "he read exhaustively on farming methods, hired a helper and worked from morning to night" (*PH* 14–15).

In this text's allegory of agricultural modernization, the old-fashioned farmers are portrayed as inarticulate foreigners and the all-American as an urban back-to-the-lander. The property's haunting indicates the persistence of something alien at the heart of California's agricultural history. "The deserted farm was situated not far from the middle of the narrow valley. On both sides it was bounded by the best and most prosperous farms in the Pastures of Heaven. It was a weedy blot between two finely cultivated, contented pieces of land" (*PH* 5). The peculiar combination of natural fertility and cultural unassimilability characterizes the land's hauntedness. The land could be read as being haunted by the dependence of Californian agricultural productivity on the presence of aliens ineligible to citizenship, whose banishment in 1924, or perhaps the wish for it, continues to exert a curse in displaced forms. The Munroe curse, then, derives from the "impenetrable mystery" of land "well watered and fertile" (*PH* 5) built upon the contributions of disappeared aliens.

The stories in *Pastures of Heaven* undermine a binary opposition between native and alien by subverting our expectations of their ready recognition. The weird story of Tularecito, for example, concerns an abnormal Indian boy who is unteachable in the classroom yet naturally talented in animal husbandry and farming. Discovered in the woods one night when he was just a baby and raised by a local farmer, Tularecito believes that he is really a gnome. Setting off one night in search of his real kin, he starts tunneling beneath a peach tree on the Munroe farm. When Bert Munroe, puzzled, persists in filling up the hole, Tularecito attacks him and, tragically, cannot be saved from subsequent arrest and incarceration. Tularecito's fate preaches the social violence of conformity: "All his life he had been an alien, a lonely outcast, and now he was going home. As always, he heard the voices of the earth—the far off clang of cow bells, the muttering of the disturbed quail, the little whine of the coyote who would not sing this night, the nocturnes of a million insects" (*PH* 44). As is typical of Steinbeck, textual sympathy favors nature's symbolic representative, even as his image of nature assumes grotesque shapes. Tularecito has "short, chubby arms, and long-loose jointed legs"; his "large head sat without interval of neck between the deformedly broad shoulders;" his "eyes were ancient and dry; there was something trogloditic about his face" (*PH* 36). Tularecito's deformities indicate a particular suitability to farmwork. Reminiscent of George Battle, whose "hands were permanently hooked [and] had become sockets" and who was "yearly bending his body lower over his earth," Tularecito "had planting hands, tender figures that never injured a young plant nor bruised the surfaces of a grafting limb" (*PH* 36).

Pastures of Heaven repeatedly presents us with physically deviant individuals who are organically connected to the soil, compared with the normal look of those who come to farming secondhand and belatedly. This rural world turns out to be populated with native aliens. It is a place, finally, where no one is really native because of an original colonial history, or where those who are the most native look the most alien. The text ensures we do not miss the racial corollary of its challenge to agrarian populism. The tragedy of the Whitesides is that though their family tree "was mingled with the good true blood of New England" (*PH* 146), they have only ever managed to produce one son per generation. The limited reproductivity of those representatives of an Anglo-Saxon aristocracy can be read as yet another way in which this wilderness stubbornly resists frontier settlement. The Anglo-Saxon turns out to be simply one among a host of disappearing figures—savages and farmers—in a landscape of ongoing colonization and recolonization.

In a textual universe where oppositions between native and alien cannot be sustained, we are not surprised to find that there should room for the Asian American. The story of Junius Maltby and his son Robbie features the sole Asian American character in Steinbeck's pre–World War II fiction: Takashi Kato, a schoolboy who is at first the target of his classmates' game of anti-Japanese espionage. Another game the boys enjoy playing is rescuing the president of the United States from Indian kidnappers. These patriotic games are ironically led by Robbie Maltby, who is widely pitied for having been raised by his father as a virtual savage but who turns out to be far worse off when brought under the tutelage of civilization. The Maltby story shares with the story of Tularecito a deep skepticism of the superiority of civilization over savagery. The text's coupling of "yellow peril" and Indian war games works to align alien Asiatic and native Indian as joint Others of the frontier's expansion, indigenizing the Asiatic within a regional ecology, in a signal departure from the discourse of California alien land law fiction. Steinbeck's staging of the yellow peril as a children's game functions as a devastating parody: the result of the game is Takashi's social integration rather than exclusion. At first, since "no one would consent to be left behind to watch" him, Takashi "found himself invited everywhere" (PH 73). Then, after a while, Takashi demands admission to the B.A.S.S.F.E.A.J, or the Boys' Auxiliary Secret Service for Espionage Against the Japanese, on the basis that "I was born here, the same as you. . . . I'm just as good American as you, ain't I?" (PH 73). The club's leader, Robbie, consents, not wanting to be cruel, and creates a special role for Takashi as the club's only bilingual intelligence officer. "[I]f you guys want," Takashi volunteers enthusiastically "we'll spy on my old man" (PH 73).

The critic Cliff Lewis has uncovered a remarkable connection between this fictional story, in which the character Robbie predicts the inevitability of a coming war with Japan, and the subsequent events around World War II, when Steinbeck entered into intelligence discussions with Franklin Roosevelt. Documents in the Roosevelt Library indicate the existence of exchanges between Roosevelt and Steinbeck, who in 1940 reported to the president on Nazi activities in Mexico and recommended that a propaganda agency separate from the FBI be created to safeguard U.S. interests in Latin America.[99] Steinbeck was offered an actual intelligence job by Roosevelt, which he declined, but he continued to be in contact with William Donovan, head of a newly formed spy agency in Washington (later to become the O.S.S.), in this period on the matter of a propaganda department. After the Pearl Harbor bombing, a December 15, 1941, memo from Donovan to the president forwarded some suggestions from Steinbeck regarding the Japanese community in California. Steinbeck's recommendation affirmed the loyalty of Japanese Americans as a group to the United States, questioned the plausibility of the existence of any mass conspiracy, and proposed a cheap and effective method of surveillance on the Japanese American community through the use of reliable Nisei informants (Lewis, 57–58).

In an example of life imitating art, Lewis observes, Steinbeck's recommendation to Donovan "adopts the fictitious Robbie's idea of using Takashi Kato in an adult version of the 'Boys' Auxiliary' to spy upon his Japanese-American community" (Lewis, 57). Steinbeck's proposal posits the loyalty of the majority of Japanese Americans and assumes the possibility of discerning political attitudes on an individual basis, which the government at the time, as we know, considered racially impossible. Indeed, among the various members of the West Coast Japanese community, the Nisei were considered by many government officials to be especially suspicious (Daniels, *Concentration Camps*, 76). A prevailing belief in an essential Asiatic unassimilability meant that their American speech and manners could be interpreted as evidence of Oriental deception. In splitting the Nisei from "unknown or strange Japanese" (in Donovan's memo on Steinbeck's recommendation)—or Takashi Kato, "good American," from his Issei father—Steinbeck's viewpoint anticipates what was later to be the WRA practice of promoting the Nisei over the Issei to positions of camp leadership as a way to facilitate Americanization. In 1942 his recommendations went unheeded and did not prevent the tragedy of mass evacuation. Yet they are of a piece with the administration of internment itself, which expected to be able to screen disloyal from loyal elements of the population through a loyalty questionnaire, to enlist Nisei in visible combat against Japan, and to transform the internees into "projectiles of democracy" in American postwar readjustment (James, 112).[100]

Steinbeck's intelligence communiqué and *Pastures of Heaven* point to an involvement in a discursive process of Asian Americanization that, like his enfleshment of the Dust Bowl migrant, crossed between the realms of policy making and fiction. The textual context for this unusual prewar appearance of a Nisei character as a "good American," moreover, suggests the extent to which the prominence of the New World's colonial status facilitated Asian American representation. Exploring the eccentricity of California's rural world to the mythic American frontier, Steinbeck's critical exploration of California's mode of production worked through different literary modes. Sometimes his text's surface reality pictured a largely gridded territory and a diminished green world, as in *Of Mice and Men*, and other times the text projected an archaic pastoralism of small family farms on the border of a resplendent nature, as in *Pastures of Heaven*; however, never did an agrarian ideal provide a moral guarantee. As much as the parody of yellow perilism as a children's game allows Steinbeck to mock racism as immature, the terms of this intervention also reflect the constraints that allow for the figuration of the Asian American as a child and not an economic agent. The condition of Takashi's enlistment as a "good American" depends upon shifting the target of yellow perilism to his adult father. Similarly, in the education discourse of the WRA that constructed internment itself as an accelerated, salutary process of Americanization, the policy's ideal subjects were the Nisei, the confusion of whose citizenship rights and biological youth enabled the agency to lay claim to their national molding.

The Maltby story is itself a story centrally about education, but one in which autodidacticism is preferred to an institutional mode, which is shown to be primarily concerned with producing social conformity rather than intellectual enlightenment. The Maltby homestead, which under Junius reverts from farmland back to wilderness, approximates a state of nature where food is gathered, not grown. Sometimes the Maltbys may go hungry "because they failed to find a hen's nest in the grass when it came to suppertime" (*PH* 66), but most of the time all it takes is burrowing "into a perfect thicket of mallow weeds" in order to "emerge carrying a pale cucumber" (*PH* 66). Instead of working, the Maltbys pass their time discussing history and literature. Upon coming of age, Robbie is made to enroll in school, but for a halcyon period, the power of his unconventional upbringing works its magic over even this environment. In this garden of natural abandon, a happy existence of innocent play scripts a notable, if small, part for an Asian American. The necessarily Edenic terms of Asian American appearance, though, indicate its episodic transience, just as childhood is impermanent and the state of nature must inevitably give way to human cultivation. Where an industrial order reigns, the Asiatic exists as a fragmented presence: a spectral figure on the margins of narrative vision ("Johnny Bear") or a somatic feature of the migrant worker whose body alludes to the racialized structure of California's economic development *(Of Mice and Men)*.

Steinbeck's Okie, Inside and Out

On first appearance, Steinbeck's writing on Dust Bowl migrants suggests a turn away from a critical engagement with modernity's universalization of alienation to a more redemptive narrative afforded by the arrival of true Americans from the frontier. It is no accident that, with *The Grapes of Wrath*, the author's departure from the naturalistic pessimism of his earlier work should have coincided with his increasing involvement with agents and allies of the New Deal.[101] Yet we cannot be all too certain of the effects of the collision between the patriotic culture of the Joads and the alienated world of California. On this point, the fiction is more ambiguous than the journalism. *The Grapes of Wrath* gives us two legends of land ownership, one in which private property is a natural right and another in which there is no original possession without theft:

> Grampa took up the land, and he had to kill the Indians and drive them away. And Pa was born here, and he killed weeds and snakes. . . . it's our land. We measured it and broke it up. (*GW* 45)

> Once California belonged to Mexico and its land to Mexicans; and a horde of tattered feverish Americans poured in. And such was their

hunger for land that they took the land—stole Sutter's land, Guerrero's land, took the grants and broke them up and growled and quarreled over them, those frantic hungry men; and they guarded with guns the land they had stolen. They put up houses and barns, they turned the earth and planted crops. And these things were possession, and possession was ownership. (*GW* 315)

The coexistence of two different moral accounts of the origins of private property in the New World could be read as underscoring California's aberrational violence, one in need of national rescue from the social deformations left by a historical foundation in Spanish colonialism. This would comport with the text's perspective on the unjust consolidations of large-scale agriculture based on the eternal belief that "[if] a man owns a little property, that property is him, it's part of him, and it's like him" (*GW* 50). Yet the violence that inheres in the assertion of property rights in California cannot help but darken the heroism of Anglo-Saxon Indian-killers in Oklahoma; the heightened visibility of colonialism in Californian history defamiliarizes the naturalized violence of the nineteenth-century frontier. *The Grapes of Wrath* retains elements of skepticism toward the benefits of civilization over savagery reminiscent of Steinbeck's earlier work that are at odds with the novel's dominant discourse of nationalism.

The novel's California setting estranges the presentation of American bodies as well. The insistent documentary drive structuring Okie representation discloses the urgency of ascertaining labor's necessary conditions of reproduction. Steinbeck's 1936 article for the *Nation* adopts an investigative eye, taking the reader on a narrative journey through squatter camps and various kinds of migrant-labor housing. An anthropological attitude permeates the 1938 pamphlet Steinbeck published with the Simon J. Lubin Society, which reprinted a series of articles he had originally written for the *San Francisco News* based on visits to Farm Security Administration (FSA) camps at Arvin and Marysville and squatter camps in Tulare and Kern Counties.[102] In *Their Blood Is Strong: A Factual Story of the Migratory Agricultural Workers in California* (1938), Steinbeck's written text is accompanied by five photographs shot by Dorothea Lange for the Farm Security Administration. The human subjects of the photography are all blessed with regular and well-proportioned features and are almost cinematically handsome in spite of their reduced social condition. On the cover is a shot of an attractive woman suckling a fairly healthy-looking child under a makeshift tent and the partial shade of a tree, surrounded by the meager possessions of transient life. The photo calls to mind the powerful identification between maternity and vitality in *The Grapes of Wrath*.[103] As Ma Joad famously says, "Man, he lives in jerks—baby born an' a man dies, an' that's a jerk—gets a farm an' loses his farm, an' that's a jerk. Woman, it's all one flow, like a stream, like eddies, little waterfalls, but the river, it goes right on. Woman looks at it like that. We ain't gonna die out. People is goin' on—changin' a little, maybe, but goin' right on" (*GW* 577). In the Lange photo, the beautiful woman and the blond child firmly meet our gaze under the bold title "Their Blood is Strong." The message their look sends is clear: despite hardship and deprivation, a genetic superiority promises a future.[104] While the racial populism inhering within Steinbeck's syncretic rhetorics of "the people" and the necessarily national limits of his welfare imaginary have been well observed,[105] they have not been fully explained. The centrality of maternal and familial figurations in this 1930s documentary genre points partly, in my view, to the necessary engagement of Asiatic racial form by any Americanist rewriting of California agricultural migrancy.

The inside text of the pamphlet continues the cover theme of a countervailing biology with the identification of the "new kind of migrants," who are small farmers used to "living in close touch with the land" and people of "English, German and Scandinavian descent"—that is to say, of "the best American stock."[106] The emphasis on the new migrants' mythic Anglo-Saxonism makes a pointed allusion to the foreignness of the old migrants. Okie representation is a re-racialization of a customary labor form, whose prospective documentation depends upon dissecting the "human structure" of agricultural migrants and exposing "how they live and what kind of people they are, what their living standard is, what is done for them and to them, and what their problems and needs are" (*TBS* 5). Our confrontation with such particular details of living indicate the pamphlet's double function—to describe the conditions in which the migrants live and to prove that they cannot live in these conditions. The same material urgency animates Steinbeck's intent with the novel, as we may glean from the evidence of his writing process left by his working journal. An October 7, 1938, entry notes, frantically: "The drop to starvation level of the wages. The trapped quality. Must get it in—difficulty of getting clean. No Soap. No money to buy soap."[107] In his fictional and nonfictional publications both, the Hoovervilles comprise a typical scene of "filth, flies, flu" (*TBS* 7). The investigation of the housing provided by corporate farms uncovers one-room shacks in which whole families are squeezed, "no rug, no water, no bed" and "a toilet with a septic tank to serve 100 to 150 people" (*TBS* 11). These dismal findings on rural living echo 1920 state reports on Japanese farmers "who do not come within the labor camp act, living in shack houses, not fit for human habitation." As the measure to curb the rural spread of aliens was then being debated, the public was presented with the horrifying picture of "open toilets, open drains from the kitchen sink, unscreened dining and cooking quarters, and living quarters generally littered with boxes, bags, etc."[108]

Steinbeck's pamphlet turns from the migrants' squalid environment to

their physical health, discussing the deficiencies of income, diet, and medical care with minute specificity. The preoccupation with such details
does not suggest an effort to sensationalize the mundane, but just the opposite—the domestication of the unknown by documentary dissection.
Typical diets for families of varying sizes are listed, from at best "boiled
cabbage, baked sweet potatoes, creamed carrots, beans, fried dough,
jelly, tea," to sometimes nothing but cornmeal mush (*TBS* 21–22). The
text dwells at such length upon dietary details since, after all, the mystification of diet has long been central to the notion of essentially disparate
standards of living among migrant groups. As if to undermine any justification for low wages, the text engages the notion at its most biological
level, insisting upon a uniform standard of income required for the maintenance of "one healthy man." Any drop below the standard is quantifi-
able according to a range of effects upon the human body, now displayed
in all its frailty: pain in the stomach, burst appendix, weakness from
measles, influenza, "hookworm," malnutrition, and mortality (*TBS* 20–
21). *Their Blood Is Strong* participates in a longstanding discourse that
articulates the social form of agricultural migrancy through an accounting of the body, one that it seeks to reinvent by formulating universal biological standards. No longer are we presented with essential differences
between bodies that operate on meat and those that operate on rice.

Still, there is always a threat of degeneration, or glimpses of an Asiatic
palimpsest, in the malnourished man whose "spirit is losing caste rapidly" (*TBS* 7), in the people who are "cut down to a kind of sub-human-
ity" (*TBS* 9). In a sense, the written and visual representations of the
Okies work against each other. Whereas Lange's photographs pay tribute
to an almost iconic physical beauty, Steinbeck's language describes a
wasted condition that hearkens to a coolie ancestry. In another sense, it is
perhaps precisely their combination—the tense juxtaposition between
the migrants' potential for racialization *and* for aestheticization—that
feeds the text's muckraking energy. The apocalyptic danger of alien
takeover is still possible, in the dangers presented by a migratory mass
"with starvation close behind them. . . . For while California has been
successful in its use of migrant labor, it is gradually building a human
structure which will certainly change the state, and may, if handled with
the inhumanity and stupidity that have characterized the past, destroy
the present system of agricultural economics" (*TBS* 5).

The New Deal text of rural labor reform and an earlier discourse of
Asian exclusionism afforded alternative approaches to the low standard
of living imposed by a system of agricultural migrancy. The system of seasonal labor produced a biological life form described by Progressive reformer Chester Rowell in 1909 as "a man with two qualities; he shall be
a hibernating man and a squatting man."[109] Rowell thought he was de-

scribing the Japanese who "exists somehow, without bothering us, during the season of no work, and [who] can do as much work squatting as he can standing up" (Rowell, 13). In a way the Okie is simply the name for the Asiatic who won't go away. On a new turn in public consciousness in the summer of 1937 Carey McWilliams wrote:

> The transients, herded together like cattle, were permitted to eke out an existence in the fantastic hope that they would ultimately disperse, vanish into the sky or march over the mountains and into the sea or be swallowed up by the rich and fertile earth. But they did not move, and with the winter season came heavy rains and floods. Soon a major crisis was admitted to exist, with over 50,000 workers destitute and starving.[110]

The images of overcrowded squatters' camps recall for good reason Japanese "shacks" or Chinatown ghettoes: they are mysterious dwelling places of a labor force for whose cost of reproduction California agribusiness does not pay. We are in a better position to appreciate Steinbeck's elevation of a family form dominated by a maternal "citadel" (*GW* 100) as a defining distinction between the new migrants and the old. In "Dubious Battle in California," he writes of the Dust Bowl migrants, "having their families with them, they are not so mobile as the earlier immigrants are" (DBC 304). *The Grapes of Wrath*'s graphic interest in the processes of natural reproduction, as the novel follows the course of Rose of Sharon's pregnancy from conception to breastfeeding, might be racially contextualized by the mystery of teeming Chinatown bachelor societies—whose ungendered appearance were the result of U.S. restrictions on Asian female immigration in order to limit the birth of Asian Americans.[111] In a sense, our documentary tour of the migrant camps provides entry at last into the mysterious abode of Asiatic labor power, mastering it with the recording of precise inventories.

McWilliams's "Oriental Agriculture"

Until the 1938 gubernatorial election of Culbert Olsen, the first Democrat to gain the state's top post in the twentieth century, power at the state and local level was held by a conservative leadership closely tied to agribusiness interests for most of the decade.[112] Thus, though the subject matter of *The Grapes of Wrath* may have concerned a political sea change that had begun as early as 1933 with the rise of Mexican-Filipino farm labor strikes and the entry of the first wave of Dust Bowl refugees, the novel's publication at the end of the decade coincided with the delayed arrival of the New Deal at the level of state politics. Coinciding as well with the onset of the Sino-Japanese War and the encroaching advance of fascism in Europe, a Californian New Deal was perhaps bound to come draped in an Americanist rhetoric of national defense. Just two months after *The Grapes of Wrath* appeared, Olsen's newly appointed official in charge of the welfare of migrants, Carey McWilliams, published an impassioned indictment of California's "farm fascism," entitled *Factories in the Field: The Story of Migratory Farm Labor in California* (1939), which backed the accusations of Steinbeck's novel with statistical documentation, historical analysis—and the power of potential government intervention. In this section, we will be concerned with the terms of McWilliams's diagnosis of California's farm labor problem and the framing context it provides for understanding the peculiar consistency of Japanese American evacuation with a federal "emancipation" of California from an agribusiness-dominated state polity.

Like Steinbeck's "Dubious Battle in California," *Factories in the Field*'s history of California agriculture is written from the standpoint of a new epoch, whose potential for a radical break from the past is heralded by the joint arrival of Dust Bowl migrants and federal programs of social remedy. Among the various groups that have historically comprised California's agricultural workforce, McWilliams draws no essential differences: "Today the army has new faces as recruits have swarmed in from the dust-bowl area eager to enlist for the duration of the crops at starvation wages. But, in substance it is the same army that has followed the crops since 1870."[113] At the same time, McWilliams believes that there is good reason to hope that "with the arrival of the dustbowl refugees, a cycle of exploitation had been brought to a close" (*FF* 306). Precisely to the extent that racial persecution has been a dominant dimension of vigilantism—that "peculiarly Californian phenomenon" (*FF* 9) so crucial to keeping an oppressed laboring class in its place—a "day of reckoning" now awaits the farm industrialists who will be unable to treat these "despised 'Okies' and 'Texicans'" as yet "another minority alien racial group" (*FF* 306). Present-day migrant workers are "American citizens familiar with the usages of democracy" (*FF* 306). Whether the term "American" is meant to emphasize a more plausible legal or cultural basis for vigorous political resistance, its assignation bears the promise of revolutionary change, the redemption of California from a cyclical or degenerative history marked by the relentless "tightening of the system of ownership and control" and "degradation of farm labor" (*FF* 7). If McWilliams thus presents California's past as essentially unchanging regardless of its periodic upheavals, this atemporal quality is consistent with a premodern characterization of California's mode of production as an "anachronistic system of landownership dating from the creation, during Spanish rule, of feudalistic patterns of ownership and control"

(*FF* 7). The signal change the Dust Bowl migrants potentially bring is thus the possibility of historical change itself.

But if *Factories in the Field* so far recalls Steinbeck's 1936 article for the *Nation,* its political vision differs importantly by demanding radical economic transformation. In "Dubious Battle in California," Steinbeck pleads for social amelioration in order to contain the sharpening of class antagonism.[114] *The Grapes of Wrath* could be read to be more openly ambivalent about the panacea of government reform, given the limitations of Weedpatch Camp, which provides the Joads with sanitary housing but no employment, thus requiring the continuation of their narrative journey. Ultimately the novel moves toward a transcendence of the social through a double symbolic gesture—toward Tom's spiritualized merging with an amorphous populist force, and toward a biologization, through Rose of Sharon, of welfare's succor.[115] By contrast, *Factories in the Field* welcomes the federal camps for their provision of important services (water, sanitation, et cetera), but more importantly for prefiguring a new social order yet to come.[116] Small collective communities, the federal camps in part function to instruct a rough peasantry in a national tradition of self-government through a committee and town hall-like system; as safe havens from grower vigilantism, they provide a space for workers to organize freely. Government assistance is just an "initial step toward" (*FF* 304) a new rural social order that depends on the organization of agricultural workers. Ultimately, "the real solution involves the substitution of collective agriculture for the present monopolistically owned and controlled system" (*FF* 324).

As war with Japan increasingly loomed on the horizon, both McWilliams and Steinbeck worried about the scapegoating of Japanese Americans, even if the former did it more publicly than the latter.[117] Both embraced principles of equality and fair treatment for Japanese Americans. Yet whereas Steinbeck's recommendation to Roosevelt on the use of Nisei informers presumed that Japanese Americans were no different from other Americans, McWilliams worried about the prominence of racially marked population concentrations. In other words, where McWilliams saw geographical pockets of unassimilated racial difference Steinbeck did not—or, extrapolating from *Pastures of Heaven,* perhaps he questioned if the West Coast Japanese looked alien any more than did their surrounding environment. I suggest that an explanation for these authors' differing perceptions of Japanese Americans' racial prominence can be found in their respective modes of representing California's state of economic alienation in the 1930s.

As we have seen, Steinbeck's strategic approach to the representation of colonial capitalism found expression in the symbolization of the Asian American as an indigeneous life form in California scenery and subverted nationalistic distinctions between native and alien. McWilliams was much less willing to naturalize a social condition. The radicalness of his demand for social transformation was partly to be seen in a willingness to entertain vast projects of social engineering on the scale of Japanese American relocation. McWilliams's extensive preoccupation with the issue of racism—during the war few worked as tirelessly to produce public awareness of the injustices of internment, in writing and on radio—was a reflection of how the existence of racial differentiation was for him a primary expression of California's system of exploitation. Compared with Steinbeck, in whose texts the history of Asian American existence is highly mediated and figurally displaced, McWilliams's writing of California trains our gaze directly onto the racially diverse bodies that populate the state. California's "strange army in tatters" numbers "200,000 workers and a more motley crew was never assembled in this country by a great industry. Sources of cheap labor in China, Japan, the Philippine Islands, Puerto Rico, Mexico, the Deep South, and Europe have been generously tapped to recruit its ever-expanding ranks" (FF 7–8). Strangeness and Orientalness are linked in the heterogeneous constitution of this labor army by "Chinese ex-prostitutes, deaf mutes, orphaned children, women and conscripted labor" (FF 184). The only racial term in the series, "Chinese" serves to augment the exoticism emphasized by a whole circus of non-normative workers.[118] The Oriental helps embellish the aberrant quality of a scene that McWilliams, far more than Steinbeck, is convinced can and must be corrected.

The form as well as the content of McWilliams's California is arguably "Oriental." The text introduces the topic of its investigation by proposing to take us on a journey beneath the "surface placidity" (FF 4) of the great inland farm valleys, making visible the existence of a "hidden history" (FF 3). Building suspense around a putatively mundane subject, the text opens with a compelling description of a scene that overturns our rural expectations:

> One looks in vain for the incidents of a rural life: the schoolhouse on the hilltop, the comfortable homes, the compact and easy indolence of the countryside. Where are the farmers? Where are the farmhouses? Occasionally the highway passes within view of a row of barracklike shacks which the traveler mistakenly identifies as, perhaps, the hovels of section hands. In the harvest seasons, the orchards are peopled with thousands of workers; and, in the great fields, an army of pickers can be seen trudging along, in the dazzling heat, in the wake of a machine. The impression gained is one of vast agricultural domains, huge orchard and garden estates, without permanent occupants. (FF 4)

Directly attacking agrarian illusions of a core distinction between city and country life, McWilliams' description would have us recognize California farms for the factories they really are: there are no farmers to be seen, only an army of workers, no real dwellings, because the land has no permanent inhabitants. The mystery of the landscape's appearance is that it is at once full of bodies yet empty of true residents.

The mystery of landscape repeats in the mystery of California labor's means of reproduction: "No one has ever been able to fathom the mystery of how this army supports itself or how it has continued to survive" (*FF* 8). This general mystery of labor reproduction is exemplified by a specifically Chinese and Japanese capacity for self-perpetuation under impossible circumstances. The Chinese were "employed at sub-subsistence wages," "had no families, and consequently were satisfied with 'the cheapest, meanest quarters,'" "boarded themselves in a mysterious manner," and when the season was over, "vanished into San Francisco and obliging re-appeared when required" (*FF* 70–71). In spite of this all, "they were extremely efficient workers" (*FF* 71). What is more, Japanese farm laborers, "were, if anything, even more efficient than the Chinese and more industrious" (*FF* 107); they met the eccentric requirements of California's seasonal agriculture both by being able to "move about quickly without incurring much transportation expense" and by being able to "hibernate" during the off-season, vanishing as soon as the crops were harvested (*FF* 107).

Given the special fit between the biological feats of Chinese and Japanese bodies and the impossible labor requirements of seasonal agriculture, we are not surprised to find that McWilliams's general designation for the industry—despite the globally diverse sources of its labor pool—is "Our Oriental Agriculture" (the name for chapter 7 of *Factories in the Field*). The term "Oriental" as it is used thus operates on different semiotic levels: it signifies the Asiatic labor that is the secret basis of a vast economic empire (one reliant on coolies or peon labor rather than workers proper); it is the metonym for an epistemological object that resists "casual inspection" (*FF* 5) and refers to the form of secrecy itself; it designates the arrested or non-normative social relations that sets California apart from the rest of the nation, or at least the nation as it is typically imagined:

> California agriculture has been . . . to a large degree "Oriental agriculture." Its mammoth farm factories have been built by cheap Oriental and peon labor, imported for particular purposes and discarded as soon as that purpose has been achieved. For over half a century this sordid business of race exploitation has been going on in the State and it would be difficult to find a meaner record of exploitation in the his-

tory of American industry. In the Eastern industrial districts, the theory of the "melting pot" has had at least limited application and to a certain extent assimilation has been achieved. But, in California, the idea of the "melting pot" never prevailed. Here the practice has been to use a race for a purpose and then to kick it out, in preference for some weaker racial unit. In each instance the shift in racial units has been accompanied by a determined effort to drive the offending race from the scene. Up to a certain point, therefore, it can be said that California has solved the difficult social problems involved in the use of alien labor by the simple expedient of driving the alien groups, one after the other, from the State. But important vestiges of the problem remain and the experience undergone with each group has definitely, and perhaps permanently, affected the social structure of the State. (*FF* 134)

As an economy characterized by permanent mass subordination and historical immutability, McWilliams's "Oriental agriculture" calls to mind Marx and Engels's mythic concept of the Asiatic mode of production (AMP).[119] In the Asiatic mode of production, the state is the sole landholder and there is no privately held property. McWilliams's California is ruled, of course, by private growers, but their utter control of local government and their connection to entrenched patterns of land monopoly add up to a totalizing entity that here knows no separation between state and civil society. Just as the concept of the Asiatic mode of production situates Oriental society outside the progress of universal history, McWilliams's California also represents an anomaly according to the normative standards of East Coast industry and an American "melting pot." Indeed, its eccentricity would seem to lie in the uneven combination of economic and social characteristics, in which the very advance of an industrial efficiency is paradoxically dependent upon a castelike social formation (sometimes McWilliams uses the term "feudal") where racial differences are exploitatively preserved rather than democratically dissolved.[120] Not unlike Russian and Chinese intellectuals who, at various moments from the late nineteenth century to the early 1930s, wondered if the concept of the AMP might provide sanction for revolutions at the periphery—questioning the necessity for "Oriental societies" to pass through a normative stage of capitalism before achieving socialism[121]—McWilliams speculated whether the collectivization of agricultural ownership would be so difficult since, in a way, in the current system, the "collective principle is [already] there" (*FF* 325).

McWilliams writes in the tradition of a California Orientalism propelled by the mystery of the political economy of the post-frontier, a tradition that includes disparate genres of texts—antimonopoly fiction from the early years of the twentieth century; government documents such as

Lt. General DeWitt's report concerning the army's evacuation of West Coast Japanese Americans; examples of film noir such as Roman Polansky's *Chinatown*; and academic studies of the western region such as Donald Worster's *Rivers of Empire*.[122] The instrumentality, in McWilliams's diagnosis, of racial distinctions to a pernicious social system provides a context for understanding the emancipatory reasoning for their eradication, even to the extent of accommodating extreme governmental coercion. If in 1939 *Factories in the Field* recommended union recognition and collectivization, it is possible to see how the negation of the "unassimilable alien" might have beckoned as the other half of the solution to a "wasteful, vicious, undemocratic and thoroughly antisocial system" (*FF* 325). In McWilliams's vision of social remedy, the transformation of aliens into Americans and the recognition of migrants as workers were flip sides of each other.

In other ways, McWilliams's structural analysis of racial formation also marked his departure from an earlier tradition of Orientalist diagnoses of land monopoly that could only conceive of a utopia premised on Asian exclusion. It may have seemed that a strong reason for McWilliams's optimistic belief in 1939 that it was "now theoretically possible to solve the farm-labor problem in California" (*FF* 324) was that, with white Americans now composing a majority of California migratory workers, he believed that "the race problem has, in effect, been largely eliminated" (*FF* 324). Yet the enduring value of *Factories in the Field* is that its materialist perception of race ultimately prevented it from taking comfort in such illusions:

> Although the change had been taking place for some time, it was suddenly realized in 1937 that the bulk of the State's migratory workers were white Americans and that the foreign racial groups were no longer a dominant factor. . . . The first reaction to this discovery was rather naïve: "Our Race Problems Vanish," editorialized the *San Francisco News,* pointing out that the possibility of a "permanently stratified society in California" would probably cease with the elimination of the minority racial groups. But the pattern of exploitation has not been altered; it remains exactly the same (*FF* 305).

Perceiving race to be an integral dimension of the social relations of capitalism, McWilliams understood that the exclusion of aliens did not banish the "race problem," or what it stood for. The insertion of Dust Bowl refugees into an established pattern of minority exploitation made the inadequacies of disenfranchisement ever more apparent. *Factories in the Field* makes the case that, despite the apparent whitening of the agricultural workforce over the course of the 1930s, the social mechanics that effect racialization are still in operation. As it turns out, strangely enough, U.S. entry into the Second World War was to provide another opportunity for their address.

How, finally, are we to judge the emancipatory narrative of Japanese American dispersal from the West Coast? On the one hand, the targeted elimination of West Coast Japanese communities was inevitably conditioned by a habitual displacement of economic transformation. On the other hand, with the 1930s, the terms of racial elimination had shifted, not insignificantly, from national exclusion to national assimilation— from the constitutive necessity of the opposition between American and alien, to the imperative of universal Americanization.[123] This process of Americanization had begun with the arrival of refugees from the old frontier along with social offices of the federal government. Its object extended to the whole region of California, which, as we have seen, was represented by reform advocates to be more Oriental than American. Like Steinbeck's character who, gesturing toward the island of democracy established by the FSA, says "This here's United States, not California" (GW 456), McWilliams figures federal intervention as the national incorporation of an alien territory. Establishing a continuity between the vigilante character of earlier yellow peril agitation and present-day "farm fascism," whose leadership has "many points of similarity with . . . Nazi Germany" (FF 231), McWilliams constructs a California whose foreign Orientalness merges all too easily with a foreign fascism. McWilliams's call for national attention to a regional situation gone awry rhetorically sets rural California on a global stage of urgent, antifascist struggle.

Such Popular Front symbolization of the battlelines between federal and local authorities in rural California clearly affected, at times, McWilliams's powers of observation. In a 1942 article on a Japanese American assembly center, he felt that "It would not be accurate to characterize Santa Anita as a 'concentration camp'" since "[for] the first time in their lives, the Issei, or first-generation Japanese, had been permitted to vote in an election" (MWJ 360–61). The article also extolled the center's orderliness, quietness, cleanliness, and good food. It was as if, when McWilliams looked at any federally operated camp, all he could see was a collective community where people were being provided "for the first time, with an adequate supply of decent drinking water and proper sanitation" and instructed in a "'town-hall' type of government" (FF 300–301). Grower-provided migrant housing, by contrast, was evidence that "[c]oncentration camps are to be found in California today" (FF 236). *Factories in the Field* asks us, "When is a concentration camp not a concentration camp?" (FF 237) and turns our gaze meaningfully to examples of "fortified camps under military surveillance" (FF 238) where migratory workers are essentially held prisoner whenever there is suspicion of a strike. Two years into the advent of internment, after the various illusions of creating utopian rural colonies had been shed, McWilliams still held that to call the internment centers "'concentration camps' after the pattern of Dachau and Oranienburg would be a gross exaggeration" (*P* 158), though it was now obvious to him that they were carceral institutions, a weird hybrid of "army camps . . . Indian reservations . . . FSA resettlement projects . . . [and] internment camps for dangerous enemy aliens" (*P* 158).[124]

In an address delivered on June 16, 1940, and published as a pamphlet by the ACLU entitled *Liberals and the War Crisis*, McWilliams directly sought to counteract what he feared to be a "profound crisis in liberal thought" brought on by the dilemma of expanding fascism.[125] Contrary to increasing numbers of prominent intellectuals and writers who were beginning to bid "farewell to liberalism" in the interest of national defense, McWilliams insisted upon the necessary compatibility of being nationally "prepared" *and* remaining "free" (*LWC* 15). He suspected that those who were decrying liberal appeasement of fascism were really readying the public for the "acceptance of a totalitarian America" (*LWC* 13). In light of the events of 1942, it may seem ironic that as part of the "strong arm processes in the making" (*LWC* 13), McWilliams should have warned of the imminent rise of anti-alien campaigns and proposals for more "effective control over aliens," including complete registering and fingerprinting, developments in which a "sickening travesty of Americanism"—of the traditional belief in equality and justice for "men of all races and creeds"—was in danger of becoming reality (*LWC* 13–14).

Yet this 1940 speech underscores the extent to which for McWilliams, a defense of democracy had to go beyond the mere protection of civil liberties to a more affirmative effort of national planning. "The imperative which we face as a nation is the imperative of planning, social planning, to take charge of our national economic life, to control it, to reorganize and if necessary reconstruct it, to point it in the direction of social progress." (*LWC* 17) McWilliams expected greater "regimentation and control . . . to come to this country" (*LWC* 14) regardless, because the "operation of undemocratic forces in our industrial society" had shown itself to result in "disorder, waste and impoverishment" (*LWC* 21). It was only a matter of who was going to be in charge of a more centrally organized national economic life—those "foes of democracy" who would use an external menace as "a pretext to justify the seizure of power" (*LWC* 21), or "the people." Though McWilliams saw through the rhetoric of those who, under the guise of "protect[ing] us, so they announce, from the Fifth Column," will ensure that "we will be railroaded into totalitarianism" (*LWC* 17), his warnings of home-grown capitalist dictatorship shares with that rhetoric the fear of a too intimate enemy. "Only the people can defend democracy, and our task is to see to it that they, not their enemies, are assigned to the task" (*LWC* 22).

Who are the people? Who are their enemies? McWilliams's speech is peppered with the specific examples of "interests who have proven themselves incapable of disinterested statesmanship" (*LWC* 22)—big business leaders such as Ford Motor Company and the Associated Farmers of California, and their political allies—but leaves the defense of democracy to a populist abstraction. Under the circumstances of a borderless war, it was perhaps all too necessary to fall back upon the proven political record of various entities, to trust in the FSA and to inscribe the actions of the U.S. Army into a New Deal narrative of federal rescue. As McWilliams wrote in September 1942:

> Great issues are at stake in the evacuation program: the question, of whether a democracy can fight a total war and preserve its freedom. The issue is fraught also with great international significance in terms of our relations with colored people generally. There is no reason why the relocation projects cannot be successful, cannot in fact reflect great credit upon us as a nation—provided a majority of American people will insist upon fair treatment of the Japanese and not succumb to demagogues and race-baiters. (MWJ 369)

By 1944 it was finally the establishment of federal jurisdiction over what was once a regional concern that could redeem an action no longer justifiable "even as a war measure" (*P* 5). "The relocation of the evacuees has taken the 'Japanese issue' away from the West Coast bigots," McWilliams wrote, "The problem has now become part of a national minority question for the solution of which the federal government has begun to assume a measure of responsibility" (*P* 278–79). As a result, "There is more interest in, and more intelligent discussion of, the race question today than at any time in our history. Over two hundred interracial committees have been established in American urban communities since the war" (*P* 283). In *Prejudice*, McWilliams still hoped that a "[w]ide dispersal of the evacuees should reduce some of the prejudice against them" and make Japanese Americans better "known to Americans in the East and Middle West" (*P* 279). In a way, the wartime commitment of military and civilian resources to a racial project—by no means "as exciting as bombing Japanese warships in the Coral Sea" (MWJ 359), yet at the time seeming as crucial to national security—met the imperative of "press[ing] forward with those basic social reforms" as "the best, most necessary, . . . most essential condition of national defense" (*LWC* 15).

CONCLUSION: TOWARD A PACIFIC RIM

Around the time of the Second World War, the sense of an increasingly borderless world pointed to the waning possibilities of imagining complete alien exclusion. Dreams of universal assimilation instead heralded the emergence of a postwar American global order. Though Axis espionage activity in Latin America should logically have focused attention to the Mexican border, it was Pacific geography that occupied the center of national security worries. A fantastic zone of national insecurity, a regional object of social scientific diagnosis and government rehabilitation, the border between American and alien was also the territory of a cultural war, to be reconstituted by the triumphal rhetoric of national defense mobilization. If in 1942 government officials had first rested upon the impossibility of distinguishing disloyal aliens from loyal Americans, not only were such official distinctions soon to be upheld, but the trope of Oriental inscrutability could even be harnessed to U.S. interests. Roger Baldwin, the national director of the ACLU tarnished historically by his wartime failure to defend Japanese American rights, referred to Nisei individuals he met in Japan during the MacArthur occupation as "typical American youth[s] with a Japanese face."[126] In fact, so secure did Baldwin seem to rest in the belief that the U.S.-born people of Japanese descent are "at heart . . . loyal Americans" that he accorded a privileged ambassadorial role to Nisei members of the U.S. occupation in Japan for constituting "a bridge between Americans and Japanese invaluable in the process of democratization" (Baldwin, 27). Special agents of Americanization, Japanese Americans could now serve as middlemen useful to U.S. geopolitical interests. In a world made safe by, or for, America, the ability to be "at home with both Americans and Japanese" (Baldwin, 27) could now be of invaluable national service.

But even before the war ended, McWilliams already envisioned the utility of the Nisei as "living proofs of the universality of America" to a "new world [which] is coming into existence in the Pacific, a world of which our West Coast is an integral part; a world which we have ushered into being" (P 313, 328). Linking the overseas and domestic fronts of the U.S. war in the Pacific, McWilliams saw an analogous victory in the liberation of Japan from its own militarism and the "liberation for the Nisei—liberation from doubt, suspicion, hatred, and distrust" (P 281). Paradoxically, the suspension of the civil rights of U.S. citizens of Japanese descent occasioned the concerted production of the unassimilable alien as a model American—not simply by the handful of religious, socialist, and dissident union organizations willing to criticize federal discrimination,[127] but by the liberal allies of the administration and the WRA, which devoted itself to promoting the integration of Japanese

Americans into communities throughout the United States. Historical scholarship that emphasizes the essential continuity of internment with "a century of anti-Oriental fears, prejudice and misunderstanding" (Daniels, *Concentration Camps*, 2) lack explanations for what appears to be a sudden turnaround in the behavior of liberal leaders, particularly in California, who helped whip up public hysteria in 1942 and worked to facilitate public acceptance of Japanese American return just three years later.[128]

In the process of internment, Japanese Americans became a significant subject of documentary representation for the first time.[129] The FSA photographic archive, for example, indicates scant interest in documenting Asian subjects in the 1930s until Executive Order 9066, when suddenly Japanese Americans became a focus of photographic attention—if not immediately for the public at large, from whom the photographs of Lange and others were famously withheld until after the war, then of the state apparatus.[130] Echoing their collaborative work on Dust Bowl migration in *An American Exodus,* Dorothea Lange's photo illustrations of Paul Taylor's written text in "Our Stakes in the Japanese Exodus," published in the September 1942 issue of *Survey Graphic,* assimilates the hardship of Japanese American removal to Depression-era themes of forced migration and displacement.[131] As a photographer for the WRA, Lange's critical images of people pressed into cramped and unhealthy camp quarters reflect a visual idiom informed by her work on migrants for the FSA (Davidov, 239–40).

In 1944 Ansel Adams published a collection of photographs taken of the Manzanar Center in Owens Valley, California, which also exhibited at the New York Museum of Modern Art. Adams's images and accompanying text typified the contradictory elements of liberal internment. *Born Free and Equal: The Story of Loyal Japanese Americans* took for granted the original military necessity of evacuation, but opposed continued detention; it assumed the existence of real Japanese American saboteurs, but sought to rescue the minority group as a whole from being stigmatized by disloyalty.[132] Adams reiterated the WRA's resettlement logic that the recognition of Japanese Americans' rights as individuals depended upon their disappearance as a group: ". . . the scattering of the loyal Japanese-Americans throughout the country is far better for them than re-concentration into racial districts and groups. They wish to prove their worth as individuals, free to move about the land in pursuit of occupation, education and recreation" (*BFE* 102). In individual close-up after close-up, Adams's striking photographs perform precisely that—the representation of his subjects as enlarged individuals, many of whom are smiling or looking directly into the camera (giving the impression of a consenting portrait rather than a candid snapshot). The photographs are captioned with sayings such as "Americanism is a matter of the mind and heart" (*BFE* 59).[133]

In the front of the book, a two-page photo shows the profile of a man, presumably one of the camp internees but situated in an expansive setting, gazing into the distance at the mountains of the Sierra Nevada. Though Adams is known for his monumental, crystalline photographs of the mountains' beauty, in this particular image the mountains form a dimunitive and hazy background to a towering, impassive human figure in the foreground. The image exemplifies the representational intervention Adams was making in choosing to shoot the Manzanar camp and its residents, located at the eastern base of the very mountain range Adams had made famous as a subject of nature photography. With written text praising the internees' cultivation of crops from the "harsh and barren land" on which they seem to be all alone, *Born Free and Equal* gestures toward presenting the internees as reincarnated pioneers of the old frontier. Yet ultimately the imagery is more natural than agrarian, and the rugged permanence of the mountains lends itself to more of a parallel than an opposition between man and nature. The shots of dreary camp barracks set against the majestic mountains evoke, at first glance, the shock of human intrusion into nature, the ironic fact of incarceration in open space. After a while, one notices that the barracks' monotonous rooftops visually echo the harsh mountain peaks themselves, linking the camp to its striking setting. The photographs propose a secret harmony between the camp residents and their unlikely surroundings, whose majesty now seems to thematize the people's noble spirit of survival. By inserting the internees into the customary frame of nature photography, the images visually indigenize its subjects as Californians.

A reading of Popular Front literature set in China and Steinbeck's *Cannery Row* in the next chapter will explore the linkage between the emergent representation of Asian American character and the discourse of U.S. globalism. Toward demonstrating the historical development of that link, I have here sought to undermine the certainty of seeing internment as the teleological expression of the history of Asian exclusionism. In an important way, internment was part of a federal reconstruction of California, whose "Asiatic problem" was joined to the enlargement of the nation's global stakes. Whatever his blindnesses, McWilliams was not wrong to perceive a historical departure in the institutional assumption of federal responsibility for the management of West Coast "aliens." Until the "war of liberation for the Nisei," racial measures directed at Asians in the United States tended to clash with U.S. interests in promoting international trade. Historians have viewed this in terms of a traditional conflict between regional politics and national politics, exemplified by repeated (if weak) presidential opposition to Asian exclusionist leadership emanating from the West Coast—from Theodore Roosevelt's disapproval of the 1906 San Francisco school segregation measure to Woodrow Wilson's opposition to the 1913 Webb-Heney Bill.

The construction of California as an antifascist front in the late 1930s and early 1940s, by contrast, proposes a radically different imagination of the Pacific Coast, one that situates the Far West once again not only in line with national interest but at the leading edge of an expansionist futurity. Paradoxically, Japanese American internment marked the border's symbolic conversion from the mongrel unassimilated zone imagined by Asian exclusionism to a new frontier of U.S. power and opportunity in the Asia-Pacific. McWilliams urged his readers to embrace the recognition that "the Pacific unites rather than separates the peoples around its rim. It is a highway as a well as a barrier; bridge as well as an abyss" (*P* 302–3). In the figure of the Asian American, a legitimate ethnic identity and the U.S. nation-form were now hegemonically aligned.

CHAPTER FIVE

One World

PEARL S. BUCK, EDGAR SNOW, AND JOHN STEINBECK ON
ASIAN AMERICAN CHARACTER

UPON THE 1931 PUBLICATION of *The Good Earth* (1931), which sold a million and a half copies in its first year and was subsequently translated into thirty languages, Pearl S. Buck became the premier interpreter of China for a generation of American readers. In 1958 Harold Isaacs's study of American opinions about Asia found that a majority of interviewees still identified Buck as the source of their images of China.[1] In the view of Maxine Hong Kingston, Buck's achievement was no less than to have made "Asian voices heard, for the first time, in Western literature."[2] Buck authored an astounding number of novels (more than seventy), short stories, film scripts, magazine articles, nonfiction books, and volumes of speeches, though her reputation as a writer ultimately stemmed from the remarkable success of *The Good Earth*. Though its author had impressed her audience as an American whose long residency in China and life experiences gave her unique insight into Chinese culture, in fact soon after the novel's publication Buck returned to the United States and never again set foot in China for the remaining thirty-nine years of her life. Her career as a leading China commentator in the 1930s and 1940s, was thus founded largely on the authority of a single work—and, moreover, a single work of fiction. The unprecedented popularity of a novel about so unlikely a subject as the life of a Chinese peasant formed the basis for an area expertise that was superseded only by the changed conditions of the Cold War.[3] After the 1970s the view of Buck as a leader in promoting cross-cultural understanding between the United States and Asia yielded to a view of her as a leading example of American Orientalism. But I will argue that the racial politics of an author once hailed by the NAACP as one of the most reliable white friends of the Civil Rights movement are not so easily categorized.

Buck's claim to an intimate knowledge of the Chinese, whose virtues she extolled, no doubt depended on a blindness to issues of paternalism and power.[4] In addition to her contaminated position as the daughter of Presbyterian missionaries, critics have faulted the accuracy of her Chinese portrait. The editors of *Aiiieeeee!* (1974), the first published anthology of Asian American writing, grouped Pearl S. Buck together with other main sources of racial stereotypes in American popular culture, such as Harriet Beecher Stowe and Earl Derr Biggers. To Frank Chin, Lawson Inada, Jeffrey Paul Chan, and Shawn Wong, Buck's Wang Lung followed in the footsteps of characters such as Uncle Tom and Charlie Chan, whose popular reception lay chiefly in their submissive service to white superiors, reflecting "racist white supremacy passed off as love and acceptance."[5] One domestic context for Buck's invention—part of a tradition of sympathetic representations of the Chinese in the early twentieth century—was certainly the nostalgia of a western regional elite for its faithful Chinese servants, the supply of which had been cut off by nineteenth-century Chinese exclusion legislation.[6] Nevertheless, if we reduce Wang Lung's appeal to the flattery of a subordinate's servility, we overlook the complexity of *The Good Earth*'s iteration of the myth of self-made man. Though Wang Lung is a Chinese peasant, the story of his fortune arguably marks the first significant literary appearance of an Asian American Horatio Alger.

It was precisely in departing from existing modes of representing Chineseness that *The Good Earth* attracted so much contemporary attention. Reviewers particularly praised Buck for creating characters that were realistically human. Malcolm Cowley wrote that "[s]he has a truly extraordinary gift for presenting the Chinese, not as quaint and illogical, yellow-skinned, exotic devil-dolls, but as human beings merely, animated by motives we can always understand even when the background is strange and topsy-turvy."[7] In the words of another contemporary reviewer, "I can recall no novel that frees the ordinary, flesh-and-blood, everyday Chinaman so satisfyingly from those screens and veils and mirrors of artistic and poetic convention which nearly always make him, to the Western reader's eye, a flat and unsubstantial figure of a pale-coloured ballet. . . ."[8] The perception that Buck's innovation lay in realistic human portraiture lasted through the 1960s. In 1967 at least one critic still felt that "[h]er characters are embodied with both good and bad—but always credible—human qualities. True to life, they are neither idealized nor intrinsically evil. They behave the way they do not because they are moved in puppet-like fashion by their literary creator; their actions are a consequence of their inner nature reacting to and upon external forces."[9]

The celebrated credibility of Buck's Chinese characters does not, of course, attest to the actual verisimilitude of her representation. It indicates the novelty of encountering Asian protagonists in a realist novel, instead of in their customary domiciles of fantasy and pulp fiction.[10] As an instance of American writing about Asians, *The Good Earth* was notable in that it strove for a reality effect. In this endeavor it was apparently successful enough to allow Americans to say "[a]t last we read, in the pages of a novel, of the real people of China."[11] More than for an isolable aesthetic achievement—despite demurrals by the academy to the contrary—it was for what was perceived as her anti-Orientalist intervention that in 1938 Buck became the fourth woman and the third American to win the Nobel Prize for literature.[12]

The Good Earth was valued by its contemporary readers for both its putative empirical fidelity and the universal truths it purportedly revealed. Some readers who had previously lived in China enjoyed the novel for imaginatively returning them there, but perhaps even more startling is the conviction held by those who had never been to China of its absolute accuracy. Reviewers lavished praise on the novel for not being a "synthetic romanticization of the Oriental as an 'escape' from our own daily lives" and for its pedagogic value to those who have "never lived in China or know anything about the Chinese."[13] *The Good Earth*'s reality effect, enabling readers to feel as if they "have lived for a long time in China," lay in making an "alien civilization" seem more culturally proximate and elevating China to the condition of an abstract universal.[14]

The credibility of *The Good Earth* was also supposedly based on its popularity with Chinese readers, who on record at least were mostly admiring and who were reported to have recognized themselves in a Western literary text for the first time. The Chinese version of *The Good Earth* appeared in serial form in 1932, less than a year after its original publication in the United States, and within four years it became available in four different Chinese editions. Michael Hunt writes that most Chinese critics praised the work because the "Chinese could recognize Wang Lung as one of them, a claim they did not care to make for Fu Manchu, Charlie Chan, or any of the other Western stereotypes with which they were acquainted" (Hunt, 47–48). Even the terms on which some of Buck's contemporary Chinese detractors formulated their objections inadvertently reinforced her cultural authority, as illustrated in a famous exchange between Buck and a Chinese scholar, Kiang Kang-Hu, in the pages of the *New York Times Book Review*.

Against American critics who praised *The Good Earth*'s authenticity, Kiang argued that the novel was at least partly derived from a twelfth-century classical Chinese romance and not at all, as Buck claimed, from the observation of contemporary Chinese life. Kiang charged Buck with promulgating erroneous facts of Chinese custom and for exaggerating its superstitiousness and barbarism for the sake of exotic thrill. She was, he wrote, "more of a caricature cartoonist than a portrait painter."[15] Kiang's cultural critique lost credibility, however, by wearing its class biases on its sleeve:

Mrs. Buck in her works portrays her own young life in China as much under the influence of Chinese coolies and amahs, who are usually from the poorest families of the lowest class north of the Yangtse-Kiang Valley. There are of course, among them many honest and good country folk, hard working and faithfully serving as domestic helpers. Their idea of life is inevitably strange and their common knowledge is indeed very limited. They may form the majority of the Chinese population, but they are certainly not representative of the Chinese people. (Kiang, 2)

In her published reply, it was all too easy for Buck to defend her representational authority with populist rhetoric, turning Kiang's criticisms into an example of the traditional divorce of Chinese intellectuals from the people. Buck claimed a superior intimacy with the Chinese peasantry, among whom she had long lived. "I write because it is my nature to do so, and I can write only what I know, and I know nothing but China having only lived there. I have few friends of my own race, almost none intimate, and so I do write about the people I do know."[16] From the perspective of the twenty-first-century reader, Kiang's distaste for the novel's "pornographic" treatment of the "animal functions" of eating, sexuality, and childbearing disables his own case for the automatic advantage of the Chinese male intellectual over the American white woman in the task of representing China to the West. As for the target American audience of the 1930s, Buck's cultural ambassadorship certainly proved more instrumental to improving diplomatic relations than Kiang's.

The significance of the praise of *The Good Earth* for being realistic is all the more complicated in light of Buck's dubious status as a serious literary realist. In the view of the elite critical establishment of the 1930s, Buck was guilty of sentimentalism and propaganda.[17] Her plots were seen as wildly improbable, and her plain style failed to validate her as an innovative artist. The award of the Nobel Prize for literature to Buck in 1938 provoked disbelief and outrage in New York's literary world. Buck's biographer, Peter Conn, attributes her unpopularity among contemporary literati in part to her mass-market readership (*Cultural Biography*, 207–11). Eventually, *The Good Earth* was "too sentimental and too improbable, too slick and too facile, too lacking in poetic sensibility and complexity."[18] Over the years Buck's novels gradually slipped into the young adult category. In fact, in choosing to lecture on "The Chinese Novel" in her Nobel Prize acceptance speech in 1938, Buck herself attributed her work's simple vocabulary and absence of psychological interiority to Chinese literary influences, situating *The Good Earth* outside the Western literary tradition as a whole.[19] Some critics have compared

Buck's prose style to modes of folk storytelling across cultures (whether Icelandic, Homeric, or Chinese), in which characters are portrayed through their actions and words.[20]

Writing Buck's obituary in the *New Republic* in 1973, Helen Snow was no doubt partly accurate in sensing that *The Good Earth*'s "fantastic popularity" derived from a general Western fascination with "humankind in a primitive setting."[21] And yet there was also a specific historical context for the novel's reception in the 1930s, when literary trends pointed toward fiction's focus on ordinary lived experience.[22] With the rediscovery of America that characterized the new populism of the 1930s came an interest in the peasantry as the site of the "real"—an orientation influenced by Russian nationalistic emphasis on the peasantry and the land and also fostered by the WPA projects in the arts (M. Klein, 150–51). Literary histories of the dominant realist modes of the 1930s— studies of the proletarian novel or of the radical novel more generally— tend to neglect Buck's work perhaps for the reason that its Chinese subject matter fell outside the typical period locales of social struggle, such as the Dust Bowl or the Spanish Civil War. Nevertheless, the ambiguity of the category of proletarian literature in the U.S. context—where its definition was never settled[23]—and its close affinity with (some would say development into) the collective novel of the Popular Front after 1935, suggest the relevance of the framework of radical fiction as a form that sought to represent a "new protagonist, the most imposing of all: the masses."[24] Radical fiction of the 1930s shared with turn-of-the-century naturalism the aim of dramatizing the unsmiling realities of capitalist modernity and the lives of the downtrodden, but whereas high naturalism was drawn to the grotesque, the realism of the Great Depression era tended toward the plainspoken.[25] To the degree that it subordinated style to matter, some critics argue that the proletarian novel could even be seen as an extension of naturalism (Madden, xxxii).

Despite the fact that Buck did not strictly qualify either as an author of proletarian literature or as a "fellow traveler" whose literary perspective was sympathetic to revolution, I suggest that her writing can be situated within the framework of 1930s realism, whose developments have been alternatively grouped under the categories of the radical novel, Great Depression literature, or even late naturalism.[26] Chinese peasants are not explicitly listed among the marginal groups famously celebrated by this literary mode—"the 'Bottom Dogs,' the adventures of young Irish delinquents, the 'Neon wilderness' of Chicago's North Side Poles, the Negro slum dwellers, the poor East Side Jews, Georgia's crackers, California fruit pickers, toilers on the Detroit assembly lines, Gastonia's textile workers, decaying Southern families, rebellious farmers, department-store wage slaves, or 'boxcar' hoboes" (Aaron, 152). Nevertheless, in supplying a biography to an unindividuated race—one whose cultural and social figuration had been closely interchangeable with the form of the mass itself—*The Good Earth* merits consideration in these terms. Its addition to the body of work identified with the 1930s, first, reinstates the Asian American into a major episode of American literary radicalism, and, second, expands the international contexts for what we know of the cultural politics of the Great Depression.

This chapter explores the textual emergence of Chinese characters in American popular culture at mid-century, a process that displaced the usual binary opposition between Oriental despot and Asiatic coolies. For this representational endeavor, the United States' geostrategic interest in Chinese national independence supplied a major condition. As we will see, the possibility of transforming the alien ineligible to citizenship into an American was in part an effect of the globalizing extension of American territory. The writings of leading cultural figures of the 1930s and 1940s—Buck's Depression-era fiction and wartime political advocacy, Edgar Snow's newsbreaking chronicles of the Chinese revolution, and Steinbeck's World War II California—will reveal the flexible uses of agrarian fiction, retooled in the service of globalization projects.

THE POLITICAL ECONOMY OF *THE GOOD EARTH*

The Good Earth begins with the marriage of Wang Lung, a Chinese peasant farmer, to O-lan, a woman he meets for the first time on his wedding day. Having been a kitchen servant in the Hwang household, a wealthy landowning family, O-lan proves to be a resourceful, industrious, and obedient wife, who bears Wang Lung two sons and a daughter. Through his diligence and his wife's, Wang Lung grows prosperous enough to increase his holdings, buying land from the decadent and spendthrift House of Hwang. Natural plenty, however, turns to scarcity when a long drought brings the family to the brink of starvation. Though they part with every other possession, they refuse to sell their land, and set off on a southward trek away from the famine-stricken area in search of an alternative livelihood. Their journey, aided by the miracle of railway transport, lands them in Kiangsu, which is full of the wonders and horrors of the big city.

Here for the first time, Wang Lung encounters Christian missionaries, Europeans, student nationalists, and Communists—all social types who symbolize ancient China's conjunctural meeting with Western modernity.[27] Wang Lung becomes a member of the lumpenproletariat, earning barely enough to feed his family by pulling a rented rickshaw everyday. The Wang family scrapes by in this manner, until one day the city's invasion by an unidentified troop of soldiers unleashes disorder, resulting in a mass ransacking of wealthy homes. Wang Lung and O-lan are swept up in the riotous crowd, and each comes away with stolen loot—Wang Lung with some gold pieces and O-lan with a pouch of precious jewels. With the gold, Wang Lung buys an ox and crop seed, enabling the family's return home. With O-lan's jewels, Wang Lung acquires more land from the Hwangs, hires farm help, and grows ever more wealthy. A set of twins, a son and daughter, is added to the household. For a time, all is well.

One year, excessive rains flood the fields, bringing farm work to a halt. As a result of prolonged idleness, Wang Lung turns to amusements offered by the nearby town, including visiting the local brothel, where he develops an obsession with a prostitute named Lotus. Lotus's feminine beauty and taste for luxury stand in sharp contrast to O-lan's plain style and habits. Wang Lung begins to spend lavishly on gifts for Lotus and on his own personal grooming. He neglects his farm and treats O-lan cruelly, making a gift of her only remaining jewels, a pair of pearls, to his new mistress. Asserting the customary privilege of a rich man, Wang Lung takes Lotus as his concubine and moves her into separate quarters newly added to his house. Wang Lung is also forced to provide for his uncle's unpleasant family after being threatened by his uncle with retribution from local bandits. The expansion of the household's numbers is followed by the disintegration of the family proper. One day Wang Lung discovers his eldest son secretly frequenting Lotus's quarters and angrily banishes him from home. O-lan dies of a long illness, and with her goes the last guarantee of the family's moral integrity.

Subsequent plot episodes revolve around Wang Lung's relationship to his children, for whom he has devised neatly diversified marriage and career plans. He arranges an eligible match for his second daughter, but must permanently care for the elder girl, whose mental development was arrested due to prolonged starvation during the famine. He sends his two older sons to school, with the intention of making the first a scholar and the second a merchant. For the third he provides no formal education because he wishes him to be a farmer, like himself. The first son has turned out to be idle and self-indulgent, and the third resists his father's plans, eventually running away to join the nationalist revolution. Only the second proves to be naturally suited to his assigned occupation and grows up to be a canny merchant. The Wangs move to town, assuming the residence of the former House of Hwang. There they conduct a life as decadent and internally divisive as that of their predecessors. In his dotage, Wang Lung falls in love with one of Lotus's young servants, Pear Blossom, and the two, along with his elder daughter, move back to the original country house. There Wang Lung is reunited with the soil he has always loved. The final scene of the novel bears melancholy witness to a conversation between the two elder sons concerning plans to sell off the land after their father's death, despite their promises to the contrary.

The Good Earth can be read as either the retelling of the Horatio Alger myth or a warning against the decadent potential of accumulation, though it is more usually remembered as a story of the former.[28] Stocked with internally unchanging characters who remain true to type, the novel gives the distinct effect of allegory, though what exactly it allegorizes is not so easy to say. Signs of hectic change intruding upon an eternal rural life, such as the "fire breathing" railroad and the commencement of international trade, suggest the novel's concern with matters of economic transition from feudalism, or the process of the peasants' detachment from the land.[29] The intergenerational conflict between peasant father and his merchant and nationalist sons lends itself to a reading of the clash between tradition and modernity. When exactly Chinese modernity began is a vexed question, however. Even when narrowly restricted to the level of official politics, the establishment of the modern nation-state was a protracted process, dominated by chaos and civil war for the better part of four decades from the 1911 establishment of Sun Yat-Sen's republican government to the eventual victory of the Communist Party in 1949. The social status of the Manchurian queue in *The Good Earth* helps to locate the story historically. In an early scene, Wang Lung is mocked by the village barber for his attachment to his queue, which marks him as out-of-date. Later in the story, after he has grown rich and vain, his new fashion consciousness dictates its removal. The sartorial clue provided by the anachronistic queue allows us to date the story to the post-dynastic republican era.

Yet the strong presence of cyclical narrative structures works against the story's historical placement. Wang Lung's travails and fortunes do not follow a linear progression. When forced off the land into wage slavery by natural disaster, his proletarianization turns out to be only temporary. His fantastic accumulation of wealth might be taken to symbolize the dissolution of feudalism's fixed social classes, except that the Wang family's reenactment of the Hwangs' earlier decline implies an eternal pattern. References to revolution (the presence of student demonstrations in Kiangsu, the political aspirations of his third son) allude to a broader background of stirring social change, but the events of Wang Lung's repeated rise and fall seem to occur outside history. One occasion presents the potential for Wang Lung to grasp himself as a member of a social class, but this is only momentary:

And then he thought of his land and he cried out passionately.

"Shall I never see it again! With all this labor and begging there is never enough to do more than feed us today." Then out of the dusk there answered him a voice, a deep burly voice,

> "You are not the only one. There are a hundred hundred like you in this city."
>
> . . . "Well, and is it forever?" asked Wang Lung bitterly.
>
> The man puffed at his pipe thrice and then spat upon the ground. Then he said,
>
> "No, and not forever. When the rich are too rich there are ways, and when the poor are too poor there are ways. . . ." (*GE* 119)

In representing class conflict as a matter of cyclical upheaval, the text reflects a conventional Western view of the Chinese past—prevalent at least until the 1960s shift in American sinology—as a series of dynastic cycles punctuated by peasant rebellion but involving no real structural transformation.[30] Buck's masses of disenfranchised workers, even as they engage in a discussion of resistance, are a disaggregated "swarm" that fails to congeal as a social formation (*GE* 122). Their political aspirations are narrowly restricted to substitutive fantasy. Ultimately, rather than identify with his class, Wang Lung separates himself from "this scum which clung to the walls of a rich man's house," maintaining the belief "that he was not truly one of them" (*GE* 123). The potential for this individuation is rooted in the fact that "[h]e owned land and his land was waiting for him" (*GE* 123), whereby differences between rich and poor are displaced by a dichotomy drawn between the city and the country.

As a space of freedom from class conflict or even class identity as such, Wang Lung's land bears a great deal more resemblance to the mythic American frontier than to any recognizable Chinese countryside, an infamous zone of social oppression at that time.[31] Wang Lung's agrarian identification revolves around a primary relationship to the land set apart from the web of social community. "At first and for a long time it seemed to Wang Lung that he wished to see no human being but only to be alone on his land" (*GE* 143). The land is metaphorically a maternal body that comforts, nurtures, and heals, a place where the farmer can rest "with the good warmth of his own land against flesh" (*GE* 145). O-lan's symbolic association with the land throughout the novel—her name being a homynym for "O Land"—elaborates its feminine associations.

The call of the land evokes a call of the wild that Wang Lung simply cannot resist answering. In a way reminiscent of Jack London's trials of masculinity, the land in *The Good Earth* affords renewal through strenuous physical activity. "Come, Ching, my friend—come—call the men—I go out to the land!" (*GE* 213). And yet unlike London's unexplored Klondike and ocean, Wang Lung's cultivated fields afford freedom from the social not through adventure but work. "He ate his evening rice all stained as he was with the earth and unwilling he washed himself even before he slept. And washing his body he laughed again, for he washed it now for no woman, and he laughed because he was free" (*GE* 215). Labor frees Wang Lung from enervating captivity to sexual desire. Wang Lung's moral superiority to other farmers (such as his uncle) and to other workers (the rest of the rickshaw pullers) lies in his compulsion to "bring forth harvests from the land!" (*GE* 124) beyond a level of practical necessity. The text's bourgeois moralization of work is reflected in the deceit and licentious dangers that arise from idleness.

Plot developments certainly preach the risks of converting land into liquid forms of property that can be easily spent or lost. The Hwang family meets its downfall by spending its land as "carelessly as water" (*GE* 154). Wang Lung's best instincts lie with treasuring "the feel of the soil under [his] feet, and the feel of the hoe hard in [his] hands" (*GE* 156–57). Though the drought may have compelled him to part with his last moveable possession, Wang Lung can still take comfort in the fact that "[t]hey cannot take the land away from me. The labor of my body and the fruit of the fields I have put into that which cannot be taken away. If I had the silver, they would have taken it" (*GE* 75). Excessive consumption is imagined as the loss of vital bodily fluids, as if spent silver were like "life blood draining from a wound" (*GE* 172). Wang Lung's purchase of Lotus, the realization of sexual "dreams . . . into flesh" (*GE* 176), substitutes the unhealthy possession of a woman's body for proper masculine self-possession. The sexualization of the evils of over-expenditure admonishes against the dangers of economic exchange, and suggests a textual attitude of romantic anticapitalism.

Yet from the outset Wang Lung already has one foot in the market: he owns his farm, sells his excess harvest to town folk, and uses the cash to pay for other necessities. The peasant's social aspiration that "he would be more than equal to these people in the foolish, great, wasteful house" (*GE* 37) reflects an economic principle of equivalence on which class mobility depends. Wang Lung would appear to reflect a precapitalist attachment to the land as "one's flesh and blood" (*GE* 37), but the land he desires more of works to expand his productive capacity. In pointed contrast to O-lan's hoarding, his acquisitive behavior functions as capital reinvestment. Wang Lung's perpetual longing for the land represents a romantic attachment to home *and* it functions as a mechanism of accumulation. In this sense, Wang Lung embodies the virtues of Jeffersonian agrarianism, which would have ownership without alienation. As we have seen in chapter 2, in the discussion of nineteenth-century Populist leader Ignatius Donnelly, agrarian critiques of monopoly capital distinguished good from evil on the basis of property size. *The Good Earth* reflects a similar perspective by idealizing Wang Lung the small farmer and condemning Wang Lung the absentee landlord, despite the fact that both are steeped in market relations.

Yet at another level the text is not blind to logical connections between small farming and big business. Nor does it illustrate the automatic rewards brought by hard work. Wang Lung's exceptional escape from the nightmare of wage slavery is actually enabled by theft, not thrift and diligence. The Wang family's city interlude marks the divide between two different kinds of social existence, the first as farmers who depend entirely on their own labor and the second as owners of an expanding business. Their class ascension occurs not as a linear process of building wage savings into seed capital, but as a mystified leap forward. As if to acknowledge the impossibility of emplotting upward mobility according to the ethics it preaches, the text resorts to an accidental plot device—a sudden riot—to enable Wang Lung's capital accumulation.[32] Moreover, though the text imagistically returns to the nurturing relation between soil and peasant, the drought dramatizes the impossibility of surviving on earth alone:

> The extreme gnawing in his stomach which he had at first was now past and he could stir up a little of the earth from a certain spot in one of his fields and give it to the children without desiring any of it for himself. This earth they had been eating in water for some days— goddess of mercy earth, it was called, because it had some slight nutritious quality in it, although in the end it could not sustain life. But made into a gruel it allayed the children's craving for some time and put something into their distended, empty bellies. (*GE* 84)

The nutritive failure of the "good earth" literally demonstrates the impossibility of an unmediated relation to the earth, a substance that cannot be directly consumed. The nature that is seemingly romanticized is one that must be socially supplemented.

The text celebrates the reciprocal image of human beings working within nature and nature transformed by human work. This idealized reciprocity proposes a balanced symmetry between what is given and what is received on both sides. Conversely, narrative crises are moments of economic imbalance. Excessive consumption is a predictable sin. More surprisingly, so is excessive production, since it is the generation of surplus that continually lands Wang Lung in trouble. An over-accumulation of energy, or silver—one of energy's currencies—marks moments of grave moral danger. "When the eldest son was gone, Wang Lung felt the house was purged of some surcharge of unrest and it was a relief to him" (*GE* 248). On the surface *The Good Earth* seems to speak from a simplified Lockean perspective, yet it anxiously anticipates the negative consequences of overproduction.[33] Since Wang Lung's increasing alienation from the land ironically results from his relentless drive to farm it, excess turns out to be the product of an internal systemic tendency. While explicitly extolling the virtue of productivity, the story of Wang Lung also considers the problem of systemic imbalances through natural metaphors of economic catastrophe: drought, flood, locusts.

It has been observed that *The Good Earth* resonated with Depression-era readers who could identify with the tale of hardship and struggle (Conn, "American Literary Culture," 111). I would further suggest that we read the novel within the framework of changing notions of conservationism, which as a result of the Depression, retreated from the gospel of efficiency.[34] The vision of Franklin D. Roosevelt's first secretary of agriculture, Henry Wallace, whose task it was to implement the New Deal's farm program, suggests the propagation of a sinological metaphor for 1930s agricultural remedy. As editor of the weekly *Wallaces' Farmer* (Des Moines, Iowa) before serving under Roosevelt, Wallace's concern with the problem of how to regulate the flow of commodities from farmer to consumer led him on three occasions to allude to "an ancient Chinese system" known as the "ever normal granary" in which the government purchased crop in times of surplus which it sold to the public in times of scarcity. "If . . . we had a really intelligent comprehension of agricultural statesmanship," Wallace wrote in 1926, "We would work out in this country a combination of the Chinese idea of an ever normal granary with a common sense handling of our surplus."[35] While the Agricultural Adjustment Act (AAA) that eventually gained passage in 1933 operated differently—seeking to bolster farm prices by subsidizing farmers for undertaking voluntary acreage reduction—Wallace's association of state intervention with Chinese-originated practices provides a further political context for the unlikely status of *The Good Earth* as an emblematic 1930s text of American agricultural crisis and remedy.[36] The AAA and *The Good Earth* both sought to achieve a harmonious balance between production and consumption.

On an overt level, Buck's novel does not, of course, prescribe state interventionism, nor for that matter does it record much of a state presence at all affecting a Chinese way of life. Indeed, compared to a tradition of sinological representations, *The Good Earth*'s unusualness lies precisely in its departure from state-oriented depictions of Oriental society. According to notions of Oriental society dating from the eighteenth century, the traditional Chinese agrarian system featured state centralization, through a repressive use of corvée labor, control of irrigation works, and the extraction of surplus.[37] Such ideas of the Orient as a state-dominated society persisted into the twentieth century with Karl Wittfogel's classic derivation of modern "totalitarianism" from the political economy of "Oriental despotism."[38] In *The Good Earth* the portrait of an essentially stateless China is disturbed only once, by a small anecdote about a corrupt tax collector and ill-maintained levees result-

ing in a flood disaster. As I have argued above, a primarily frontier representation of the Chinese countryside imparts an anticipatory nostalgia
for the primitive freedoms about to be sacrificed to civilization's incipient advance rather than a frustration with overcivilization. Yet what are
the racial implications of using American frontier tropes to dramatize
the ambivalence of modernization in a Chinese setting? Though *The
Good Earth* mourns the vanishing Chinese as a kind of noble savage,
Wang Lung's loss of innocence is ironically depicted as a process of increasing Orientalization, not Westernization.

Wang Lung's social rise shifts him from predominantly producing to
predominantly consuming, and to the addictive pleasures of a more culturally marked set of activities. The acquisition of wealth infuses Wang
Lung's world with increasing signs of Chineseness: silk garments,
polygamy and concubinage, opium (which Wang Lung gives to his uncle
and aunt), culinary delicacies, bonded female servants (or "slaves"), and
a generally increasing hierarchization of gender relations. In their early
peasant existence, Wang Lung and O-lan have a marriage that is, despite
its obvious inequalities, paradoxically more companionate, based as it is
upon a united passion for the land. An image of the two tilling the soil by
each other's side evokes some sense of partnership. In the course of events,
we are transported from the transcultural terrain of open wheat and rice
fields and placed within confining, ornate interiors.

Besides environmental differences, Wang Lung's class ascension is also
registered by a physiological transformation. Opening with a description
of the farmer as he prepares to take a bath, the novel shows us a body
that is robust, "dark," and "slender" (5). Later, as Wang Lung succumbs
to corruption, his skin turns "yellow as clay" (132). Buck's moral distinction between poor and rich folk is shaded in browns and yellows. In
contrast to the farmer's children, who "tumbled like brown puppies upon
his threshold" (146), Old Lady Hwang's skin is "stretched over her little
bones as smooth and as yellow as the gilt upon an idol" (16); yet another
rich lord in Kiangsu had "great yellow rolls of . . . flesh doubled over his
breasts and over his belly" (139). Accompanying the adoption of Orien-
tally marked customs, Wang Lung's epidermal re-coloration carries
racial, not just health, connotations.

Depicting the metamorphosis of the universal (American) farmer into
an Oriental lord, *The Good Earth* is ultimately less a celebration of upward mobility than a populist declamation against oligarchy. To this extent, it bears a resemblance to California land monopoly novels of the
post-frontier, in which modernization and Orientalization are so often
coupled together.[39] Yet unlike these, *The Good Earth* offers no comforting displacements, no promise of expelling alienation. Given the extent to
which the end of the American frontier was imaginatively cloaked in a

necessary yet terrifying Asiatic future, the 1930s production of the Chinese peasant as a newly nostalgic subject reflects an alternative articulation of the temporality of U.S.-Asian relations. In contrast to alien land law fiction, Buck's novel acknowledges the internal logic of alienation to possession, how liquidating effects can issue from ostensibly opposite desires. The setting of a frontier narrative in China indicates the potential for a different articulation of agrarianist ideology and the contradictions of globalization. If alien land law fiction narrates agricultural class struggle through stories of racial conflict in California, *The Good Earth* in a sense does the reverse, renegotiating U.S.-Asian relations—and Asiatic representation—through the story of agricultural class ascension in China.

John Lossing Buck and U.S. Agricultural Economics in China

The daughter of southern Presbyterian missionaries, Pearl Sydenstricker was born in 1892 in Hillsborough, West Virginia. From the age of three months until college, she was raised in Zhenjiang (Chinkiang), a city near Nanjing (Nanking) on the Yangtze River in a missionary community. Returning to China after graduation from Randolph-Macon Women's College in Lynchburg, Virginia, she married an agricultural economist named John Lossing Buck in 1917 and spent the next six years in Nanxhushou (Nanhsuchow) in northern Anhui (Anhwei) province, often accompanying her husband on field research trips into the countryside. Although John Buck was not an ordained clergyman, he had obtained a China posting through the Presbyterian Board of Foreign Missions two years earlier because of his training in the new field of rural economics, representing a new generation of American educational and scientific endeavor in the early republican period. The pro-Western outlook of many of the 1911 revolution's leaders, among whom were many Christian converts, coincided with a budding U.S. academic-government nexus of scientific expertise.

John Buck was an important participant in early-twentieth-century debates among American agricultural specialists on the relative merits of Chinese versus Western agriculture. In *Farmers of Forty Centuries* (1927), F. H. King idealized Asian farmers for conserving their natural resources for thousands of years and criticized Western farmers for wastefulness and overdependency on mechanization and artificial fertilizers. John Buck took the opposite view (Conn, *Cultural Biography*, 55–56). His scientific mission was twofold—to collect data on methods of Chinese agriculture, a subject as yet to be systematically analyzed, and to help improve them through the introduction of methods of Western efficiency. He experimented with varieties of wheat, barley, cotton, corn, and beans, in order to find a durable, fast maturing strain that would help farmers avoid losing harvests to flooding (Conn, *Cultural Biography*, 58). His research, published in *Chinese Farm Economy* (1930) and *Land Utilization in China* (1937), established him as one of the foremost American scholars in agricultural economics. Buck's books became standard texts on China's rural economy in U.S. universities, and in China they were used to train agricultural economists up through World War II. He headed the Department of Agricultural Economics at Nanking University for almost two decades, consulted for the International Famine Relief Commission, and advised the Nationalist government on Yangtze River disaster relief.[40]

The Good Earth was another product of the Bucks' fieldwork in the rural north and can be read as a rejoinder to John Buck's statistical analysis of Chinese farming. Although the 1920s witnessed the beginnings of professional U.S. diplomacy in China and the establishment of institutions in the United States for the study of Asia, until World War II American writing on China was in its so-called "amateur" phase, issuing from the pens of missionaries, diplomats, customs officials, and other representatives of an expanding network of U.S. cultural and scientific institutions there (Cohen, 2–7). The writing produced by the Bucks belongs to a moment before the clear distinction between official and popular knowledges about Asia was established under the imperatives of postwar U.S. superpower and thus can be seen as foreign policy documents of a sort.

"Far too high a proportion of his meager income goes into the necessities to maintain physical life," writes John Buck of the Chinese farmer, "Even with this his food is unvaried and lacking in the nutriment he needs, his clothing is of the cheapest sort, his home a bare protection from the weather and with little comfort or beauty."[41] Discovering a low standard of living among Chinese farmers, an extreme population density compared to the West, a limited availability of good arable soil not yet cultivated, and a scenery of drab farm houses, John Buck offers nothing to surprise a reader familiar with Arthur Smith's *Chinese Characteristics*.[42] However, though these Chinese attributes may sound familiar, Buck's work suggests a different approach to the problem of U.S.-Asian relations constituted by the disparity in standards of living:

> The great question arising from the Chinese type of land utilization is what adjustment can be made in relations between China, a country of low standards and cheap production and one of high standards and expensive production such as the United States. It has been stated that the peoples who produce most efficiently will inherit the earth. China's

rural economy is one of efficient use of land in that the large consumption of vegetable products requires less land to support a given population. For this reason costs are less per unit of food and China becomes a keen competitor, with other nations producing and consuming food less efficiently. Other nations may pursue a policy of isolation, preventing Chinese immigration and foregoing sales of their expensive products to the Chinese. Presumably this is what will continue to take place at least for a very long time to come. Eventually Chinese standards will rise somewhat. The high standard countries may even raise their standard by adopting the Chinese system of producing a large proportion of food energy from vegetable products.

Having tasted a high standard of living a country like the United States is not likely to permit it to be lowered by an undue increase of its own population or by permitting the influx of peoples of a much lower standard who would eventually take the land from those having the higher standard. China cannot hope to meet her population problem by emigration. She is faced with a large population in relation to resources and she must devise means of limiting the growth of that population growth along with other improvements if she is to raise her standard very greatly.[43]

This passage reveals the intersection of a question concerning the U.S. immigration border and the project of Western developmentalism in China. In a sense the problem in John Buck's *Land Utilization in China* is the same one that appears in the writings of nineteenth-century California trade unionists that worried about declining wages as a result of globalization processes in which "the peoples who produce most efficiently will inherit the earth." Here, however, a meatless Chinese diet is no longer the sign of a more efficient "human motor" powered by fewer calories, but rather a more efficient use of land, which can produce more and feed more.[44] The distinction between meat and vegetable production signifies differences between large acreages used for grazing cattle and small acreages that support intensive farming of vegetable crops. In John Buck's text, the differences between Americans and Chinese no longer center upon the body's economy. Rather, population size is what determines a national standard of living. John Buck is gloomy about the prospects of stemming international flows. Instead of trying to patrol U.S. immigration borders, he proposes raising Chinese living standards to those of the United States.

In fact, John Buck's research discovers Chinese farm operations to be relatively inefficient. A heavier reliance on human labor and a lower degree of capitalization and mechanization in China account for the fact that Chinese farm labor is twenty-five times less productive than American. Buck recommends consolidating China's myriad small farms into larger acreages because, in principle, "a person living on a large farm is economically much better off than one on a small farm" (*CFE* 110). Farming is best rationalized according to business principles since "[f]arming is a business in which profits are as essential as in any other" (*CFE* 38). Buck justifies his business approach to agrarian reform on the basis of findings that 93 percent of farmland is privately owned, and of this "[s]omewhat less than three-fourths of the farm land is owned by the farmer himself and over one-fourth is rented" (*LUC* 194). Insufficient productivity and low profitability—not high rates of tenancy, absentee landlordism, or rural inequality—are, in his view, China's key agricultural problems.[45]

Pearl S. Buck's experience in the field, as we know, lead her to a similar focus on the farm owner as the paradigmatic Chinese subject, though she believed there was little in traditional farming methods that required improving. Her own skepticism toward the panacea of productivity may help explain why it was, in the 1930s, that it was the novelistic product of their Anhui research that achieved wider cultural influence. What her husband judges to be an unenviable life of struggle, Pearl S. Buck celebrates as an authentic form of existence. The Chinese peasants, she writes, "were the ones who bore the brunt of life, who made the least money and did the most work. They were the most real, the closest to the earth, to birth and death, to laughter and weeping. To visit the farm families became my own search for reality, and among them I found the human being as he most nearly is."[46] Pearl S. Buck's universalization of Chinese peasant reality occurs in the context of contending forces over the future of rural China: the 1920s Christian rural movement, the expanding apparatus of Western scientific aid, and Chinese nationalism. Reacting against these various modernization projects, Buck hews to the cultural superiority of rural traditionalism. In an autobiography written twenty years after the literary birth of Wang Lung, Buck makes explicit her skeptical views on the benefits of Western technology, indulging in an unmistakable jab at her ex-husband's pursuit:

> I must confess that I had often wondered secretly what a young American could teach the Chinese farmers who had been farming for generations on the same land and by the most skillful use of fertilizers and irrigation were still able to produce extraordinary yields and this without modern machinery. Whole families lived in simple comfort upon farms averaging less than five acres and certainly I had known of no Western agriculture that could compete with this. (*MSW* 139)

Not only does *The Good Earth* idealize what modern agricultural economics would like to better rationalize, but its antimodernism extends to a wholesale rejection of the Western colonial enterprise, including its religious mission. In a 1932 *Harper's* article that outraged the missionary establishment, entitled "Is there a case for Foreign Missions?" Pearl S. Buck excoriated missionaries for their fundamental disrespect for Chinese culture (Conn, *Cultural Biography*, 148–49). An episode in *The Good Earth* in which a missionary proselytizes Wang Lung is intended to show the irrelevance and incomprehensibility of Christianity to peasant concerns. One day soon after his arrival in the big city, Wang Lung encounters a foreigner with "eyes as blue as ice and a hairy face"[47] who hands him a piece of paper. When he finally summons his courage to look at it,

he saw on the paper a picture of a man, white-skinned, who hung upon a crosspiece of wood. The man was without clothes except for a bit about his loins, and to all appearances he was dead, since his head drooped upon his shoulder and his eyes were closed above his bearded lips. Wang Lung looked at the pictured man with increasing interest. There were characters beneath, but of these he could make nothing.

He carried the picture home at night and showed it to the old man. But he also could not read and they discussed its possible meaning, Wang Lung and the old man and the two boys. The two boys cried out in delight and horror,

"And see the blood streaming out of his side!"

And the old man said,

"Surely this was a very evil man to be thus hung."

But Wang Lung was fearful of the picture and pondered as to why a foreigner had given it to him, whether or not some brother or this foreigner's had not been so treated and the other brethren seeking revenge. He avoided, therefore, the street on which he had met the man and after a few days, when the paper was forgotten, O-lan took it and sewed it into a shoe sole together with other bits of paper she picked up here and there to make the soles firm. (*GE* 125–26)

Seen through the untutored eyes of the Chinese peasant, the crucifixion image is grotesque, violent, and perverse. The novel's adoption of what critics have commonly observed to be a biblical style of narration might be considered part of an overall textual strategy to represent Christianity's irrelevance to a way of life already possessed of its own inner truth. *The Good Earth*'s cultural relativism reflects the contemporary pressure upon the missionary enterprise exerted by metropolitan intellectual developments in Boasian cultural anthropology and revolutionary circumstances in China.[48] *The Good Earth* was a participant in the debate on religious ethnocentrism taking place at the time between fundamentalists and liberals within the Christian missionary community. As a descendant of American Protestant missionary discourse, Buck's critique of religious colonialism traces a path from theological salvation to a secular American universalism.

Pearl S. Buck's infatuation with Chinese peasant self-sufficiency turns her into a leading critic of Western colonialism and, as Peter Conn remarks, an early advocate of universal racial equality.[49] However, Buck was also a critic of Chinese intellectuals who "not only knew nothing about their own country people, [but] did not even know how to talk with them or address them" (*MSW* 188). Her literary enterprise is thus informed by an even more audacious rivalry. On one level, Buck writes straightforwardly as an anti-intellectual populist, privileging personal experience over text-based learning, practical wisdom over scholasticism, country simplicity over urban cosmopolitanism.

On another level, if her populism placed her at odds with the interests of the Kuomintang (KMT) Nationalist elite, her romanticization of agrarian China clashed even more directly with the views of the Communist movement. In 1949 Buck received an invitation to visit the new People's Republic, which she did not accept. In 1972, during Nixon's rapprochement with China, she applied for a visa, but it was denied. Her 1934 departure from war-torn China turned out in the end to be a permanent one, in part because, in the unrevised judgment of the Chinese Communist Party (CCP), her writing had "for a long time taken an attitude of distortion, smear and villification toward the people of China and their leaders" (Helen Snow, 28). According to James Thomson, a China historian whose family was personally acquainted with the Bucks and lived next door in the same missionary compound, "[as] China's politics polarized in the 1940s, Pearl won the enmity of both the Chinese Nationalists—whose sleazily corrupt authoritarianism she detested—and the Chinese communists—whose totalitarian assault on Chinese family values she vigorously condemned" (Thomson, "Quest," 13). Buck's quarrels with the KMT and CCP are well established in many of her articles, and ultimately what is most interesting about them is the seriousness with which she competed with both parties' claims to represent the Chinese nation.

The genesis of *The Good Earth* can be traced to the ideological split in the Chinese Nationalist movement in 1927, when right-wing forces within the KMT, backed by American and British gunboats, purged the Nationalist Party of its Communist membership during the bloody suppression of the Shanghai and Nanking workers' uprising. The counterrevolution, fictionally chronicled in André Malraux's *La Condition Humaine* (1934), marks a watershed event in the history of the Chinese Communist Party.[50] After this event, the Chinese Communists went underground and, after repeated failures to organize the urban proletariat, into the countryside where, counter to Comintern instruction from the Soviet Union, they began working to develop a primary base among the rural peasantry. The Bucks were present in Nanking during the 1927 workers' uprising and, along with other foreign residents of the city, were forced to flee, returning only after Western gunboats and Chiang Kai-Shek's military purge had succeeded in reestablishing order. Pearl S. Buck's autobiography recounts how the experience of having to hide, while Communist workers marched on Western establishments in the city, led her to a pivotal moment of racial self-recognition:

> For the first time in my life I realized fully what I was, a white woman, and no matter how wide my sympathies with my adopted people, nothing could change the fact of my birth and ancestry. In a way, I suppose, I changed my world then and there, in that tiny dark hut. I could not escape what I was. (*MSW* 212)

All the writing that Buck produced—compulsive in its abundance and repetitiveness—can be read through the lens of exilic yearning, engendered by this original trauma of racial self-recognition.[51]

I propose that we consider *The Good Earth* to be a form of diasporic Chinese nationalism born of the counterrevolution of 1927. Through the vehicle of Chinese peasant virtue, Buck's intervention sought an alternative reconciliation of two contradictory developments: anticolonial Asian nationalism and U.S. global expansion. In its geographical location, Buck's imaginative enterprise jostled for space with the work of Chinese Communist organizers who had been forced into the countryside. This is why her relationship to Communism was far more fraught than her relationship to the KMT elite, whom she could dismiss as a bunch of clever young bureaucrats "who could speak English or French or German better than they spoke Chinese" (*MSW* 252).[52] Buck's ambivalence toward the rise of Chinese revolutionary nationalism which, on the one hand, she perceived as a logical response to Western domination, and on the other hand, occasioned her own exile, exemplified the United States' double wartime alliance with European colonialism and Asian nationalism (paradigmatically Indian and Chinese) at mid-century.

Critic Gianna Quach observes that notwithstanding her indictment of missionaries, Buck essentially installed "America" in place of a Christian God (97). Because of Buck's blindness to the necessary conditions of her own epistemological claims, Quach judges her writing to be a form of Western colonial discourse. If so, what interests me is that in this case the antithetical discourses of Western colonialism and Chinese nationalism over Chinese representation should have verged so closely upon each other.[53] At least since the circulation of the Open Door Notes in 1899, the United States had officially defined itself as the self-appointed guardian of

Chinese territorial integrity and a unique friend to China. Pearl S. Buck's writing was significant in enacting the turn taken by this "sentimental imperialism" under the pressure of Chinese civil war and competing colonialisms—Japanese and Western—in Asia.[54] To evaluate fully the politics of *The Good Earth*'s peasant nationalism, it will be useful to situate it next to another influential American text of the 1930s, Edgar Snow's *Red Star over China* (1938), which is considered by many to be the "classic account of the birth of Chinese Communism."

TWO CHINESE PEASANTS: MAO TSE-TUNG AND WANG LUNG

Arriving in Shanghai in 1928 from Kansas, Edgar Snow worked as a China correspondent for thirteen years, assisting the editor of the English-language *China Weekly Review*, writing a regular column for the *New York Sun*, and eventually becoming the *London Daily Herald*'s special correspondent. In 1936 Snow became the first Western journalist to enter a Communist-controlled area and gain access to the party leadership. The book that documented his findings, *Red Star over China*, exercised unrivaled influence over the thinking and reporting on the Chinese Communist movement for the next decade. Harold Isaacs found that it was second only to *The Good Earth* as a source of American impressions of the Chinese.[55] Translated into half a dozen languages, *Red Star* was additionally remarkable for its impact on Chinese youths themselves, many of whom, because of KMT censorship, learned about the CCP's programs for the first time from Snow's writings.[56] In the American colony of the Philippines, the Anti-Japanese People's Army, or Huk guerilla movement, which flourished in parts of central and southern Luzon after March of 1942, used *Red Star* as one of its first training manuals, since the American description of Maoism was easier to obtain at the time than Chinese ones.[57] An admixture of travel notes, interviews, and biographies of members of the Red Army, including the first published biography of Mao himself, *Red Star* served as a way for Chinese Communists to finally speak to the outside world after having completed the Long March from southwest China to the remote sanctuary of Yenan in the northwest. From 1928 until Snow's newspaper reports began appearing in the mid-1930s, little of the Chinese Communist movement was known to Western observers. Many people even doubted that the Red Army had survived the Nationalist scorched-earth campaigns in Kiangsi. Snow's writing played an instrumental role in dispelling the notion of the Communists as bandits and in building Mao's persona and prestige in China, the rest of Asia, and the West. China historian John Fairbank goes so far as to say that had it not been for *Red Star over China*, the Chinese revolution might not have been victorious.[58]

Red Star's eyewitness account of a China as yet unseen by the West promises to verify the existence of a subject shrouded in mystery, in this case Chinese Communists. Snow's investigative reporting unveils before Western eyes a peasant who turns out to be wonderfully "direct, frank, simple, undevious . . . ,"[59] not unlike the appealing protagonist of *The Good Earth*. But Snow's Chinese peasant is the main actor of quite a different drama. Among the many mini-biographies of Red Army officers contained in *Red Star*, Snow's interview with Mao in a section entitled "Genesis of a Communist" is exemplary. In the story of his childhood, presented in the form of first-person narration, the Communist leader recounts the background of his father, a poor peasant who served as a conscripted soldier for some years and then "by saving carefully and gathering together a little money through small trading and other enterprise" managed to buy back his land and return to his home village in Hunan province. Over the course of time, Mao's family rose to become "middle peasants," and through savings garnered from annual crop surplus, accumulated a little capital and attained the status of rich peasants. "After he became a 'rich' peasant, he devoted most of his time to that business. He hired a full-time laborer, and put his children to work on the farm, as well as his wife" (*RSOC* 130–31). Mao describes a family configuration in which his father was the "Ruling Power" and the "Opposition was made up of myself, my mother, my brother, and sometimes even the laborer." His mother preferred a "policy of indirect attack," but Mao's conflicts with his father taught him that he could defend his rights only by open rebellion (*RSOC* 132–33).

Disgusted with farmwork, Mao later ran away from home to continue his studies, taking up law and classics. When a mass peasant uprising in the city of Changsha, prompted by famine, was harshly repressed by authorities, Mao identified with the rebels because they "were ordinary people like my own family" (*RSOC* 135). During another food shortage the following year, one of his father's rice consignments was seized by the poor. Though he was unsympathetic to his father's wrath, Mao was also ambivalent about the villagers' methods. From his reading of Chinese classical literature and old romances, Mao observed that "there was one thing peculiar about such stories, and that was the absence of peasants who tilled the land . . . I found that they all glorified men of arms, rulers of the people, who did not have to work the land, because they owned and controlled it and evidently made the peasants work it for them" (*RSOC* 134). Later Mao moved to the provincial Szechuan capital of Changsha, where he enrolled in a series of vocational schools, switching from one to the next as he became bored with a given subject's narrowness. His experiences in Changsha included police school, an apprenticeship in soap making, and a course of study at a commercial school, the last of which most pleased his father who "readily appreciated the advantages of commercial cleverness" (*RSOC* 143). In the excitement of the 1911 revolution, he joined the regular army, where he became acquainted with socialism. Later he formed a study group called the New People's Study Society, whose members were to become famous heroes in the history of the Chinese revolution.

"The Autobiography of Mao Tse-Tung, As Told to Edgar Snow" first appeared in serial form from July to October 1937 in *Asia* magazine, a periodical published by Pearl S. Buck's second husband, Richard Walsh. From Snow, Americans learned the life story of the man who would eventually become China's most famous peasant.[60] At the time, however, the Chinese peasant with the greatest American household recognition was Wang Lung; sales of *The Good Earth* exceeded *Red Star* by a factor of fifty (Hunt, 56–57). Although the novel had understandably superior mass appeal, the narrative structure of the two texts share certain similarities. Like *The Good Earth*, Snow's "autobiography" lends itself to an Oedipal interpretation of Mao's radicalization, rooting national politics in family romance. "The Autobiography of Mao Tse-Tung" might well be the story of Wang Lung's third son, the one who is intended for farmwork but who leaves to join a revolution his father cannot understand. In both texts, sexual rivalry between father and son provides a central idiom for political rebellion. Snow's partisan chronicle of the Chinese Communist movement and Buck's agrarianist novel could hardly be more ideologically antagonistic, but I suggest that we read these two popular narratives of Chinese peasant lives as parallel engagements with the question of how to represent the Chinese subaltern in the context of a growing but unfocused U.S. stake in Asian nationalism. In presenting an opportunity for Chinese peasants to speak for themselves—one by direct quotation of a first-person testimony and the other through the omniscient powers of fiction—Snow and Buck provide readers with unusual access to an uncorrupted alterity, one that is paradoxically dependent upon the privilege of their translation services. Neither the literary fame of Wang Lung nor the international stature of Mao can be detached from U.S. concerns with geopolitical management.

The Communist movement appears directly in *The Good Earth* on one occasion. This episode, like the scene involving the missionary encounter, confronts Wang Lung with another image he fails to properly understand:

But the next time one handed a paper freely to Wang Lung it was a man of the city, a young man well clothed, who talked loudly as he distributed sheets hither and thither among the crowds who swarm about anything new and strange in the street. This paper bore also a picture of blood and death, but the man who died this time was not white-skinned and hairy but a man like Wang Lung himself, a common fellow, yellow and slight and black of hair and eye and clothed in ragged blue garments. Upon the dead figure a great fat one stood and stabbed the dead figure again and again with a long knife he held. It was a piteous sight and Wang Lung stared at it and longed to make something of the letters underneath. He turned to the man beside him and he said,

"Do you know a character or two so that you may tell me the meaning of this dreadful thing?"

And the man said,

"Be still and listen to the young teacher; he tells us all."

"The dead man is yourselves," proclaimed the young teacher, "and the murderous one who stabs you when you are dead and do not know it are the rich and the capitalists, who would stab you even after you are dead. You are poor and downtrodden and it is because the rich seize everything."

Now that he was poor Wang Lung knew full well but he had heretofore blamed it on a heaven that would not rain in its season, or having rained, would continue to rain as though rain were an evil habit. When there was rain and sun in proportion so that the seed would sprout in the land and the stalk bear grain, he did not consider himself poor. Therefore he listened in interest to hear further what the rich men had to do with this thing, that heaven would not rain in its season. And at last when the young man had talked on and on but had said nothing of this matter where Wang Lung's interest lay, Wang Lung grew bold and asked,

"Sir, is there any way whereby the rich who oppress us can make it rain so that I can work on the land?"

At this the young man turned on him with scorn and replied,

"Now how ignorant you are, you who still wear your hair in a long tail! No one can make it rain when it will not, but what has this to do with us? If the rich would share with us what they have, rain or not would matter none, because we would all have money and food."

A great shout went up from those who listened, but Wang Lung turned away unsatisfied. Yes, but there was the land. Money and food are eaten and gone, and if there is not sun and rain in proportion, there is again hunger. Nevertheless, he took willingly the papers the young man gave him, because he remembered that O-lan had never enough paper for the shoe soles, and so he gave them to her when he went home. (126–28)

In the novel, each run-in with a proselytizing agent begins with an unreadable image of violence on paper and ends with the paper's insertion into peasant shoes. The peasant's formulaic response makes a pointed comment on the irrelevance of Western modes of deliverance—religious or political—to his actual, daily predicament. Wang Lung operates on a practical, individualist level because "war was a thing like earth and sky and water and why it was no one knew but only that it was" (*GE* 322).

Wang Lung's intuitive naturalization of historical forces suggests more than a stereotypic peasant lack of social consciousness. From the founding of the Chinese Communist Party in 1921 until the publication of Edgar Snow's investigative reporting, academic and journalistic debates about China's revolutionary ripeness often substituted cultural generalization for historical discussion. Although a few Western experts, such as Columbia's Paul Monroe and University of Chicago's Harley Farnsworth, considered a peasant brand of Marxism a genuine possibility, for the most part American writers assumed the exoticism of communism to China.[61] Henry Kittredge Norton deemed it highly improbable that communism would take root in the "unsympathetic soil of China." Nathaniel Peffer, a China specialist at Columbia, wrote that Chinese communism is an "exotic growth, brought in from the outside, from a different soil and climate, and thrust in barely under the surface." Grover Clark, the editor of the Peking *Leader*, concurred that China offers "only a very stony ground" for Bolshevism, and that Marxism is fundamentally antithetical to Chinese traits of property consciousness, individualism and family solidarity.[62]

Throughout the 1930s Chinese scholars were themselves debating the question of the origins of capitalism in Chinese history and the problem of conceptualizing China as an "Asiatic Society." The official view of Chinese Communist historians in the postrevolutionary era held that China in the late imperial period, prior to Western intrusion, was developing autonomously toward a capitalist system. This view, legitimized by Mao in his 1939 essay, "The Chinese Communist Revolution and the Chinese Communist Party," argued that "[t]he development of commodity economy in Chinese feudal society had already given birth to the *sprouts of capitalism*; had it not been for the influence of foreign capitalism, China would have developed slowly into a capitalist society."[63] Chinese debates were paralleled by Soviet controversies stirred by Trotsky's challenge to Stalin's unilinear, stagist concept of history with his theory of the "laws of uneven and combined development." Trotsky argued for a view of the Russian state as having developed under "semi-Asiatic conditions," with czarism representing "an intermediate form between European absolutism and Asian despotism, being, possibly closer to the latter of the two."[64] Though these discussions were transpiring in different linguistic universes, their simultaneity indicates the extent to which the prospect of revolution in a neocolonial agrarian society posits the necessary question of historical transition, with the rhetoric of organicity symptomatizing the desire for nationally autonomous historical development.

Edgar Snow's writing is an important document in the archive of international Marxist debates about "permanent revolution" in the semiperiphery, and it illustrates the presence of a significant American contribution to this debate. The strange occurrence in which a Maoist variant of revolutionary Marxism came to be first internationalized through an American journalistic text reflects American mediation of the divergences between Soviet and Chinese communism. Snow's sympathetic account of the Chinese Communists—particularly that he presents them as a politically autonomous movement more capable than their rivals of providing national leadership—was not welcome to the Comintern, whose call for the Chinese Communists to follow the KMT leadership both before and after the 1927 disaster turned out to be wrongheaded and, perhaps worse, irrelevant. For this reason, American Communist Party organs were among the few venues where *Red Star* was negatively reviewed (Shewmaker, 57).

Red Star's key intervention lay with refuting the general perception among Western observers that communism was a foreign transplant to China. In his preface to Mao's "autobiography," Snow explains, "I realized that this was not only [Mao's] story but an explanation of how communism grew—a variety of it real and indigenous to China—and why it had won the adherence and support of thousands of young men and women" (*RSOC* 125). True to this prospectus, the mini-biographies that follow—of P'eng Teh Huai, Hsu Hai-Tung, Chu-Teh, and many others—essentially reiterate that story, of the authentic peasant and proletarian origins of the generals, officers, and committed members of the Red Army. In spite of his many intellectual and political accomplishments, to the end Mao communicates the "simplicity and naturalness of the Chinese peasant, with a lively sense of humor and a love of rustic laughter" (*RSOC* 92–93). Like Wang Lung, who despite his rising fortune remains a peasant at heart, Mao "was plain-speaking and plain living, and some people might have considered him rather coarse and vulgar" (*RSOC* 92–93).

Red Star seeks to establish the absolute identity of the peasant masses and the organized Red Army. Communists are revealed to be "direct, frank, simple, undevious" peasants who just happen to also be "scientific minded" (*RSOC* 355). The Red Army's continued immersion in peasant culture explains its lack of ritual pomp and hierarchy. Even the highest officers live like the rank and file, including Mao, who "after hundreds of confiscations of property of landlords, officials, and tax collectors . . . owned only his blankets and a few personal belongings . . ." (*RSOC* 93). Pedagogic themes abound in the examples of the Red Army's cultural work among peasants through the use of political theater, whose goals include the spread of literacy and social awareness, and the end to foot binding, infanticide, child slavery, prostitution, polygamy, opium consumption, and official corruption. In fact, in his travels throughout the communist-held areas, Snow claims to find no trace of the "feudal" practices and vices we see in *The Good Earth*.[65]

Snow's observation of how the Red Army makes "men" out of peasant masses serves the important political function of testifying to Communist praxis and also the important textual function of demystifying his politically exotic subject. The purpose of his reportage is to answer basic questions such as, "How did the Reds dress? Eat? Play? Love? Work?" (*RSOC* 37). The author's presence as a character interacting with other characters in the story bears eyewitness to the ordinary daily activities that prove that they "ate and lived like men" (*RSOC* 324). And yet, as epic heroes capable of superhuman feats of courage and strength, *Red Star*'s characters no more resemble real human individuals than do *The Good Earth*'s fixed social types. Snow's adventurous journey to "Red China" for quasi-mythical creatures at times takes on the air of a quest romance. Before the gaze of the political tourist, the landscape carries the hint of exotic promise. After a couple days of suspenseful but uneventful travel, Snow sets eyes for the first time on a man dressed in the uniform of the Red Army:

> [W]e reached a lovely pool of still water set in a natural basin hollowed from great rocks, and there I saw my first Red warrior.
>
> He was alone except for a white pony which stood grazing beside the stream, wearing a vivid silky-blue saddle-blanket with a yellow star on it. (*RSOC* 65)

Seen through Snow's eyes, the Red cadre looks startlingly like a different kind of "Red"—the sort transplanted from an American Western. From this sighting onward, the future projected by the Chinese soviet is tinged with yearning for America's frontier past. Fairbank's introduction to *Red Star* draws pointed attention to Snow's pioneer origins, noting that he was "born in Kansas City in 1905, his forebears having moved westward by degrees from North Carolina to Kentucky and then into Kansas territory."[66] When Snow heads off to China in 1928 his journey seems but a logical extension of an American historical process of "westering." Snow takes an immediate liking to China's remote Northwest, and by the end of his adventure this Kansan has no trouble convincing us that having to leave Red China feels to him like leaving home (*RSOC* 368).

Even the directional symbolism of Chinese geography seems uncannily familiar, with urbanized zones lying to the east, and the west representing a remote border region populated by minority tribes. The Communist movement's recruits trek from east to west in search of a legendary utopia. Many seek refuge from Old World persecution. The industrial projects Snow visits have a friendly rustic quality. Living conditions may be harsh, but compared to "Shanghai factories where little boy and girl slave workers sat or stood at their tasks twelve or thirteen hours a day," Snow writes, "here seemed to be a life at least of good health, exercise, clean mountain air, freedom, dignity, and hope, in which there was room for growth" (*RSOC* 252). Snow assures his readers that the Chinese Communists' political program does not include communalizing land ownership (*RSOC* 224), but rather descends from the original "promise of Dr. Sun Yat Sen: 'Land to those who till it'" (*RSOC* 220). "Chinese communism as I found it in the Northwest," Snow writes, "might more accurately be called rural equalitarianism than anything Marx would have found acceptable as a model child of his own" (*RSOC* 219).

In the years following the Second World War, the McCarthyist witch-hunt of American "China hands" came to center on the contention that U.S. foreign policy in China had been subverted from within, through the propagation of the myth that the Chinese Communists were in fact harmless agrarian democrats. In truth, anyone who had expressed criticisms of the KMT's conduct of the war, and reservations about U.S. support for Chiang Kai-Shek, fell prey to accusations of subversion, fueled by a powerful China Lobby in Washington, which included such prominent individuals as U.S. Congressman Walter Judd and Time-Life publisher Henry Luce.[67] The postwar charges of a State Department conspiracy centered on a period in 1943–1944 when U.S. officials, dismayed by the paralysis of Chiang's government, began to entertain a strategic relationship with the Communists. The Communists were reported to be aggressively engaged in guerrilla warfare against the Japanese and were, moreover, established in north China, a region considered crucial for the final defeat of Japan. Two government delegations, consisting of representatives from the air corps, medical corps, signal corps, and infantry, visited Yenan in 1943 with the express purpose of evaluating Communist potential for military collaboration. Among the advocates of American aid to the Communists was General Joseph Stillwell, commander of the China-Burma-India theater of operations, whose running conflicts with Chiang eventually resulted in his removal from the post.[68] After the war, as the needs and desires of the Republican Party and the China Lobby began to converge, and the failure of U.S. foreign policy in China became unmistakable to all, the thesis began to take hold that China had been "lost" to the Communists because of a left-wing conspiracy of State Department officials and China specialists. Almost every intellectual in both the government and private sector with policy expertise on China came under investigation by the House Un-American Activities Committee (HUAC), and in many cases their careers, and the institutions that supported them, were destroyed.[69]

Because of the tragic stakes involved, the question of who was ultimately responsible for originating the so-called "agrarian reformer thesis" about the Chinese Communists has long been a matter of scholarly preoccupation.[70] The very difficulty of pinpointing the notion's original source, however, testifies to its pervasiveness as a World War II discourse. Observing the "striking uniformity" of the impressions of Chinese Communism that appeared in Western literature between 1937 and 1945, one historian writes that "[t]here is . . . practically no record of any Western visitor to red China [in that period] who came away disenchanted or hostile" (Shewmaker, 184, 269). Journalists such as James Bertram described Yenan as the "nearest thing to a complete democracy in China." Evans Carlson, a U.S. marine who was the first outside military observer to scrutinize the operations of the Red Army, thought that the Communist system approximated a "pure democracy" associated with Christian ethics.[71] Signaling an interest in broadening the U.S. military alliance to make use of the demonstrably more effective mobilizers of anti-Japanese popular resistance in 1943–1944, Franklin Roosevelt himself referred to the Yenan leaders as the "so-called Communists."[72]

No doubt the joint specter of German fascism and Japanese militarism provided the necessary conditions for a Popular Front alliance between— or, some would say, a confusion of[73]—capitalist democracy and revolutionary communism, one of whose discursive effects was this agrarian reformer thesis. In the figural convergence of Chinese Communists and American pioneers, Edgar Snow's and Pearl S. Buck's rewriting of the Chinese countryside played a large part. The implications of this frontier representation of China for U.S. global leadership as well as domestic race relations underscore the Americanizing import of such 1930s agrarian fictions.

THE WAR AGAINST RACISM AND THE SINO-JAPANESE FRONT

Until the end of the Vietnam War, the post–World War II period witnessed almost uninterrupted U.S. military involvement in Asian national politics.[74] By contrast, it is a commonplace of historical scholarship on

Depression-era U.S. foreign policy, defined by the Stimson doctrine of nonrecognition in response to the Japanese invasion of Manchuria in 1931, that international politics in general, and East Asia in particular, were a matter of little public interest in that decade.[75] Yet indirectly, 1930s culture may have helped pave the way for the nation's preparedness for overseas military engagement. A powerful intersection between the representation of Chinese national emergence in the post-dynastic era and the culture of the Depression allowed an investment in the Asian peasant to take hold. California agriculture, where an industrial exploitation found convenient figuration in an Orientalized despotism and indentured servitude, seemed to yield a mirror image of the Chinese countryside, now oddly peopled with independent farmers. In the world turned upside down of the 1930s, the Orient and the American frontier appeared to have switched places.

Snow's adventures with utopian cooperative experiments and Buck's miraculous tale of a farmer's capital accumulation presented satisfying escape from insurmountable agricultural failure. Successful back-to-the-land narratives, *The Good Earth* and *Red Star over China* addressed the anxieties of a period characterized by mass rural displacement with no prospect of urban absorption. The 1937 MGM film adaptation of *The Good Earth* reveals the refraction of the Chinese setting through the lens of domestic concerns by enlarging, visually and diegetically, the passages that describe the Wang family's southward trek. Spectacular scenes of mass rural migration are among the film's most visually memorable segments. The film also ends happily with father and elder son resolving their differences in a coordinated effort to protect their crop from a plague of locusts, in essence emphasizing the book's themes of natural disaster and eliminating altogether the story of Wang Lung's moral degeneration. If the film adaptation may be taken as one indicator of the book's dominant American interpretation, the emphasis on rural displacement and homecoming reflects the compelling fantasy of returning to the land. As for *Red Star over China,* Snow's story of the Long March in particular caught the attention of nearly every reviewer and was singled out as one of the great adventure tales of the twentieth century (Shewmaker, 60). The Red Army's determined trek to Yenan offered a thrilling counter-epic to the troubling phenomenon of mass migration in the 1930s, whose westward movement only reiterated once again the absence of a continental American frontier.[76]

While the Soviet Union in the 1920s and the embattled Spanish Republic in the '30s were well-known destinations for "political pilgrims" fleeing a Western civilization they felt to be in moral or economic crisis and decline, the importance of China as a site of leftist intellectual tourism has received somewhat less notice. After Franco's victory, the anti-Japanese front in China to some extent succeeded Civil War Spain as a leading geographic icon of the Popular Front. In the first ten months of 1938, Hangzhou (Hankow), the new capital of the refugee Nationalist government, attracted journalists, diplomats, artists, and political radicals. Veterans of the Spanish Civil War such as the Canadian doctor Norman Bethune visited, as did leaders of the U.S. Communist movement like Earl Browder and Mike Gold, filmmakers Joris Ivens and Frank Capra, and writers Agnes Smedley, Anna Louise Strong, W. H. Auden, Christopher Isherwood, and Ernest Hemingway.[77] The antifascist front in Spain, as a result of the war's political betrayals, had the primary effect of crystallizing an anti-Stalinist left. Antifascist resistance to Japan's "Greater East Asian Co-Prosperity Sphere" had the effect of broadening support for the end of colonialism.[78] Insofar as China was both a semi-colonial territory and a major ally during World War II, it occasioned an American articulation of anti-imperialism. It is in this context that Buck's liberal management of Asian nationalism can best be appreciated.

Pearl S. Buck's *The Good Earth* and John Lossing Buck's *Chinese Farm Economy* both depict a rural China absent of landlordism, excessive taxation, or perpetual landlessness. In the case of the agricultural economic text, the elision of class exploitation and comprador capitalism was plainly flattering to the project of Western development. Since Pearl S. Buck rebukes the Western advisor and diminishes his relevance, the place of the West in her fictional universe is far more discrete. At one point, however, Buck stages an encounter between her protagonist and her surrogate self:

It was only one day when he was on the street of the silk markets looking for a passenger that he learned better than he had known, that there were those who were more foreign than he in this city. He happened on this day to pass by the door of a shop from whence ladies sometime came after the purchasing of silks within, and sometimes thus he secured one who paid him better than most. And on this day someone did come out on him suddenly, a creature the like of whom he had never seen before. He had no idea of whether it was male or female, but it was tall and dressed in a straight black robe of some rough harsh material and there was the skin of a dead animal wrapped about its neck. As he passed, the person, whether male or female, motioned to him sharply to lower the shafts and he did so, and when he stood erect again, dazed at what had befallen him, the person in broken accents directed that he was to go to the Street of Bridges. He began to run hurriedly, scarcely knowing what he did, and once he called to another puller whom he knew casually in the day's work,

"Look at this—what is this I pull?"

And the man shouted back at him,

"A foreigner—a female from America—you are rich—"

But Wang Lung ran as fast as he could for fear of the strange creature behind him, and when he reached the Street of Bridges he was exhausted and dripping with his sweat.

This female stepped out then and said in the same broken accents, "You need not have run yourself to death," and left him with two silver pieces in his palm, which was double the usual fare.

Then Wang Lung knew that this was indeed a foreigner and more foreign yet than he in this city, and that after all people of black hair and black eyes are one sort and people of light hair and light eyes of another sort, and he was no longer after that wholly foreign in the city. (*GE* 108–9)

The above occasion witnesses the only appearance of a white woman in the text. The fur stole, the shopping for silks, the ignorance of local prices, and the flawed language skills all point to the kind of foreigner who would have been the antithesis of the woman who had rejected "the narrow and conventional life of the white man in Asia" and who had "lived with the Chinese people and spoke their tongue before . . . [her] own" (*MSW* 19). This scene in *The Good Earth*, in which the peasant arrives at racial self-recognition through an encounter with a white person, alludes to and inverts Buck's autobiographical narrative of her own racial awakening, discussed earlier.[79] The severity of the self-caricature registers the uncomfortable, contradictory location of the "West" in this American-authored text. In a sense, the obtrusive woman-in-fur signals a reluctant acknowledgment of the impossibility of excluding the West entirely from China.

A linguistic misunderstanding between Wang Lung and his third son toward the end of *The Good Earth* ostensibly allegorizes the imperviousness of the classic peasant to political or social forms of identification. The son informs his father: "There is to be a war such as we have not heard of—there is to be a revolution and fighting and war such as never was, and our land is to be free!" To this Wang Lung replies, perplexed: "Our land is free already—all our good land is free. I rent it to whom I will and it brings me silver and good grains and you eat and are clothed and are fed with it, and I do not know what freedom you desire more than you have" (*GE* 245). The intergenerational misunderstanding counterposes a nationalist meaning of freedom to what the peasant comprehends by the same word. When Wang Lung says that their land is free already because it generates rent income and profit, he voices the peasant's petit bourgeois ideology of freedom in its economic sense. While the son's use of "our land" invokes the notion of national liberation, Wang Lung can only understand it in terms of private property ownership. Weighing

the land's variable meanings, *The Good Earth* proposes to separate political and economic notions of independence.

With the onset of the Sino-Japanese War in 1937 and particularly after
U.S. entry into World War II, the idea of independence in Buck's articles
and speeches undergoes a shift in meaning. During the late 1930s and
early 1940s, Buck served as a prominent advocate of U.S. intervention on
China's behalf, producing hundreds of magazine articles and speeches for
governmental and citizen organizations. In "What Are We Fighting for in
the Orient?" (1943), Buck writes, "To defeat the Axis . . . is to defeat the
sort of tyranny which would forbid the growth of independence anywhere. When we make the defeat of the Axis our war aim, we are then
fighting a war of independence on a scale hitherto unknown. We like to
think that our victory would establish independence in the world."[80]
Buck's essay seeks to establish the basis for a natural alliance between the
United States and Russia, India, and China, even though these are poor
countries from which the American standard of living is as remote "as a
millionaire's is from a farmer's" (WWFO 12). Buck's invocation of dis-
parities in standards of living in this context may strike us as off the point
unless we recall the importance of the idea to the advocacy of borders between the United States and Asia historically. In the discourses of Asian
exclusion, the idea that "We must protect the American standards of living from the Orientals who live on three cents of rice a day"[81] has repeatedly been at odds with the dream of "freedom of the seas."[82] As Buck
recounts, "China was only potentially a good customer, for because of
her size, her self-sufficiency, and her low standard of living, our trade
with her never became what we hoped it would . . . It seems that trade is
only at its best between peoples whose standards of living are more
nearly equal" (WWFO 12). Although Chinese self-sufficiency may once
have been a contributing factor to the difficulties of global integration,
under the changed circumstances of the Second World War it constitutes
the very thing on which a U.S.-China alliance depends. In *The Good
Earth*, the attachment to the land (as either soil or private property) pre-
cludes nationalist identity. To join the revolution Wang Lung's son must
leave home. Yet in the context of the Sino-Japanese War, the peasant's
same stubborn inertia is presented as an act of nationalist resistance:
"[China] has had such bitter experience with Japan that nothing will
keep her from the determination to drive Japan from her soil" (WWFO
13). And again, "we may count on China until Japan is driven off her
soil" (WWFO 14).

With the inscription of the Sino-Japanese War into the wider global
conflict of the Second World War, Chinese nationalist struggle takes on
universal significance. "For such Chinese," Buck writes, referring to a
proud acquaintance, "it is not enough merely to win a military victory—

they want to establish freedom as a human principle in the world" (WWFO 14). Having come a long way from the pragmatic peasant concerned chiefly with papering the soles of his shoes, Buck's Chinese now cherishes the lofty aim of doing "away with such men [militarists], driving them first from their soil and then from the world" (WWFO 15). Subtending the tension between private possession and nationalism, peasant soil-attachment provides a flexible vehicle for the paradoxical linking of opposites: Chinese isolationism and the making of world history, pragmatism and idealism, the concrete and the abstract. Establishing a continuity between Chinese soil and "the world," the "good earth" takes on new, planetary dimensions. Buck begins the article by attributing historically restricted international ties to the existence of economic disparity and ends by concluding that political commonality now requires the flow of free trade. "Besides, freedom on the seas is a good thing for those who also have freedom on land" (WWFO 12–13). In her slippery use of the word "freedom" in wartime to mean, interchangeably, the free market, national self-determination, and democracy, Buck's literary corpus over the years traced a trajectory from idealizing agrarian independence to sloganeering for global capitalism.[83]

The identity between Chinese peasant and American pioneer enabled Wang Lung, in the American cultural imaginary, to be refigured as a stalwart freedom fighter. *The Good Earth* provided the key cultural resource for World War II's military alliance between the United States and China. The wave of antiforeignism in 1926–28 sweeping the Nationalist government to power had interrupted the ninety-three year effort of American missionaries. In 1925 there were 8,300 Protestant missionaries at work in China, more than 5,000 of whom were Americans; after 1927 the total number of Americans, excluding government officials and businessmen, never rose above 3,000, as the ripples of antiforeignism, rising criticism of missions at home, Sino-Japanese hostilities, and heavy depression cutbacks combined to reduce the number of private citizens working in China.[84] As the number of missionaries declined and the prospects for Christian conversion grew dim, the literary invention of a Chinese peasant, one who was unconvinced of anyone else's superiority but already assimilated to American ways, grew ever more instrumental. Enjoying multiple lives, Buck's peasant fiction names not one text but several. Buck's Sino-Japanese wartime "journalism" detailing the Chinese peasant response to the Japanese occupation, though written entirely in the United States, supplemented her earlier fiction: its authority derived from the fiction, even as it fed fiction's extra-literary importance.

China's continuing presence on the side of the Allies during World War II was seen by many State Department officials as the "best insurance that the present war does not become a race war."[85] While it is true that the war against Japan seemed to realize an Anglo-Saxonist identification between the United States, Britain, and Commonwealth countries in defining the terms of Pacific security, a countervailing desire among members of the administration to distance the United States from British colonialism reflected anxiety about precisely such a racial conflict. The threat presented by Japan to Western power in Asia was both military and ideological. For the United States, Japan's criticism of the hypocrisy of Western democratic values and the potential appeal of a pan-Asianist movement united domestic issues of racial discrimination with the question of formulating the appropriate stance on European colonialism in Asia. Long before the war's outbreak, the notion that an expansionist Japan might find sympathizers among African Americans had already emerged in an imaginative literature that projected a black-yellow alliance of the oppressed. In the bad conscience of white supremacy, such as Lothrop Stoddard's *The Rising Tide of Color* (1920), or in the solidarity of the oppressed imagined by W.E.B. Du Bois's interracial romance *Dark Princess* (1928), one sees the discursive beginnings of anticolonial alliances that would gain political formalization after the Bandung era.[86] With the endorsement of the cause for Indian independence by the thirty-third conference of the National Association for the Advancement of Colored Peoples (NAACP) in 1942, and evidence of pro-Japan sentiments among some African American groups, the racial implications of the war in Asia seemed to demand the renegotiation of an older white supremacy.[87] Expressing the expectation of many high-level policy makers in 1945, Roosevelt's former Under Secretary of State Sumner Welles forecast a "powerful surge toward freedom among the peoples of the East" after the war, and made a case for international trusteeship as a guard against a "general and violent upheaval" of colonial peoples.[88] The engineering of a postwar U.S. security system, which involved the military occupation of islands throughout the Pacific, depended upon a delicate negotiation of anticolonial rhetoric with the interests of American power.

Throughout the war, Buck made use of the alliance with China to campaign against discrimination at home and colonialism abroad. Her essay collection *Asia and Democracy* (1943) pinpoints racism as the Achilles' heel of U.S. military strategy against Japan. It urges the repeal of discriminatory laws; pleads with African Americans to remain loyal to the United States; condemns race riots and lynchings in the South; and criticizes Japanese American internment. In "Tinder for Tomorrow," Buck writes: "We cannot win even this war without convincing our coloured allies—who are most of our allies—that we are not fighting for ourselves as continuing superior over coloured peoples."[89] Further along in the same essay, the national identity of this "we" is specified, and distinguished from, Western Allied powers as a whole:

Are we all-out for democracy, for total justice, for total peace based on human equality, or are the blessings of democracy to be limited to white people only? The answer must be made clearly and quickly. To evade the question, to delay the answer is to reply in the negative. And the United States must take lead. (TT 5)

Buck's appeal gives voice to the war's radical potential for advancing the civil rights struggle at the same time that it rests the ideal of universal equality upon the U.S.'s moral superiority.[90]

Buck's wartime articles reveal the animation of U.S.-Asian solidarity imperatives by the nightmare of an anti-Western alliance of the colonized.[91] In hindsight, the potential for a Greater East Asian Co-Prosperity Sphere seemed to be a historical realization of the warning Jack London issued upon his return from the Russo-Japanese front in 1904. What disturbed London was not just the show of Japan's military strength, but the future portended by scenes in which, as London put it, "[o]n one side squats a Chinese civilian on his hams, on the other side squats a Japanese soldier. . . . They are talking."[92] In Buck's not-too-distant version of "Asia for the Asiatics," "the peoples of Asia are still waiting, still watchful. . . . they are lending an ear to what Japan is saying because they know there is truth in it" (TT 6). Though London and Buck actively campaigned on behalf of opposite racial policies, their shared fear of a China-Japan combination discloses what it is that U.S. nativist and globalist orientations have had in common. The nightmare of a "yellow peril" that spurs the urgency for U.S. friendship with Asia is particularly explicit in one of Buck's essays appearing at the onset of the Sino-Japanese War, in which the Oriental identity of the opponents increases the likelihood of their ferocity, treachery, and cruelty. Like London's "The Yellow Peril," Buck's "Western Weapons in the Hands of the Reckless East" (1937) projects the global risks of East Asian modernization when technology is shared, but not necessarily the West's spiritual or cultural values.[93] Warning that "[e]ither winner [of the Sino-Japanese War] will look at the world with new, triumphant eyes" (WHE 673), the essay reproduces notions of Asiatic world conquest and the apocalyptic tenor of East-West race war. Whereas London directed his energies in favor of immigration restriction, the threat of a "yellow peril" is here used to encourage greater U.S. involvement in Asian continental affairs, including a cultivation of Chinese national resistance.

The explicit themes of Oriental cruelty exploited by "Western Weapons in the Hands of the Reckless East" are a notable exception in Buck's writings, which untiringly extol the Chinese for "tolerance and wisdom about human life" and for their native liberalism and sense of justice.[94] The trajectory of her writing from *The Good Earth* to the wartime articles demonstrates a slide from emphasizing China's ahistorical frontier isolation to pointing out the world historical nature of its warfront. The Sino-Japanese front is metaphorically the "longest battle line the world has ever known," since it symbolizes the universal stakes of the internal battle lines between segregationism and civil rights within Western democracy.[95] "The front extends to millions of people within the democracies themselves who share little or none of the benefits of the form of the government for which they are now, or may be, compelled to fight."[96] In the East what transpires as a conflict between nations mirrors a conflict of ideologies within the West. Her strategic appeal for U.S. military aid to China casts the anti-Japanese resistance fighters as American pioneers, likening Chinese "armed peasants" to "those early American farmers, who, each with his squirrel gun, shaped American democracy."[97]

The wide audience Buck won for her Americanized Chinese peasant suggests its resonance with the U.S. need for developing a proxy American presence in Asia. Buck's China, moreover, provided a haven for an agrarian nostalgia that, in a U.S. setting, had become increasingly unserviceable.[98] As an instance of Depression-era literature, Buck's rural imagination stands at the extreme end of the antitechnological. Returning to the United States, Buck recounts in her autobiography her dismay at first seeing a combine harvester: "It is farming, of course, the American way, but I was dissatisfied with it. They had no touch with the earth direct, and I feel that there must be the direct touch, hands upon stones and earth and wood, in order that life may have stability" (*MSW* 133). The Chinese setting for Buck's agrarian discourse, however, allows her to displace the problematics of agricultural mechanization onto differences between East and West. Only by having located the yeoman myth in a faraway place could *The Good Earth* have earned Buck a contemporary reputation for realism. In a parable of the destruction wrought by the Western development of China, she writes:

> There I saw the monster machine, something I had never seen before nor heard of, and therefore which I could not name. A man rode upon it, a young Chinese man, not a workingman but a Western-educated man, and he was guiding it slowly along one side of the street and then the other. What was he doing? He was pushing down the houses. Those old one-story houses, made of hand-shaped brick and cemented together with lime plaster, had stood well enough for shelter through hundreds of years, but they had been built long before such a machine had been conceived in the mind of Western man, and they could not withstand the assault. They crumbled into ruins. (*MSW* 242)

This image of the monster machine is reminiscent of the invading tractors in *The Grapes of Wrath*, those "[s]nub-nosed monsters, raising the dust and sticking their snouts into it, straight down the country, across the country, through fences, through dooryards, in and out of gullies in straight lines."[99] However, as the previous chapter has argued, despite a superficial Jeffersonian agrarianism, Steinbeck's critique of colonial capitalism lays bare the violence of American frontier settlement. In *The Grapes of Wrath* and *Pastures of Heaven*, farmers are driven off the land not by the advent of some new social evil but partly as a logical consequence of their inherent divorce from nature, whose disastrous visitations issue a pessimistic verdict on the ability of human beings as a whole ever to cohabitate peaceably with the environment. Buck's droughts and floods would appear to belong to a nature even more unsparing, but its vicissitudes are assuaged by the timeless image of the farmer turning the earth in a constant, diurnal circle. Her Sino-Japanese War writings explicitly insist upon the anticolonial, rather than expansionist, essence of American nationalism. But perhaps the abundant fertility of *The Good Earth* can already be seen to have provided security against ecological exhaustion and salved the troubled conscience of territorial possession staked on the frontier claim that "Grampa killed Indians" (*GW* 45). The multiple uses of Buck's Chinese yeoman underscores the porous relation between the veiled nature of American expansion and the ideal life of agrarian national fictions.

In "Arms for China's Democracy" (1938), a piece that, for Buck, shows unusual sympathy toward the Chinese Communists, Buck welcomes the Communists' supply of arms to the peasants (otherwise withheld by the KMT) and explains her support for a peasant revolution, which she believes is likely to unfold after the war. In the political picture she paints in this article, the Red Army "cannot today be called in the strict sense Communist" (ACD 535), and Chinese peasants are just "[f]armers with guns [who] will not submit to overtaxation" (ACD 534). Therefore, the Red Army "corresponds more nearly to the post-Revolutionary Americans who shaped the beginnings of the American republic of the people, by the people, for the people" (ACD 535). Despite Buck's customary denunciation of the Communists, even they sometimes appear to her as agrarian pioneers. The convergence of writers as ideologically divergent as Buck and Snow on this point suggests the repeated refraction of Chinese national longing through the lens of the American frontier. The shock with which the final outcome of the Chinese civil war was received by U.S. politicians and media as the "loss of China" testifies perhaps not just to U.S. arrogance but to the influence of this particular Popular Front representation. Perhaps even more than U.S. patronage of the cosmopolitan, Christian leaders of the KMT, the yeoman figuration of an autochthonous rural resistance contributed to the popularly held fantasy that before 1949 China was already an imaginative extension of

U.S. territory. As the epilogue of a civil war lost to the CCP and its displaced continuation, the McCarthyist discovery of subversives everywhere in the State Department hardly revealed the deceitfulness of an agrarian reformer construction so much as its profound cultural resonance.

It is clear from Edgar Snow's report as well that the Chinese civil war affords the confrontation of traditional Oriental character with the plainspoken frontiersman. However, his cultural representation of the two Chinas grates against U.S. foreign policy, since the Americans are shown to be officially supporting the wrong side. It is the Reds who have "generally discarded much of the ceremony of traditional Chinese etiquette, and [whose] psychology and character were quite different from our old conceptions of Chinese" (*RSOC* 355). Efforts on the part of the Nationalists to introduce Western cultural models, meanwhile, such as Chiang Kai-Shek's YMCA-inspired New Life Movement, kept failing to eradicate the archaic Oriental features of KMT rule: corruption, censorship, evasiveness, and dictatorship. *Red Star* exposes the United States—which was channeling lend-lease aid exclusively to the KMT and refusing to establish consular representation in Yenan—to be unwittingly buttressing Oriental despotism against American-style democracy.

Notwithstanding his domestication of the Chinese Communists, Snow's critique of U.S. foreign policy draws in part from the figural persuasion of Asiatic modernity, in particular the historical guarantee of a rising Asiatic mass:

> The great reservoir of human material in the revolutionary Chinese people will still be pouring men ready to fight for their freedom into our front lines long after the tidal flood of Japanese imperialism has wrecked itself on the hidden reefs of Chinese resistance. (*RSOC* 113)

Exclaiming that he "had failed to realize on what almost unbelievably modest sums it was possible for a Chinese proletarian army to exist" (*RSOC* 261), Snow, in his coverage of the Red Army's achievements, highlights extraordinary powers of survival against a technologically superior enemy. Here even as a fervent spirit is responsible for Chinese physical persistence, Snow's admiring account of Chinese revolutionary nationalism draws upon an expectation of Asiatic insuperability that echoes "yellow peril" fantasy. Instead of predicting a nightmare of capitalist repression, however, Snow's revolution on the semiperiphery heralds the potential for universal socialist emancipation.

In light of what they shared and what they did not, Snow and Buck marked a range of American Popular Front positions on China, which had at their core the identification of Chinese antifascism and American anticolonialism to the mutual benefit of the two nations. In the polarized framework of the Cold War, the identity of opposites quickly became a matter of national insecurity. Though no friend of the Chinese Communists, Pearl S. Buck herself did not escape being investigated by the FBI investigation or tarred by HUAC's brush. In a 1946 report ordered by J. Edgar Hoover, she was charged with belonging to at least four "Communist Front Organizations": the Japanese-American Committee for Democracy, the East and West Association, the American Civil Liberties Union, and the Indian League of America. Among the key activities that drew the bureau's attention was, in the words of the FBI report, her campaign "to wipe out all race discrimination in the war effort."[100] Then again, in the HUAC hearings, one can also see a paranoid political style that, in its attention to Asian forecasts of an American future, shares much with the position it seeks to foreclose. Whether advocating strategies of rapprochement or nonrecognition, American discourses on China, during an era that saw, simultaneously, China's entry into the "family of nations" and the shaping of the United States into a superpower, were distinctive for their inscription of Asian politics into the very heart of American national identity.[101]

Pacific Rim Ecologies, Asian Miracle Economies

From Wendell Wilkie's encircling *One World* (1943) to Henry Wallace's internationalist campaign trail, the early 1940s proffered alternative visions of harmony between U.S. world leadership and Asian colonial emancipation.[102] Such utopian possibilities were foreclosed at the end of the decade by rising anti-Communist virulence and U.S. complicity in formal colonialism's return, but something of the intimacy between the imagined form of U.S. global presence and the assertion of Asian national independence nevertheless remained. Thus even as the creator of Wang Lung and the voices of like-minded liberals were silenced by the Cold War, in spite of the "loss of China"—or perhaps to counteract this loss—the American frontier now extended well into the Asia Pacific region. As a postwar national security concept, the Pacific Rim first materialized as a "defense perimeter" encircling a Communist-led mainland. In the language of National Security Council (NSC) document 48/1, "The United States must maintain a minimum position in Asia if a successful defense is to be achieved against future Soviet aggression. This minimum position is considered to consist of at least our present military position in the Asian offshore island chain, and in the event of war its denial to the Communists."[103] Though the geographic particulars of the cordon sanitaire changed from time to time (Korea was, until the invasion of the North Korean Army, not considered a significant point of defense), in general the postwar Asian miracle economies were spatially consistent with the old "defense perimeter." From 1955 to 1978 U.S. military deliveries to Taiwan and Republic of Korea (ROK) totaled $9.05 billion, compared with $3.2 million for all of Latin America and Africa combined; during the 1950s U.S. aid accounted for 83 percent of all ROK imports.[104] Celebrated cultural values or no, in the case of the northeast Asian region, upward mobility within the world economy was bolstered by U.S. procurements on behalf of its "grand area" military strategy.

If Wang Lung represents an early prototype for the Asian economic miracles of the 1960s and after, U.S. globalism had another valuable literary resource at mid-century, one that marks, from this side of the Pacific, the new internality of Asia to the American West. Written during the Second World War and published at its conclusion, Steinbeck's *Cannery Row* (1945) is notable for being the first serious literary work by a major American writer to include an Asian American in its character ensemble. Where *The Good Earth* thematizes the noble tiller at work, Steinbeck's Lee Chong suggests a quite different set of economic virtues. However, both foreground the economic exemplification of Asian American character.

Concerned with the exploits of the bedraggled inhabitants of the sardine canning district of Monterey, California, *Cannery Row* depicts everyday life at the edges of the world of work:

> The canneries rumble and rattle and squeak until the last fish is cleaned and cut and cooked and canned and then the whistles scream again and the dripping, smelly, tired Wops and Chinamen and Polaks, men and women, straggle out and droop their ways up the hill into the town and Cannery Row becomes itself again—quiet and magical. Its normal life returns.[105]

Here, "normal life" features a regular cast of characters who, like creatures of twilight, reemerge with the waning of the working day: unemployed bums, prostitutes, a Chinese grocer, a biologist, a painter, and assorted other "gathered and scattered" (*CR* 1). The novel's central characters are the bums, whose indisposition to work represents a philosophical alternative to "our so-called successful men . . . with bad stomachs, and bad souls" (*CR* 142). While Mack and the boys themselves may have no regular occupation, the other row denizens, on whose munificence the bums depend, do. In response to the insoluble economic catastrophe of the 1930s the novel offers more than a negation of productive discipline in the celebration of happy-go-lucky laziness. *Cannery Row*'s pastoral world posits an alternative economy, one that is perhaps less regularized than the daily factory whistle but no less eternal. Dora's brothel business, an archetype of socially invisible labor, follows the ebb and flow of clients brought in by the fishing seasons or regimental movement into the Presidio army base (*CR* 96). Doc's occupation, the collection of marine animals for scientific laboratories, heeds the schedule of the tides. The third anchor personality of Cannery Row's social community, Lee Chong, does not so much engage in a naturalized economic activity as facilitate the symbiotic exchange unique to this alternative community.

The action of the novel, small as it is, highlights the extent to which *Cannery Row*—on the surface an oddly gentle piece of fiction to succeed *The Grapes of Wrath*—continues to address the Depression's concern with crises of exchange. Essentially, the storyline involves two parties thrown by "Mack and the boys" in honor of Doc. The first is a disaster that plunges them into social disgrace, and the second is a success that brings the whole community together again. The idea for a party arises out of the bums' feeling of indebtedness toward Doc, but their lack of funds requires that they concoct a plan based upon the elaborate system of credit that structures Cannery Row society. Instead of hiring themselves out to the Hediondo cannery, Mack and his friends decide to raise money by going on a frog-gathering expedition to nearby Carmel Valley. To Doc's Western Biological Laboratory, animals are worth money, and frogs five cents a piece. Without revealing their purposes, the bums get gas on credit from Doc and borrow Lee Chong's Ford truck in exchange for fixing it. They capture about a thousand frogs, exchange them at Lee Chong's store for whiskey and party supplies, and decorate the laboratory in gleeful anticipation of Doc's return from La Jolla. As the evening develops, the party spins out of control, and Doc arrives home to find his laboratory destroyed. The frogs escape from their packing case and so, like Doc, Lee Chong suffers a total loss on his dealings with the bums.

Cannery Row's comic structure at first suggests Steinbeck's retreat from writing socially engaged fiction, but the portrait of Mack and the boys indicates an insistent continuity of 1930s subject matter. A "group of men who had in common no families, no money, and no ambitions beyond food, drink and contentment" (*CR* 9), the bums are a version of the social type engendered by the seasonal structure of California agricultural labor. But where the itinerant farmhands in *Of Mice and Men* come to tragedy, Mack and his friends "approached contentment casually and quietly, absorbed it gently" (*CR* 10). Instead of treating the agrarian dream as a tragic theme, Steinbeck's strategy here is to make a virtue of homelessness and a mockery of property values. The bums squat in a warehouse where simulated beds are drawn in chalk on the floor. "Each man had property rights inviolable in his space. He could legally fight a man who encroached on his square. The rest of the room was property common to all" (*CR* 39–40). By and large, the cannery district comprises a community of residents instead of owners, including characters such as the Malloys, who make a home out of a defunct boiler, or the gopher who digs a burrow in a vacant lot. The setting is a postindustrial scene of broken machinery that, like the Ford truck with mallows growing between its spokes, is in the process of being reclaimed by nature. Each individual is like a hermit crab that has taken up shelter in someone else's discarded shell.

The marine animal analogy is, of course, intentional to the text's design. The "Great Tide Pool" where Doc does his primary collecting, and which receives lengthy and lyrical description, provides the metaphor for the human community that borders it:

> It is a fabulous place: when the tide is in, a wave-churned basin, creamy with foam, whipped by the combers that roll in from the whistling buoy on the reef. But when the tide goes out the little water world becomes quiet and lovely. The sea is very clear and the bottom becomes fantastic with hurrying, fighting, feeding, breeding animals. Crabs rush from frond to frond of the waving algae. Starfish squat over mussels and limpets, attach their million little suckers and then slowly lift with incredible power until the prey is broken from the rock. And then the starfish stomach comes out and envelops his food. Orange and speckled and fluted nudibranchs slide gracefully over the rocks, their skirts waving like the dresses of Spanish dancers. And black eels poke their heads out of crevices and wait for prey. The snapping shrimps with their trigger claws pop loudly. The lovely, colored world is glassed over. Hermit crabs like frantic children scamper on the bottom sand. And now one finding an empty shell he likes better than his own, creeps out, exposing his soft body to the enemy for a moment, and then pops into the new shell. A wave breaks over the barrier, and churns the glassy water for a moment and mixes bubbles into the pool, and then it clears and is tranquil and lovely and murderous again. (CR 30–31)

Though it is no less "red in tooth and claw" than Jack London's version, nature here is observed with a biologist's repose and remove; viewed in miniature, life's struggle can be aestheticized, even made picturesque. *Cannery Row*'s nature is also an enclosed world, literally, the one world of the encircling tidepool: thus individual creature tragedies are leavened by a distanced perspective on life and death. If Darwinian evolutionism had informed naturalism's social critique of class struggle at the turn of the century, the ecological direction taken by this text renegotiates the central relation between nature and society. Where high naturalism depicted the viciousness of capitalist society in animal terms, in this postindustrial setting of rusting machines the main scene of conflict has shifted to nature.

Cannery Row is a story without embodied villains, and this absence is also to be seen in the lack of dramatic tension that mediates between the event of the disaster and the event of its recuperation. In the hiatus between the two parties, we are informed that "It was a bad time. Evil stalked darkly in the vacant lot" (*CR* 144–45). The bums suffer social ostracism for their irresponsible actions, but their disgrace is simply one element in a larger pattern of ill luck affecting the whole community. The subsequent dramatic turning point is just as generalized: "At last a crack had developed in the wall of evil. There were evidences of it everywhere" (*CR* 148). Mack and his friends make a mess of things, but the synchronicity of events shows that the whole community undergoes good and bad times together as a single unit. The problem underlying the failure of the party can be explained by Mack's good intentions that "I'd just like to give [Doc] something when I didn't get most of it back" (*CR* 81), yet the intricacy of social interdependence makes it impossible to give without receiving something in return. In this paradigm of social relations, a calculable balance sheet is subordinated to a higher ecological mystery. Not accidentally, the mechanism that permits the social restoration of the bums also goes by an Oriental name:

> The wall of evil and of waiting was broken. It broke away in chunks. . . . Some force wrought with Lee Chong's heart and all in an Oriental moment he forgave Mack and the boys and wrote off the frog debt which had been a monetary headache from the beginning. And to prove to the boys that he had forgiven them he took a pint of Old Tennis Shoes up and presented it to them. (*CR* 148)

As the merchant to whom "Over the course of the years everyone in Cannery Row owed . . . money" (*CR* 5), Lee Chong is the obvious candidate to play the villain's part. Instead the text offers us a gentle parody of mercantile villainy:

> [B]itterness arose as the day wore on and prices went up. Steak, for instance—the very best steak shouldn't have been more than ten frogs a pound but Lee set it at twelve and a half. Canned peaches were sky high, eight frogs for a No. 2 can. Lee had a stranglehold on the consumers. He was pretty sure that the Thrift Market or Holman's would not approve of this new monetary system. If the boys wanted steak, they knew they had to pay Lee's prices. (*CR* 118)

Lee Chong's behavior generates no resentment because "While [the bums] were mildly irritated that Lee was taking them for an economic ride or perhaps hop, two dollars' worth of bacon and eggs was in their stomachs lying right on top of a fine slug of whiskey and right on top of the breakfast was another slug of whiskey" (*CR* 119). "[F]inancial bitterness" fails to sap Mack and his friends not just because "they did not measure their joy in goods sold, their egos in bank balances" (*CR* 119), but because it is already clear from the beginning that Lee's transactions do not profit him in financial terms. As it turns out, the payments lose value through the currency's literal disappearance. Lee Chong possesses the pronounced attributes of the calculating businessman, his "little restless sausage fingers" always working "interest and discounts, addition, subtraction . . . on the abacus" (*CR* 7), and he "never had a sale, never reduced a price, and never remaindered" (*CR* 122). However, Lee Chong manages to run a successful operation somehow by converting financial losses into social credit. "Sometimes he made business errors, but even these he turned to advantage in good will if in no other way" (*CR* 6). Events always seem to escape predictability so that even Lee Chong's shrewd calculus could find nothing wrong in the original deal ("Lee's mind nosed over the proposition like a mouse in a cheese cupboard" [*CR* 118]). The text seems to urge us toward a different kind of economic logic altogether, in which catastrophic meltdown is cured by an economy of abundance.[106]

The mysterious plenitude of assets that enables the merchant's magnanimous gesture of debt forgiveness ("What he did with his money, no one ever knew. Perhaps he didn't get it. Maybe his wealth was entirely in unpaid bills" [*CR* 6]) corresponds to the fact that as the main source of commodity products in the neighborhood, the grocery store, "while not a model of neatness, was a miracle of supply" (*CR* 6). Containing in one single room a vast heterogeneity of objects, "everything [a man] needed or wanted to live and to be happy" (*CR* 6), Lee Chong's grocery store has its analogue in the other anchor institutions of the community. Dora's Bear Flag Restaraunt supplies "the one commodity Lee Chong did not keep" (*CR* 6)—women—while at Western Biological Laboratory "[y]ou can order anything living . . . and sooner or later you will get it" (*CR* 26). Putting "lovely animals of the sea" up for sale, Western Biological Laboratory's business involves converting natural things into commodities, yet these products are strangely untransformed by human labor. Collected but not reworked, the wares sold by Western Biological Laboratory are fragments of nature preserved in their original state. The social community Steinbeck constructs is one that has little to do with productive labor, though its complex interdependency foregrounds the governing centrality of exchange to all social relationships. The lesson of the two parties lies in the moral that all members of the community are indebted to one another, and that no one gains at another's expense. The relation between the human community and the tidepool ecosystem is not one of mere analogy but also proximity. Physically adjacent to the seashore, the social microcosm Steinbeck explores reflects a condition so near nature that social relations are transacted with minimal mediation. Meanwhile, frogs circulate as currency. Such proximity facilitates the representation of economic disaster in literally natural terms.

The disappearance of the frogs evokes the Dust Bowl, or the representation of economic loss through the figure of nature's dissipation. The 1930s' common reliance on a Dust Bowl metaphor for the Depression's endemic economic dysfunction comes to mind with the example of Francis Almones, who "had a sad life, for he always made just a fraction less than he needed to live. His father had left him a little money but year by year and month by month, no matter how hard Francis worked or how careful he was, his money grew less until he just dried up and blew away" (*CR* 62–63). The story of the frogs' disappearance, however, provides an important alternative to the tragic erosion of soil into lifeless dust. Their dispersion is comedic, in no small part due to the fact that when introduced in the original scene of their capture the frogs are anthropomorphized as Okie migrants:

> During the millennia that frogs and men have lived together in the same world, it is probable that men have hunted frogs. And during that time a pattern of hunt and parry has developed. . . . Frogs have every right to expect it will always be done that way. . . . But how could they have anticipated Mack's new method? . . . Hysterically the frogs displaced from their placid spots swam ahead of the crazy thrashing feet and the feet came on. . . . A few frogs lost their heads and floundered among the feet and got through and these were saved. But the majority decided to leave this pool forever, to find a new home in a new country where this kind of thing didn't happen. A wave of frantic, frustrated frogs, big ones, little ones, brown ones, green ones, men frogs and women frogs, a wave of them broke over the bank, crawled, leaped, scrambled. They clambered up the grass, they clutched at each other, little ones rode big ones. And then—horror of horror—the flashlights found them. (*CR* 92–94)

Though the frogs' disappearance from the packing crate represents someone's personal economic loss, it is impossible for us to regret altogether the prospect of their escape back home. As befitting the ethos of *Cannery Row*, home, like nature, is everywhere. "Some found the sewer and had worked their way up the hill to the reservoir and some went into the culverts and some only hid among the weeds in the vacant lot" (*CR* 127) The strange force that "all in an Oriental moment" allows for debt forgiveness is already prefigured by the frogs' equivalence with the Depression's soil *and* its migrant farmers, their dualness as both natural and social things. The text's magical solution to dire economic crisis rests upon the proximity between nature and society, such that exchange can occur in the absence of a universal equivalent. Exchange value is subordinate, money is natural, and the ruthlessness of a financial arithmetic is spared by the text's confidence in an abundant nature, from which all things come and all things return.

Steinbeck's approach to nature as a relational ecosystem gestures toward Oriental mysticism. Critics have linked his "holistic" world view to certain Taoist ideas concerning the all-inclusive nature of reality, the rejection of worldly ambition, the cultivation of simple physical enjoyments and the inner life.[107] Steinbeck's personal exposure to Taoist philosophy through his friend Ed Ricketts, on whom the character Doc is based, lends support to a view of Doc as the embodiment of the sage himself, the "wordless teacher" of the community, and the appreciator of Sanskrit poetry (Lisca, 25). In this reading, the major themes of *Cannery Row* as a whole—the escape from material values and the escape from action—derive from the *Tao Teh Ching* (Lisca, 27). Though Steinbeck's interest in relationality was already present in his earlier critiques of industrialization, such as *Pastures of Heaven*, its Orientalist undertones are most audible now, beginning with his partnership with Edward F. Ricketts, and their expedition to the Sea of Cortez in 1940. First published as a part of a collaborative volume *Sea of Cortez* (1941) and reissued separately a decade later under the title *The Log from the Sea of Cortez*, Steinbeck's account of this marine collecting trip down the coast and around the bays and estuaries of the Gulf of California forms a pre-text to the 1945 novel about Monterey's tidepool community. In the travel narrative and in *Cannery Row*, Steinbeck's adoption of a more explicitly philosophical language counterposes Western materialistic values to Eastern holism, which he refers to as "non-teleological thinking":

> This deep underlying pattern inferred by non-teleological thinking crops up everywhere—a relational thing, surely, relating opposing factors on different levels, as reality and potential are related. . . . The whole picture is portrayed by *is,* the deepest word of deep ultimate reality, not shallow or partial as reasons are, but deeper and participating, possibly encompassing the Oriental concept of being.[108]

My own interest lies less in assessing the rigorous usages of Eastern philosophy and more in the fact itself that the Oriental should have come to demarcate the "green world" of gentle respite from the ravages of industrial competition—and, by the time of Hitler's invasion of Poland, the horrors of total global war. *The Log from the Sea of Cortez* is vividly mindful of the symbolic excursion away from the world that this 1940 marine expedition represents. With no small measure of satisfaction, Steinbeck notes: "Hitler marched into Denmark and into Norway, France had fallen, the Maginot Line was lost—we didn't know it, but we knew the daily catch of every boat within four hundred miles" (*LSC* 756). In *The Log*, this "green world" is both an actual space—the bays and estuaries of the Baja peninsula—and an alternative outlook, one associated with Eastern holism or ecological relationality as in the quote above. In *Of Mice and Men*, the forest glen is a parallel universe to the ranch world of industrial farming, though it offers but limited sanctuary and is hedged in by irrigation dykes, highways, and other signposts of human cultivation. With *The Log*, Steinbeck's shift of setting to a coastal environment enables a continued attention to local community, but one shielded from industrial extinction through a constant connection to the infinite. This infinite—in philosophical name "Oriental," in imagery oceanic—provides Steinbeck's imaginative wartime response to the past decade's crisis of market relations and class struggle.[109]

A Taoist reading *Cannery Row* would assign a secondary position to the Chinese grocer, whose tutelage in Li Po appreciation by Doc attests to Doc's symbolic status as the Eastern sage of this text.[110] While it has been noted that Lee Chong manages to convert a "parasitic" relationship with the community into a "commensal" one,[111] insufficient emphasis has been placed on the significance of the text's racial inflection of its economic argument. In a text putatively "Oriental" as a whole, where does a Chinese grocer fit? Why, indeed, a Chinese grocer?

> The word is a symbol and a delight which sucks up men and scenes, trees, plants, factories and Pekinese. Then the Thing becomes the Word and back to Thing again, but warped and woven into a fantastic pattern. The word sucks up Cannery Row, digests it and spews it out. And the Row has taken the shimmer of the green world and the sky-reflecting seas. Lee Chong is more than a Chinese grocer. He must be. Perhaps he is evil balanced and held suspended by good—an Asiatic planet held to its orbit by the pull of Lao Tze and held away from Lao Tze by the centrifugality of abacus and cash register—Lee Chong suspended, spinning, whirling among groceries and ghosts. A hard man with a can of beans—a soft man with the bones of his grandfather. For Lee Chong dug into the grave on China Point and found the yellow bones, the skull with gray ropy hair still sticking to it. And Lee carefully packed the bones, femur, and tibias really straight, skull in the middle, with pelvis and clavicle surrounding it and ribs curving on either side. Then Lee Chong sent his boxed and brittle grandfather over the western sea to lie at last in ground made holy by his ancestors. (*CR* 14–15)

Some students of the Oriental stereotype in American culture have taken Steinbeck at his word ("Lee Chong is more than a Chinese grocer"), applauding him for creating a "cartoon Oriental exterior [that] masks a creature of broader function, greater scope, and perhaps hints at universal significance" (Bedford, 10). The point, however, is not just that Lee Chong may be one vehicle among others for the expression of the text's universal humanism, but rather—as the passage above suggests—a central instance of the text's interest in denaturalizing representation. In constituting Lee Chong as the impresario of economic mystery (just as Doc holds the key to the enigmas of the sea), Steinbeck makes pointed reference to a traditional modality of Asiatic racial form. In the passage above, the selection of a Chinese grocer works to emphasize the dichotomy between the material and the spiritual, since Lee Chong is suspended between the abacus and Lao Tze, groceries and ghosts, a can of beans and a box of ancestral bones—in a sense, between the Asiatic and the Oriental. The inclination to liberate the Asiatic from a reduction to "groceries" surfaces within a textual context rife with the literalization of economic metaphors.

Back to the tidepool where Doc does his collecting:

Then the creeping murderer, the octopus, steals out, slowly, softly, moving like a gray mist, pretending now to be a bit of weed, now a rock, now a lump of decaying meat while its evil goat eyes watch coldly. It oozes and flows toward a feeding crab, and as it comes close its yellow eyes burn and its body turns rosy with pulsing color of anticipation and rage. Then suddenly it runs lightly on the tips of its arms, as ferociously as a charging cat. It leaps savagely on the crab, there is a puff of black fluid, and the struggling mass is obscured in the sepia cloud while the octopus murders the crab. (*CR* 31)

Among the members of the oceanic food chain, the octopus is the only one that kills with emotional fervor. That the aim of collecting octopuses takes Doc out of town assigns special notice to this animal. At the very same moment that the bums are collecting frogs en masse, Doc is collecting octopuses, but Steinbeck makes it clear that, in this case, we are not to pity the animals: "He turned over the boulders with his crowbar and now and then his hand darted quickly into the standing water and brought out a little angry squirming octopus which blushed with rage and spat ink on his hand. Then he dropped it into a jar of sea water with the others and usually the newcomer was so angry that it attacked its fellows" (*CR* 108). Mean-spirited, competitive and murderous, the octopus retains the qualities designated by Frank Norris's treatment of monopoly capital. Here, though, the octopus's predations mark the site of displaced social struggle in an otherwise idyllic world. However, it is a struggle suddenly reduced to dimunitive proportions—harmless and humorous, as viewed from the transcendent perspective of a larger whole.

The Asiatic is also given organic life in this text. Its personification is doubled by a mysterious "old Chinaman" who is sighted only at dusk or at dawn, Steinbeck's "time of magic in Cannery Row," when few people are about, and "cats drip over the fences and slither like syrup to look for fish heads," "dogs parade majestically," "sea gulls come flapping in," and gophers "creep out and drag flowers into their holes" (*CR* 85–86). Making his appearance exactly when "the street is silent of progress and business," this "Old Chinaman comes out of the sea and flip-flaps across the street and up past the Palace" (*CR* 85–86). Since no one knows where he comes from exactly and where he goes, the "old Chinaman" is evocative of Lee Chong himself, who would go "secretly to San Francisco" whenever there was a "price on his head . . . until the trouble blew over" (*CR* 6). In this intensely local setting, San Francisco exists as much outside the coordinates of the familiar world as the land across the western sea to which Lee Chong sends his grandfather's bones. On the one hand, the lifeworld of the Chinese in California is as mysteriously rendered as ever, but, on the other hand, no more so than the wondrous animal world. The mystery of Oriental domicile and the "larger whole" whose nature "we could begin to feel . . . but not its size" (*LSC* 875) are aligned.

In characterization, the "Old Chinaman" strikes a distinct contrast to Lee Chong. One is pointedly old while the other seemingly unmarked by age; one is a solitary creature while the other exists in a network of community. The purposeless presence of the "Old Chinaman" thematizes obsolescence, in contrast to Lee Chong's social functionality. The two can be seen as temporal correlates, their location in the same neighborhood, where they are the only racial Others, providing an allegory of racial integration. The "Old Chinaman" points to an older social type, even as Lee Chong retains many stereotypic attributes. Showing the social alien to be fading away, Steinbeck locates the racial figure in what he calls the "hour of the pearl," the magical in-between moment between day and night ruled by the animals who inhabit the fringe of human communities. As a creature among these biological life forms, the "Old Chinaman" marks Steinbeck's insertion of the Asiatic into a local ecology, and a strategy of the alien's indigenization.

It seems to me not accidental that the text, which offers a happy fix to the Depression's economic crisis that Steinbeck so influentially depicted, should so prominently feature the theme of Asian inclusion. The flip-flapping Chinaman echoes the sound made by the invisible Chinese farmhand in Steinbeck's earlier short story "Johnny Bear" (1938), but *Cannery Row* also has a Asian character who exists inside the borders of this Californian community, a project he will expand through the principal character of *East of Eden* (1952).[112] From the eclectic inventory of Lee Chong's store to the cornucopia of life forms in the tidepool, heterogeneity characterizes the new California border community. Lee Chong functions as a valve between inside and outside—through his store's "miracle of supply" of commodities from the outside world, through his travel links to San Francisco, and even to China "across the western sea." Though just as assertive in its sense of the local as Steinbeck's other work, this text opens a connection to the world beyond, insists that this locale and others form part of one world. As Steinbeck writes in his travelogue, "All things are one thing and that one thing is all things—plankton, a shimmering phosphorescence on the sea and the spinning planets and an expanding universe, all bound together by the elastic string of time. It is advisable to look from the tide pool to the stars and then back to the tide pool again" (*LSC* 929). Imagining homologous and contiguous relations between the local (the tidepool) and the global (the sea)—and even the universal (the stars)—the Pacific Rim at last overtakes a fin de siècle sense of California as a barricaded Western outpost.

Notes

1. Mitsuye Yamada, *Camp Notes*, 39.
2. For an influential argument that stresses the "heterogeneity, hybridity, and multiplicity" of Asian American culture as the basis of its counterhegemonic potential, see Lowe, *Immigrant Acts*, 60–83. For an institutional and activist history that argues for the strategic necessity of Asian American panethnicity, see Espiritu, *Asian American Panethnicity*.
3. Kitano and Sue, "The Model Minorities," 1.
4. On how the Asian American admissions controversy at top universities informed a shift in affirmative-action policy away from race, see Takagi, *The Retreat from Race*. On the phenomenon of the "Asian Tigers" presaging the conceptual dismantling of the "Third World," see Harris, *The End of the Third World*.
5. Said, *Orientalism*.
6. For the classic periodizing approach to positive and negative images of Asia in the Western imagination, see Isaacs, *Scratches on Our Mind*. William Wu's pioneering study of the American literary representation of Chinese Americans attributes its failure of realism in the period 1850 to 1940 to the predominance of a yellow peril imagination in that era. See Wu, *The Yellow Peril*, 1–5. A commonplace of Asian American studies is to view "model minority" discourse as having originated in the 1960s as a result of a conservative backlash to the black Civil Rights movement. For a representative account, see Keith Osajima, "Asian Americans as the Model Minority," 165–74. More recently, Gary Okihiro has argued that "yellow peril" and "model minority" can be seen to share a set of characteristics—"singleness of purpose, patience and endurance, cunning, fanaticism and group loyalty"—across time. See Okihiro, *Margins and Mainstreams*, 141–43. Robert G. Lee traces "model minority" discourse to the Cold War liberalism of the 1950s, and David Palumbo-Liu dates the early origins of the discourse to the 1930s, when he begins to detect some "historical crossings of the racial frontier" in the academic conclusions that Asians were as mentally capable as whites. See Lee, *Orientals*, 145–79; and Palumbo-Liu, *Asian/American*, 152. Lee observes that "yellowface coolie" and "model minority" coexist and are "mutually reinforcing at critical junctures," but for him the basis of their similarity is that "neither is created by the actual lives of Asians in America." See Lee, 12. Lee's six images of the Oriental—pollutant, coolie, deviant, yellow peril, model minority, and gook—are periodized chronologically, despite the extent to which they share obvious overlapping characteristics. Palumbo-Liu argues that the "impossibility of actualizing and stabilizing 'Asian/American' is directly linked to the distinction made between 'Asian' and 'American,' the premise of the mutual exclusion." The impossibility is rooted in the inherent contradiction that informs the constitution of the Other in a situation where the democratic and universal premises of the na-

tion's image of its ideal self are contradicted by its white supremacist ideology. See Palumbo-Liu, 171. For how the Asian as object and the abject can be thought of as "two sides of the same alien" in a psychoanalytic vein, see Li, *Imagining the Nation*, 10.

7. The formal and historical specification of American Orientalism is attracting the energies of a generation of brilliant young scholars, many of whom I have been fortunate to encounter as graduate students at Berkeley: Josephine Park, Misa Oyama, Hoang Phan, Jodi Kim, and Sylvia Chong. For a recent account of Orientalism and its critique in American poetry from the perspective of culture as a translingual practice, see Huang, *Transpacific Displacement*.

8. Here I use the term "form" as distinct from "formation" in the sense used by Etienne Balibar to describe that which, more than an effect of capital accumulation, is also a privileged terrain of the management of social struggle. Balibar writes: "The world-economy is not a self-regulating, globally invariant system, whose social formations can be regarded as mere local effects; it is a system of constraints, subject to the unforeseeable dialectics of its internal contradictions. It is globally necessary that control of the capital circulation in the whole accumulation space should be exercised from the core; but there has always been struggle over the *form* in which this concentration has been effected. The privileged status of the nation form derives from the fact that, locally, that form made it possible (at least for an entire historical period) for struggles between heterogeneous classes to be controlled and for not only a 'capitalist class' but the *bourgeoisies* proper to emerge from these. . . ." See Balibar, "The Nation Form," 90.

9. Hagedorn, ed., *Charlie Chan Is Dead*.

10. See Chin et al., eds., *Aiiieeeee!* xi–38. The quarrel I refer to is Frank Chin's criticisms of Maxine Hong Kingston, David Henry Hwang, and Amy Tan for reproducing exoticizing and emasculating stereotypes of Asian Americans. The war of newspaper interview quotations has found its way into literary production as well. Frank Chin has written a parody of *The Woman Warrior* called "The Unmanly Warrior," in his "Afterword." To Chin's effort, Kingston has responded rather more wittily by modeling the noisy, profane, and rambunctious protagonist of *Tripmaster Monkey* on Chin.

11. Homi Bhabha writes: "For it is the force of ambivalence that gives the colonial stereotype its currency; ensures its repeatability in changing historical and discursive conjunctures; informs its strategies of individuation and marginalization; produces that effect of probabilistic truth and predictability which, for the stereotype, must always be in excess of what can be empirically proved or logically construed." See Bhabha, "The Other Question," 66.

12. Scott, "The Evidence of Experience."

13. For a critique of Asian American historiography focusing too much on anti-Asian activities and not enough on Asian Americans themselves, see Daniels, "Westerners from the East: Oriental Immigration Reappraised," 375.

14. Friedman and Selden, eds., *America's Asia*, x.

15. For the nontransparency of representation, see Spivak, "Can the Subaltern Speak?" For some good reasons why, even as Asian American studies goes transnational, we ought to remember that thinking globally is constrained by acting locally, see S. L. Wong, "Denationalization Reconsidered."

16. Robert G. Lee observes that the Chinese immigrants who were compared favorably by employers to Irish workers could be viewed as a nineteenth-century model minority. See Lee, 67.

17. The upshot of Stuart Miller's history of American attitudes toward Chinese immigrants, for example, which makes an important contribution by showing that anti-Asianism was a national, not just regional, sentiment, is that Americans were always already racist. See *The Unwelcome Immigrant*. Ronald Takaki's influential multicultural approach to U.S. history has the effect of analogizing different kinds of racisms. See *Iron Cages*. Even Yuji Ichioka, who crucially connects Japanese immigrant history with American and Japanese labor history, makes use of his historical evidence ultimately to unveil the existence of indelible racism in American labor and socialist leadership. See *The Issei*.

18. On the historically tenuous relationship between Asian American studies and Marxism, as well as for potentially fruitful areas of overlap, see Liu and Cheng, "A Dialogue on Race and Class."

19. In my view, Omi and Winant somewhat overemphasize the theoretical rescue of race from class reductionism at the expense of focusing on the precise ways in which race and class have indeed intersected historically. See Omi and Winant, *Racial Formation in the United States*. From within literary and cultural studies, Lowe's *Immigrant Acts* follows in a post-Marxist vein. See Lowe, 1–36. Perhaps because of the inhibiting effect of race-versus-class debates on materialist approaches, in recent years some of the most powerful theoretical accounts of racialization have issued from psychoanalytic perspectives. See Anne Cheng, *The Melancholy of Race*.

20. David Liwei Li, for example, periodizes the representation of Asian America in two phases, 1882 to 1943 or 1965, and 1943 or 1965 to the present. The dates correspond to significant turning points in immigration legislation. In Phase I, Asian Americans were the object (or Other) of the national imaginary. In Phase II, the abject (or the not-yet-possible representative of the national imaginary) is neither radical enough for institutional enjoinment nor competent enough to enjoy the subject status of citizens. See Li, 5–10. It is unclear, however, how the temporal movement from phase I to phase II is explained by the Kristevan notion of abjection derived from Judith Butler, which Li uses to theorize the difference between object and abject. For a sociological history of the period 1924 to 1965, when a "regime of immigration restriction" produced the "impossible subject" of the illegal alien, see Ngai, *Impossible Subjects*. The priority of the law in racialization studies can, in large part, be explained by the fact that it is Asian American critical race theory that has led the way in studying the production of the Asian alien. See, for example, Matsuda, "Looking to the Bottom"; Saito, "Alien and Non-Alien Alike"; Aoki, "Foreign-ness and Asian American Identities"; and Lesser, "Always Outsiders."

21. Saxton, *The Indispensable Enemy*.

22. See Marchetti, *Romance and the "Yellow Peril"*; Hamamoto, *Monitored Peril*; and Moy, *Marginal Sights*. For the study of Chinese American representation in American literature, see Wu; See also Kim's *Asian American Literature*, 3–22. Recent studies of Asian representation by Palumbo-Liu and Robert G. Lee cover a wide range of American cultural material, including literature.

23. Lukács, *The Historical Novel*, 171–250; also "Narrate or Describe?"

24. Naturalism's taxonomies match sociology's discursive emergence. See Mizruchi, "Cataloguing the Creatures of the Deep." See also Horwitz, "Maggie and the Sociological Paradigm."

25. Trachtenberg, *The Incorporation of America*.

26. Sklar, *The Corporate Reconstruction of American Capitalism*, 83.

27. For proximate but somewhat different arguments about Asian American racialization, see Lowe, Li, and Palumbo-Liu. For Li, "Asian America" is the product of the contradictions of racial democracy, or "America's universalist promise of democratic consent and its race-, gender-, and culture-specific practice of citizenship." See Li, 6. For Lowe and Palumbo-Liu, racialization emerges from the contradictions between democracy and racial capitalism, between the "promise of political emancipation and the conditions of economic exploitation," between arguments for "egalitarianism, as well as class distinction," and between white supremacy and assimilation. See Lowe, 23, and Palumbo-Liu, 181. My argument shares more with Lowe's and Palumbo-Liu's than with Li's in moving beyond a "merely political" sphere of analysis. But whereas Lowe locates the contradiction (of which race is an attempted resolution) *between* the political and the economic, my approach is to view race as the effect of a contradiction *of* political economy, where a diachronic dimension is crucial, and politics and economics constitute interrelated rather than antithetical domains. Compared with that of Palumbo-Liu, my argument is more invested in how to narrate a process of Asian American racialization that requires that we rethink the category of white supremacy as a racial ideology.

28. On how Japan's "late industrialization" produced a "dyad of incommensurable judgement" along the lines of "Are the Japanese a threat or a model? . . . Are they inventors or purloiners?" see Cumings, *Parallax Visions*, 18–19.

29. On how the strategy of an Open Door policy presented an alternative to war by emphasizing shares instead of spheres, an investment expansion—which transformed basic class relations, social structures, and extended property relations—instead of older, territorial, settler, or commercial forms of imperialism, see Sklar, 80. See also LaFeber, *The New Empire*, 30–32. On the marketplace consciousness that fueled American empire, see Williams, *The Roots of the Modern American Empire*.

30. Bright and Geyer, "Where in the World is America?" 80.

31. Here my argument departs from approaches to Asian American racialization that essentially follow Said in positioning the East as the West's Manichean Other. See Marchetti, 6; Robert G. Lee, 8; and Lowe, 18. My argument comes closest to Okihiro's conceptualization of model minority and yellow peril, which sees them as linked moments of ideological attestation to and deconstruction of the "West"; however, for Okihiro, even as the model minority highlights compatible cultural norms, it basically positions Asia and America as antipodes. See Okihiro, *Margins*, 140. For many cultural critics of Asian America, including Okihiro, Lowe, and Li, it is the gap or "contradiction" between the American rhetoric of equality and the reality of racial hierarchy (however theorized) that results in the reification of the Asian American as antithetically alien.

32. See Cumings, *Parallax Visions*, 18–33; also Cumings, "The Origins and Development."

CHAPTER ONE

1. All three are from *Jack London's Tales of Adventure*.

2. Britain and the United States agreed to Japan's takeover of the Bonin (Osagawara) islands in 1873.

3. London was dubbed the "American Kipling" by early reviewers. In the 1890s Kipling was extolled by Americans as the preeminent English writer of short fiction, and his work appeared in many American magazines. London embarked on his writing career by deliberately emulating the most popular magazine fiction and the advice of short-story handbooks at the time. See McClintock, *White Logic*, xi, 6–7.

4. When London actually ventured beyond the safe bounds of U.S. territorial administration, to the South Seas, for instance, his travel texts did not retrieve the tropical paradise of his Hawaii writings, but a Conradian world that was dark and full of horror. See *Cruise of the Snark*. Nevertheless, London reserved his most scathing contempt for the tourist. See the discussion of London's "dual Pacific Worlds" in Labor's "Jack London's Pacific World." For London's Hawaii and Alaska as America's "remote and internal colonies," see Howard, *Form and History*, 173.

5. The natives in London's Northland and Hawaii fiction are considered, at times, inferior to Anglo-Saxons yet admirable for their primitive warrior qualities of resourcefulness, honesty, loyalty, and self-sacrifice. See the Yukon stories collected in *The Son of the Wolf* and his *Stories of Hawaii*. Labor makes the observation that London's fame as a storyteller of the Klondike notwithstanding, it is the Pacific which engages London's earliest interest and informs the exotic imagination of his other settings. See Labor, "London's Pacific World." However, the "Pacific World" Labor analyzes is a Manichaean one, split between a bucolic paradise despoiled by white men and a fiendish jungle that turns whites into savages—not the space of the Asiatic that concerns me here.

6. London, *The Iron Heel* from *Novels and Writings*, 473–74 (hereafter cited as *IH*).

7. In 1919 *The Iron Heel* was hailed by the American news media for having anticipated the government suppression of radicals, and in 1923 it was hailed by Anatole France in its first French edition. See Joan London, *Jack London and His Times*, 311.

8. With the exceptions of Eugene V. Debs, Bill Haywood, and Mary Marcy, Socialist Party leaders ignored it or sought to distance themselves from the novel. See Philip Foner, *Jack London*, 95–96. For an example of a contemporary socialist response, see the review of *The Iron Heel* by Spargo in *The International Socialist Review*, 628–29.

9. Johnston, *Jack London—An American Rebel?* 68.

10. Joan London, *Jack London*, 122. Among California socialists, many were

former Populists. However, the Oakland membership was primarily utopian and reformist rather than radical, and London was among the few who considered themselves revolutionary socialists. See Johnston, 70.

11. Work that emphasizes London's radicalism tends to downplay his racism. For example, Philip Foner, who celebrates London as an "American rebel," reconciles the contradiction by temporally separating London's "socialistic" moments from his "racist ones"; London's socialist writings lowered race barriers, Foner argues, but when London drifted away from socialism, his racism returned. See Foner, 36. Work that attends to questions of race in London, conversely, tends not to take his socialism very seriously. See Cain, "Socialism, Power, and the Fate of Style." In their introduction to a recent anthology of critical essays on London, many of which concern his colonial and racial representations, Cassuto and Reesman refer to London's "eccentric vision of individualistic socialism." See their introduction in *Rereading Jack London*, 4. Noting that London's socialism was for "whites only," Johnston characterizes London as having a naïve understanding of socialism. See Johnston, 31–32, 48.

12. For the former, see Joan London, 285. For the latter, see Auerbach's excellent *Male Call*.

13. In *Revolution and Other Essays* and *Jack London Reports* (cited hereafter as YP and JWC, respectively).

14. See Mallan, "Roosevelt, Brooks Adams and Lea," 216–30.

15. For the link between monopoly capitalism and imperialism, see Lenin, "Imperialism, the Highest Stage of Capitalism."

16. As quoted in Perry, *Jack London: An American Myth*, 174.

17. For an alternative account of the American version of the yellow peril that gives relatively more weight to the influence of Brooks Adams and Pierton Dooner, see Okihiro, *Margins and Mainstreams*, 129–31.

18. Theodore Roosevelt was awarded the Nobel Peace Prize for arbitrating the terms of the peace between Russia and Japan at Portsmouth.

19. See the essays in Kaplan and Pease.

20. Miller, *The Unwelcome Immigrant*, 110.

21. Offner, "'Pacific Rim' Societies," 228. In the United States, Chinese immigration exclusion was passed in 1882.

22. According to Neu, the "Pacific Cruise" served three purposes: to display American power and preparedness to Japan and Europe; to make Japan realize the United States wanted settlement of the immigration question; and to symbolize the unity of English-speaking peoples of the Pacific against Japanese encroachments. Australian reception of the cruise, Neu writes, as exemplified in the proclamation by the *Melbourne Age* of "the common trust of the two white races whose destinies are bound up in Pacific dominance," constituted the first outward sign of Australia's disposition to lean for support on the U.S. instead of Britain. The West Coast, likewise, received the cruise as a validation of it as part of the United States after a period of building tension with federal officials over the question of Japanese immigration and school segregation. See *An Uncertain Friendship*, 216. For the specifically U.S.-character of the "Pacific Rim" idea, see Dirlik, "The Asia-Pacific Idea," 61. For the "Pacific Rim" as a symptom of a par-

ticular crisis of U.S self-imagining toward the end of the Cold War, see Connery, "Pacific Rim Discourse."

23. Saxton, *The Indispensable Enemy*.

24. See, for instance, an article in the official journal of the American Federation of Labor that makes the parallel argument that the Japanese "cannot be unionized" and "cannot be Americanized." Pio, "Exclude Japanese Labor," 274–76.

25. For a representative text, see Commons, *Race and Immigrants in America*. This was published as a contribution to early congressional debates on immigration restriction, and was reissued in 1920, in the era when the last and most restrictive of the Progressive immigration bills was debated and passed. For a discussion of Commons in relation to the Turnerian frontier, see Slotkin, *Gunfighter Nation*, 190.

26. Hall, "Race, Articulation and Societies Structured in Dominance."

27. See Lucie Cheng and Bonacich, eds., *Labor Immigration*.

28. Robert G. Lee observes that there is little to support the nineteenth-century claim that the Chinese arrived in the U.S. as unfree labor, similar to the thousands who were transported as contract labor to Cuba and Peru. The Chinese actually arrived as free labor in an economic and legal sense, but once here were proletarianized and racially excluded as "coolies." See Lee, 58.

29. Roediger, *The Wages of Whiteness*, 78–97.

30. Roediger appends the anti-Chinese issue to the anti-black racism of trade unions. See Roediger, 168, 179. Stuart Miller holds that Easterners' hostility to Chinese immigration was solidified on the basis of the slavery issue. The fear that Chinese slavery was being instituted on the West Coast was expressed in a Boston paper as early as 1853, and in 1862 Congress passed a law stipulating that all Chinese immigration had to be voluntary and prohibiting American vessels from transporting coolies anywhere. See Miller, *Unwelcome Immigrant*, 150, 153.

31. Almaguer, *Racial Faultlines*, 7, 205–6. Current scholarship, however, is only just beginning to develop this comparative question. The work of Hoang Phan addresses the question of how the "Chinese race" figures as that form of labor that threatens the status of "free labor" in ways historically and ideologically distinguished from slavery. Phan, "Civic Identity and the Invention of the Asiatic," chapter of unpublished UC Berkeley English dissertation (in progress), "The Labors of Difference." On how "coolieism" helped to preserve "free labor" as an ideological refuge for the white workingman in ways largely analogous to "Nigger work," see Robert G. Lee, 57, 82.

32. U.S. acquisition of the Philippines immediately expanded the space of Chinese exclusion to Southeast Asia, with the exclusion policy on Chinese contract labor applied to the Philippines (as well as Puerto Rico and Cuba) in 1899. The renewal of the act in 1904 extended exclusion laws without time limit and applied them to U.S. insular possessions: the Chinese populations of Hawaii and the Philippines, unless U.S. citizens, were barred from the U.S. mainland.

33. Brooks Adams, "The New Industrial Revolution," 162.

34. Marx, "Revolution in China and Europe," in *On Colonialism*, 19.

35. "Revolution in China and Europe," 24. It should be noted that by "Chinese

revolution" Marx does not mean a political revolution by a developed Chinese working class. Marx seems to be referring, alternatively, to the disruption engendered by the dissolution of the authority of the emperor and "old China;" to the "chronic rebellions subsisting in China for the ten years past, and now gathered together in one formidable revolution," resulting in the resistance to the British sale of opium; or to the Chinese demand for "precious metals" in return for tea and silk, resulting in the following for England: a rise in the price of tea, a chief article of consumption; a drain of bullion; and "a great contraction of an important market for her cotton and woolen goods." Interestingly, Marx attributes the Chinese demand for payment in "hard money" to an "Oriental behavior" of hoarding and failure to consume: "The Chinese, ready though they may be, as are all people in periods of revolutionary convulsion, to sell off to the foreigner all the bulky commodities they have on hand, will, as the Orientals are used to do in the apprehension of great changes, set to hoarding. . . ." Thus Marx is not suggesting that revolution in Europe, in the proper Marxian sense, is to be preceded by one in China, but rather that China functions as the market that accelerates the crisis of capital likely to bring on revolution in Europe. Marx, 19, 21, 23.

36. Mahan, *The Problem of Asia*, 19, 86.

37. McKee, *Chinese Exclusion*, 17. Individuals such as U.S. China expert William Rockhill, U.S. Minister to China Charles Denby, Henry Cabot Lodge, and New Hampshire Congressman Jacob Gallinger all thought China offered a vast market for American goods that would propel the United States ahead of other Western nations. See McClellan, *The Heathen Chinee*, 168–72.

38. Tyler Dennett provides a history that portrays the United States as a critic of British and European imperialism in China and as an example of the forging of a different kind of relation. Indeed, Dennett goes so far as to claim that at the end of the century the United States was more nearly allied, by commercial and political necessity, to Asia and to Asiatic aspirations than to Europe. See *Americans in East Asia*, 632.

39. Mahan's thinking had great influence on the build up of the American navy under the Roosevelt administration.

40. Sir Henry Rawlinson was a leading Russophobe of the day—a proponent of the Forward School who argued that the British occupy Herat in order to preempt a potential Russian seizure of this valuable "gateway to India." See *England and Russia in the East*. For British representations of Russians, see Hopkirk, *Quest for* Kim and *The Great Game*.

41. Hauner, *What Is Asia to Us?* 49. This racial property disqualification in the interests of Russian colonial appropriation of areas in which Chinese and Koreans were resident might be fruitfully compared to the U.S. 1913 Alien Land Bill, aimed at the Japanese, which prohibited the purchase or leasing for longer than three years of any land by aliens ineligible for citizenship. Such a parallel between the anti-Asian legislations of two expanding colonial powers, Russia and the United States, underscores the necessity of locating the U.S. Asian exclusion movement within the context of Pacific Rim imperialisms.

42. The 1895 painting was accompanied by the caption: "Nations of Europe, Guard Your Most Precious Possessions." For a discussion of the painting, see McClellan, 230.

43. See Dennett, *Theodore Roosevelt and the Russo-Japanese War*, 26, 120.

44. To give one example among many magazine articles of the period, see Proctor, "Saxon or Slav?" 1179.

45. See Mahan, *The Influence of Sea Power on History* and Mackinder, "The Geographical Pivot of History." Note that in Brooks Adams's reading, this new Orientalist geographical discourse becomes so spatially flexible that even France and Germany are constituted as Others to Britain by being identified as "continental powers." See Adams, *America's Economic Supremacy*. Geopolitics clearly informs racial ideology in the way France also gives trouble to wishful fantasies of consolidating the Anglo-Saxon nations. See Dos Passos, *The Anglo-Saxon Century*.

46. For a discussion of Mackinder's views on this subject, see Hauner, 122–46. Note that the "Western seapower" versus "Eastern landpower" model persists in American Cold War discourse on the Soviet Union, as in Gray, "Keeping the Soviets Landlocked." Hauner argues that the containment strategy credited to George Kennan Jr., during the Cold War actually originates with Mackinder's "heartland" theory. See Hauner, 161.

47. See also the construction of Nish's study, *The Anglo-Japanese Alliance*.

48. For instance, Maxey, "Why We Favor Japan in the Present War," 505–10; Boulger, "Russia, Japan and Ourselves," 368–74. For a dissenting Korean (American) point of view on Japanese imperialism, see Chung, *Oriental Policy of the United States*. Chung seeks to convince his American audience that Japan is not the "Britain of the East" so much as the "Prussia of the East." Chung prefers the "crude and brutal" forms of Russian conquest to the "subtle and insidious" tactics of the Japanese, who have received no U.S. censure for their actions in Korea and China. See Chung, 168, 113.

49. Historical analysis of American attitudes toward Japan has sometimes split this ambivalence into a conflict between an official state sentiment depicted as "pro-Japan" and a popular sentiment depicted as anti-Asian. But to do so, I think, is to exonerate the state and other hegemonic discourses associated with it from racial ambivalence. At the level of the state, the U.S. reflects, borrowing the words of Neu, an "uncertain friendship" with Japan, given that the Russo-Japanese War left Japan with hegemony over Korea, extensive rights in Manchuria, and unknown ambitions in China. See Neu, 19.

50. Dennett writes that Theodore Roosevelt approached Europe through the Pacific, and Asia formed the United States's "back door" to European politics. See *Theodore Roosevelt*, 5–6. For an authoritative account of the rise of U.S. imperialism in the period, see Beale, *Theodore Roosevelt and the Rise of America to World Power*.

51. According to Neu, the Russo-Japanese War marked the end of an uncomplicated view of Japan as an American protégé. See Neu, 19. For the peak of U.S.-Japan tension from 1900 to the signing of the Root-Takahira Agreement of 1908, see Bailey, *Theodore Roosevelt and the Japanese-American Crisis*.

52. In works such as *Valor of Ignorance* and *Day of the Saxon*, Homer Lea laments the loss of the martial spirit among the "Saxon nations" and sees its strongest modern embodiment in the New Japan. A plea for the United States to create a standing army, *Valor of Ignorance* concludes with a fantasy of Japanese invasion of the West Coast which catches the U.S. offguard.

53. Travis, *George Kennan and the Russian-American Relationship*, 294–96, 264–65. George Kennan is an older relative of George Kennan Jr., the architect of U.S. Cold War containment policy.

54. Kennan, "The Story of Port Arthur, VI," 998 (hereafter cited as VI).

55. Kennan, "The Story of Port Arthur, I," 526–27 (hereafter cited as I). See also, "The Story of Port Arthur, II," 631–32 (hereafter cited as II).

56. Kennan, "The Story of Port Arthur, III," 779 (hereafter cited as III). This move is not unique to Kennan. In *Arena*, another writer argues that while Russia and Japan present examples of isolated countries "suddenly" brought face-to-face with European civilization, the Russian worker and capitalist are less capable of understanding European industries than are the Japanese. See Albrecht, "The Situation in the Russian Interior," 225–31.

57. Kennan, "The Story of Port Arthur, VIII," 178 (hereafter cited as VIII).

58. Kennan, "The Story of Port Arthur, IV," 893 (hereafter cited as IV).

59. Kennan, "The Story of Port Arthur, X," 426 (hereafter cited as X).

60. Kennan, "The Story of Port Arthur, XI," 628 (hereafter cited as XI).

61. "I was interested in making the discovery that it was possible to see the shell, and even to photograph it, in one particular part of its course." See Kennan, "The Story of Port Arthur, IX," 228 (hereafter cited as IX).

62. Kennan, "The Destruction of the Baltic Fleet," 814 (hereafter cited as DBF).

63. Riis, *How the Other Half Lives*, 6.

64. Kennan, IX: 230.

65. Nothing, Riis writes, "can dam the stream of homelessness that issues from a source where the very name of home is a mockery." See Riis, 153. For the idea of modernity as the loss of totality in which "the world is wide and yet it is like home," see Lukács, *The Theory of the Novel*, 29. Reading the realist novel in relation to the problem of exerting control over increasingly threatening urban spaces, Kaplan writes: "The project of the realist novel is to make these rented spaces inhabitable and representable. While realistic narratives chart the homelessness of their characters, they thereby construct a world in which their readers can feel at home." See Kaplan, *Social Construction of American Realism*, 8.

66. Kennan's experience is evocative of the sensation that Freud has called the "uncanny," defined as "that class of the frightening which leads back to what is known of old and long familiar." See the 1919 essay, "The 'Uncanny,' " in Freud, *Standard Edition of the Complete Psychological Works*, 17:220.

67. The Japanese government did indeed impose strict military censorship upon foreign correspondents, with long delays before visits to the front. This military censorship, however, reflected a wider international trend. For an early example of British military censorship in the battle of Omdurman in 1898, see Springhall, "Up Guards and at Them!" 58.

68. Hereafter cited as JCMS and JPUC, respectively. Citations are taken from articles reprinted in *Jack London Reports*.

69. Jack London, "Japanese in Invisible War," 108 (hereafter cited as JIW).

70. Jack London, "Japanese Supplies Rushed to Front by Man and Beast," 95 (hereafter cited as JSRF).

71. Jack London, "The Monkey Cage," 114 (hereafter cited as MC).

72. Jack London, "Give Battle to Retard Enemy," 100 (hereafter cited as GBRE).

73. See Jack London, "Dr. Moffett." Since the *Examiner* claimed never to have received this dispatch, the text was obtained by the editors of *Jack London Reports* from a holograph in the London archives at the Huntington Library.

74. Isabella Bird Bishop (1831–1904) was an English explorer and the author of such travel books as *Journeys in Persia and Kurdistan* (1891) and *Chinese Pictures* (1900).

75. Jack London, "Americans Praise Japan's Army," 47–48 (hereafter cited as APJ).

76. See, for example, Jack London, "Vivid Description of Army in Korea," 42 (hereafter cited as VDAK).

77. "Royal Road a Sea of Mud," 47 (hereafter cited as RSM).

78. Jack London, "The Sufferings of the Japanese," 78 (hereafter cited as SJ).

79. Auerbach, 16. Also see Seltzer's reading of London's *Call of the Wild* in *Bodies and Machines*, 166–72. For the professionalization of turn-of-the-century American writers, see Wilson, "American Naturalism and the Problem of Sincerity."

80. Furer approaches the question of region in London differently than I do. Pointing to London's depiction of the Anglo-Saxon tendency to conquer peoples of various climatic "zones," Furer counterposes London's racist Yukon writings to what he perceives as his antiracist Pacific tales in which stories such as "Chun Ah Chun" (1908) and "Koolau the Leper" (1908) valorize characters of Chinese and Hawaiian ancestry. Furer argues that with the publication of *The House of Pride* (1912), London's fear of the yellow peril appears to subside. See Furer, "'Zone Conquerors' and 'White Devils,'" 158–59, 163. While I would question the antiracist reading of these portraits, it is certainly the case that London's writings set in the Pacific islands are contradictorily governed by the logic of his Asiatic geography.

81. Jack London, "Letter" (March 8, 1904), 14.

82. Jack London, "Letter" (February 11, 1904), 9.

83. Jack London, "Letter" (February 9, 1904), 8–9.

84. Jack London, "Letter" (April 1, 1904), 18.

85. Jack London, "Letter" (March 29, 1904), 18.

86. Jack London, "Letter" (May 22, 1904), 23–24. The censor to whom he refers is the Japanese one.

87. Joan London's biography of her father describes him as essentially a fiction writer who turned to journalism only when financially necessary. Muckraking had no appeal to him, she writes, as he viewed it as the voice of the middle class that stood by unmoved during the Populist outcry of the late nineteenth century (Joan London, 242).

88. For this period as defined by the problematic of the "corporate form," see Trachtenberg, *The Incorporation of America*. For the centrality of efficiency to the social reform imagination of Progressivism, see Hays, *Conservation and the Gospel of Efficiency*.

89. Jack London, "Goliah."

90. Jack London, "The Unparalleled Invasion."

91. At least one critic has attempted to recuperate London from charges of

racism by reading "The Unparalleled Invasion" as a critical representation of the Western invasion of the non-West, with biological germs being used to stand in for the unseen yet thoroughgoing operations of cultural imperialism. See Berkove, " A Parallax Correction," 33–39.

92. In 1937 Leon Trotsky wrote that *The Iron Heel*'s foresight made it more real and sharp in the 1930s than in 1905, and that the class warfare that once appeared pessimistically brutal, in the era of fascism felt progressively hopeful. See Trotsky, 95.

93. On naturalism and Progressivism's shared condescension toward the working classes, see Howard, 127.

94. Portelli, "Jack London's Missing Revolution," 187.

95. Joan London, 284. Tsuji notes the calming of London's racial animus between his 1904 "The Yellow Peril" and his 1909 "If Japan Wakes China." See Tsuji, "Jack London and the Yellow Peril," 96–99.

96. See Glancy, "Socialist with a Valet," 33–34. Manyoungi, with whom London was henceforth never to be without, was the first of his personal servants, all of whom were Asian (Joan London, 286).

97. Johnston notes London's thwarted quest for adventure in Korea and return in July of 1904 to Oakland, where he again looked to the socialist struggle for romance. See Johnston, 96.

98. Jack London, "Cossacks Fight then Retreat," 51–53.

99. The essay entitled "The Yellow Peril," though composed in Manchuria in June 1904, was not published in the *San Francisco Examiner* until September 25, 1904, after London's return to the United States.

CHAPTER TWO

1. Ferrero-Lombroso, *Criminal Man*, 24. The original text in Italian appeared in 1876, and the French edition in 1887. Nordau's *Degeneration*, which helped to acquaint American readers with Lombroso, appeared in March 1895 and was the much discussed book of the year. Frank Norris's explicit enthusiasm for Lombroso is evidenced in his story "A Case for Lombroso," which appeared in *The Wave*, Sept. 11, 1897.

2. Quoted in Pick, *Faces of Degeneration*, 216 (hereafter cited as *Faces*).

3. Howard, *Form and History in American Literary Naturalism*, 93.

4. Norris, "She and the Other Fellow," 242.

5. Norris, "After Strange Gods," 379 (hereafter cited as ASG).

6. "Death of Asia" is James Moy's term. See Moy, *Marginal Sights*, 82–94.

7. Norris, "Thoroughbred," 197 (hereafter cited as T).

8. Robert G. Lee characterizes the coolie as having represented a "third sex"—ambiguous, inscrutable, and hermaphroditic. This gender representation is traceable to the anti-Chinese movement's precipitation in the 1870s partly by the establishment of family life and the arrival of white women, with many services provided by Chinese immigrant men now performed by families. See *Orientals*, 85, 94.

9. For late nineteenth- and early-twentieth-century Anglo-Saxonism, see

Higham, *Strangers in the Land* (hereafter cited as *Strangers*). For early-nineteenth-century Anglo-Saxonism, see Horsman, *Race and Manifest Destiny*.

10. The key text giving voice to the idea that the end of the nineteenth century also brings to a close the unique conditions of the American frontier is Frederick Jackson Turner's "The Significance of the Frontier in American History," delivered as a lecture at the World's Columbian Exposition in Chicago before a group of historians, July 12, 1893.

11. Ross, "The Causes of Race Superiority," 87. Ross was one of the most prominent sociologists of his day. For a like-minded view of the dangers of immigration, see Walker, "Immigration and Degradation." For the popularity of Anglo-Saxon "race suicide" as social scientific notion at the time, see Wald, *Constituting Americans*, 245–46.

12. Though the discourses of degeneration travel from Europe to America via criminal anthropology, the development of this discourse into a grand thesis of the decline of the West is pioneered in America vis-à-vis the Asiatic encounter, before being transported back to Europe. Charles Beard observes that Brooks Adams's *The Law of Civilization and Decay* (1896) anticipated Oswald Spengler's *Decline of the West* (1932; originally published in German in 1922). See Beard, introduction to *The Law of Civilization and Decay*, vii.

13. The nineteenth-century California socialist Henry George has similar difficulty rationalizing his support for free trade and his opposition to Asian immigration, but in his case the result is an incoherent distinction between the economic effects upon U.S. wages by Chinese labor in America and Chinese labor in China. George's position takes for granted that the two simply cannot be engaged in producing the same goods: free trade, in his logic, is defended to the degree that it is grasped as a foreign exchange of different commodities—American cigars, for instance, for Chinese tea—and not as part of a forced modernization process rapidly integrating China into a capitalist world system. See Henry George's testimony before the Congressional Joint Special Committee's investigation of Chinese immigration in 1876, which lent substantial impetus to the ensuing exclusion laws, in Philip Foner and Rosenberg, eds., *Racism, Dissent, and Asian Americans*, 26–29. For Friedrich Engels's critique of George for his failure to see a contradiction between capital and labor and his misplaced emphasis on landed private property as the sole cause of social inequality, see Engels, "The Labor Movement in the United States," 287–89. Engels's essay originally appeared as the appendix to the American edition of *The Conditions of the Working Class in England* (1887), which was the first edition of the book in English.

14. In his study of how "savage war" substituted for "class war" in America, Slotkin addresses the coincidence between the closure of the old "agrarian/artisanal/entrepreneurial" frontier with a crisis in American social and political history in which class conflict could no longer be disarmed by the frontier myth. In taking a continental view of American space, Slotkin privileges a discourse of savagery for providing the terms of representation for the Others of industrial modernity: strikers, the urban mob, et cetera. For him, the Spanish-American War and the war in the Philippines are logical extensions of the Indian wars. See *Gunfighter Nation*, 31, 51. Although complicating the convention of frontier violence by viewing it through the lens of U.S. imperial adventures in the period,

Amy Kaplan emphasizes aspects of continuity between the victims of continental conquest and victims of imperialism, writing that the "spectacle of American manhood and nostalgia for the American past" denies "political agency and visibility to the subjects of the American empire." See "Romancing the Empire," 661.

15. Justification for reading Ross within the discursive context of Chinese Asia-Pacific labor migration becomes even clearer when we compare to his disquisition on Chinese immigration and Anglo-Saxon race suicide the writings of Charles Pearson, an Australian author concerned with Chinese southward expansion who lamented the "unchangeable limits of the higher races." In Pearson, as in Ross, these limits have to do with climatic adaptability, which prevents the Aryan race from being able to "stamp out or starve out all their rivals on the face of the earth." See Pearson, *National Life and Character*, 31.

16. In *The Law of Civilization and Decay*, Brooks Adams lays out the connections between the modern tendency of the West toward centralization and decline, and the rise of Asia in the world. Through the appreciation of gold, the value of the dollar has declined against eastern currency, "and the effect is the same as though the tenacity of life of the Asiatic has been increased four-sixths." "The cheapest form of labour is thus being bred on a gigantic scale, and this labour is being accelerated by an industrial development which is stimulated by eviction of the farmers, as the 'industrial revolution' was stimulated in England one hundred and thirty years ago." See Adams, *The Law of Civilization and Decay*, 292. As Henry Adams comments to his brother after reading the book, "On your wording of your Law, it seemed to me to come out, in its first equation thus, in the fewest possible words: All civilization is Centralization. All Centralization is Economy. Therefore all Civilization is the survival of the most economical (cheapest). Darwin called it fittest, and in one sense fittest is the fittest word. Unfortunately it is always relative, and therefore liable to misunderstanding. Your other formula is more difficult. Under economic centralization, Asia is cheaper than Europe. The world tends to economical centralization. Therefore Asia tends to survive, and Europe to perish . . ." (quoted in Beard). See Beard, xlii–xliii. Likewise, Jack London demonstrates a concern with the "shrinkage of the planet" as a result of the fact that the "favored portions of the earth are occupied," leaving no more places to explore, and because of the advances in technology annihilating "space and time" so that all parts of the world are "accessible and drawn . . . closer together." See London, "The Shrinkage of the Planet," 148, 155. Following Adams, London writes, "From man's drawing the world closer and closer together, his own affairs and institutions have consolidated. Concentration may typify the chief movement of the age—concentration, classification, order; the reduction of friction between the parts of the social organism." Planetary shrinkage is inaugurated by the fact that "in 1869 the East was made next door neighbor to the West." See 154, 146.

17. Smith, *Chinese Characteristics*, 96–97.

18. Brooks Adams, "The New Industrial Revolution," 165.

19. Stout, *Chinese Immigration and the Physiological Causes of the Decay of a Nation*, 14. Arthur Stout was a prominent physician with connections to the American Medical Association.

20. "American Manhood against Asiatic Coolieism. Which Shall Survive?" is the subtitle of Samuel Gompers's 1902 pamphlet submitted as congressional testimony. See Gompers, *Meat versus Rice*.

21. Cf. Edward Said's account of how the "West" constructs the "East" in *Orientalism*.

22. White, "The Forms of Wildness," 21. McTeague is an example of a Norris character whose decline into brutishness is symbolized as the unleashing of animal impulses of lust and violence. London's famous dog stories, *Call of the Wild* and *White Fang*, also locate brutishness on the axis of wilderness and civilization.

23. For the degradation of work under monopoly capitalism, see Harry Braverman's classic *Labor and Monopoly Capital*.

24. Lenin, "Imperialism, the Highest Stage of Capitalism." Lenin followed the liberal J. A. Hobson in making the epochal link between the rise of imperialism and the rise of monopoly finance capitalism.

25. For naturalism as a literature of market culture, see Michaels, *The Gold Standard and the Logic of Naturalism*. For realism and naturalism as structured by the contradictions of class conflict and mass culture, see Kaplan, *The Social Construction of American Realism*. For naturalism as a literature of machine culture, see Seltzer, *Bodies and Machines*. My argument most resembles Howard's account of naturalism in relation to the increasing dominance of "market relations in a national and even global economy; and the presence of class struggle in a nation with a constantly increasing, largely immigrant urban proletariat that was both very vulnerable to the recurrent economic depressions and relatively visible to other classes." See Howard, 71–72.

26. A basis for the racial articulation of this contradiction may be discoverable in Martin J. Sklar's suggestion that the Open Door strategy offered an alternative to war as a way of resolving the disequilibrium caused by surplus capital and that the model of investment expansion it entailed marked a general transformation of basic class relations, social structures, and the extension of property relations characteristic of the era's "corporate reconstruction." See Sklar, *The Corporate Reconstruction of America*, 80. Wu is perhaps the first to have noted the special intimacy between naturalism and labor unionism in forging the discourse of Asian exclusionism, though his formulation of the relationships among these three terms differs from mine. "Between 1882 and 1908," he writes, "naturalism replaces labor issues as the force behind hostility to the Chinese immigrants in fiction." See Wu, *The Yellow Peril*, 78. For the relatively peripheral character of ideological anti-Semitism in the United States before World War I, see Higham, *Send These to Me*, 95–116.

27. See Saxton, *The Indispensable Enemy*. Saxton argues that anti-Asianism was a symptom of a conservative mainstream labor movement whose craft bias mobilized a racial and ethnic rhetoric to justify exclusion of the unskilled proletarian majority.

28. See Postone, "Anti-Semitism and National Socialism," 303.

29. Hofstader, *Age of Reform*, 61–62.

30. Riis, *How the Other Half Lives*, 98.

31. Preston, *Aliens and Dissenters*.

32. For the popularization of this notion, see Lowe, *Immigrant Acts*, 4.

33. Koshy, "Morphing Race into Ethnicity," 155.

34. Roediger, *The Wages of Whiteness*. On anti-Chinese feeling, he writes: "Labor and anti-Chinese movements overlapped so thoroughly as to be indistinguishable, with the exclusion issue providing the basis for labor unity at key points." See 179. Susan Koshy takes her lead from Roediger's position.

35. See Mink, *Old Labor and New Immigrants*.

36. Eric Foner, "Why is there no socialism in the United States?"

37. In defining itself so much against the Chicago school of sociology, Asian American studies from early on has tended to polarize race and ethnicity on the basis of permanent difference versus potential assimilation. For a nuanced intellectual history of ethnic studies that stresses the ambiguous continuities between the Chicago school of sociology and post-1960s Asian American studies, see Yu, *Thinking Orientals*, 104–5, 193, 198–99.

38. Saxton uses a "Close the Ports" article in the *American Federationist* that year to date this shift, though there isn't a clear-cut correspondence between speech making and policy adoption. For example, by 1892 or so, AFL organs began to stress the evils of "unrestricted immigration," but in 1894 the AFL still officially favored free entry for all except Asians. See Saxton, 273–77.

39. The 1924 Immigration Act installed a quota system based on national origins and stopped the admission of any alien ineligible for citizenship. Among immigrant groups, this extended only to those categorized as "Mongolian." For excerpts of the relevant court opinions, see Hing, *Making and Remaking Asian America*, 226–31.

40. Powderly, "Exclude Anarchist and Chinaman!" 5.

41. Powderly's articulation of "anarchism" to the new European immigration is not idiosyncratic. Take, for example, a quote from the *Los Angeles Times* (August 23, 1893): "If we can keep out the Chinese, there is no reason why we cannot exclude the lower classes of Poles, Hungarians, Italians and some other European nations which people possess most of the vices of the Chinese and few of their good qualities, besides having a leaning toward bloodshed and anarchy which is peculiarly their own." Quoted in Saxton, 234. See also Preston.

42. On the former, take for example, the San Francisco *Truth* (July 5, 1882): "Voted out, drowned out by beer and gin, and pauperized out with the general drunkenness and misery, and beggary that would be entailed upon us . . . The last thing but one this country wants is to be flooded by hordes of Chinese and Malays, and that one is to be similarly flooded by hordes of ignorant, barbarous, incompetent, incapable, intractable slaves from the Mediterranean. If we want millions of brute labor, the Chinamen and the donkey are the best brutes we have." Quoted in Saxton, 275. As regards the latter, Yuji Ichioka's chronicle of the organizing efforts by Japanese workers and the existence of Japanese socialist activity in the San Francisco Bay Area demonstrates that the AFL certainly did have an alternative to viewing Asians as scab labor. See *The Issei*.

43. The period 1901–1906 marked the height of official government persecution of Chinese entering the United States who were uniformly assumed to be laborers in disguise. In 1903 the Immigration Bureau adopted the Bertillon system for the inspection of Chinese immigrants. Developed by criminal anthropology, the system was a "scientific method of identifying criminals by the accurate mea-

surement and inspection of the naked body." See McKee, *Chinese Exclusion versus the Open Door, 1900–1906*, 74, 143. 1901 also marked the rise of the Japanese and Korean Exclusion League and the effort to extend the 1882 Exclusion Act to these groups.

44. The 1903 Immigration Act for the first time excluded aliens because of their beliefs, but this meant that the state was taking on the difficult task of determining which beliefs were un-American. Preston observes that although Roosevelt thought that "when compared with suppression of anarchy, every other question sinks into insignificance," the state was never able to discover very many anarchists. Between 1903 and 1921, thirty-eight persons were excluded for holding anarchistic beliefs, and between 1911 and 1919, when the red scare deportations began, fourteen aliens of the "anarchistic classes" were deported. The vagueness of the 1917 law as to what exactly constituted advocacy of radicalism coupled with the assignation of broad power to the Immigration Bureau to deport radicals placed federal officers in the position of constantly trying to uncover "passive and insidious forms" of radical activity. See Preston, 33, 84.

45. On southern and eastern Europeans, the San Francisco *Truth* held that "The trouble with this class is not that it does not assimilate (the objection urged against the Chinese) but that it does, and the assimilation has the same effect as that of poisonous weeds growing among wheat" (September 27, 1882). Quoted in Saxton, 275.

46. David D. Anderson, *Ignatius Donnelly*, 67–68.

47. Donnelly, *Caesar's Column*, 110 (hereafter cited as CC).

48. Note that the rhetoric of diet figures heavily into Asian exclusionist discourse in the period. See Gompers.

49. See F. W. Taylor, *The Principles of Scientific Management*. See also, Rabinbach, *The Human Motor*.

50. George, "The Chinese in California."

51. Warren, *Black and White Strangers*, 129.

52. A phrase Warren uses to describe the image of the black African in the eyes of the white audiences of plantation fiction and minstrelsy in the 1890s. See Warren, 119.

53. For a similar argument, see Robert G. Lee, 16, 32, 49, 53, 61.

54. Convention resolution, cited in Saxton, 222 (emphasis added).

55. Jack London, *The Iron Heel*, 371 (hereafter cited as *IH*).

56. George, *Progress and Poverty*, 539 (hereafter cited as *PP*).

57. Perry Anderson, *Lineages of the Absolutist State*, 472.

58. Hindess and Hirst, *Pre-Capitalist Modes of Production*, 198–200.

59. For naturalism's aestheticization of disintegrating reality, see Baguley, "The Nature of Naturalism," 18.

60. See Jack London, *The People of the Abyss*, 234–35, 316–17. For an analysis of how *The People of the Abyss* asserts Americanness as a subject-position from which to judge the English poor at a distance, see Peluso, "Gazing at Royalty," 59. Peluso reads the book to participate in a contest of positional superiority for imperial dominance.

61. Joan London, *Jack London and His Times*, 379. In the January 1929 issue of *New Masses*, Martin Russak celebrated London as a "real proletarian writer"

who wrote about the working class, was read by the working class, used his own proletarian life as material, and whose writing burned with the spirit of revolt. See Philip Foner, *Jack London: American Rebel*, 7. Foner praises London for knowing how to simplify a difficult subject for politically illiterate audiences and for applying Marxism to American conditions. See Foner, 55.

62. Norris, *The Octopus* (hereafter cited as *TO*). All citations will be taken from this edition.

63. Walker, *Frank Norris: A Biography*, 273.

64. Henderson, *California and the Fictions of Capital*, 5–7.

65. James Machor points to critics' worry about the disjuncture between the final rhapsodic faith in the wheat and moral optimism, and the amoral determinism and pathos pervading the story of the ranchers and the railroad. See "Epic, Romance and Norris's *The Octopus*," 42.

66. Pizer represents the view of 1960s critics who viewed *The Octopus* as "more a novel about man's relationship to nature than a story of man as a social being. . . ." See Pizer, *The Novels of Frank Norris*, 121. Some of this earlier critical discussion is fascinating. In an intriguing reading of the novel's theory of nature, James Folsom collapses the opposition between railroad and ranchers by showing how they both symbolize an animal nature at odds with the wheat's vegetable nature. See "The Wheat and the Locomotive," 68–70.

67. See Starr's introduction to *The Octopus*, xxv.

68. The physical proximity of Bonneville and Guadalajara is a geographical invention of *The Octopus* that reflects the thematic importance of the U.S.-Mexico border to symbolic representations of Californian political economy.

69. I place "new immigrants" in quotation marks because *The Octopus* does not seem to differentiate recent European arrivals from Mexicans and Indians. To some extent the basis of difference among the various social groupings in the novel is more consistently religious: Jews and Catholics against Protestants.

70. Howard mentions the exclusion of Chinese workers from the scene as part of the text's erasure of the laborer in general. See Howard, 122–23. I approach a reading of Asian exclusion in the text differently.

71. See Williams, *The Roots of American Empire*.

72. For the China market as an imaginary solution to the nation's problems of overproduction in this period, see Eperjesi, "The American Asiatic Association," 209.

73. Norris, "The Frontier Gone At Last," 1183 (hereafter cited as FGL). Norris's reference to the U.S. marine suggests that the event he has in mind is American military participation in the suppression of the 1901 Boxer Rebellion.

74. In a March 1899 letter to William Dean Howells, who had just reviewed *McTeague* favorably in *Literature*, Norris wrote: "I think there is a chance for somebody to do some great work with the West and California as background, and which will be at the same time thoroughly American. My idea is to write three novels around the one subject of *Wheat*. First, a story of California (the producer), second, a story of Chicago (the distributor), third, a story of Europe (the consumer) and in each to keep to the idea of this huge Niagara of wheat rolling from West to East. I think a big Epic trilogy could be made out of such a

subject, that at the same time would be modern and distinctly American." Quoted in Starr, "Introduction," vii–viii.

75. In a virtuoso reading of *The Octopus*, Michaels keenly observes the novel's concern with consumption, noting the exchangeability of Asiatic hunger and corporate greed as figures of consumer desire. See Michaels, 185–86. Michaels's approach to consumption, however, is to oppose it to production and distribution, and to note the extent to which these are displaced by the question of desire. Michaels's handling of production and consumption as binary, rather than relational, terms reduces his political stake to that of showing how the agrarian producer ethos of the novel ends up being overwhelmed by the logics of consumer capitalism.

76. In *The American Novel*, Carl Van Doren wrote that "what was elemental in Frank Norris became abysmal in Jack London. He carried the cult of red blood in literature to an extreme at which it began to sink into the ridiculous, as in his lineal descendants of the moving pictures." Quoted in McClintock, 151. Alfred Kazin writes that London's "thick slabs of bleeding meat were essentially only a confession of despair." See Kazin, *On Native Grounds*, 115. The wide impact of Upton Sinclair's muckraking exposure of the meat industry, compared with the California socialist author's other endeavors, might also be reconsidered in this light. Though *The Jungle* (1906) is set in Chicago, it should be considered another example of California naturalism. London's publicity on behalf of the novel was instrumental to its reception. On the connection between London and Sinclair, see Philip Foner, *Jack London*, 80.

77. Quoted in Howard, 73.

78. Pizer criticizes Norris's "excessive symbolization" of the railroad. See Pizer, 159.

79. Because the eastern United States was already glutted with Great Plains wheat, California tapped foreign markets for wheat sales, mainly Great Britain. Another factor was that routes to distant markets were already defined during the Civil War, when California was forced to buy manufactures from Europe. The wheat economy was based on California's own indigeneous sources of capital and also British capital. See Henderson, *California and the Fictions of Capital*, 5.

80. Rothstein, "Frank Norris and Popular Perceptions of the Market," 62.

81. For the logic of national socialism's figuration of the Jew as the abstract form of capital that was reflected in the way the death camps could be understood to have sought the reduction of exchange value to use value, see Postone, "Anti-Semitism and National Socialism."

82. Besides *The Iron Heel*, see "The Unparalleled Invasion" and "Goliah."

83. Parrington writes that naturalism's discovery of background, environment, and the economic basis of society depicts characters as "figures of men and women encompassed by the great stream, carried along on a resistless current." See Parrington, *The Beginning of Critical Realism in America*, 180–81. Lee Clark Mitchell writes that realist characters manage to withstand forces that pressure them into action, while naturalist characters always accede to their strongest desire, whatever it is they resolve to do. See Lee Clark Mitchell, *Determined Fictions*, 9. Contrasting market culture and machine culture—and realism and nat-

uralism—Seltzer argues that what is a sign of agency in the former is a sign of automaticism in the latter. See Seltzer, 17–18.

84. Lukács, *The Historical Novel*, 183–89.

85. Jack London, "The Plague Ship," 90 (hereafter cited as PS).

86. See frontispiece to Gompers.

87. Hofstader, *Social Darwinism in American Thought*.

88. Norris, *Moran of the* Lady Letty, 194 (hereafter cited as *MLL*).

89. The phrase was Madison Grant's. See *Passing of the Great Race*.

90. Wilson's *The Boys in the Back Room,* quoted in Martin, *California Writers,* 6–7.

91. For a different account of racial representation and capital, see Henderson, *Fictions of Capital*, 21. Wu identifies Norris as "the most important naturalist to write about Chinese Americans." See Wu, 126.

92. Trachtenberg, *The Incorporation of America, 5.* For the conflicts and modes of reconciliation between large-scale corporate capitalism and American individualism in the period, see also Sklar, 71, 92.

93. *Valley of the Moon*, 22, 155. That novel's heroine is in fact named Saxon.

94. Unlike the thousands of Chinese transported as contract labor to Cuba and Peru in the nineteenth century, the Chinese that arrived in the U.S. came as free labor in an economic and legal sense. Once here, however, they were proletarianized and racially excluded as "coolies." See Robert G. Lee, 58.

95. For the characterization of the genre of "late imperial romance" as reflecting the desire for re-enchanting a globe already thoroughly mapped, see McClure, *Late Imperial Romance.*

96. The notion of an Asian disenchantment of nature reverses the valuation of Asian immigrant labor by its supporters for transforming the Californian "wasteland" into a "paradise." Contemporary sources in support of Japanese labor attested that "whatever the colonization of the State of California is to-day is due, of course, to a greater extent to the efforts of the Japanese immigrants. And yet they are being excluded for that very reason. The only fault to be found with them is that they are too efficient" (quoted in Iichiro Tokutomi). See Tokutomi, *Japanese-American Relations*, 86.

97. Labor, "Jack London's Symbolic Wilderness."

98. It is true that Jack London's Asiatic characters who reside in Pacific island settings lose their overt villainy, as if even they are softened by an Edenic Polynesian effect. Andrew Furer sees this as part of London's diminution of "Anglo-Saxon" bias in general when the environment is less harsh. Furer upholds "Chun Ah Chun" and "Koolau the Leper" as examples of Pacific tales that valorize those of Chinese and Hawaiian ancestry. See Furer, " 'Zone Conquerors' and 'White Devils,' " 158–59, 163. My argument cannot take up London's Hawaiian Asiatic, which is not fully described by the logic of representation I am pursuing. However, it is worth noting that in "Koolau the Leper," the leprosy that afflicts the handsome Polynesian native has been brought to the islands by Chinese indentured labor. See Jack London, "Koolau the Leper," 1443.

99. Jack London, "King of the Greeks," 825 (hereafter cited as KG).

100. Jack London, "White and Yellow."

101. Jack London, "Yellow Handkerchief," 887–88.
102. Jack London, "The Chinago," 1405–1417.

CHAPTER THREE

1. Executive Order No. 9066, appendixed in Select House Committee Investigating National Defense Migration, *Fourth Interim Report*, 314. In 1941 there were 127,000 Japanese Americans living in the continental United States. Over 112,000 lived in the three Pacific Coast states of Washington, Oregon, and California. Of these, 93,000, or nearly 80 percent lived in California alone. See Weglyn, *Years of Infamy*, 36.

2. Daniels, *The Decision to Relocate the Japanese Americans*, 56. More recently, Robert Shaffer has sought to show that "opposition to the removal and internment policy was more widespread in white, liberal, left-wing, and religious publications and organizations, and among African-American activists, than historians have heretofore acknowledged." See Shaffer, "Cracks in the Consensus," 85.

3. Commission on Wartime Relocation, *Personal Justice Denied*, 18, (hereafter cited as *PJD*).

4. DeWitt, *Final Report*, 8.

5. Kumamoto, "The Search for Spies," 55–56.

6. Yang Murray, "Introduction: The Internment of Japanese Americans," 6.

7. On December 15, after the Pearl Harbor bombing, Secretary of the Navy Frank Knox launched unfounded allegations of Japanese American subversion in public by declaring, "I think the most effective Fifth Column work of the entire war was done in Hawaii with the possible exception of Norway." Knox's remarks were then followed by the January 25, 1942, release of the Roberts Commission Report on the Pearl Harbor attack that alleged the role of resident traitors in aiding a spy operation centered in the Japanese consulate. See Weglyn, 49.

8. Daniels, *Concentration Camps: North America*, xvi.

9. See Lane Hirabayashi and James Hirabayashi, "A Reconsideration of the United States Military's Role;" and Robinson, *By Order of the President*.

10. For a survey of the historiography from the 1940s to the 1990s, see Yang Murray, 20–26.

11. For internment literature focused on the event as civil rights violation, see Weglyn; Irons, *Justice at War*; Daniels, *Prisoners without Trial*; and Daniels, *The Decision to Relocate the Japanese Americans*. For the culture of resistance in the camps, see, for example, Okihiro, "Japanese Resistance in America's Concentration Camps," 20–34. For the administration of and life in the camps, see Taylor, *Jewel of the Desert*; and James, *Exile Within*.

12. Grodzins, *Americans Betrayed*, 58.

13. TenBroek, Barnhart, and Matson, *Prejudice, War, and the Constitution*.

14. For a brief account of the effort by University of California to suppress the publication of Grodzins's work, see Yang Murray, 23.

15. Drinnon, *Keeper of Concentration Camps*, 272.

16. See Daniels, *The Politics of Prejudice*, 77, 64.

17. Lucie Cheng and Bonacich, "Introduction," 1.

18. Okihiro and Drummond, "The Concentration Camps and Japanese Economic Losses," 168.

19. Note that their use of the term "exclusionism" in separate historical instances is inconsistent. In the 1900–1924 period, it specifically denotes a technique of guaranteeing a migrant labor force. In 1942 this is not the case.

20. Aoki, "No Right to Own," 68. In the end, the article retreats to making a more general type of claim—that the practice of institutionalized racism represented by the earlier legislation made racial scapegoating possible later—and does not explore how Alien Land Laws may have specifically "paved the way" to internment.

21. This despite the fact that a Japanese surprise attack on Pearl Harbor was prophesied in at least seven military strategic plans between 1911 and 1941. Approximately two dozen formal plans were drawn up prior to World War II under War Plan Orange, the most prominent of the color plans developed in the early twentieth century. Japan was assigned the color code name Orange, and the United States, blue. Although Edward Miller's study goes far toward establishing a military expectation of Japanese attack on U.S. territories, it does not point to specific plans for Japanese American removal. In its one mention of the 1942 removal, *War Plan Orange* implies a sharp disparity between the hysteria of political leaders and the sober pragmatism of military strategic planners who by 1911 were confident that an invasion was too fantastic to be seriously contemplated. See Miller, *War Plan Orange*, 1–2, 14, 39, 41, 48.

22. For an example of the former, see Lea, *Valor of Ignorance*; for the latter, Bywater, *The Great Pacific War*.

23. For the war against Japan as a racial war, see Dower, *War without Mercy*. On frontier war, see Drinnon, *Facing West*; see also Slotkin, *Gunfighter Nation*.

24. Quoted in Kumamoto, 61.

25. California State Board of Control, *California and the Oriental*, 93 (hereafter cited as *CO*). In particular, attention was drawn to a settlement of around 2,000 Japanese fishermen who lived in shantytowns on Terminal Island in Los Angeles' San Pedro Bay. In 1935 amendments to the California Fish and Game Code discriminating against Japanese fishermen were proposed, though eventually dropped. In late 1940 the Office of Naval Intelligence sought to evacuate them from Terminal Island by declaring it a "defensive Naval operating area" but was stumped by laws protecting private property from federal intrusion. See Kumamoto, 59–60.

26. Rutherford, "Do We Need the Japanese Farmers?" 107. For an example of the argument that economic exigency dictated maintaining the Japanese in production, see Bendiner, "Cool Heads or Martial Law," 185–86.

27. Fisher and Nielsen, *The Japanese in California Agriculture*, 2.

28. Costigan, "The Plight of the Nisei," 184.

29. S. V. Christierson to William Cecil; and S. V. Christierson to Congressman John Z. Anderson.

30. McWilliams, *Prejudice*, 65 (hereafter cited as *P*).

31. See Saxton, *The Indispensable Enemy*.

32. For the "wages of whiteness" enjoyed by the American working class, including those of ethnic Irish descent, who distinguished themselves from blacks, see Roediger, *The Wages of Whiteness*.

33. Note that Omi and Winant's critical overview of the sociological field of class conflict theories of race counterposes a theory of labor segmentation (Michael Reich, David Gordon, and Richard Edwards)—which argues for a capitalist class interest in racial inequality—to a theory of the split labor market (Edna Bonacich)—which argues for a working-class interest therein. Ultimately, Omi and Winant dismiss both so-called classical Marxist approaches for economism, in the former case because it dismisses racial identification as a form of false consciousness, and in the latter case because the alignment of class and racial identity in the formation of a white labor aristocracy preempts a more contingent understanding of racial and class articulation. See Omi and Winant, *Racial Formation in the United States*, 29–35. Their critique imputes an unnecessary rigidity to Marxist analysis, I think, without actually demonstrating the superior explanatory power of Laclau and Mouffe's notion of articulation in affording an understanding of the historical relationship between race and class in the U.S. example. The argument for contingent articulation—here and elsewhere in post-Gramscian-inflected cultural studies—often provides an easy out for theoretical failure disguised as a refusal of (deterministic) theory. The case of Asian exclusionist history would suggest that capital's tactics of labor disorganization and white working-class racism need not be grasped as mutually exclusive readings.

34. I am suggesting neither that Chinese in California did not also work in agriculture, nor that all Japanese did. I am concerned with the sites of Asian exclusion discourse, not with making claims about Japanese and Chinese American social history. The question is how class and sectoral positions have been iconically racialized as Chinese or Japanese. For a history of Californian Chinese farming, see Chan, *This Bittersweet Soil*; see also, Leung and Ma, "Chinese Farming Activities." For Japanese American labor history, see Modell, "Class or Ethnic Solidarity;" see also Yoneda, "One Hundred Years of Japanese Labor."

35. McWilliams, *Factories in the Field*, 102 (hereafter *FF*).

36. Higgs, "The Wealth of Japanese Tenant Farmers," *Agricultural History*, 488.

37. See Matsumoto, *Farming the Home Place*, 21–22.

38. Chuman, *The Bamboo People*, 79–80.

39. McGovney, "The Anti-Japanese Land Laws of California," 7.

40. In this way, superior Asiatic industry in the agricultural sector also takes on a different quality from its customary presentation in discussions of labor immigration. When it comes to Chinese coolies, we do not take seriously the rhetorical inflation of a superior Asiatic industry: the attribution strikes us as a necessary ideological effect of a system designed to guarantee an industrial surplus army of labor. But when it comes to the rhetoric about Japanese farmers, superior Asiatic industry has an objective quality. It is the very thing that explains the shifting social location of Asian exclusionism.

41. Iwata, "The Japanese Immigrants in California Agriculture," 29.

42. Modell, *The Economics and Politics of Racial Accommodation*, 36–37.

43. Ichioka, "Japanese Immigrant Response," 174.

44. Bloom and Riemer, *Removal and Return*, 70.

45. Higgs, "Landless by Law," 223.

46. Bloom and Riemer also report the same but observe that the acreage in 1940 was far less than in 1920. See Bloom and Riemer, 70.

47. Bunje, *The Story of Japanese Farming*. This study was produced on a WPA project under the direction of the University of California, Berkeley, 1937.

48. Until 1983, $400 million (in 1942 dollars) was the assumed estimate of evacuee property losses, but that figure is now thought to be apocryphal. Originally attributed to the Federal Reserve Bank but now untraceable in any of its documents, the figure is "shrouded in myth." See Sandra C. Taylor, "Evacuation and Economic Loss," 165. Under the Japanese-American Evacuation Claim Act of 1948, 26,568 claims totaling $148 million were filed; the government disbursed approximately $37 million. See *PJD* 118. The Civil Liberties Act of 1988 allotted $1.2 billion to a fund from which each surviving Japanese American affected by Executive Order 9066 was entitled to receive $20,000. See *PJD* xx. According to the report of the Commission on Wartime Relocation and Internment of Civilians, by 1954 the best evidence of economic losses no longer existed. See *PJD* 119.

49. Chiba, "Truth of the Japanese Farming in California," in *CO* 220.

50. For the discussion of the Asiatic horde and the mixed crowd of urban modernity, see chapters 1 and 2.

51. Daniel, *Bitter Harvest*, 88–89.

52. Mowry, *California Progressives*, 152–53, 295–97.

53. From the Progressive *California Weekly* in 1909 (quoted in Mowry). See Mowry, 154.

54. Of all the commentators on Japanese exclusionism, McWilliams is still the one to have pursued this question most thoroughly. See McWilliams, 102. The next chapter will take up McWilliams's analysis of race and class as symptomatic of New Deal liberalism.

55. See Rosenberg, "The IWW and the Organization of Asian Workers," 77–79.

56. On how the IWW's "internationalist vision and professions were sorely tested by American racial realities," see Dreyfus, "The IWW and the Limits of Inter-ethnic Organizing," 452; on the IWW's failure to enlist Japanese members, see also Daniel, *Bitter Harvest*, 82–83. For a corroboration of Rosenberg's contention regarding IWW's commitment to interracial class solidarity, see Choi, "The Rhetoric of Inclusion." Choi is careful to draw the distinction between the IWW's rhetoric and practice. "Much more study needs to occur before evaluating the depth of the IWW's commitment to include Asian workers," she writes. See Choi, 5.

57. See O'Brien and Fugita, "Mobilization," 522–37.

58. See Rosenberg, 80–81.

59. As Choi writes, Asian Americans have generally been marginalized in the historiography of American radicalism, and even in studies of the IWW surprisingly few scholars have focused on the organization's relationship to workers of color. See Choi 1, 5.

60. See Yuji Ichioka's work as a whole for an exceptional and sustained inter-

est in writing the early history of the Japanese immigrant left. See Ichioka, *The Issei*. In an influential study of union organizing among L.A. retail produce workers in the 1930s, Modell tells the story of two unions, an AFL local (in effect segregated) and a Nisei-organized union that survived for a brief three years. See Modell, "Class or Ethnic Solidarity," 193–206.

61. Azuma, "Japanese Immigrant Farmers," 14.

62. In their foundational annotated bibliography of Japanese American historical sources, Ichioka et al. write that "the entire corpus of the historical literature on Japanese Americans (excluding those in Hawaii) is tied directly or indirectly to the past exclusion movement," such that we know "very little about how the Japanese immigrants, the excluded, felt and thought about being excluded." See Ichioka et al., *A Buried Past*, 4–5.

63. See Matsumoto; see also Lukes and Okihiro, *Japanese Legacy*, and Hayashi, *For the Sake of our Brethren*.

64. See, for example, Daniels, *Politics of Prejudice*, 92–93. According to McWilliams, both novels were in high demand for a long time at California public libraries and were widely circulated, if not instigated, by anti-Japanese propaganda groups. See McWilliams, *P* 60–61.

65. Peter Kyne (1880–1957) was San Francisco born and raised. He wrote twenty-five novels, some selling 100,000 copies, and hundreds of short stories and articles for *Cosmopolitan, American Magazine, Sunset, Collier's*, and particularly the *Post*. Some of his novels were adapted into movies; he also wrote original material for silent movies and scripts for "talkies." His most memorable character creation is Cappy Ricks, a rags-to-riches sea captain who is the protagonist of a 1916 collection of tales named for him. Kyne served in the infantry during the Spanish-American War, participating in the repression of the Philippine national insurrection led by Emilio Aguinaldo, and as an army captain in World War I. See Dillon, "Kyne, Peter Bernard." Wallace Irwin (1876–1959) was born in New York and spent most of his life there, with the exception of a stint in California during 1895–1904, when he attended Stanford University, then wrote for the *San Francisco Examiner*, and served as the editor of *Overland Monthly* magazine. See Irwin's obituary, *New York Times*, February 15, 1959, 87. His greatest literary success came with *Letters of a Japanese Schoolboy*, which first appeared in *Collier's Weekly*. Published in book form in 1909, it was subsequently developed into a series that was syndicated in forty leading American papers. For *Letters*, he was praised by his contemporaries for achieving a "subtle sympathy with the Japanese mental attitude, evidenced by a clever employment of false syntax that is amusing in itself while not so grotesque as to confuse the reader." See *The National Cyclopedia of American Biography*, 185.

66. McWilliams attributes the stereotype of Japanese American speech—such as the use of honorifics and the "so sorry, please"—and other "Jap" conventions of comic strips and pulp magazines to Irwin's invention. According to McWilliams, *Letters* was inspired by the San Francisco school board incident. See McWilliams, *P* 44.

67. Kyne, *Pride of Palomar*, 315 (hereafter cited as *POP*).

68. Cf. George Kennan's praise of the gardens planted by Japanese soldiers fighting the Russo-Japanese War, in chapter 1.

69. Okada's body seems to be Semitically stereotyped: he is described as wearing highly tailored clothes, an expensive hat, and a gold band ring with diamond and sapphires; he has pudgy fingers. See *POP* 26–27. The character is based upon a historical person, George Shima (1864–1926), one of the most successful entrepreneurs in the history of California agriculture and popularly known as the "Potato King." At his death, he left an estate estimated at between $15 and $17 million. See Don Hata and Nadine Hata, "George Shima: 'The Potato King' of California."

70. See Hays, *Conservation and the Gospel of Efficiency.*

71. Cf. the discussion of Jewish villainy in the novels of Ignatius Donnelly and Frank Norris in chapter 2.

72. *POP* 254. Capitalization in the original.

73. My argument here is strongly influenced by Moishe Postone's reading of Nazi personification of the Jew as the abstract side of capital and his analysis of the death camps in those terms. See "Anti-Semitism and National Socialism."

74. The town of Bly is based upon Florin, California, one of two rural communities in the state well known at the time to be composed in majority of Japanese residents. The other was Livingston. For a 1920s profile of Florin and Livingston, see Rauschenbush, "Their Place in the Sun."

75. Irwin, *Seed of the Sun*, 128 (hereafter cited as *SS*).

76. See, for example, *POP* 39. On this note, it may be worth mentioning the case of the June 1941 arrest in Hollywood of Itaru Tachibana, language officer with the Imperial Japanese, for a "conspiracy to obtain national defense information for a foreign power." Tachibana was accused of securing naval intelligence reports through one Al Blake, an American go-between, who made his living imitating department store dummies and freelancing as an amateur counterespionage agent. See Kumamoto, 55.

77. Note the significance of calling a white man who does business with Japanese a "so-called white man" as opposed to a "Jap lover" (following "nigger lover"). In the former case, the racial identity of the white subject itself comes into question.

78. McWilliams, "Once Again the Yellow Peril," 736.

79. Edwards, "The Industrial Side of the Alien Land Law Problem," 199.

80. The constant foregrounding of Irish (and in Kyne, also Spanish) ethnicity suggests a different kind of white racial formation produced on the West Coast than from that influentially posited by Roediger and others based on studies of the South or Northeast. See also Ignatiev, *How the Irish Became White*. In California, whiteness may not depend upon the necessary disappearance of Irishness, but rather the show of ethnic culture.

81. George Henderson writes, "while racial categories existed outside capitalism and certainly outside agriculture, it is also true that capitalism and agriculture were among the many sites where race was made and 'racializing' performed. . . . [C]apitalist agriculture . . . was an opportunity to further (and further specify) the idea and practice of race: without it, in other words, race would have meant that much less." See Henderson, *California and the Fictions of Capital*, 91.

82. See the novels by Ignatius Donnelly and Jack London on monopoly capitalism, discussed in chapter 2.

83. At least since the commissioner-general of immigration's 1901 campaign against anarchists and "Chinamen," the political and racial dimensions of alienness have enwrapped Asiatic racial form in the ideological currents of American politics. Government crackdown on political dissenters and on resident aliens after the McKinley assassination is the subject of Preston's study, *Aliens and Dissenters*. Though there is evidence that in the 1930s the F.B.I. suspected Japanese agents of stirring black and labor unrest, it is not until the era of McCarthyism that the ideological and racial meanings are neatly condensed into a single Asiatic figure. On Cold War Orientalism, see Pietz, "The 'Post-Colonialism' of Cold War Discourse." See also C. Klein, *Cold War Orientalism*.

84. Steffens, "California and the Japanese," 35. A walking delegate was a union representative who visited workers on their jobs to see whether agreements were upheld.

85. For further background on Elwood Mead, see Lawrence B. Lee, *Reclaiming the American West*, 22–23.

86. Mead, "What Should be the Next Step in Rural Development?"

87. For a short of biography of Adams, see Erdman, Ryerson, and Tinsley, *In Memoriam: Richard Laban Adams*, 3–5. For a brilliant account of R. L. Adams's racialized Progressivism, see Henderson, *Fictions of Capital*, 92–96.

88. Salvage, directed by R. L. Adams, *A Survey*, 14.

89. As Henderson writes, the fact that agriculture became a version of capitalism "did not spell the end of agrarian fantasies, which were too tenacious and flexible, too capable of being appropriated and transformed, to come to quick ends." See Henderson, 180.

90. Mears, "The Land, the Crops, and the Oriental," 206.

91. This topic will be taken up in chapter 4.

92. Rowell, "Orientophobia," 13.

93. See War Relocation Authority, "The Western Growers Association," 6.

94. See interview with Chester Moore conducted by Grodzins, Report No. 11, 8 October 1942, *JERS* 67/14C A16.200.

95. See letters to William Cecil, director of agriculture, California State Department of Agriculture from E. M. Seifert Jr., and from S. V. Christerson, president of the Western Growers Protective Association.

96. See for example, Rutherford. The author concludes, no.

97. Farm Security Administration, *Final Report*, 42.

98. The retreat of Jeffersonian agrarianism among federal agency officials and congressional legislators by the end of the 1930s has been noted, for example, in the exemptions of various federal reclamation projects in the West from the 160-acre limit imposed by the 1902 Newlands Act on recipients of federal largess as an official policy of encouraging small family farms. Donald C. Swain writes that "the Reclamation Bureau's Jeffersonian objectives were somewhat less compelling in 1940 than in 1902. . . ." See Swain, "The Bureau of Reclamation," 145.

99. On the color line in Progressive thought, see Van Nuys, "A Progressive Confronts the Race Question." See also Henderson, *Fictions of Capital*.

100. In Irwin's *Seed of the Sun*, Anna Bly consoles herself with the thought that "all the faces in the world were not yellow, smiling and unfathomable." See

SS 125. In "The Industrial Side of the Alien Land Law Problem," Edwards uses the term "smiling Jap." See Edwards, 191.

101. The term "Cadillac desert" is Marc Reisner's. *Chinatown* makes a detective mystery out of a famous 1905 episode in the history of California water development, involving the swindling of Los Angeles and the farmers of Owens Valley by a group of high-level speculators. Why the film should be named *Chinatown* is not obvious unless one contextualizes the film within the history of California's racialized discourse of speculative irrigation.

102. For the application of Karl Wittfogel's model of "hydraulic civilization" to the American West, see Worster, *Rivers of Empire*, 4–6. Reisner also makes comparisons between the American West and Oriental civilization. See Reisner, 3. For the classic theory linking the irrigation public works and totalitarianism, see Wittfogel, *Oriental Despotism*.

103. Japanese Association of America, statement appended to California State Board of Control, *California and the Oriental*, 207.

CHAPTER FOUR

1. Petersen, *Japanese Americans*, 73. A 1966 article he wrote on Japanese Americans in the *New York Times Magazine* is usually cited by scholars today as an inaugural moment of 1960s model minority discourse. See Petersen, "Success Story." Petersen was a social demographer at Ohio State University and the author of, among other works, *Planned Migration* (1955), *The Politics of Population* (1964), and *Population* (1969).

2. Petersen, "The Incarceration of the Japanese-Americans," 1367.

3. In fact, the notion of "totalitarian liberals" mobilized by Petersen in the 1960s can be found in Norman Thomas's original 1942 critique of the ACLU and Congress's acquiescence to the executive branch's "totalitarian theory of justice." See Thomas, "Dark Day for Liberty," 929–31. The overall historiographical picture is thus one of exceptional dissent or compromised support for Japanese American rights. For an overview of the elements of the left-liberal Roosevelt coalition that supported or criticized the internment order, see Shaffer, "Cracks in the Consensus." Shaffer offers a revisionist account that argues that "opposition to the removal and internment policy was more widespread in white liberal, left-wing, and religious publications and organizations, and among African-American activists, than historians have heretofore acknowledged." See Shaffer, 84.

4. Gordon Chang, for example, writes of "the limits, even bankruptcy, of liberals who thought themselves passionate opponents of racism but who also endorsed mass forced relocation of aliens and citizens alike solely on the basis of race." See Chang, "Superman Is About to Visit," 37. Writing of Dillon Myer's "extraordinary alliance with leading civil libertarians," Richard Drinnon contrasts the heroic minority efforts of the director of the American Civil Liberties Union of Northern California and Korematsu defense counsel Wayne Collins against the pro-FDR position of the ACLU's national leadership. See *Keeper of Concentration Camps*, 117–59.

5. For a study that takes seriously the contradictory, liberal New Deal dimension of internment, see Thomas James's analysis of progressive education policy in the camps in *Exile Within*.

6. Quoted in Drinnon, 3. Dorothy Swaine Thomas was the director of the Japanese Evacuation and Relocation Project, which sent anthropologists into the camps for "community analysis."

7. For example, in the same study, internment's leading scholar, Roger Daniels, writes that internment "reflected one of the central themes of American history—the theme of white supremacy, of racism," that its liberal administrators were culpable by "the stern standards of the Nuremberg Tribunal" of an atrocity, *and* that "New Deal liberals were not the prime policy makers during the war; the military and its civilian bosses were in the saddle." See Daniels, *Concentration Camps*, xvi, 102, 144–45.

8. On the New Deal and African Americans, see Sitkoff, *A New Deal for Blacks*; see also Natasan, *The Black Image in the New Deal*. The Asian American working-class subject of the 1930s has been a topic of study, particularly in the case of Filipinos. Though the history of 1930s labor strikes and unionization movements necessarily enters the discursive field of the New Deal, it is not one with it. On Filipino labor radicalism, see Cordova, *Filipinos: Forgotten Asian Americans*; see also DeWitt, *Violence in the Fields*. Also, for African American civil rights activism and African diasporic anticolonial politics in the pre–WW II period, see Von Eschen, *Race against Empire*.

9. In Los Angeles County, for example, perhaps twenty-five Japanese were on relief before the war, of a county population of almost 37,000. Daniels writes: "The various New Deal relief agencies, so crucial to the livelihood of most recent immigrant groups during the depression, had very little impact on Japanese Americans." See Daniels, "Japanese America, 1930–1941," 35. Citing similar statistics, John Modell makes the stronger allegation that needy Japanese were kept from white charity. According to him, at the depth of the depression only eleven families were on county relief and fifty received unemployment benefits. See *Economics and Politics of Racial Accommodation*, 86. The percentage of Chinese Americans receiving federal unemployment relief in 1933 was higher than that of Japanese Americans but lower than that of blacks and whites. See Light, *Ethnic Enterprise in America*, 87.

10. In developing our present-day critical consciousness of this fact, the pioneering works of Alexander Saxton and that of David Roediger were key. See Saxton, *The Indispensable Enemy*, and *The Rise and Fall of the White Republic*; see also Roediger, *The Wages of Whiteness*, and *Towards the Abolition of Whiteness*.

11. See Du Bois, *Black Reconstruction in America, 1860–1880*.

12. Starr, *Endangered Dreams*, 270.

13. Appearing in April 1939, *The Grapes of Wrath* sold 429,000 copies in hardcover in the first year of publication, and 543,000 in hardcover by 1941, despite the availability then of an inexpensive reprint issued by *Sun Dial Press*. In 1940 John Ford made a film of the novel starring Henry Fonda. See Starr, 256. The remarkable success of the Okie exodus in achieving cultural mythic status is not to be confused with political victory for migrant farmworkers. The bill proposed by the La Follette Senate Civil Liberties Committee, which held hearings on

farm labor repression in the winter of 1939, failed in Congress, and the CIO agricultural union, UCAPAWA, was crushed in the fields. See Denning, *The Cultural Front*, 261–62.

14. Exploring how "Okie" came to be a generic term for poor whites, James Gregory notes the extension in the 1930s of the application of "racial slurs" from non-Anglo foreigners and people of color, to "white, old-stock American natives, Protestant Americans, rural Americans, heartlanders." See *American Exodus*, 100–102.

15. The 1935 state bill was invalidated by the Supreme Court in *Edwards* vs. *California*, 314 U.S. 160 (1941). See *Edwards* vs. *California*, 160–86.

16. Paul S. Taylor, "Again the Covered Wagon," 350.

17. Daniel, *Bitter Harvest*, 87–99.

18. California State Board of Control, *California and the Oriental*, 108–9 (hereafter cited as *CO*).

19. For an argument on the racial politics of Progressive reform that emphasizes the elimination of racialized landscape, see Don Mitchell, *The Lie of the Land*, 99.

20. Hing, *Making and Remaking Asian America*, 33–34.

21. On the deportation practices of the INS during the 1930s, see Dinwoodie, "Deportation." On the "unlikely coalition of exclusionists, anti-colonialists, and Filipino nationalists [who] managed to band together" in support of the Tydings-McDuffie Act, see Hing, 35–36. On Filipinos' reputation for militancy and its impetus for granting Philippine independence, see Don Mitchell, 127; see also, Daniel, 109. Also see Takaki, *Strangers from a Different Shore*, chapter 9. On Filipinos as initiating an Asian American turn toward unionization and away from a contract system and the search for ethnic advancement within that, see Friday, *Organizing Asian American Labor*, 124–39. On the participation of Japanese workers in interracial strike actions at Vacaville and El Monte in the early 1930s, see Daniel, 136–47.

22. Benson, *True Adventures of John Steinbeck*, 278–300.

23. For example, "With Dakin in the tent sat Burke, a lowering, sullen Irishman, and two short Italian men who looked very much alike. Mrs. Dakin had retired to the other side of the partition. Under the white light of the gasoline lamp Dakin's pink scalp showed through his blond hair." See Steinbeck, *In Dubious Battle*, 143.

24. Steinbeck's Indians are represented along the same lines, as one with the land and equally endangered by modernity, as in *To a God Unknown* (1933). For critiques of Steinbeck for stereotyping minorities as primitives, see Ortega, "Fables of Identity;" and Owens, "Grandpa Killed Indians." For a defense of Steinbeck for his sympathy to minorities that is of a piece with his sympathy for Okies, working stiffs, bums, and anti-Nazi resisters—in other words, all kinds of marginal groups—see Shillingshaw, "Steinbeck and Ethnicity."

25. Steinbeck, "Fingers of Cloud," 161–64.

26. The term Asian American today includes Asian and Pacific Islanders, immigrants and U.S.-born people of Chinese, Japanese, Filipino, Korean, East Indian, Southeast Asian, and various Pacific Islander ancestry. The historical term Asiatic referred paradigmatically to people of Chinese and Japanese ancestry.

Though the category expanded and contracted at different moments, Filipinos were generally constructed in discursively distinct ways. Japanese workers did participate in the cross-racial farm labor strikes of the early 1930s but were by this time a relatively minor element of the demography.

27. Paul Taylor and Tom Vasey, "Contemporary Background of California Labor," 404–5 (hereafter cited as CBCL).

28. Paul Taylor and Vasey, "Historical Background of California Farm Labor," 289, 295 (hereafter cited as HBCL).

29. R. L. Adams, "Farm Labor," 4 (hereafter cited as FL).

30. Bunje, *The Story of Japanese Farming*, 39. This study was produced on a WPA project under the direction of the University of California, Berkeley (hereafter cited as *SJF*).

31. Paul Taylor and Clark Kerr, "Uprisings on the Farms," 22 (hereafter cited as UF).

32. Edwards, "The Industrial Side," 197.

33. Paul Taylor, "Again the Covered Wagon," 351.

34. Steinbeck, *The Grapes of Wrath*, 301 (hereafter cited as *GW*).

35. See Etheridge Jr., "Changing Attitudes Toward Steinbeck's Naturalism."

36. On Steinbeck's "non-teleological" view of nature, see Benson, 244.

37. For a particularly interesting engagement and reversal of the sentimentalism in *The Grapes of Wrath*, see Szalay, *New Deal Modernism*, 166–67.

38. Steinbeck, "Dubious Battle in California," 303 (hereafter cited as DBC).

39. Steinbeck, *In Dubious Battle*, 252.

40. Denning sees Carey McWilliams as a leading voice of Popular Front antiracism. See Denning, 449.

41. Carey McWilliams, "California and the Japanese," *New Republic* (March 2, 1942): 297 (hereafter cited as CJ).

42. McWilliams, "Moving the West-Coast Japanese," 359, 364 (hereafter cited as *MWJ*).

43. McWilliams, *Prejudice*, 140 (hereafter cited as *P*).

44. Daniels writes that "[I]t is now clear that a major source for these persistent and mendacious stories were American military officers, especially those connected with the Western Defense Command with headquarters in San Francisco's Presidio." None of these stories of subversive activity had any basis in fact. As it turned out, no Japanese American was ever demonstrated to have committed sabotage or espionage in the continental United States during the entire war. See Daniels, *The Decision to Relocate*, 12–13.

45. Furthermore, in California, by early 1942 there were 314 classified Japanese American civil service employees (all citizens), and there were others working for subordinate branches of government. In L.A. County, there were ninety-five city and county employees. Though a substantial number of Nisei were trained as teachers, not one had been hired by any school board in Los Angeles. A few had been hired in Seattle. See Daniels, "Japanese America" 39, 45.

46. See chapter 3 for this genealogy.

47. Conkin, "The Vision of Elwood Mead," 88.

48. For Elwood Mead, see chapter 3.

49. See, for example, Kelly, *A Survey of Procedures*. See also, in the same series, William Salvage's study on sugar beets.

50. Quoted in McWilliams, *Prejudice*, 79–80.

51. Irwin, *Seed of the Sun*, 107 (hereafter cited as *SS*).

52. See, for example, Mears, "The Land, the Crops, and the Oriental," 146; see also, Rauschenbush, "Their Place in the Sun," 141.

53. Hays, *Conservation and the Gospel of Efficiency*, 2–5.

54. War Relocation Authority, *A Story of Human Conservation*. The WRA was dissolved on June 30, 1946.

55. Executive Order 9106, printed in the Select House Committee Investigating National Defense Migration, *Fourth Interim Report*, 16 (hereafter cited as *FIR*).

56. Wording of *Fourth Interim Report*, 7.

57. Linehart, "Japanese American Resettlement," 56–57.

58. War Relocation Authority, Transcript of "Conference on Evacuation of Enemy Aliens," 18.

59. Wallinger, "Dispersal of the Japanese Americans," 78. Wallinger points out that only three of the centers—Gila River, Granada, and Tule Lake—were placed on lands that did not have serious agricultural setbacks.

60. Reed, "Termination Report on Proposed Agricultural Program," 1 (hereafter cited as PAP).

61. Myer, from his "Problems of Evacuee Resettlement in California," Eagle Rock, California, June 19, 1945, WRA papers, 6, quoted in Wallinger, 373.

62. From the War Relocation Authority's *Myths and Facts about Japanese Americans*, June 1945, quoted in Wallinger, 373.

63. Newspaper report of speech made May 22, 1942; quoted in War Relocation Authority, *A Story of Human Conservation*, 7.

64. In actuality, by January 1946, 50 percent of the Japanese American population were back on the West Coast, with another 25 percent expected to return gradually from the Midwest and East. See Girdner and Loftis, *The Great Betrayal*, 424.

65. See, for example, War Relocation Authority, *Story of Human Conservation*, 193.

66. Leuchtenburg, *Franklin D. Roosevelt*, 174.

67. Baldwin, *Poverty and Politics*, 48.

68. The protectionist climate of the post-WW I era in Europe and the United States damaged the consumer purchasing power of American farmers, who exported less while having to pay more for manufacturing products.

69. Lowitt, *The New Deal and the West*, 180.

70. Don Mitchell writes that the "Bracero Program was a peculiarly 'premodern' form of labor control, predicated as it was on the careful control of individual, contractual laborers, often carefully guarded in fields and camps." See Mitchell, 195.

71. Farm Security Administration, *Final Report*, 2. (hereafter referred to *FSA Report*).

72. Farm Security Administration, Press Release, 1.

73. Department of Agriculture Program, "Keeping Up Production on Japa-

nese Farms," p. 5 of radio script. Emphasis in the original. (hereafter cited as KPJF).

74. Farm Security Administration, Press Release, 1.

75. Farm Security Administration, Press Release, 1.

76. Farm Security Administration, Press Release, 1.

77. Bendiner, "Cool Heads or Martial Law," 181–82.

78. For a superb reading of the novel as a modernist text that privileges abstraction, see Szalay, 162–200.

79. Don Mitchell credits *The Grapes of Wrath* with a canny juxtaposition of scenic ideology and regimental spatial reality in his discussion of the passage when the Joads, upon reaching the top of Tehachapi Pass, first glimpse the California of which they have been dreaming. In the Steinbeck text: "and then they stood, silent and awestruck, embarrassed before the great valley. The distance was thinned with haze, and the land grew softer and softer in the distance. A windmill flashed in the sun, and its turning blades were like a little heliograph, far away. Ruthie and Winfield looked at it, and Ruthie whispered, 'It's California.'" See *Grapes of Wrath*, 310. Mitchell writes, "The dream itself is impossible without a certain haze that closes off perspective, that hides the struggle that goes into making landscape. . . . Hidden in the bushes along the creeks and irrigation ditches is the other side of the California Dream, a side that has been there all along, but is easy to overlook from atop the hill: the invisible army of migrant workers who make the landscape of beauty and abundance that awed the Joads." See Mitchell, 13–14. My own reading argues that migrant labor is not hidden by the ideology of 1930s California representation but is in fact openly refigured by it.

80. As George Henderson argues, "Steinbeck's primary thesis, in geographical terms, was that you cannot understand what is going on inside California unless you know what is occurring outside." For a persuasive reading of Steinbeck's keen awareness of the social effects of modern farming in Oklahoma and California, and his dismantling of the myth of "the family farm as a basic unit of democracy," see Henderson, "John Steinbeck's Spatial Imagination."

81. For a concise overview of the institutional and philosophical conflict between George Peek, an advocate of export dumping, and Henry Wallace, an advocate of production controls, see Skocpol and Finegold, "State Capacity and Economic Intervention."

82. At Topaz, there were only 248 farmers; the rest were professionals, semiprofessionals, managers and office workers, nursery workers, fishermen, and forestry and unskilled workers. See Sandra Taylor, *Jewel of the Desert*, 104.

83. Reed, "The Agricultural Program," 6 (hereafter cited as AP).

84. As John Modell writes, agriculture was the backbone for an ethnic economy that sustained the Japanese American community until World War II. See Modell, *Economics and Politics*, 26–27.

85. More forcefully than any other WRA speaker, Powell placed blame for the Japanese American problem solely on the nation, see John Powell, "America's Refugees: Exodus and Diaspora," (St. Louis, Missouri, April 14, 1943), quoted in Wallinger, 229.

86. Whereas during the Depression there had been just twenty-five Japanese

Americans on L.A. County relief, after the war, there were four thousand and rising. See Daniels, *Concentration Camps*, 164.

87. WRA representative Katherine French, for example, stressed the differences between residents of Poston and those elsewhere in America, differences which were either highly desirable or inconsequential for membership in American communities. The main attributes were that "many of the families were more closely knit than most ordinary American families." Another was the fact that in spite of negative incentives imposed by the WRA wage scale, the evacuees still persevered in their former ways as industrious workers. See French, "Talk Made by Katherine French of WRA, Poston," at Claremont [California], November 3, 1944, quoted in Wallinger, 296.

88. Japanese farmers were urged by the military to continue tending their fields until the eve of evacuation so as to demonstrate their loyalty. According to David Mas Masumoto, despite offering an attractive deal, the government had trouble finding operators to take over the evacuee farms. See *Country Voices*, 48. Quoting Gary Okihiro's 1989 observation that the "rural dimension of Asian American Studies" was still a "fallow field, 'uncultivated yet rich with possibilities,'" Valerie Matsumoto points to the relatively underdeveloped understanding of "the degree to which class considerations really affected anti-Asianism" in the rural towns of Livingston and Cortez, given the predominance of urban studies of anti-Asianism. See *Farming the Home Place*, 11, 36–37.

89. See Lisca, "*Cannery Row* and the Tao Teh Ching"; Hayashi, "The 'Chinese Servant' in *East of Eden*"; and Bedford, "Steinbeck's Uses of the Oriental."

90. Steinbeck, *Of Mice and Men*, 807 (hereafter cited as *MM*).

91. The compensatory brutality of McTeague's hands can be read in terms of craft labor's displacement by the twin processes of foreign labor immigration and mechanization in the late nineteenth century. McTeague's antithesis is Trina Sieppe, the daughter of German immigrants, whose "industry was a constant reproach to him" and who annoyed him because she was so small, so prettily made, so invariably correct and precise." This productionist reading of the antagonism between the married couple has an echo in the tale of Augustine, their French cook, about whom all that was known was "that she was a decayed French laundress, miserably poor, her trade long since ruined by Chinese competition." Augustine's physical lack of self-control, resulting in a state of automaticity, bears a striking similarity to McTeague's condition: "Trina's anger promptly reduced her to a state of nervous collapse, wherein she lost all power of speech, while her head began to bob and nod with an incontrollable switching of the muscles, much like the oscillations of the head of a toy donkey. Her timidity was exasperating, her very presence in the room unstrung the nerves, while her morbid eagerness to avoid offense only served to develop in her a clumsiness that was at time beyond belief." See Norris, *McTeague*, 477, 400.

92. See Paul Taylor and Vasey, "Historical Background," 282.

93. "Maybe he ain't bright, but I never seen such a worker. He damn near killed his partner buckin' barley. There ain't nobody can keep up with him. God awmighty I never seen such a strong guy." (*Of Mice and Men*, 825); "He's a good skinner. He can rassel grain bags, drive a cultivator. He can do anything. Just give him a try" (812).

94. Steinbeck, "Johnny Bear," 100 (hereafter cited as JB).

95. On this topic, see chapter 2.

96. Owens, *John Steinbeck's Revision of America*, 78–89. See also, Lisca, *John Steinbeck: Nature and Myth*, 54; Fontenrose, *John Steinbeck: An Introduction and Interpretation*, 28; Levant, *The Novels of John Steinbeck*, 37; and Ditsky, "Faulkner Land and Steinbeck Country."

97. Steinbeck, *Pastures of Heaven*, 4 (hereafter cited as *PH*).

98. For the first view, see French, "The 'California Quality' of Steinbeck's Best Fiction," 12–13. For the latter, see Owens, *Steinbeck's Revision*, 78–87.

99. See Lewis, "John Steinbeck's Alternative to Internment Camps," 56.

100. The loyalty determination process allowed for a change of mind from disloyal to loyal but not the other way around; those who declared loyalty were assumed to be permanently loyal. Myer at first wanted a completely integrated draft but from the public relations perspective, a volunteer battalion would serve as better proof of Japanese American loyalty, while a segregated unit would also provide better potential for its visibility. In this case, Myer felt that what was needed was proof of group, rather than individual, loyalty. See Wallinger, 98, 208.

101. On Steinbeck's contact with federal officials of the regional headquarters of the Resettlement Administration starting in 1936, and his friendship with Tom Collins, the real life model for the FSA camp manager of Weedpatch in *The Grapes of Wrath*, see Benson, 332–50.

102. The Simon J. Lubin Society was the creation of the Progressivist founder and first director of the California Commission on Immigration and Housing (CCIH) as an advocacy group for rural reform. Established in 1913 under the Progressive gubernatorial reign of Hiram Johnson, the California Commission on Immigration and Housing (CCIH) exemplified both Progressivism's campaign against the abuses of corporate monopoly and its hostility to organized labor. The CCIH was complicitous in the crackdown on the IWW, and after World War I, it took a leading role in the immigration restriction movement on behalf of "the social health of the state." See Daniel, *Bitter Harvest*, 99; see also Don Mitchell, 103.

103. According to the photographer Horace Bristol, whom Steinbeck accompanied into the field in early 1938, the ending of *The Grapes of Wrath* was inspired by Lange's photography as well as his own. Dorothea Lange's *Migrant Mother*—the most famous of the over 270,000 negatives collected by her Resettlement/Farm Security Administration photographic team—first appeared in *Survey Graphic* in 1936. In 1938 the picture of an even more robust nursing Oklahoma woman shot by Bristol appeared in *Life*. See Starr, *Endangered Dreams*, 250–51. For a reading of the novel that emphasizes the New Deal's opposition between pregnancy and sympathy, and the ultimate displacement of female reproductivity by an abstract (read: masculinist) notion of public good, see Szalay, 162–82.

104. For a scathing critique (and in my view too quick a dismissal) of Steinbeck's "racial populism," see Denning, 267.

105. For an incisive account of the tensions between various rhetorics of the people in *The Grapes of Wrath*—a Popular Front laborism, a conservative vitalism, a New Deal technocracy, and a racial populism—see Denning, 265. For Steinbeck's national welfarism, see Szalay, 181–82.

106. Steinbeck, *Their Blood is Strong*, 3, 30 (hereafter cited as *TBS*).

107. October 7, 1938, entry. See Robert Demott, ed., *John Steinbeck: Working Days*, 84.

108. See statement by Edward Brown, "Japanese Immigration," printed in California State Board of Control, *California and the Oriental*, 109. Brown was the chief sanitary engineer of the California State Commission of Immigration and Housing.

109. Chester Rowell, "Orientophobia," 13.

110. McWilliams, *Factories in the Field*, 315.

111. Through overzealous enforcement, the 1875 Page Law prohibiting the importation of Chinese female prostitutes effectively barred Chinese women and resulted in a radically imbalanced sex ratio among Chinese immigrant communities. See Hing, 23.

112. See Burke, *Olson's New Deal for California*.

113. McWilliams, *Factories*, 8 (hereafter cited as *FF*).

114. Steinbeck's confluence with socialist ideas often led him to be accused of being a socialist or a communist, but he never advocated or endorsed it as a system and was, according to his biographer Benson, never a political radical. See Benson, 44, 69.

115. For a reading of the novel with a somewhat different emphasis on the displacement of familial (read: maternal) care by an abstract (read: masculine) figuration of a national public, see Szalay, 167–82. Rose of Sharon's suckling of a dying old stranger in place of her miscarried child points to altered forms of sympathy and sentiment and "situates *The Grapes of Wrath* in the context of broadly welfarist, New Deal concerns about the operation of a resolutely national domestic economy." See Szalay, 171.

116. For a reading of McWilliams as a genuine Popular Front figure—in whose work the representation of government reforms prefigured more radical visions of a democratic and collective social order—against Steinbeck's relative conservativism, see Denning, 266–67.

117. In a November 7, 1940, letter to Edward G. Robinson, Steinbeck referred to a growing "hysteria" toward Japanese Californians and his fear of a "witch hunt" conducted through "the formulated and calculated oppression of aliens by men of power, and . . . the generalized hatred of uninstructed people who must be sacrificial victims." See Demott, 178.

118. The attachment of the term "Chinese" to "ex-prostitute" points to the originary figure of Asian exclusion, constituted by the 1875 Page Law, which barred the importation of Chinese "prostitutes"—effectively Chinese women as such—and formed a precursor to the more sweeping 1882 Chinese Exclusion Act.

119. Marx and Engels's concept of the AMP draws from a complex of ideas about Asian political and economic systems in the Enlightenment. The complex contains the following features: state property of land, lack of judicial restraint, religious substitution for law, absence of hereditary nobility, servile social equality, isolated village communities, agrarian predominance over industry, public hydraulic works, torrid climatic environment, and historical immutability. See Perry Anderson, *Lineages of the Absolutist State*, 472.

120. The caste concept of California's political economy recurs in more recent attempts to grapple with the "mutual constitutiveness" of race and class. Tomás Almaguer, for instance, describes a hierarchical society characterized by white immigrants at the top, and, in descending order, Mexicans, blacks, Asians, and Indians. See Almaguer, *Racial Faultlines*, 9.

121. See Anne M. Bailey and Josep R. Llobera, "Editors' Introduction," 49–52.

122. For more on this, see chapter 3.

123. Robert Weiss writes that "[e]ven before international developments influenced policy, the Franklin D. Roosevelt administration evinced some sensitivity to the plight of aliens." Although little was done to alter preexisting legislation concerning aliens, in implementing these laws, "the executive branch shifted from a posture of hostility in the 1920s to one of sympathy under Roosevelt. Anti-immigrant feeling persisted, but it no longer had the government stamp of legitimacy." "Much of this assault on racism," however, "centered on peoples of European origin. . . ." See Weiss, "Ethnicity and Reform," 566–67.

124. My point is not whether the Japanese American camps should appropriately be called concentration camps, but the alien vs. American figuration McWilliams uses to represent them. Among post-1970s scholars, Daniels has led the way in insisting that Japanese Americans were confined in "concentration camps," quoting President Roosevelt and Chief Justice Owen Roberts's use of the term when talking about Japanese Americans. Daniels acknowledges that unlike European Jews, Japanese Americans were never subjected to systematic execution, and that more Japanese Americans were born in camps than died there. However, Daniels insists on the parallel between American and German camps for confining individuals within barbed-wire compounds under military patrol, simply on the basis of ancestry, without charge or trial. See Yang Murray, "Introduction: The Internment of Japanese Americans," 23–24.

125. McWilliams, *Liberals and the War Crisis*, 3 (hereafter cited as *LWC*).

126. See Baldwin, "Nisei in Japan," 24. Note that the phrase "American with a Japanese face" derives from Louis Adamic. See Adamic, "American with a Japanese Face."

127. On the critics of the administration's internment policy, see Shaffer, 88–107.

128. Among such leaders were Earl Warren—California attorney general at the time of evacuation and governor during the return of Japanese Americans—Los Angeles Mayor Bowron Fletcher, and California Attorney General Robert W. Kenny. Daniels suggests that some factors were a federal policy of racial tolerance and the 1945 location of the United Nations conference in San Francisco, which emphasized principles of racial equality. See Daniels, *Concentration Camps*, 149–58, 162.

129. Richard and Maisie Conrat, who published *Executive Order 9066* in 1972, discovered some 25,000 photographs of Japanese American evacuation and internment taken by Dorothea Lange, Ansel Adams, Clem Albers, J. D. Bigelow, Russell Lee, Francis Stewart, and others. Caroline Chung Simpson takes a March 20, 1944, piece by Carl Mydans on the Tule Lake camp in *Life* magazine to mark an "inaugural moment of postwar visibility for Japanese Ameri-

cans." See Chung Simpson, *An Absent Presence*, 9. Following Marita Sturken's discussion of Japanese American internment's absent presence in postwar national memory, Simpson's study emphasizes the relative absence of national media coverage until 1944, except in the West Coast media in the initial period of evacuation. See Chung, 21–22; Sturken, "Absent Images of Memory." My argument, which situates internment in relation to the prewar era, emphasizes the relative presence of representation as linked to the state's assumption of an Americanization project. Even as Chung Simpson tends to view the community analysis projects in the camps, for example, as having maintained "the constructed alienation of the Nisei" by "affirming the resilience of Japanese culture," there is also an acknowledgment that the camps were seen as a "new stage in the modernization of Japanese Americans" whereby the "prewar pathology" of residual Japaneseness in Japanese Americans might be reformed. See Chung Simpson, 48, 71.

130. FSA chief Roy Stryker sent Russell Lee to photograph agency projects involving evacuee farm transfer and the assignation of a few hundred Japanese Americans to migrant labor in eastern Oregon, eastern Washington, and Idaho. Although Lange was hired by the WRA to photograph the process of evacuation, including the inside of the assembly centers, her photographs were impounded during the war and none were published in the "Pictorial Summary" of the U.S. Army Western Defense Command and Fourth Army's *Final Report: Japanese Evacuation from the West Coast, 1942*. See Davidov, " 'The Color of My Skin,' " 226–27. In Davidov's analysis, while Lange's images "demanded an emotional response that seemed to some to be inimical to national security," Lee's were more circumspect (Davidov, 229, 228).

131. Paul Taylor, "Our Stakes in the Japanese Exodus."

132. Ansel Adams, *Born Free and Equal*, 34–36 (hereafter cited as *BFE*). Lange was critical of what she saw to be Adams's overly accommodationist portrait of the camp. See Davidov, 233.

133. There are also other kinds of shots: individuals at work in middle distance, group scenes in middle distance, and shots that show the contextual backdrop of camp scenes. However, I mention the individual close-up shots because it is this composition of an Asian (American) subject that strikes me as novel. See, by comparison, the anthropological style of the 1913 photographs shot by Arnold Genthe with text by Will Irwin, *Old Chinatown*. Genthe's photos have been reprinted in John Tchen, *Genthe's Photographs of San Francisco's Old Chinatown*.

CHAPTER FIVE

1. See Isaacs, *Scratches on Our Mind*.

2. Conn, "Introduction: Rediscovering Pearl S. Buck," 2.

3. Hunt, "Pearl S. Buck—Popular Expert in China, 1931–1949," 33, 40.

4. For a critique of Pearl S. Buck's Orientalism, see Quach, "Chinese Fictions."

5. Chin, et al., eds., *Aiiieeeee!* xxii. They write: "For the generations of Asian Americans born and raised since the '20s, the Christian conversion, Charlie Chan, Fu Manchu, Shangri-la, Pearl S. Buck, and the camps, Asian American his-

tory, like the Asian and the Asian American, has been and is real only as a product of white fiction and fantasy." See xxxviii–xxxix.

6. See, for example, Hauser, "Chinaman's Chance," and Stewart Edward White, "My Ming Collection." For an excellent feminist analysis of the ambivalence of literature concerning Chinese domestics, see Robert G. Lee, *Orientals*, 83–105.

7. Cowley, "The Good Earthling," 251–52.

8. Proteus, "Review of *The Good Earth*," 430.

9. Cevasco, "Pearl S. Buck and the Chinese Novel," 447.

10. As Elaine Kim writes, "Anglo-American writers of some literary merit" have made use of caricatures of Asians, "although usually not as a focus for their work"; "But, for the most part, the enormous body of Anglo-American literature containing these caricatures, particularly those dealing with Asians as a theme, are of much lesser stuff—pulp novels and dime romances of varying degrees of literary quality." See Kim, *Asian American Literature*, 3

11. Florence Ayscough's review of *The Good Earth*, entitled "The Real China," 676.

12. Officially, the academy's citation referred to her Chinese novels as pioneering, and specifically praised her biographies of her parents, *The Exile* (1936) and *Fighting Angel* (1936)—made available also as a two-volume set under the title *The Flesh and the Spirit*—as her finest "literary works of art." See Conn, *Pearl S. Buck: A Cultural Biography*, 212.

13. Nathaniel Peffer, "Review of *The Good Earth*," 1.

14. Quoted in Nancy Evans, "Review of *The Good Earth*," 324.

15. Kiang, "A Chinese Scholar's View," 2.

16. Pearl S. Buck, "Mrs. Buck Replies," 17.

17. For Pearl S. Buck's sentimentalism, see Thomson Jr., "Pearl S. Buck and the American Quest for China," 13–14; see also Bellman, "Popular Writers in the Modern Age," 362.

18. Doyle, "Pearl S. Buck's Short Stories," 68.

19. Pointing out that Pearl S. Buck learned to speak Chinese before English, though she did study English first when it came to reading and writing, Yu Yuh-Chao argues that classic Chinese novels such as *Shui Hu Chuan* (*The Water Margin*), *San Kuo* (*The Romance of the Three Kingdoms*) and *Hung Lou Meng* (*Dream of the Red Chamber*) comprise Buck's formative influences. See Yuh-Chao, "Chinese Influences on Pearl S. Buck."

20. Thompson, "Pearl S. Buck," 100–101.

21. Helen Snow, "An Island in Time," 28.

22. Klein, "Roots of Radicals," 138.

23. Proletarian literature was a contested term, taken variously to refer to authorship, audience, subject matter, or political perspective. See Foley, *Radical Representations*, 80.

24. This is Foley's description of the collective novel. See Foley 400, 410.

25. See Madden, "Introduction," xxxii. Also see Aaron, *Writers on the Left*, 151–52.

26. Curiously, Buck herself sometimes referred to *The Good Earth* as a "proletarian" novel. See Conn, "Pearl S. Buck and American Literary Culture," 111.

27. Given the extensive rural basis of American Protestant missionary work in China since the 1830s, the implausibility of Wang Lung's "first encounter" as staged by Pearl S. Buck should at least be noted. In the so-called Nanking decade, 1928–1937, dating from the Kuomintang (KMT) suppression of the Communists to the outbreak of the Sino-Japanese War, American personnel in China—present through the various instruments of mission stations, Christian colleges, the National Christian Council, the YMCA, private Chinese institutions, international relief agencies, and foundations—was largely concentrated in the effort of rural reconstruction. See Thomson, *When China Faced West*, 204.

28. The MGM film, for example, ends at the novel's halfway point on the triumphal note of Wang Lung's success, eliminating the depiction of his decline. *The Good Earth* (1937, Metro Goldwyn Mayer).

29. Pearl S. Buck, *The Good Earth*, 359 (hereafter cited as *GE*).

30. In his influential intellectual history and critique of American Sinology, Paul Cohen points to the Vietnam watershed in the historiographical profession which initiated a critique of Western imperialism and the recognition of the limits of Western power, resulting in a double shift—first, of taking socioeconomic causation seriously and, second, to a more genuinely Other-centered historiography. See Cohen, *Discovering History in China*, xiv–7. The 1950s and 1960s were characterized by an "impact-response" approach to the question of Chinese modernization, whereby virtually all historians divided Chinese history into the "traditional" and the "modern," with the latter designating the beginning of the period when the motion of history was governed primarily by forces exogenous to Chinese society and tradition. See Cohen, 11, 58, 68. Beginning in the late 1960s with the intervention of Benjamin Schwartz and, under the influence of Lloyd and Susanne Rudolph's critique of the "modernity of tradition" in the field of Indian political development, China scholars began to question the presuppositions of modernization theory in its construction of an ahistorical premodern China. See Cohen, 80–81. On the other side of the tradition/modernity divide, modernization theory was also guilty of subordinating history to an essential culture in explaining the structural conditions of the present. See Cohen, 189. Cohen's own desire is for a "truly interior, China-centered view of recent Chinese history." See Cohen, 153. While I find Cohen's critical overview of post–World War II sinology useful, I remain skeptical of this desire for pure, autochthonous origins.

31. Between 1911 and 1949, China experienced a marked and continuous trend toward an increase in rural tenancy. By 1937 it was estimated that almost two-thirds of Chinese farmers rented land from others. Among the prevailing conditions of tenancy were: high rents, insecurity of tenure, excessive charges, and absence of written agreements. Besides increased tenancy, the rural crisis characterizing interwar China also involved the fact of heavy, inequitable taxation and widespread official corruption, which subjected the peasant proprietor and, in particular the poor peasant, to varieties of graft and squeeze in the collection of land tax. See Thomson, *When China Faced West*, 44.

32. This is even more the case in the film version of *The Good Earth*, in which O-lan comes by the jewels not through her own agency, but wakes up with them magically in her hand after being trampled by a mob. Wang Lung does not enter the house at all and therefore has no part in the mechanism of capital accumulation.

33. Here I am following C. B. MacPherson's reading of Locke as the basis for the classical liberal theory of possessive individualism. See MacPherson, "Introduction."

34. Starting with the shrinkage of European export markets at the end of the First World War, American agricultural prices experienced severe deflation, but it was not until the first year of the New Deal that federal officials sought to address the persistent problem of agricultural surplus by trying to reward production controls for major staple crops (cotton, wheat, corn, and hogs) instead of trying to discover solutions along market avenues. The Agricultural Adjustment Act launched in the spring of 1933 was actually a meld of both approaches. See Skocpol and Finegold, "State Capacity and Economic Intervention," 268.

35. Henry Wallace, weekly column, 1314.

36. For more on the linkage between New Deal agricultural reform as inspired by "Chinese agricultural statesmanship," see Bodde, "Henry Wallace and the Ever-Normal Granary."

37. Perry Anderson, *Lineages of the Absolutist State*, 472–83.

38. See Wittfogel, *Oriental Despotism*.

39. For a discussion of alien land law fiction, see chapter 3, and also my discussion of Frank Norris's *The Octopus* in chapter 2.

40. Stross, *The Stubborn Earth*, 161–85.

41. John Lossing Buck, *Chinese Farm Economy*, 420 (hereafter cited as *CFE*).

42. See chapter 2 for a discussion of Smith.

43. John Buck, *Land Utilization in China*, 20 (hereafter cited as *LUC*).

44. For the conceptualization of the working body as the "human motor" in late-nineteenth to early-twentieth-century physical and social science, see Rabinbach, *The Human Motor*.

45. As such, John Buck's authoritative assessment of rural conditions might be interestingly set alongside Mao Tse-Tung's radically different diagnosis set out in his "Report on an Investigation of the Peasant Movement in Hunan." The very first page of *Land Utilization in China* makes clear that it will not address "the so-called agrarian situation which may be thought of in terms of the political, economic and social relationships between farmers and other classes of society." See *Land Utilization*, 1. But Buck's assessment of the objective rate of tenancy also derives from his over-sampling of more prosperous owner-cultivated regions north of the Yangtze River. See Thomson, *When China Faced West*, 211. As late as 1970 Buck's data continued to inform American historiographical claims that Chinese peasant living standards rose in the period between 1890 and 1970. Paul Cohen points out that if there was any part of China which escaped agrarian crisis, it was the region studied by Buck, where between 1911 and 1933 the tenancy rate remained stable at 13 percent, compared to an increase from 28 percent to 32 percent for China as a whole. See Cohen, 128. For a stringent critique of the research validity of Buck's surveys, see Stross, 176–87.

46. Pearl S. Buck, *My Several Worlds*, 146 (hereafter cited as *MSW*).

47. The description of the missionary resembles that of Pearl S. Buck's father Absalom Sydenstricker. See Pearl S. Buck, "The Giants Are Gone."

48. A 300-page report commissioned by a confederation of Protestant denominations, entitled *Re-Thinking Missions* (1932), denounced most evangelical

practices as irrelevant and obsolete and issued a series of liberal recommendations. See Conn, *Cultural Biography*, 149–50.

49. Conn dates Pearl S. Buck's long association with the Civil Rights movement from the fall of 1932, when she first made contact with leading African American organizers and journalists. See Conn, *Cultural Biography*, 151.

50. For a historical account of the event, see Isaacs, *Tragedy of the Chinese Revolution*. The Counterrevolution of 1927 is also central to the history of Soviet Communism because the substantive content of the debate between Stalin's policy of "socialism in one country" and Trotsky's theory of a permanent revolution is staged around Comintern responsibility for the 1927 counterrevolutionary disaster in China.

51. Critics have noted that Pearl S. Buck's lack of contact with China after settling in the United States in the 1930s helps explain her static image of China. See Hunt, "Popular Expert," 39.

52. For example, this barely checked condescension toward the KMT under the exigencies of U.S.-China wartime alliance is readable in her remarks on Madame Chiang Kai-Shek during Madame Chiang's celebrated tour of the United States in 1943. Pearl S. Buck speaks about the event from the perspective of an interested party who shares with Madame Chiang the desire to drum up American support for the Chinese anti-Japanese resistance, but in carefully praising the visit as a "personal triumph" achieved through her "beauty and charm," Buck registers the feeling that the visit "has done something less than it might have done." Buck is careful to blame the political limitations of the visit on the ignorance of the American people about Chinese reality, but the implication of a yawning gap between charming beauty and real struggle insinuates that the failure of Madame to enlighten her American audience devolves at least partly from her own ignorance of the real China. See Pearl S. Buck, "A Warning about China," 53.

53. The complicities of colonial discourse and nationalist discourse in representing the subaltern subject have been most far reachingly explored by Indian historians associated with the Subaltern Studies project and their theoretical commentators, such as Gayatri Chakravorty Spivak. See *Selected Subaltern Studies*, ed. Ranajit Guha and Spivak. See also Spivak, "Can the Subaltern Speak?" To my knowledge, the influence of Indian Subaltern Studies upon the contemporary field of Chinese historiography remains as yet minimal, though there is evidence that a general notion of subalternity has been picked up in some limited ways. See Gail Hershatter's critique of Guha and Spivak framed in terms of a theoretical (in)appropriateness to the China context in her essay "The Subaltern Talks Back."

54. Thomson, *Sentimental Imperialists*.

55. Isaacs, *Images of Asia*, 155 n, 162–63. Within the first year of publication, *Red Star over China* (1938) sold more than 100,000 copies in Great Britain. Though the first American edition sold only about 15,000 copies, subsequent printings brought this total up to 65,000, making Edgar Snow's book the most successful nonfiction work about the Far East hitherto published in the United States.

56. Schram, *Mao Tse-Tung*, 193.

57. Woodside, "The Rise and Fall," 315.

58. Fairbank, *The People's Middle Kingdom*, 84–85.

59. Edgar Snow, *Red Star over China* (1938; rev. and enlarged ed., New York: Grove Press, 1968), 355 (hereafter cited as *RSOC*).

60. See Edgar Snow "The Autobiography of Mao Tse-Tung, As Told to Edgar Snow" in four parts.

61. See McNail, *China's International Relations*; see also Monroe, *China: A Nation in Evolution*.

62. Norton, *China and the Powers*; Peffer, "The Chinese Idea of Communism;" Grover Clark, *The Great Wall Crumbles*. All quoted in Shewmaker, *Americans and Chinese Communists*, 30–31.

63. Dirlik, "Chinese Historians," 106 (italics added).

64. From Leon Trotsky, *1905*, published in Russian for the first time in 1922 (quoted in Samuel H. Baron). See Baron, "Plekhanov, Trotsky, and the Development of Soviet Historiography," 391. For an overview of Soviet historiography, see Shteppa, *Russian Historians and the Soviet State*. For the history of the Asiatic mode of production debate, see Dunn, *Fall and Rise of the Asiatic Mode of Production*; see also, Anne M. Bailey and Josep R. Llobera, eds., *The Asiatic Mode of Production*. For the derivations and analysis of the AMP in Marx, see Krader, *The Asiatic Mode of Production*.

65. See *Red Star*, 225.

66. Fairbank, "Introduction," *Red Star*, 11.

67. Koen, *The China Lobby*.

68. See Tuchman, *Stillwell and the American Experience*.

69. The first public knowledge of "conspiracy" came on June 7, 1945, when the FBI arrested six suspects in conjunction with the *Amerasia* affair when someone in the Office of Strategic Services noticed a similarity between a restricted OSS document and an article appearing in *Amerasia* magazine. Although the investigations came to naught, myths concerning it continued to appear in China Lobby sources. See Koen, 69–74. In July 1948 the House Committee on Un-American Activities (HUAC) began a series of hearings on Communist espionage activities in the United States prior to and during World War II. In 1951 HUAC targeted the State Department officers who had been present on an American military mission to Yenan in July 1944 to explore a strategic alliance with Mao. See Koen, 90–91. Though a rival of *Amerasia*, the Institute of Pacific Relations was also a major target of attack. See Koen, 153. China specialists whose national loyalty was questioned in some way included: John Fairbank, Owen Lattimore, Lawrence Rosinger, T. A. Bisson, Derk Bodde, Harold M. Vinacke, Charles P. Fitzgerald, Benjamin Schwartz, Kenneth S. Latourette, William C. Johnstone, W. W. Lockwood, and Dorothy Borg. Journalists were also targeted, including: Theodore H. White, Richard Lauterbach, Edgar Snow, Harrison Forman, Israel Epstein, and Brooks Atkinson. See Koen, 133.

70. Isaacs claims that *Red Star* is the birthplace of the agrarian reformer myth, but Shewmaker questions this. See Shewmaker, 255.

71. Carlson, *Twin Stars of China*, 231.

72. See Roosevelt's correspondence with Evans Carlson (quoted in Tuchman, 486).

73. For example, see Shewmaker, 319.

74. On the historical emergence of globalism as an idea, Akira Iriye writes that the succession of the international system of the British empire by a bipolar universe inhabited by two global superpowers can be dated to the Yalta Conference, when "[b]oth the Soviet Union and the United States perceived themselves as global powers, and they recognized the desirability of outlining the limits of each other's spheres of influence outside the national boundaries." See Iriye, *The Cold War in Asia*, 98.

75. Robert Ferrell writes that throughout the 1930s Roosevelt was reluctant to take a strong foreign policy stand due to the prioritization of domestic affairs. Ferrell, *American Diplomacy*, 243. Robert Divine has tried to counteract the domestic orientation of 1930s historiography by pointing to the significance of the neutrality legislation passed by Congress to keep the U.S. out of future wars, though the content of that significance would still suggest that the 1930s was "the high tide of American isolationism in the twentieth century." See Divine, *The Illusion of Neutrality*, vii. On the subject of East Asian marginality to the United States' other geopolitical concerns, Waldo Heinrichs writes, ". . . with all its rhetoric, illusion and befuddlement, American East Asian policy tended in fact to be cautious, conservative, and founded on the view that American interests in East Asia, considered alone, were marginal. . . . When East Asia assumed critical importance it was for larger, worldwide reasons or because of its relation to European concerns." See Heinrichs, "The Middle Years," 91.

76. The Tolan Committee convened by the House of Representatives states in its 1941 report: "Something fundamental has occurred to render the haphazard shifts of residence by the average American family a matter for national study and investigation." The report identifies migrancy—or the phenomenon of persons in perpetual motion—as a new social problem of the times. See Select House Committee to Investigate the Interstate Migration of Destitute Citizens, *Preliminary Report*, 9.

77. Janice R. MacKinnon and Stephen R. MacKinnon, *Agnes Smedley*, 202. See also Auden and Isherwood, *Journey to a War*; and Ernest Hemingway's Letter to Henry Morgenthau.

78. Orwell's *Homage to Catalonia* (1938) is the influential text that centers on the tragic fate of the Trotskyist P.O.U.M. fighters. The ideological significance of Maoism, as a critique of Soviet revolutionary retreat, surfaces later as an influential current within the Western left in the 1960s. Until the heyday of Third World nationalisms, sectarian readings of the antifascist warfront in Asia were submerged beneath its predominantly racialized meaning.

79. Cf. Fanon, *Black Skin, White Masks*.

80. Pearl S. Buck, "What Are We Fighting For in the Orient?" 10 (hereafter cited as WWFO).

81. Wallace, *New Frontiers*, 72.

82. For a critique of the economic coercion of "free trade," see Gallagher and Robinson, "The Imperialism of Free Trade."

83. William Appleman Williams is the key thinker to have suggested an inexorable link between the American agricultural lobby and the push for U.S. overseas economic expansion. As an industry whose profits in the nineteenth century were early dependent upon an export market, U.S. farmers consistently opted for

lower tariffs and free marketplace expansion and were key to the development of a U.S. policy of imperialism without formal colonies. *"The American farmer, rather than the American manufacturer or financier, alerted the rest of the world to the power and the dangerous challenge of the American economy.* The specter of an Americanization of the world, as it came to be called in the 1890s, was initially created by the sodbuster, the swineherd, the cattleman, and the cotton-chopping sharecropper." See Williams, *The Roots of the Modern American Empire*, 22–23 (emphasis in original).

84. Thomson, *While China Faced West*, xi, 35, 206.

85. Thorne, *Allies of a Kind*, 291.

86. African American identification with Japanese imperialism was not without its political contradictions, of course. See the special issue of *Positions,* "The Afro-Asian Century," edited by Jones and Singh, especially articles by Widener, Koshiro, and Mullen.

87. Walter White, *A Rising Wind*, 144–48. See also Janken, "From Colonial Liberation to Cold War Liberalism." For a history of the relationship between civil rights activism and anticolonial movements in the 1940s, see Von Eschen, *Race Against Empire.*

88. Welles, *New York Herald Tribune* (March 28, 1945), quoted in Louis, *Imperialism at Bay, 1941–1945*, 498.

89. See Pearl S. Buck, "Tinder for Tomorrow," 3 (hereafter cited as TT).

90. NAACP President Walter White cites Pearl S. Buck's essay "Tinder for Tomorrow" as an eloquent warning against the catastrophic consequences of blindness to the liabilities of racism to U.S. global power. See White, 150–52.

91. Gary Okihiro argues that the idea of a yellow peril fundamentally derives from non-whites' contestation of white supremacy. To this extent, U.S. government concerns about African American sympathy for Japan's cause during World War II involves the combination of two historically related fears of anticolonial resistance. "In the postbellum period, that domestic fear of African-American resistance to white supremacy would eventually merge with the international fear of the yellow peril, as exemplified in the government surveillance of African-American leaders and organizations after World War I." See Okihiro, *Margins and Mainstreams*, 127.

92. Jack London, "The Yellow Peril," 279.

93. Pearl S. Buck, "Western Weapons," 673 (hereafter cited as WHE).

94. See Pearl S. Buck, "An Open Letter to the Chinese People," 126 (hereafter cited as OLCP).

95. Pearl S. Buck, "Thanks to Japan," 280 (hereafter cited as TJ).

96. Second quotation taken from Pearl S. Buck, "A Warning to Free Nations," 161 (hereafter cited as WFN).

97. Pearl S. Buck, "Arms for China's Democracy," 534 (hereafter cited as ACD).

98. On this point, see chapter 4.

99. Steinbeck, *The Grapes of Wrath*, 47 (hereafter cited as *GW*).

100. Conn, *Cultural Biography*, 270, 299.

101. Koen communicates a sense of this inscription through an unselfconscious replication of his subject's paranoia in chronicling the China Lobby's

sweeping subversion of American national institutions. Koen writes, "United States policy toward China is more deeply involved in domestic politics than any other aspect of American foreign affairs. It was the one area specifically excluded by Senator Vandenberg in 1947 from the scope of bipartisan agreement. Partly as a result of this exclusion from bipartisan consideration, contention over China policy has virtually become a permanent feature of Republican-Democratic party battles and, at least since 1953, of somewhat less intensive battles between the conservative and moderate wings of the Republican party." See Koen, vii.

102. Similar to Buck's wartime writings, Wendell Wilkie's *One World* projects a postwar internationalism where Asia and America will be part of one world and the liberation of Asia is simultaneously the overturning of racism in America. See Wilkie, 202. Wilkie argues that the League of Nations had failed because it had taken "inadequate account of the pressing needs of the Far East"; his visit to China left him "with the feeling that if all Chinese Communists are like [Chou En-Lai], their movement is more a national and agrarian awakening than an international or proletarian conspiracy" (Wilkie, 196, 132). For a like-minded vision of a post-Pacific world, where a rising Asian standard of living and U.S. economic prosperity go hand in hand, see Wallace, *Our Job in the Pacific*.

103. NSC 48/1, "The Position of the United States with Respect to Asia," December 23, 1949, U.S. Department of Defense, vol. 8, *United States–Vietnam Relations 1945–1967* (Washington, D.C., 1971), quoted in John Lewis Gaddis; see "'Defense Perimeter' Concept," 65.

104. Cumings, "The Origins and Development," 67.

105. Steinbeck, *Cannery Row*, 2 (hereafter cited as *CR*).

106. For an influential Depression-era expression of catastrophic wastefulness resulting from American assumptions about living in an "economy of abundance," see Stuart Chase, *Economy of Abundance*. An important publicist of New Deal philosophy, Chase authored numerous books on such topics as government in business and environmental waste. See also Chase, *Rich Land, Poor Land*.

107. See Lisca, "*Cannery Row* and the Tao Teh Ching;" and Bedford, "Steinbeck's Uses of the Oriental," 7–11. On Steinbeck and Ed Ricketts as holistic thinkers, see Astro, *Steinbeck and Ricketts*, 48.

108. Steinbeck, *The Log from the Sea of Cortez*, 875 (italics in the original; hereafter cited as *LSC*).

109. On the ocean as capital's myth medium, particularly in Pacific Rim discourse, see Connery, "The Oceanic Feeling and the Regional Imaginary."

110. See Lisca, "Tao Teh Ching," 24.

111. Lisca, *The Wide World of John Steinbeck*, 201–2.

112. For commentary on the character of Lee, see Hayashi, "The 'Chinese Servant' in *East of Eden*."

Works Cited

Aaron, Daniel. *Writers on the Left: Episodes in American Literary Communism.* New York: Columbia University Press, 1992.

Adamic, Louis. *From Many Lands.* New York: Harper & Bros., 1940.

Adams, Ansel. *Born Free and Equal: The Story of Loyal Japanese-Americans.* New York: U.S. Camera, 1944.

Adams, Brooks. *America's Economic Supremacy.* New York: Macmillan, 1900.

——. *The Law of Civilization and Decay.* 1896. Reprint, New York: Vintage, 1959.

——. "The New Industrial Revolution." *Atlantic Monthly* (January 1901): 157–65.

Adams, R. L. [Richard Laban]. "California Farms: To Buy or Not to Buy?" California Agricultural Experiment Station Circular No. 358, March 1944. Berkeley: University of California.

——. "Farm Labor." Address before the California State Chamber of Commerce, aired on KSFO radio, January 26, 1936. Transcript. In the library of The Giannini Foundation of Agricultural Economics, University of California at Berkeley.

Adams, R. L., and William H. Smith Jr. "Farm Tenancy in California and Method of Leasing." The Giannini Foundation of Agricultural Economics, Bulletin No. 655, Paper No. 95. Berkeley, Calif.: Agricultural Experiment Station, 1941.

Albrecht, Adalbert. "The Situation in the Russian Interior." *Arena* 32 (September 1904): 225–31.

Almaguer, Tomás. *Racial Faultlines: The Historical Origins of White Supremacy in California.* Berkeley and Los Angeles: University of California Press, 1994.

Anderson, David D. *Ignatius Donnelly.* Boston: Twayne, 1980.

Anderson, Perry. *Lineages of the Absolutist State.* London: Verso, 1974.

Aoki, Keith. "Foreign-ness and Asian American Identities: Yellowface, World War II Propaganda, and Bifurcated Racial Stereotypes." UCLA *Asian Pacific American Law Journal* 4, no. 1 (Fall 1996): 1–71.

——. "No Right to Own: The Early Twentieth-Century 'Alien Land Laws' as a Prelude to Internment." *Boston College Law Review (Boston College Third World Law Journal)* 11, no. 1 (December 1998): 37–72.

Astro, Richard, and Tetsumaro Hayashi, eds. *Steinbeck: The Man and His Work.* Corvallis: Oregon State University Press, 1971.

Astro, Richard. *Steinbeck and Ricketts: The Shaping of a Novelist.* Minneapolis: University of Minnesota Press, 1973.

Auden, W. H., and Christopher Isherwood. *Journey to a War.* New York: Random House, 1939.

Auerbach, Jonathan. *Male Call: Becoming Jack London.* Durham, N.C.: Duke University Press, 1996.

Ayscough, Florence. "The Real China." *Saturday Review* (March 7, 1931): 676.

Azuma, Eiichiro. "Japanese Immigrant Farmers and California Alien Land Laws: A Study of the Walnut Grove Japanese Community." *California History* 73 (Spring 1994): 14–29, 84–89.

Baguley, David. "The Nature of Naturalism." In *Naturalism in the European Novel: New Critical Perspectives.* New York: Berg, 1992.

Bailey, Anne M., and Josep R. Llobera, "Editors' Introduction to the Fate of the AMP from Plekhanov to Stalin." In *The Asiatic Mode of Production: Science and Politics.* London: Routledge, 1981.

Bailey, Thomas. *Theodore Roosevelt and the Japanese-American Crisis.* Gloucester, Mass.: P. Smith, 1964.

Baldwin, Roger. "Nisei in Japan." *Common Ground* (Summer 1948): 24–29.

Baldwin, Sidney. *Poverty and Politics: Rise and Decline of the Farm Security Administration.* Chapel Hill: University of North Carolina Press, 1968.

Balibar, Etienne. "The Nation Form: History and Ideology." In *Race, Nation, Class: Ambiguous Identities* by Etienne Balibar and Immanuel Wallerstein. New York: Verso, 1991.

Baron, Samuel H. "Plekhanov, Trotsky, and the Development of Soviet Historiography." *Soviet Studies* 26 (July 1974): 380–95.

Barthes, Roland. *Image-Music-Text.* New York: Hill and Wang, 1977.

Beale, Howard. *Theodore Roosevelt and the Rise of America to World Power.* Baltimore: Johns Hopkins University Press, 1956.

Beard, Charles. Introduction to *The Law of Civilization and Decay,* by Brooks Adams, 3–56. 1896. Reprint, New York: Vintage, 1959.

Beauchamp, Gorman. "Resentment and Revolution in Jack London's Sociofantasy." *Canadian Review of American Studies* 13 (Fall 1982): 179–90.

Bedford, Richard C. "Steinbeck's Uses of the Oriental." *Steinbeck Quarterly* 13 (Winter–Spring 1980): 5–19.

Behdad, Ali. *Belated Travelers: Orientalism in the Age of Colonial Dissolution.* Durham, N.C.: Duke University Press, 1994.

Bellman, Samuel. "Popular Writers in the Modern Age: Constance Rourke, Pearl Buck, Majorie Kinnan Rawlings, and Margaret Mitchell." In *American Women Writers: Bibliographic Entries,* edited by Maurice Duke, Jackson R. Bryer, and M. Thomas Inge, 353–78. Westport, Conn.: Greenwood Press, 1983.

Bendiner, Robert. "Cool Heads or Martial Law." *Nation* (February 1942): 183–85.

Benson, Jackson. *The True Adventures of John Steinbeck, Writer.* New York: Viking, 1984.

Beresford, Charles. *Break-Up of China.* New York: Harper & Bros., 1899.

Berkove, Lawrence I. "A Parallax Connection in London's 'The Unparalleled Invasion.'" *American Literary Realism* 24, no. 2 (Winter 1992): 33–39.

Bhabha, Homi. "The Other Question: Stereotype, Discrimination, and the Discourse of Colonialism." In *The Location of Culture,* 66–84. London: Routledge: 1994.

Blauner, Robert. "Colonized and Immigrant Minorities." In *Racial Oppression in America.* New York: Harper, 1972.

Bodde, Derk. "Henry Wallace and the Ever-Normal Granary." *Far Eastern Quarterly* 5 (August 1946): 411–26.

Bonacich, Edna. "A Theory of Middleman Minorities." *American Sociological Review* 38 (October 1973): 583–94.

Borg, Dorothy, and Shumpei Okamoto, eds. *Pearl Harbor as History: Japanese-American Relations 1931–1941*. New York: Columbia University Press, 1973.

Boulger, Demetrius. "Russia, Japan, and Ourselves." *Nineteenth Century* (March 1904): 368–74.

Braverman, Harry. *Labor and Monopoly Capital*. New York: Monthly Review Press, 1974.

Bright, Charles, and Michael Geyer. "Where in the World is America?" In *Rethinking American History In a Global Age,* edited by Thomas Bender, 63–99. Berkeley and Los Angeles: University of California Press, 2002.

Brown, Edward. "Japanese Immigration." In *California and the Oriental,* Report of the State Board of Control of California, 1920. Reprint, New York: Arno Press, 1978.

Buck, John Lossing. *Chinese Farm Economy: A Study of 2866 Farms in Seventeen Localities and Seven Provinces in China*. Chicago: University of Chicago Press, 1930.

———. *Land Utilization in China: A Study of 16,786 Farms in 168 Localities and 38,256 Farm Families in Twenty-Two Provinces in China, 1929–1933*. Chicago: University of Chicago Press, 1937.

Buck, Pearl S. "Arms for China's Democracy." *Asia* 38 (September 1938): 534–35.

———. "The Giants Are Gone." *Asia* 36 (November 1936): 711–14.

———. *The Good Earth*. 1931. Reprint, New York: Pocket Books, 1994.

———. "Mrs. Buck Replies to Her Chinese Critic." *New York Times* (January 15, 1933): 17.

———. *My Several Worlds: A Personal Record*. New York: John Day, 1954.

———. "An Open Letter to the Chinese People." *Asia* 38 (February 1938): 126–28.

———. "Thanks to Japan." *Asia* 38 (May 1938): 279–80.

———. "Tinder for Tomorrow." In *Asia and Democracy*, 1–8. London: Macmillan, 1943.

———. "A Warning about China." *Life* 14 (May 10, 1943): 53–54, 56.

———. "A Warning to Free Nations." *Asia* 41 (March 1941): 161.

———. "Western Weapons in the Hands of the Reckless East." *Asia* 37 (September 1937): 672–73.

———. "What Are We Fighting for in the Orient?" In *Asia and Democracy,* 9–17. London: Macmillan, 1943.

Bunje, Emil T. H. *The Story of Japanese Farming*. Berkeley: University of California, 1937.

Burgam, Edwin Berry. "The Sensibility of John Steinbeck." In *Steinbeck and His Critics: A Record of Twenty-Five Years,* edited by E. W. Tedlock and C. V. Wicker, 104–18. Albuquerque: University of New Mexico Press, 1957.

Burke, Robert. *Olson's New Deal for California*. Berkeley and Los Angeles: University of California Press, 1953.

Burkhart, Gilbert, and James Burkhart. *Writers and Partisans: A History of Literary Radicalism in America.* New York: John Wiley and Sons, 1968.

Bywater, Hector. *The Great Pacific War.* Boston: Houghton Mifflin, 1920.

Cain, William E. "Socialism, Power, and the Fate of Style: Jack London in His Letters." *American Literary History* 3 (Fall 1991): 603–13.

California, State Board of Control of. *California and the Oriental.* Sacramento: California State Printing Office, 1920. Reprint, New York: Arno Press, 1978.

Carlson, Evans. *Twin Stars of China: A Behind the Scenes Story of China's Valiant Struggle for Existence by a U.S. Marine Who Lived and Moved with the People.* New York: Dodd, Mead, 1940.

Cassuto, Leonard, and Jeanne Campbell Reesman, eds. *Rereading Jack London.* Stanford, Calif.: Stanford University Press, 1996.

Cevasco, G. A. "Pearl Buck and the Chinese Novel." *Asian Studies* 5 (December 1967): 437–50.

Chan, Sucheng. "Asian American Historiography." *Pacific Historical Review* 65 (August 1996): 363–99.

———. *This Bittersweet Soil: The Chinese in California Agriculture, 1860–1910.* Berkeley and Los Angeles: University of California Press, 1986.

Chang, Gordon. "'Superman is about to Visit the Relocation Centers' and the Limits of Wartime Liberalism." *Amerasia* 19 (1993): 37–59.

Chase, Richard. *The Novel and Its Traditions.* Garden City, N.Y.: Doubleday Anchor Books, 1957.

Chase, Stuart. *Economy of Abundance.* New York: Macmillan, 1934.

———. *Rich Land, Poor Land: A Study of Waste in the Natural Resources of America.* New York: Whittlesey House, 1936.

Cheng, Anne Anlin. *The Melancholy of Race.* New York: Oxford University Press, 2000.

Cheng, Lucie, and Edna Bonacich, eds. *Labor Immigration under Capitalism: Asian Workers in the United States before World War II.* Berkeley and Los Angeles: University of California Press, 1984.

Chiba, Toyoji. "Truth of the Japanese Farming in California." Appendix to *California and the Oriental,* Report of the State Board of Control of California, 216–28. 1920. Reprint, New York: Arno Press, 1978.

Chin, Frank. "Afterword." In *Chinaman Pacific and Frisco R.R. Co.,* i–v. Minneapolis, Minn.: Coffee House Press, 1988.

Chin, Frank, Jeffrey Paul Chan, Lawson Fusao Inada, and Shawn Wong, eds. *Aiiieeeee! An Anthology of Asian American Writers.* New York: Mentor, 1991.

Choi, Jennifer Jung Hee. "The Rhetoric of Inclusion: The I.W.W. and Asian Workers," *Ex Post Facto* 8, 1999. http://www.sfsu.edu/~epf/1999/choi.html (May 2001).

Christierson, S. V. Letter to Congressman John Z. Anderson, January 22, 1942. Japanese American Evacuation and Resettlement Records, 1930–1974 (MSS 67/14c), A16.16. Bancroft Library, University of California at Berkeley.

———. Letter to Director of California Department of Agriculture William Cecil, January 10, 1942. Japanese American Evacuation and Resettlement Records, 1930–1974 (MSS 67/14c), A16.201. Bancroft Library, University of California at Berkeley.

Chuman, Frank. *The Bamboo People: The Law and Japanese Americans.* Del Mar, Calif.: Publisher's Inc., 1976.

Chung, Henry. *Oriental Policy of the United States.* New York: Fleming H. Revell, 1919.

Clark, Grover. *The Great Wall Crumbles.* New York: Macmillan, 1935.

Cohen, Paul. *Discovering History in China: American Historical Writing on the Recent Chinese Past.* New York: Columbia University Press, 1984.

Cohen, Warren. "American Perceptions of China." In *Dragon and Eagle. United States–China Relations: Past and Future,* edited by Michael Oksenberg and Robert Oxnam, 54–86. New York: Basic Books, 1978.

———, ed. *New Frontiers in American–East Asian Relations.* New York: Columbia University Press, 1983.

Commission on Wartime Relocation and Internment of Civilians. *Personal Justice Denied.* Seattle: University of Washington Press, 1997.

Commons, John. *Race and Immigrants in America.* New York: Macmillan, 1907.

Conkin, Paul. "The Vision of Elwood Mead." *Agricultural History* 34 (April 1960): 88–97.

Conn, Peter. "Introduction: Rediscovering Pearl S. Buck." In *The Several Worlds of Pearl S. Buck,* edited by Elizabeth J. Lipscomb, Frances E. Webb, and Peter Conn, 1–5. Westport, Conn.: Greenwood Press, 1994.

———. "Pearl S. Buck and American Literary Culture." In *The Several Worlds of Pearl S. Buck,* edited by Elizabeth J. Lipscomb, Frances E. Webb, and Peter Conn, 111–17. Westport, Conn.: Greenwood Press, 1994.

———. *Pearl S. Buck: A Cultural Biography.* Cambridge: Cambridge University Press, 1996.

Connery, Christopher. "The Oceanic Feeling and the Regional Imaginary." In *Local/Global: Cultural Production and the Transnational Imaginary,* edited by Rob Wilson and Wimal Dissanayake, 284–311. Durham, N.C.: Duke University Press, 1996.

———. "Pacific Rim Discourse: The U.S. Global Imaginary in the Late Cold War Years." *Boundary 2* 21, no. 1 (1994): 30–56.

Conrad, Joseph. "Autocracy and War." *North American Review* (July 1905): 833–55.

Cook, Sylvia. "Steinbeck, the People, and the Party." *Steinbeck Quarterly* 15 (Winter–Spring 1982): 11–23.

Cordova, Fred. *Filipinos. Forgotten Asian Americans: a Pictorial Essay, 1763–circa 1963.* Dubuque, Iowa: Kendall, Hunt, 1983.

Costigan, Howard. "The Plight of the Nisei." *Nation* (February 14, 1942): 184.

Cowley, Malcolm. "The Good Earthling." (1935). Reprinted in *Think Back On Us . . . A Contemporary Chronicle of the 1930's,* edited by Henry Dan Piper. Carbondale: Southern Illinois University Press, 1967: 251–53.

Cumings, Bruce. "The Origins and Development of the Northeast Asian Political Economy: Industrial Sectors, Product Cycles and Political Consequences." In *The Political Economy of the New Asian Industrialism,* edited by Frederic Deyo, 149–88. Ithaca, N.Y.: Cornell University Press, 1987.

———. *Parallax Visions: Making Sense of American–East Asian Relations.* Durham, N.C.: Duke University Press, 2002.

Daniel, Cletus. *Bitter Harvest: A History of California Farmworkers, 1870–1941*. Ithaca, N.Y.: Cornell University Press, 1981.

Daniels, Roger. "American Historians and East Asian Immigrants." *Pacific Historical Review* 53 (November 1974): 449–72.

———. *Concentration Camps: North America*. 1971. Reprint, Malabar, Fla.: Robert E. Krieger, 1981.

———. *The Decision to Relocate the Japanese Americans*. 1975. Reprint, Malabar, Fla.: Robert E. Kreiger, 1986.

———. "Japanese America, 1930–1941: An Ethnic Community in the Great Depression." *Journal of the West* 24 (October 1985): 35–49.

———. *The Politics of Prejudice: The Anti-Japanese Movement in California and the Struggle for Japanese Exclusion*. New York: Antheneum, 1973.

———. *Prisoners without Trial: Japanese Americans in World War II*. New York: Hill & Wang, 1993.

———. "Westerners from the East: Oriental Immigration Reappraised." *Pacific Historical Review* 35 (1966): 373–83.

Davidov, Judith Fryer. "'The Color of My Skin, the Shape of My Eyes': Photographs of the Japanese-American Internment by Dorothea Lange, Ansel Adams, and Toyo Miyatake." *Yale Journal of Criticism* 9, no. 2 (1996): 223–44.

Demott, Robert, ed. *John Steinbeck: Working Days*. New York: Penguin, 1989.

Dennett, Tyler. *Americans in East Asia*. New York: Macmillan, 1922.

———. *Theodore Roosevelt and the Russo-Japanese War*. Garden City, N.Y.: Doubleday Page, 1925.

Denning, Michael. *The Cultural Front: The Laboring of American Culture in the Twentieth Century*. London: Verso, 1996.

Department of Agriculture Program in Cooperation with Agricultural Colleges. "Keeping Up Production on Japanese Farms." Transcript of a radio program broadcast on KGO and associated stations of the Western Blue Network, National Broadcasting Company at 6:45 a.m., P.S.T., on March 27, 1942. Japanese American Evacuation and Resettlement Records, 1930–1974 (MSS 67/14c), A8.03. Bancroft Library, University of California at Berkeley.

DeWitt, Howard. *Violence in the Fields: California Filipino Farm Labor Unionization during the Great Depression*. Saratoga, Calif.: Century Twenty One Publishing, 1980.

DeWitt, J. L. *Final Report: Japanese Evacuation from the West Coast, 1942*. Washington, D.C.: Government Printing Office, 1943.

Dillon, Richard. "Kyne, Peter Bernard." *American National Biography Online*, February 2000. http://www.anb.org/articles/16/16-00944.html (February 2002).

Dinwoodie, D. H. "Deportation: The Immigration Service and the Chicano Labor Movement in the 1930s." *New Mexico Historical Review* 52 (1977): 193–206.

Dirlik, Arif. "The Asia-Pacific Idea: Reality and Representation in the Invention of a Regional Structure." *Journal of World History* 3 (Spring 1992): 55–79.

———. "Chinese Historians and the Marxist Concept of Capitalism." *Modern China* 8 (January 1982): 105–32.

Ditsky, John. "Faulkner Land and Steinbeck Country." In *Steinbeck: The Man and His Work*, edited by Richard Astro and Tetsumaro Hayashi, 11–23. Corvallis: Oregon State University Press, 1971.

Divine, Robert. *The Illusion of Neutrality*. Chicago: University of Chicago Press, 1962.

Donnelly, Ignatius. *Caesar's Column: A Story of the Twentieth Century*. Chicago: F. J. Schulte, 1891.

Dooner, P. W. *Last Days of the Republic*. San Francisco: Alta California Publishing House, 1880.

Dos Passos, John R. *The Anglo-Saxon Century and the Unification of the English-Speaking People*. New York: Knickerbocker Press, 1903.

Dower, John W. *War Without Mercy: Race and Power in the Pacific War*. New York: Pantheon Books, 1986.

Doyle, Paul A. *Pearl S. Buck*. Boston: Twayne, 1965.

———. "Pearl S. Buck's Short Stories: A Survey." *English Journal* 55 (January 1966): 62–68.

Dreyfus, Philip J. "The IWW and the Limits of Inter-ethnic Organization: Reds, Whites, and Greeks." *Labor History* 38, no. 2 (Fall 1997): 450–70.

Drinnon, Richard. *Keeper of Concentration Camps: Dillon S. Myer and American Racism*. Berkeley and Los Angeles: University of California Press, 1987.

———. *Facing West: The Metaphysics of Indian-Hating and Empire Building*. Minneapolis: University of Minnesota Press, 1981.

Dubois, W.E.B. *Black Reconstruction in America, 1860–1880*. New York: Antheneum, 1992.

Dunn, Stephen. *The Fall and Rise of the Asiatic Mode of Production*. London: Routledge, 1987.

Edwards vs. *California*. In *United States Reports: Cases Adjudged in the Supreme Court* 314 (October term, 1941), 160–86. Washington, D.C.: Government Printing Office, 1942.

Edwards, Percy. "The Industrial Side of the Alien Land Law Problem." *Overland Monthly* (August 1913): 190–200.

Engels, Frederich. "The Labor Movement in the United States." In Karl Marx and Frederich Engels, *Letters to Americans 1848–1895*, 285–91. New York: International Publishers, 1953.

Eperjesi, John. "The American Asiatic Association and the Imperialism Imaginary of the American Pacific." *Boundary 2* 28, no. 1 (Spring 2001): 195–219.

Erdman, H. E., K. A. Ryerson, and J. M. Tinsley. *In Memoriam: Richard Laban Adams*. Berkeley and Los Angeles: University of California Press, 1959.

Esperitu, Yen Le. *Asian American Panethnicity: Bridging Institutions and Identities*. Philadelphia: Temple University Press, 1992.

Etheridge, Charles Jr. "Changing Attitudes toward Steinbeck's Naturalism and the Changing Reputation of *East of Eden*." In *The Steinbeck Question: New Essays and Criticism*, edited by Donald Noble, 250–59. Troy, N.Y.: Whitsun Publishing Co., 1993.

Evans, Nancy. "Review of *The Good Earth* [Pearl S. Buck]." *Bookman* 73 (May 1931): 324.

Fairbank, John. *The People's Middle Kingdom and the U.S.A.* Cambridge: Harvard University Press, Belknap Press, 1967.

Fanon, Frantz. *Black Skin, White Masks.* New York: Grove Press, 1968.

———. *Wretched of the Earth.* New York: Grove Press, 1963.

Farm Security Administration, U.S. Department of Agriculture, and Wartime Civil Control Administration. Press Release. San Francisco, May 23, 1942. Japanese American Evacuation and Resettlement Records, 1930–1974 (MSS 67/14c), A8.03. Bancroft Library, University of California at Berkeley.

Farm Security Administration. *Final Report of the Participation of the FSA in the Evacuation Program of the . . . Western Defense Command, Covering the Period March 15, 1942–May 31, 1942.* San Francisco, June 5, 1942. Japanese American Evacuation and Resettlement Records, 1930–1974 (MSS 67/14c), C1.0316. Bancroft Library, University of California at Berkeley.

Ferguson, Edwin. "The California Alien Land Law and the Fourteenth Amendment." *California Law Review* 35 (1947): 61–90.

Ferrell, Robert. *American Diplomacy in the Great Depression: Hoover-Stimson Foreign Policy 1929–1933.* New Haven: Yale University Press, 1957.

Ferrero-Lombroso, Gina. *Criminal Man, according to the Classification of Cesare Lombroso.* New York: G. P. Putnam, 1911.

Fields, Barbara. "Slavery, Race and Ideology in the United States of America." *New Left Review* 181 (1990): 95–118.

Fisher, Lloyd, and Ralph Nielsen. *The Japanese in California Agriculture.* Berkeley, Calif.: U.S. Bureau of Agricultural Economics, 1942.

Foley, Barbara. *Radical Representations: Politics and Form in U.S. Proletarian Fiction, 1929–1941.* Durham, N.C.: Duke University Press, 1993.

Folsom, James. "The Wheat and the Locomotive: Norris and Naturalistic Esthetics." In *American Literary Naturalism: A Reassessment,* edited by Yoshinobu Hakutani and Lewis Fried, 57–74. Heidelberg, Germany: Carl Winter, 1975.

Foner, Eric. "Why Is There No Socialism in the United States?" *History Workshop* 17 (Spring 1984): 57–80.

Foner, Philip. *Jack London: American Rebel.* New York: Citadel Press, 1947.

Foner, Philip, and Daniel Rosenberg, eds. *Racism, Dissent, and Asian Americans from 1860 to the Present: A Documentary History.* Westport, Conn.: Greenwood Press, 1993.

Fontenrose, Joseph. *John Steinbeck: An Introduction and Interpretation.* New York: Barnes and Noble, 1964.

French, Warren. "The 'California Quality' of Steinbeck's Best Fiction." *San Jose Studies* 1 (November 1975): 9–19.

Freud, Sigmund. "The Uncanny." In *Standard Edition of the Complete Psychological Works.* Translated into English by James Strachey et al., 217–52. Vol. 17. 1919. Reprint, London: Hogarth Press, 1953.

Friday, Chris. "Asian American Labor and Historical Interpretation." *Labor History* 35 (Fall 1994): 524–46.

———. *Organizing Asian American Labor: The Pacific Coast Canned Salmon Industry, 1870–1942.* Philadelphia: Temple University Press, 1994.

Friedman, Edward, and Mark Selden, eds. *America's Asia: Dissenting Essays on Asian-American Relations.* New York: Pantheon Press, 1971.

Furer, Andrew. "'Zone Conquerors' and 'White Devils': The Contradiction of Race in the Works of Jack London." In *Rereading Jack London*, edited by Leonard Cassuto and Jeanne Campbell Reesman, 158–71. Stanford, Calif.: Stanford University Press, 1996.

Gaddis, John Lewis. "'Defense Perimeter' Concept." In *Uncertain Years: Chinese-American Relations 1947–1950,* edited by Dorothy Borg and Waldo Heinrichs, 61–118. New York: Columbia University Press, 1980.

Gallagher, John, and Ronald Robinson. "The Imperialism of Free Trade." *The Economic History Review* 2d ser., 6, no. 1 (1953): 1–15.

George, Henry. "The Chinese in California." *New York Daily Tribune* 39 (May 1, 1869): 1–2.

———. "Chinese Immigration." In *Cyclopedia of Political Science, Political Economy, and of the Political History of the United States,* edited by John Lalor, 409–14. Chicago: Melbert B. Cary, 1883.

———. *Progress and Poverty.* 1879. Reprint, New York: Modern Library, 1929.

Girdner, Audrie, and Anne Loftis. *The Great Betrayal: The Evacuation of Japanese-Americans during World War II.* London: Macmillan, 1969.

Glancy, Donald R. "Socialist with a Valet: Jack London's 'First, Last, and Only' Lecture Tour." *Quarterly Journal of Speech* 49, no. 1 (February 1963): 31–39.

Gompers, Samuel. *Some Reasons for Chinese Exclusion. Meat versus Rice: American Manhood against Asiatic Coolieism. Which Shall Survive?* Washington, D.C.: American Federation of Labor, 1902.

Graebner, Norman A. "Hoover, Roosevelt, and the Japanese." *Pearl Harbor as History: Japanese-American Relations 1931–1941,* edited by Dorothy Borg and Shumpei Okamoto, 25–52. New York: Columbia University Press, 1973.

Grant, Madison. *The Passing of the Great Race.* New York: Charles Scribner's Sons, 1916.

Gray, Colin. "Keeping the Soviets Landlocked: Geostrategy for a Maritime America." *National Interest* 4 (Summer 1986): 24–36.

Greenblatt, Stephen. "Invisible Bullets: Renaissance Authority and its Subversion, *Henry IV* and *Henry V.*" In *Political Shakespeare: New Essays in Cultural Materialism,* edited by Jonathan Dollimore and Alan Sinfield, 18–47. Ithaca, N.Y.: Cornell University Press, 1985.

Gregory, James. *American Exodus: The Dust Bowl Migration and Okie Culture in California.* New York: Oxford University Press, 1989.

Griswold, A. Whitney. *The Far Eastern Policy of the United States.* New Haven: Yale University Press, 1938.

Grodzins, Morton. *Americans Betrayed: Politics and the Japanese Evacuation.* Chicago: University of Chicago Press, 1949.

Guha, Ranajit, and Gayatri Spivak, eds. *Selected Subaltern Studies.* New York: Oxford University Press, 1988.

Hagedorn, Jessica, ed. *Charlie Chan is Dead: An Anthology of Contemporary Asian American Fiction.* New York: Penguin, 1993.

Hall, Stuart. "Race, Articulation and Societies Structured in Dominance." In *Black British Cultural Studies,* edited by Houston Baker Jr., Manthia Diawara, and Ruth Lindeborg, 16–60. Chicago: University of Chicago Press, 1996.

Hamamoto, Daniel. *Monitored Peril: Asian Americans and the Politics of TV Representation.* Minneapolis: University of Minnesota Press, 1994.

Hamilton, David Mike. "Some Chin-Chin and Tea—Jack London in Japan." *Pacific Historian* 23 (Summer 1979): 19–25.

Harris, Nigel. *The End of the Third World: Newly Industrializing Countries and the Decline of an Ideology.* New York: Penguin Books, 1986.

Hata, Don, and Nadine Hata. "George Shima: 'The Potato King of California.'" *Journal of the West* 25 (January 1986): 55–63.

Hauner, Milan. *What Is Asia to Us? Russia's Heartland Yesterday and Today.* Boston: Unwin Hyman, 1990.

Hauser, Ernest O. "Chinaman's Chance." *Saturday Evening Post* 213, no. 23 (December 7, 1940): 14–15, 82–87.

Hayashi, Brian. *For the Sake of Our Brethren: Assimilation, Nationalism, and Protestantism among the Japanese of Los Angeles, 1895–1942.* Stanford, Calif.: Stanford University Press, 1995.

Hayashi, Tetsumaro. "The 'Chinese Servant' in *East of Eden.*" *San Jose Studies* 18 (Winter 1992): 52–60.

Hays, Samuel. *Conservation and the Gospel of Efficiency: The Progressive Movement, 1890–1920.* Cambridge: Harvard University Press, 1959.

Heinrichs, Waldo. "The Middle Years 1900–1945 and the Question of a Large U.S. Policy for East Asia." In *New Frontiers in American–East Asian Relations,* edited by Warren Cohen, 77–106. New York: Columbia University Press, 1983.

Hemingway, Ernest. Letter to Treasury Secretary Henry Morgenthau, July 30, 1941. In "Morgenthau Diary (China)" by Henry Morgenthau, a report prepared for the Committee on the Judiciary, United States Senate. 1:457–62. Washington, D.C.: Government Printing Office, 1965.

Henderson, George. *California and the Fictions of Capital.* Oxford: Oxford University Press, 1999.

———. "John Steinbeck's Spatial Imagination in *The Grapes of Wrath*: A Critical Essay." *California History* 68 (Winter 1989/90): 211–223, 262.

Hendricks, King, and Irving Shepard, eds. *Jack London Reports.* Garden City, N.Y.: Doubleday, 1970.

Hershatter, Gail. "The Subaltern Talks Back: Reflections on Subaltern Theory and Chinese History." *Positions* 1 (Spring 1993): 103–30.

Higgs, Robert. "Landless by Law: Japanese Immigrants in California Agriculture in 1941." *Journal of Economic History* 38 (March 1978): 205–25.

———. "The Wealth of Japanese Tenant Farmers in California, 1909." *Agricultural History* 53 (April 1979): 488–93.

Higham, John. *Send These to Me: Immigrants in Urban America.* Rev. ed. Baltimore: Johns Hopkins University Press, 1984.

———. *Strangers in the Land: Patterns of American Nativism 1860–1925.* New Brunswick, N.J.: Rutgers University Press, 1955.

Hindess, Barry, and Paul Hirst. *Pre-Capitalist Modes of Production.* London: Routledge & Kegan Paul, 1975.

Hing, Bill Ong. *Making and Remaking Asian America through Immigration Policy, 1850–1990.* Stanford, Calif.: Stanford University Press, 1993.

Hirabayashi, Lane, and James Hirabayashi. "A Reconsideration of the United States Military's Role in the Violation of Japanese-American Citizenship." In *Ethnicity and War*, edited by Winston A. Van Horne, 87–110. Milwaukee: University of Wisconsin System American Ethnic Studies Coordinating Committee, 1984.

Hofstader, Richard. *Age of Reform: From Bryan to F.D.R.* New York: Knopf, 1969.

———. *Social Darwinism in American Thought, 1865–1915.* Philadelphia: University of Pennsylvania Press, 1944.

Hopkirk, Peter. *The Great Game: On Secret Service in High Asia.* London: Murray, 1990.

———. *Quest for* Kim. Ann Arbor: University of Michigan Press, 1997.

Horsman, Reginald. *Race and Manifest Destiny: The Origins of American Racial Anglo-Saxonism.* Cambridge: Harvard University Press, 1981.

Horwitz, Howard. "Maggie and the Sociological Paradigm." *American Literary History* 10, no. 4 (Winter 1998): 606–38.

Howard, June. *Form and History in American Literary Naturalism.* Chapel Hill: University of North Carolina Press, 1985.

Huang, Yunte. *Transpacific Displacement: Ethnography, Translation, and Intertextual Travel In Twentieth-Century American Literature.* Berkeley and Los Angeles: University of California Press, 2002.

Hunt, Michael. "Pearl Buck—Popular Expert in China, 1931–1949." *Modern China* 3 (January 1977): 33–64.

Ian-Ruban, Wanda. "What Defeat Would Mean to Russia." *Outlook* 19 (March 19, 1904): 687–94.

Ichioka, Yuji. *The Issei: The World of the First Generation Japanese Immigrants 1885–1924.* New York: Free Press, 1988.

———. "Japanese Immigrant Response to the 1920 California Alien Land Law." *Agricultural History* 58 (April 1984): 157–78.

Ichioka, Yuji, Yasuo Sakata, Nobuya Tshuchida, and Eri Yasuhara. *A Buried Past: An Annotated Bibliography of the Japanese American Research Project Collection.* Berkeley and Los Angeles: University of California Press, 1974.

Ignatiev, Noel. *How the Irish Became White.* New York: Routledge, 1995.

Iriye, Akira. *The Cold War in Asia: A Historical Introduction.* Englewood Cliffs, N.J.: Prentice-Hall, 1974.

Irons, Peter. *Justice at War.* New York: Oxford University Press, 1983.

Irwin, Wallace, and Arnold Genthe. *Old Chinatown.* New York: M. Kennerly, 1913.

Irwin, Wallace. *Seed of the Sun.* New York: George H. Doran, 1921.

Isaacs, Harold. *Images of Asia: American Views of China and India.* New York: Capricorn Books, 1962.

———. *Scratches on Our Minds: American Images of China and India.* New York: John Day, 1958.

———. *Tragedy of the Chinese Revolution.* 2d rev. ed., Stanford, Calif.: Stanford University Press, 1961.

Iwata, Masakazu. "The Japanese Immigrants in California Agriculture." *Agricultural History* 36 (January 1962): 25–37.

James, Thomas. *Exile Within: the Schooling of Japanese Americans 1942–1945.* Cambridge: Harvard University Press, 1987.

Janken, Kenneth R. "From Colonial Liberation to Cold War Liberalism: Walter White, the NAACP, and Foreign Affairs, 1941–1955." *Ethnic and Racial Studies* 21:6 (November 1998): 1074–1095.

Johnston, Carolyn. *Jack London—An American Rebel?* Westport, Conn.: Greenwood Press, 1984.

Jones, Andrew F. and Nikhil Pal Singh, eds. The Afro-Asian Century. *Positions* 11, no. 1 (Spring 2003).

Kang, Younghill. "China Is Different." *New Republic* (July 1, 1931): 185–86.

Kaplan, Amy. "Romancing the Empire: The Embodiment of American Masculinity in the Popular Historical Novel of the 1890s." *American Literary History* 2 (Winter 1990): 659–90.

———. *Social Construction of American Realism.* Chicago: University of Chicago Press, 1988.

Kaplan, Amy, and Donald Pease, eds. *The Cultures of United States Imperialism.* Durham, N.C.: Duke University Press, 1993.

Kazin, Alfred. *On Native Grounds: An Interpretation of Modern American Prose Literature.* New York: Reynal & Hitchcock, 1942.

Kelly, Lynwood J., under the direction of R. L. Adams, *A Survey of Procedures and Possible Ways on Maintaining or Increasing the Crop Producing Powers of California Lands (With Special Reference to Irrigated Truck and Field Crops).* Berkeley: The Giannini Foundation of Agricultural Economics for the Technical Advisory Committee of the Soil Conservation and Domestic Allotment Administration for California, July–August 1936.

Kennan, George. "The Destruction of the Baltic Fleet." *The Outlook* (July 29, 1905): 811–19.

———. "The Japanese in San Francisco Schools." *The Outlook* (June 1, 1907): 246–52.

———. "Russian Views of Kuropatkin and his Army." *The Outlook* (February 18, 1905): 425–31.

———. "The Social and Political Condition of Russia." *The Outlook* (January 30, 1904): 261–66.

———. "The Story of Port Arthur: I. A Journey to Dalny." *The Outlook* (March 4, 1905): 523–28.

———. "The Story of Port Arthur: II. In Dalny and at the Front." *The Outlook* (March 11, 1905): 629–36.

———. "The Story of Port Arthur: III. With the Besieging Army." *The Outlook* (April 1, 1905): 777–84.

———. "The Story of Port Arthur: IV. The Assault that Failed." *The Outlook* (April 8, 1905): 888–95.

———. "The Story of Port Arthur: VI. The Second Attempt to Storm the Fort." *The Outlook* (April 22, 1905): 994–1001.

———. "The Story of Port Arthur: VIII. In The Advanced Trenches." *The Outlook* (May 20, 1905): 173–83.

———. "The Story of Port Arthur: IX. The Progress of the Siege." *The Outlook* (May 27, 1905): 228–33.

———. "The Story of Port Arthur: X. Life in the Japanese Trenches." *The Outlook* (June 17, 1905): 419–27.

———. "The Story of Port Arthur: XI. Saps, Mines, and Assault." *The Outlook* (July 8, 1905): 622–29.

Kiang, Kang-Hu. "A Chinese Scholar's View of Mrs. Buck's Novels." *New York Times Book Review* (January 15, 1933): 2, 16–17.

Kim, Elaine. *Asian American Literature: An Introduction to the Writings and Their Social Context.* Philadelphia: Temple University Press, 1982.

Kingston, Maxine Hong. *Tripmaster Monkey.* New York: Knopf, 1989.

Kitano, Harry, and Stanley Sue. "The Model Minorities." *Journal of Social Issues* 29, no. 2 (1973): 1–9.

Kitano, Harry. "Japanese Americans: The Development of a Middleman Minority." *Pacific Historical Review* 53 (November 1974): 500–19.

Klein, Christine. *Cold War Orientalism: Asia in the Middlebrow Imagination, 1945–1961.* Berkeley and Los Angeles: University of California Press, 2003.

Klein, Marcus. "Roots of Radicals: Experience in the Thirties." In *Proletarian Writers of the Thirties,* edited by David Madden, 134–57. London: Southern Illinois University Press, Feffer & Simmons, 1968.

Koen, Ross Y. *The China Lobby in American Politics.* New York: Macmillan, 1960.

Koshy, Susan. "Morphing Race into Ethnicity: Asian Americans and Critical Transformations of Whiteness." *Boundary 2* 28, no. 1 (Spring 2001): 134–57.

Krader, Lawrence. *The Asiatic Mode of Production: Sources, Development and Critique in the Writings of Karl Marx.* Assen, The Netherlands: Van Gorcum, 1975.

Kumamoto, Bob. "The Search for Spies: American Counterintelligence and the Japanese American Community, 1931–1942." *Amerasia* 6, no. 2 (1979): 45–75.

Kyne, Peter. *Pride of Palomar.* New York: Cosmopolitan Book Corp., 1921.

Labor, Earle. "Jack London's Mondo Cane: 'Batard,' *The Call of the Wild,* and *White Fang.*" In *Critical Essays on Jack London,* edited by Jacqueline Tavernier-Courbin, 114–30. Boston: G. K. Hall, 1983.

———. "Jack London's Pacific World." In *Critical Essays on Jack London,* edited by Jacqueline Tavernier-Courbin, 205–22. Boston: G. K. Hall, 1983.

———. "Jack London's Symbolic Wilderness: Four Versions." *Nineteenth Century Fiction* 17, no. 2 (September 1962): 149–61.

LaFeber, Walter. *The New Empire: An Interpretation of American Expansion.* Ithaca, N.Y.: Cornell University Press, 1963.

Lange, Dorothea, and Paul S. Taylor. *An American Exodus: A Record of Human Erosion.* New York: Reynal & Hitchcock, 1939.

Lea, Homer. *Day of the Saxon.* New York: Harper & Bros., 1912.

———. *Valor of Ignorance.* New York: Harper & Bros., 1909.

Lee, Lawrence B. *Reclaiming the American West: An Historiography and Guide.* Santa Barbara, Calif.: ABC-Clio, 1980.

Lee, Robert G. *Orientals: Asian Americans in Popular Culture.* Philadelphia: Temple University Press, 1999.

Lenin, V. I. "Imperialism, the Highest Stage of Capitalism." In *The Lenin Anthology,* edited by Robert Tucker, 204–74. New York: Norton, 1975.

Lesser, Jeff H. "Always 'Outsiders': Asians, Naturalization, and the Supreme Court." *Amerasia* 12, no. 1 (1985–86): 83–100.

Leuchtenburg, Willaim. *Franklin D. Roosevelt and the New Deal 1932–1940.* New York: Harper & Row, 1963.

Leung, Peter C. Y., and L. Eve Armentrout Ma. "Chinese Farming Activities in the Sacramento–San Joaquin Delta: 1910–1941." *Amerasia* 14 (1988): 1–18.

Levant, Howard. *The Novels of John Steinbeck: A Critical Study.* Columbia: University of Missouri Press, 1974.

Lewis, Cliff. "Art for Politics: John Steinbeck and FDR." In *After* The Grapes of Wrath: *Essays on John Steinbeck in Honor of Tetsumaro Hayashi,* edited by Donald Coers et al., 23–39. Athens: Ohio University Press, 1995.

———. "John Steinbeck's Alternative to Internment Camps: A Policy for the President, December 15, 1941." *Journal of the West* 34, no. 1 (January 1995): 55–61.

Li, David Liwei. *Imagining the Nation: Asian American Literature and Cultural Consent.* Stanford, Calif.: Stanford University Press, 1998.

Light, Ivan H. *Ethnic Enterprise in America: Business and Welfare among Chinese, Japanese, and Blacks.* Berkeley and Los Angeles: University of California Press, 1972.

Linehart, Thomas. "Japanese American Resettlement in Cleveland During and After World War II." *Journal of Urban History* 20 (November 1993): 54–80.

Lipscomb, Elizabeth J., Frances E. Webb, and Peter Conn, eds. *The Several Worlds of Pearl S. Buck.* Westport, Conn.: Greenwood Press, 1994.

Lisca, Peter. "*Cannery Row* and the Tao Teh Ching." *San Jose Studies* 1 (November 1975): 21–27.

———. *John Steinbeck: Nature and Myth.* New York: Crowell, 1978.

———. *The Wide World of John Steinbeck.* New Brunswick, N.J.: Rutgers University Press, 1958.

Liu, John M. and Cheng, Lucie. "A Dialogue on Race and Class: Asian American Studies and Marxism." In *The Left Academy: Marxist Scholarship on American Campuses,* Vol. 3, edited by Bertell Ollman and Edward Vernoff, 139–163. New York: Praeger, 1986.

London, Jack. "Americans Praise Japan's Army" (March 5, 1904). In *Jack London Reports,* edited by King Hendricks and Irving Milo Shepard, 47–51. Garden City, N.Y.: Doubleday, 1970.

———. "Bonin Islands: An Incident of the Sealing Fleet of '93" (1897). In *Jack London's Tales of Adventure,* edited by Irving Milo Shepard, 59–63. Garden City, N.Y.: Hanover House, 1956.

———. *Call of the Wild.* New York: Macmillan, 1903.

———. "The Chinago" (July 1909). In *The Complete Short Stories of Jack London,* edited by Earle Labor, Robert C. Leitz III, and Irving Milo Shepard, 2:1405–17. Stanford, Calif.: Stanford University Press, 1993.

———. "Cossacks Fight then Retreat" (March 5, 1904). In *Jack London Reports,* edited by King Hendricks and Irving Milo Shepard, 51–54. Garden City, N.Y.: Doubleday, 1970.

———. *Cruise of the Snark.* New York: Macmillan, 1911.

———. "Demetrios Contos" (1903). In *The Complete Short Stories of Jack Lon-

don, edited by Earle Labor, Robert C. Leitz III, and Irving Milo Shepard, 2:874–84. Stanford, Calif.: Stanford University Press, 1993.

———. "Dr. Moffet" (March 13, 1904). In *Jack London Reports,* edited by King Hendricks and Irving Milo Shepard, 82–90. Garden City, N.Y.: Doubleday, 1970.

———. "Give Battle to Retard Enemy" (May 1, 1904). In *Jack London Reports,* edited by King Hendricks and Irving Milo Shepard, 99–107. Garden City, N.Y.: Doubleday, 1970.

———. "Goliah" (1907). In *The Complete Short Stories of Jack London*, edited by Earle Labor, Robert C. Leitz III, and Irving Milo Shepherd, 2:1201–21. Stanford, Calif.: Stanford University Press, 1993.

———. "If Japan Wakens China" (December 1909). In *Jack London Reports,* edited by King Hendricks and Irving Milo Shepard, 358–61. Garden City, N.Y.: Doubleday, 1970.

———. *The Iron Heel* (1907). In *Novels and Writings*, 315–553. New York: Library of America, 1982.

———. *Jack London's Tales of Adventure*, edited by Irving Milo Shepard. Garden City, N.Y.: Hanover House, 1956.

———. "Japan in Invisible War" (May 2, 1904). In *Jack London Reports,* edited by King Hendricks and Irving Milo Shepard, 107–11. Garden City, N.Y.: Doubleday, 1970.

———. "Japan Puts an End to the Usefulness of Correspondents" (July 1, 1904). In *Jack London Reports,* edited by King Hendricks and Irving Shepard, 122–26. Garden City, N.Y.: Doubleday, 1970.

———. "Japanese Officers Consider Everything a Military Secret" (June 2, 1904). In *Jack London Reports,* edited by King Hendricks and Irving Shepard, 118–22. Garden City, N.Y.: Doubleday, 1970.

———. "Japanese Supplies Rushed to Front by Man and Beast" (April 21, 1904). In *Jack London Reports,* edited by King Hendricks and Irving Shepard, 93–5. Garden City, N.Y.: Doubleday, 1970.

———. "Just Meat." In *When God Laughs and Other Stories,* 93–128. New York: Macmillan Co., 1911.

———. "King of the Greeks" (1902). In *The Complete Short Stories of Jack London*, edited by Earle Labor, Robert C. Leitz III, and Irving Milo Shepherd, 2:823–32. Stanford, Calif.: Stanford University Press, 1993.

———. "Koulau the Leper" (1908). In *The Complete Short Stories of Jack London*, edited by Earle Labor, Robert C. Leitz III, and Irving Milo Shepherd, 2:1441–1454. Stanford, Calif.: Stanford University Press, 1993.

———. "Letter to Charmian Kittredge" (February 9, 1904). In *Jack London Reports,* edited by King Hendricks and Irving Shepard, 8–9. Garden City, N.Y.: Doubleday, 1970.

———. "Letter to Charmian Kittredge" (February 11, 1904). In *Jack London Reports*, edited by King Hendricks and Irving Shepard, 9. Garden City, N.Y.: Doubleday, 1970.

———. "Letter to Charmian Kittredge" (March 8, 1904). In *Jack London Reports,* edited by King Hendricks and Irving Shepard, 14–15. Garden City, N.Y.: Doubleday, 1970.

———. "Letter to Charmian Kittredge" (March 29, 1904). In *Jack London Reports,* edited by King Hendricks and Irving Shepard, 18. Garden City, N.Y.: Doubleday, 1970.

———. "Letter to Charmian Kittredge" (April 1, 1904). In *Jack London Reports,* edited by King Hendricks and Irving Shepard, 18–19. Garden City, N.Y.: Doubleday, 1970.

———. "Letter to Charmian Kittredge" (May 6, 1904). In *Jack London Reports,* edited by King Hendricks and Irving Shepard, 22. Garden City, N.Y.: Doubleday, 1970.

———. "Letter to Charmian Kittredge" (May 22, 1904). In *Jack London Reports,* edited by King Hendricks and Irving Shepard, 23–24. Garden City, N.Y.: Doubleday, 1970.

———. "The Monkey Cage" (May 10, 1904). In *Jack London Reports,* edited by King Hendricks and Irving Shepard, 113–18. Garden City, N.Y.: Doubleday, 1970.

———. *Novels and Writings.* New York: Library of America, 1982.

———. *The People of the Abyss.* 1907. New York: Lawrence Hill Books, 1995.

———. "The Plague Ship" (1897). In *The Complete Short Stories of Jack London*, edited by Earle Labor, Robert C. Leitz III, and Irving Milo Shepherd, 1:84–96. Stanford, Calif.: Stanford University Press, 1993.

———. *Revolution and Other Essays.* New York: MacMillan, 1910.

———. "Royal Road a Sea of Mud" (March 5, 1904). In *Jack London Reports,* edited by King Hendricks and Irving Shepard, 42–47. Garden City, N.Y.: Doubleday, 1970

———. "The Run Across" (1895). In *Jack London's Tales of Adventure,* edited by Irving Shepard, 57–58. Garden City, N.Y.: Hanover House, 1956.

———. "The Shrinkage of the Planet" (January 1900). In *Revolution and Other Essays,* 141–57. New York: Macmillan Co., 1910.

———. *The Son of the Wolf.* New York: Garrett Press, 1969.

———. *The Star Rover.* 1914. Reprint, Gloucester, U.K.: Alan Sutton, 1986.

———. "Story of a Typhoon Off the Coast of Japan" (1893). In *Jack London's Tales of Adventure*, edited by Irving Shepard, 54–57. Garden City, N.Y.: Hanover House, 1956.

———. *Stories of Hawaii.* Edited by A. Grove Day. Honolulu, Hawaii: Mutual Publishing, 1965

———. "The Sufferings of the Japanese" (March 13, 1904). In *Jack London Reports,* 77–82. Garden City, N.Y.: Doubleday, 1970.

———. *Tales of the Fish Patrol.* Oakland, Calif.: Star Rover House, 1982.

———. "Travel in Korea" (March 10, 1904). In *Jack London Reports,* edited by King Hendricks and Irving Shepard, 63–73. Garden City, N.Y.: Doubleday, 1970.

———. "The Unparalleled Invasion" (1906). In *Curious Fragments: Jack London's Tales of Fantasy Fiction,* edited by Dale Walker, 109–20. Port Washington: Kennkat Press, 1975.

———. "Vivid Description of Army in Korea" (March 4, 1904). In *Jack London Reports,* 40–42. Garden City, N.Y.: Doubleday, 1970.

———. *Valley of the Moon.* 1913. Reprint, Santa Barbara, Calif.: Peregrine Smith, 1975.

————. "White and Yellow" (1902). In *The Complete Short Stories of Jack London,* edited by Earle Labor, Robert C. Leitz III, and Irving Milo Shepherd, 1:800–808. Stanford, Calif.: Stanford University Press, 1993.

————. *White Fang.* New York: Macmillan, 1906.

————. "Yellow Handkerchief" (1903). In *The Complete Short Stories of Jack London,* edited by Earle Labor, Robert C. Leitz III, and Irving Milo Shepherd, 2:885–95. Stanford, Calif.: Stanford University Press, 1993.

————. "The Yellow Peril" (June 1904). In *Revolution and Other Essays,* 269–89. New York: Macmillan, 1910.

London, Joan. *Jack London and His Times.* New York: Doubleday, 1939.

Louis, William Roger. *Imperialism at Bay, 1941–1945: The United States and the Decolonization of the British Empire.* Oxford: Clarendon Press, 1977.

Lowe, Lisa. *Immigrant Acts: On Asian American Cultural Politics.* Durham, N.C.: Duke University Press, 1996.

Lowitt, Dick. *The New Deal and the West.* Bloomington: Indiana University Press, 1984.

Lukács, Georg. *The Historical Novel.* 1962. Lincoln: University of Nebraska Press, 1983.

————. "Narrate or Describe?" In *Writer and Critic,* edited by Arthur Kahn, 110–48. 1970. Reprint, New York: Grosset & Dunlap, 1971.

————. *The Theory of the Novel.* Cambridge: MIT Press, 1971.

Lukes, Timothy, and Gary Okihiro. *Japanese Legacy: Farming and Community Life in California's Santa Clara Valley.* Cupertino: California History Center, 1985.

Machor, James. "Epic, Romance, and Norris's *The Octopus.*" *American Literary Realism* 18, nos. 1–2 (Spring–Autumn 1985): 42–58.

Mackinder, Halford. "The Geographical Pivot of History." *The Geographical Journal* 23:4 (April 1904): 421–45.

MacKinnon, Janice R., and Stephen R. MacKinnon. *Agnes Smedley: the Life and Times of an American Radical.* Berkeley and Los Angeles: University of California Press, 1988.

MacPherson, C.B. "Introduction" in *The Second Treatise of Government,* by John Locke, vii–xxi. Indianapolis: Hackett, 1980.

Madden, David, ed. *Proletarian Writers of the Thirties.* London: Southern Illinois University Press, Feffer & Simons, 1968.

Mahan, Alfred T. *The Influence of Sea Power on History.* 1894. Reprint, London: Methuen, 1965.

————. *The Problem of Asia and Its Effects Upon International Policies.* London: Sampson Low, Marston, 1900.

Mallan, John P. "Roosevelt, Brooks Adams and Homer Lea: The Warrior Critique of Business Civilization." *American Quarterly* 8 (Fall 1956): 216–30.

Mao, Tse-Tung. "On Contradiction." In *Selected Works of Mao Tse-Tung,* 1:311–47. Peking: Foreign Languages Press, 1975.

————. "Report on an Investigation of the Peasant Movement in Hunan." In *Selected Works of Mao Tse-Tung,* 1:23–59. Peking: Foreign Languages Press, 1975.

Marchetti, Gina. *Romance and the "Yellow Peril": Race, Sex, and Discursive Strategies in Hollywood Fiction.* Berkeley and Los Angeles: University of California Press, 1993.

Martin, Stoddard. *California Writers: Jack London, John Steinbeck, the Tough Guys.* New York: MacMillan Press, 1983.

Marx, Karl, and Frederick Engels. *On Colonialism.* New York: International Publishers, 1972.

Masumoto, David Mas. *Country Voices: The Oral History of a Japanese American Family Farm Community.* Del Rey, Calif.: Inaka Countryside Publications, 1987.

Matsuda, Mari. "Looking to the Bottom: Critical Legal Studies and Reparation." In *Critical Race Theory: The Key Writings that Formed the Movement,* edited by Kimberlé Crenshaw, Neil Gotanda, Gary Peller, and Kendall Thomas, 63–79. New York: The New Press, 1995.

Matsumoto, Valerie. *Farming the Home Place: A Japanese American Community in California, 1919–1982.* Ithaca, N.Y.: Cornell University Press, 1993.

Matthews, Blayney. *The Specter of Sabotage.* Los Angeles: Lymanhouse, 1941.

Matthews, Fred. "White Community and 'Yellow Peril.'" *Mississippi Valley Historical Review* 50 (March 1964): 612–33.

Maxey, Edwin. "Why We Favor Japan in the Present War." *Arena* 32 (August 1904): 505–10.

McClellan, Robert. *The Heathen Chinee: A Study of American Attitudes toward China.* Columbus: Ohio State University Press, 1971.

McClintock, James I. *White Logic: Jack London's Short Stories.* Grand Rapids, Mich.: Wolf House Books, 1975.

McClure, John. *Late Imperial Romance.* London: Verso, 1994.

McGovney, Dudley O. "The Anti-Japanese Land Laws of California and Ten Other States." *California Law Review* 35 (1947): 7–60.

McKee, Delbert. *Chinese Exclusion versus the Open Door, 1900–1906.* Detroit: Wayne State University Press, 1977.

McNair, Harley Farnsworth. *China's International Relations and Other Essays.* Shanghai: Commercial Press, 1926.

McWilliams, Carey. "California and the Japanese." *New Republic* (March 2, 1942): 295–97.

———. *Factories in the Field: The Story of Migratory Farm Labor in California.* Boston: Little, Brown, 1939.

———. "Japanese Evacuation: Policy and Perspectives." *Common Ground* (1942): 69–70.

———. *Liberals and the War Crisis.* Los Angeles: ACLU, 1940.

———. "Moving the West-Coast Japanese." *Harper's* (September 1942): 359–69.

———. "Once Again the Yellow Peril." *Nation* (June 26, 1935): 735–36.

———. *Prejudice: Japanese-Americans, Symbol of Racial Intolerance.* Boston: Little, Brown, 1944.

Mead, Elwood, R. L. Adams, and J. W. Gregg. *Colonization and Rural Development in California.* Circular No. 247. Berkeley: University of California College of Agriculture, Agricultural Experiment Station, 1922.

Mears, Eliot Ginnell. "The Land, the Crops, and the Oriental." *Survey Graphic* (May 1, 1926): 146–49, 203–6.

Michaels, Walter Benn. *The Gold Standard and the Logic of Naturalism*. Berkeley and Los Angeles: University of California Press, 1987.

Miller, Edward S. *War Plan Orange: The U.S. Strategy to Defeat Japan*. Annapolis, Md.: Naval Institute Press, 1991.

Miller, Stuart. *The Unwelcome Immigrant: The American Image of the Chinese, 1785–1882*. Berkeley and Los Angeles: University of California Press, 1969.

Mills, Nicholas. *Arguing Immigration: Are New Immigrants a Wealth of Diversity . . . Or a Crushing Burden?* New York: Touchstone, 1994.

Mink, Gwendolyn. *Old Labor and New Immigrants in American Political Development: Union, Party, and State*. Ithaca, N.Y.: Cornell University Press, 1986.

Mitchell, Don. *The Lie of the Land: Migrant Workers and the California Landscape*. Minneapolis: University of Minnesota Press, 1996.

Mitchell, Lee Clark. *Determined Fictions: American Literary Naturalism*. New York: Columbia University Press, 1989.

Mizruchi, Susan. "Cataloguing the Creatures of the Deep: 'Billy Budd, Sailor' and the Rise of Sociology." *Boundary 2* 17 (1990): 272–304.

Modell, John. "Class or Ethnic Solidarity: The Japanese American Company Union." *Pacific Historical Review* 38 (1969): 193–206.

———. *The Economics and Politics of Racial Accommodation: The Japanese of Los Angeles, 1900–1942*. Urbana: University of Illinois Press, 1977.

Monroe, Paul. *China: A Nation In Evolution*. Chautauqua, N.Y.: The Chautauqua Press, 1927.

Moore, Barrington. *Social Origins of Dictatorship and Democracy: Lord and Peasant in the Making of the Modern World*. Boston: Beacon Press, 1966.

Moore, Chester. Interview by Morton Grodzins. Report No. 11 (October 8, 1942). Japanese American Evacuation and Resettlement Records, 1930–1974 (MSS 67/14c), A16.200. Bancroft Library, University of California at Berkeley.

Mowry, George E. *The California Progressives*. Berkeley and Los Angeles: University of California Press, 1951.

Moy, James S. *Marginal Sights: Staging the Chinese in America*. Iowa City: University of Iowa Press, 1993.

Natasan, Nicholas. *The Black Image in the New Deal: The Politics of FSA Photography*. Knoxville: University of Tennessee Press, 1992.

Neu, Charles. *An Uncertain Friendship: Theodore Roosevelt and Japan, 1906–1909*. Cambridge: Harvard University Press, 1967.

Ngai, Mai. *Impossible Subjects: Illegal Aliens and the Making of Modern America*. Princeton, N.J.: Princeton University Press, 2004.

Nish, Ian. *The Anglo-Japanese Alliance: The Diplomacy of Two Island Empires, 1894–1907*. London: Athlone, 1966.

Noble, Donald, ed. *The Steinbeck Question: New Essays in Criticism*. Troy, N.Y.: Whitson Publishing Co., 1993.

Norris, Frank. "The Frontier Gone At Last." In *Norris: Novels and Essays*, 1183–90. 1902. Reprint, New York: Library of America, 1986.

———. *McTeague*. In *Norris: Novels and Essays*, 261–572. 1899. Reprint, New York: Library of America, 1986.

———. *Moran of the* Lady Letty. New York: P. F. Collier & Son, 1898.

————. *The Octopus.* 1901. Reprint, New York: Penguin, 1986.

————. "Outward and Visible Signs: I. She and the Other Fellow," *Overland Monthly* 23 (March 1894): 241–46.

————. "Outward and Visible Signs: IV. After Strange Gods," *Overland Monthly* 24 (October 1894): 375–79.

————. "Outward and Visible Signs: V. Thoroughbred," *Overland Monthly* 25 (February 1895): 196–201.

————. "A Plea for Romantic Fiction." In *Norris: Novels and Essays*, 1165–69. 1901. Reprint, New York: Library of America, 1986.

————. "Zola as a Romantic Writer." In *Norris: Novels and Essays*, 1106–8. 1896. Reprint, New York: Library of America, 1986.

Norton, Henry Kittredge. *China and the Powers.* New York: John Day, 1927.

O'Brien, David J., and Stephen S. Fugita. "Mobilization of a Traditionally Petit Bourgeois Ethnic Group." *Social Forces* 63 (December 1984): 522–37.

Oehling, Richard A. "The Yellow Menace: Asian Images in American Film." In *The Kaleidoscopic Lens: How Hollywood Views Ethnic Groups*, edited by Randall M. Miller, 182–206. Englewood, N.J.: Ozer, 1980.

Offner, Avner. "'Pacific Rim' Societies." In *The Rise of Colonial Nationalism*, edited by John Eddy and Deryck Schreuder, 227–47. Boston: Allen & Unwin, 1988.

Okihiro, Gary. "Japanese Resistance in America's Concentration Camps: A Re-Evaluation." *Amerasia* 2 (Fall 1973): 20–34.

————. *Margins and Mainstreams: Asians in American History and Culture.* Seattle: University of Washington Press, 1994.

Okihiro, Gary, and David Drummond. "The Concentration Camps and Japanese Economic Losses in California Agriculture, 1900–1942." In *Japanese Americans: From Relocation to Redress*, edited by Roger Daniels, Sandra C. Taylor, and Harry H. L. Kitano, 168–175. Salt Lake City: University of Utah Press, 1986.

Oksenberg, Michel, and Robert Oxnam, eds. *Dragon and Eagle: United States–China Relations, Past and Future.* New York: Basic Books, 1978.

Omatsu, Glenn. "'The Four Prisons' and the Movements of Liberation: Asian American Activism from the 1960s to the 1990s." In *The State of Asian America: Activism and Resistance in the 1990s*, edited by Karin Aguilar–San Juan, 19–69. Boston: South End Press, 1994.

Omi, Michael, and Howard Winant. *Racial Formation in the United States: From the 1960s to the 1990s.* 2d ed., New York: Routledge, 1994.

Ortega, Philip D. "Fables of Identity: Stereotype and Caricature of Chicanos in Steinbeck's *Tortilla Flat*." *Journal of Ethnic Studies* 1 (1973): 39–43.

Osajima, Keith. "Asian Americans as the Model Minority: An Analysis of the Popular Press Image in the 1960s and 1980s." In *Reflections on Shattered Windows: Promises and Prospects for Asian American Studies*, edited by Gary Okihiro et al., 165–74. Pullman: Washington State University Press, 1988.

Owens, Louis. "Grandpa Killed Indians, Pa Killed Snakes: Steinbeck and the American Indian." *Melus* 15 (1988): 85–92.

————. *John Steinbeck's Re-Vision of America.* Athens: University of Georgia Press, 1985.

Palumbo-Liu, David. *Asian/American: Historical Crossings of a Racial Frontier.* Stanford, Calif.: Stanford University Press, 1999.

Parrington, V. L. *The Beginning of Critical Realism In America: 1860–1920.* New York: Harcourt, Brace, Jovanovich, 1930.

Pearson, Charles. *National Life and Character: A Forecast.* London: MacMillan, 1893.

Peffer, Nathaniel. "The Chinese Idea of Communism." *Current History* 36 (July 1932): 400–4.

———. "Review of *The Good Earth* [Pearl S. Buck]." *Books* (March 1, 1931): 1.

Peluso, Robert. "Gazing at Royalty: Jack London's *The People of the Abyss* and the Emergence of American Imperialism." In *Rereading Jack London*, edited by Leonard Cassuto and Jeanne Campbell Reesman, 55–74. Stanford, Calif.: Stanford University Press, 1996.

Perry, John. *Jack London: An American Myth.* Chicago: Nelson Hall, 1981.

Petersen, William. *Japanese Americans: Oppression and Success.* New York: Random House, 1971.

———. "The Incarceration of the Japanese-Americans." *National Review* 8 (December 1972): 1349–50, 1367–69.

———. "Success Story, Japanese-American Style." *New York Times Magazine* (January 1966): 20–21, 33, 36, 38, 40–41, 43.

Pick, Daniel. *Faces of Degeneration: A European Disorder, c. 1848–1918.* Cambridge: Cambridge University Press, 1989.

Pietz, William. "The 'Postcolonialism' of Cold War Discourse." *Social Text* 18 (Summer 1988): 55–75.

Pio, Augusta. "Exclude Japanese Labor." *American Federationist* (May 1905): 274–76.

Pizer, Donald. *The Novels of Frank Norris.* Bloomington: Indiana University Press, 1960.

Pletsch, Carl. "The Three Worlds, or the Division of Social Scientific Labor, circa 1950–1975." *Comparative Study of Society and History* 23 (October 1981): 565–90.

Portelli, Allesandro. "Jack London's Missing Revolution: Notes on *The Iron Heel*." *Science Fiction Studies* 9, no. 2 (1982): 180–94.

Postone, Moishe. "Anti-Semitism and National Socialism." In *Germans and Jews since the Holocaust: The Changing Situation in West Germany*, edited by Anson Rabinbach and Jack Zipes, 302–14. New York: Holmes & Meier, 1986.

Powderly, Terence V. "Exclude Anarchist and Chinaman!" *Collier's* (December 14, 1901): 5–7.

Preston, William, Jr. *Aliens and Dissenters: Federal Repression of Radicals, 1903–1933.* New York: Harper Torchbooks, 1963.

Proctor, John. "Saxon or Slav?" *Harper's* (November 25, 1899): 1179.

Proteus. "Review of *The Good Earth* [Pearl S. Buck]." *New Statesman and Nation* (May 16, 1931): 430.

Quach, Gianna. "Chinese Fictions and the American Alternative: Pearl Buck and Emily Hahn." *Tamkang Review* 24 (Fall 1983): 75–116.

Rabinbach, Anson. *The Human Motor: Energy, Fatigue and the Origins of Modernity.* Berkeley and Los Angeles: University of California Press, 1992.

Rauschenbush, Winifred. "Their Place in the Sun: Japanese Farmers Nine Years after the Land Laws." *Survey Graphic* 56 (May 1926): 141–45, 203.

Rawlinson, Henry. *England and Russia in the East.* London: John Murray, 1875.

Reed, Ernest. "The Agricultural Program of the War Relocation Authority." Draft, May 31, 1943. Japanese American Evacuation and Resettlement Records, 1930–1974 (MSS 67/14c), E2.752. Bancroft Library, University of California at Berkeley.

————. "Termination Report on the Nature and Extent of Proposed Agricultural Program." Japanese American Evacuation and Resettlement Records, 1930–1974 (MSS 67/14c), E2.753. Bancroft Library, University of California at Berkeley.

Reisner, Marc. *Cadillac Desert: The American West and Its Disappearing Water.* New York: Penguin, 1986.

Rideout, Walter Bates. *The Radical Novel in the United States, 1900–1954.* Cambridge: Harvard University Press, 1956.

Riis, Jacob. *How the Other Half Lives.* 1890. Reprint, New York: Dover Publications, 1971.

Robinson, Greg. *By Order of the President: FDR and the Internment of Japanese Americans.* Cambridge: Harvard University Press, 2001.

Roediger, David. *Towards the Abolition of Whiteness: Essays on Race, Politics, and Working-Class History.* New York: Verso, 1994.

————. *The Wages of Whiteness: Race and the Making of the American Working Class.* New York: Verso, 1991.

Root, Elihu. "The Real Questions Under the Japanese Treaty and the San Francisco School Board Resolution." *American Journal of International Law* 1, no. 2 (April 1907): 273–86.

Rosenberg, Daniel. "The IWW and the Organization of Asian Workers in Early-20th-Century America." *Labor History* 36, no. 1 (Winter 1995): 77–87.

Ross, Edward. "The Causes of Race Superiority." *Annals of the American Academy of Political and Social Science* 18 (July 1901): 67–89.

Rothstein, Morton. "Frank Norris and Popular Perceptions of the Market." *Agricultural History* 56, no. 1 (January 1982): 50–66.

Rousseau, Jean-Jacques. *Second Discourse on the Origin and Foundations of Inequality.* In *The First and Second Discourses,* edited by Roger D. Masters, 77–181. New York: St. Martin's Press, 1964.

Rowell, Chester. "Orientophobia." *Collier's* (February 1909): 13, 29.

Rutherford, D. M. "Do We Need the Japanese Farmers?" *Pacific Rural Press* 143, no. 4 (February 21, 1942): 107.

Said, Edward. *Orientalism.* New York: Vintage, 1979.

Saito, Natsu Taylor. "Alien and Non-Alien Alike: Citizenship, 'Foreignness,' and Racial Hierarchy in American Law." *Oregon Law Review* 76, no. 2 (Summer 1977): 261–345.

Salvage, William, under the direction of R. L. Adams. *A Survey of Procedures and Possible Ways of Maintaining or Increasing the Crop Producing Powers of California Lands (With Special Reference to Sugar Beets).* Berkeley: The Giannini Foundation of Agricultural Economics for the Technical Advisory Committee of The Soil Conservation and the Domestic Allotment Administration for California. July–August 1936.

Saxton, Alexander. *The Indispensable Enemy: Labor and the Anti-Chinese Movement in California*. Berkeley and Los Angeles: University of California Press, 1971.

———. *The Rise and Fall of the White Republic: Class, Politics and Culture in Nineteenth-Century America*. New York: Verso, 1991.

Schram, Stuart. *Mao Tse-Tung*. New York: Simon & Schuster, 1967.

Scott, Joan. "The Evidence of Experience." *Critical Inquiry* 17 (Summer 1991): 773–97.

Select House Committee Investigating National Defense Migration. *Fourth Interim Report: National Defense Migration*. 77th Cong., 2d sess., May 1942.

Select House Committee to Investigate the Interstate Migration of Destitute Citizens. *Preliminary Report*. 76th Cong., 3rd sess., 1941.

Seltzer, Mark. *Bodies and Machines*. New York: Routledge, 1992.

———. "The Naturalist Machine." In *Sex, Politics, and Science in the Nineteenth-Century Novel*, edited by Ruth Bernard Yeazell, 116–47. Baltimore: Johns Hopkins University Press, 1986.

Shaffer, Robert. "Cracks in the Consensus: Defending the Rights of Japanese Americans During World War II." *Radical History Review* 72 (1998): 85–120.

Shewmaker, Kenneth. *Americans and Chinese Communists, 1927–1945: A Persuading Encounter*. Ithaca, N.Y.: Cornell University Press, 1971.

Shillinglaw, Susan. "Steinbeck and Ethnicity." In *After the Grapes of Wrath*, edited by Donald V. Coers et al., 40–57. Athens: Ohio University Press, 1995.

Shteppa, Konstantin F. *Russian Historians and the Soviet State*. New Brunswick, N.J.: Rutgers University Press, 1962.

Shuyan, Li. "Jack London in China." *Jack London Newsletter* 19 (January–April 1986): 42–46.

Siefert, E. M., Jr. Letter to Director of California Department of Agriculture William Cecil, January 10, 1942. Japanese American Evacuation and Resettlement Records, 1930–1974 (MSS 67/14c), A16.201. Bancroft Library, University of California at Berkeley.

Simpson, Caroline Chung. *An Absent Presence: Japanese Americans in Postwar Culture, 1945–1960*. Durham, N.C.: Duke University Press, 2001.

Sitkoff, Harvard. *A New Deal for Blacks: The Emergence of Civil Rights as a National Issue*. New York: Oxford University Press, 1978.

Sklar, Martin J. *The Corporate Reconstruction of American Capitalism, 1890–1916*. Cambridge: Cambridge University Press, 1988.

Skocpol, Theda, and Kenneth Finegold. "State Capacity and Economic Intervention in the Early New Deal." *Political Science Quarterly* 97 (Summer 1982): 255–78.

Slotkin, Richard. *Gunfighter Nation: The Myth of the Frontier in Twentieth-Century America*. New York: Antheneum, 1992.

Smith, Arthur. *Chinese Characteristics*. New York: Fleming H. Revell, 1894.

Snow, Edgar. "The Autobiography of Mao Tse-Tung: Boyhood of a Chinese Red." *Asia* 37 (July 1937): 481–85.

————. "The Autobiography of Mao Tse-Tung: How the Red Army Began." *Asia* 37 (September 1937): 619–22.

————. "The Autobiography of Mao Tse-Tung: The Red Army in Action." *Asia* 37 (October 1937): 683–88.

————. "The Autobiography of Mao Tse-Tung: Schooling of a Chinese Red." *Asia* 37 (August 1937): 570–76.

————. *Red Star over China.* 1938. Rev. ed., New York: Grove Press, 1968.

Snow, Helen. "An Island in Time." *New Republic* 24 (March 1973): 28–29.

Spargo, John. Review of *The Iron Heel* [Jack London]. *International Socialist Review* 8, no. 10 (April 1908): 628–29.

Spivak, Gayatri. "Can the Subaltern Speak?" In *Marxism and the Interpretation of Culture,* edited by Cary Nelson and Lawrence Grossberg, 271–313. Urbana: University of Illinois Press, 1988.

Springhall, John. "Up Guards and at Them! British Imperialism and Popular Art, 1880–1914." In *Imperialism and Popular Culture,* edited by John Mackenzie, 49–72. Manchester: Manchester University Press, 1986.

Starr, Kevin. *Endangered Dreams: The Great Depression in California.* Oxford: Oxford University Press, 1996.

————. Introduction to *The Octopus,* by Frank Norris, vii–xxxi. New York: Penguin, 1986.

Steffens, Lincoln. "California and the Japanese." *Collier's* (March 25, 1916): 5–6, 32–36.

Steinbeck, John. *Cannery Row.* 1945. Reprint, New York: Penguin, 1992.

————. "Dubious Battle in California." *Nation* 12 (September 12, 1936): 302–4.

————. *East of Eden.* 1952. Reprint, New York: Penguin, 1979.

————. "Fingers of Cloud." *Stanford Spectator* 2 (February 1924): 161–64.

————. *The Grapes of Wrath.* 1939. Reprint, New York: Penguin Books, 1992.

————. *In Dubious Battle.* 1936. Reprint, New York: Penguin, 1992.

————. "Johnny Bear." From *The Long Valley.* In *Steinbeck: The Grapes of Wrath and Other Writings, 1936–1941,* 93–110. 1938. Reprint, New York: Library of America, 1996.

————. *The Log from the Sea of Cortez.* In *Steinbeck: The Grapes of Wrath and Other Writings, 1936–1941,* 697–973. 1941. Reprint, New York: Library of America, 1996.

————. *Of Mice and Men.* In *Novels and Stories, 1932–1937,* 795–878. 1938. Reprint, New York: Library of America, 1994.

————. *Pastures of Heaven.* In *Novels and Stories, 1932–1937,* 1–169. 1932. Reprint, New York: Library of America, 1994.

————. *Their Blood is Strong: A Factual Story of the Migratory Agricultural Workers in California.* San Francisco: Simon J. Lubin Society of California, 1938.

Stimson, Henry L. *The Far Eastern Crisis.* New York: Harper & Bros., 1936.

Stout, Arthur, *Chinese Immigration and the Physiological Causes of the Decay of a Nation.* San Francisco: Agnew & Deffebach, 1862.

Strong, Edward, *The Second Generation Japanese Problem.* Stanford, Calif.: Stanford University Press, 1934.

Stross, Randall E. *The Stubborn Earth: American Agriculturalists on Chinese*

Soil, 1898–1937. Berkeley and Los Angeles: University of California Press, 1986.

Sturken, Marita. "Absent Images of Memory: Remembering and Reenacting the Japanese Internment." *Positions* 5, no. 3 (Winter 1997): 687–707.

Swain, Donald C. "The Bureau of Reclamation and the New Deal, 1933–1940." *Pacific Northwest Quarterly* 61 (July 1970): 137–46.

———. *Federal Conservation Policy, 1921–1933.* Berkeley and Los Angeles: University of California Press, 1963.

Szalay, Michael. *New Deal Modernism: American Literature and the Invention of the Welfare State.* Durham, N.C.: Duke University Press, 2000.

Takagi, Dana Y. "Asian Americans and Racial Politics." *Social Justice* 20 (Spring–Summer 1993): 115–28.

———. *The Retreat from Race: Asian-American Admissions and Racial Politics.* New Brunswick, N.J.: Rutgers University Press, 1992.

Takagi, Paul. "The Myth of 'Assimilation in American Life.'" *Amerasia* 2 (Fall 1973): 149–58.

Takaki, Ronald. *Iron Cages: Race and Culture in Nineteenth-Century America.* 1979. Reprint, New York: Oxford University Press, 1990.

———. *Strangers from a Different Shore: A History of Asian Americans.* New York: Penguin Books, 1989.

Taylor, F. W. *The Principles of Scientific Management.* New York: Harper & Bros., 1929.

Taylor, Hannis. "Representative Government for Russia." *North American Review* (January 1905): 19–26.

Taylor, Paul S. "Again the Covered Wagon." *Survey Graphic* 24, no. 7 (July 1935): 348–51, 368.

———. "Our Stakes in the Japanese Exodus." *Survey Graphic* 31 (September 1942): 373–97.

Taylor, Paul S., and Clark Kerr. "Uprisings on the Farms." *Survey Graphic* 24:1 (January 1935): 19–44.

Taylor, Paul S., and Tom Vasey. "Contemporary Background of California Labor." *Rural Sociology* 1, no. 4 (December 1936): 401–19.

———, and Tom Vasey. "Historical Background of California Farm Labor." *Rural Sociology* 1, no. 3 (September 1936): 281–95.

Taylor, Sandra C. "Evacuation and Economic Loss: Questions and Perspectives." In *Japanese Americans: From Relocation to Redress,* edited by Roger Daniels, Sandra C. Taylor, and Harry H. L. Kitano, 163–167. Salt Lake City: University of Utah Press, 1986.

———. *Jewel of the Desert: Japanese American Internment at Topaz.* Berkeley and Los Angeles: University of California Press, 1993.

Tchen, John. *Genthe's Photographs of San Francisco's Old Chinatown.* New York: Dover, 1984.

tenBroek, Jacobus, Edward N. Barnhart, and Floyd W. Matson. *Prejudice, War, and the Constitution.* Berkeley and Los Angeles: University of California Press, 1954.

Thomas, Norman. "Dark Day for Liberty." *Christian Century* (July 29, 1942): 929–31.

Thompson, Dody Weston. "Pearl Buck." In *American Winners of the Nobel Literary Prize,* edited by Warren G. French and Walter E. Kidd, 85–110. University of Oklahoma Press, 1968.

Thomson, James C., Jr. "Pearl S. Buck and the American Quest for China." In *The Several Worlds of Pearl S. Buck,* edited by Elizabeth J. Lipscomb, Frances E. Webb, and Peter Conn, 7–15. Westport, Conn.: Greenwood Press, 1994.

———. *Sentimental Imperialists: The American Experience in East Asia.* New York: Harper & Row, 1981.

———. *When China Faced West: American Reformers in Nationalist China, 1928–1937.* Cambridge: Harvard University Press, 1969.

Thorne, Christopher. *Allies of a Kind: The United States, Britain and the War Against Japan, 1941–1945.* New York: Oxford University Press, 1978.

Tokutomi, Ichiro. *Japanese-American Relations.* 2d rev. ed., New York: Macmillan, 1922.

Tong, Ben. "The Ghetto of the Mind." *Amerasia* 1 (November 1971): 1–31.

Trachtenberg, Alan. *The Incorporation of America: Culture and Society in the Gilded Age.* New York: Hill and Wang, 1982.

Travis, George. *George Kennan and the Russian-American Relationship, 1865–1924.* Athens: Ohio University Press, 1990.

Trotsky, Leon. "Trotsky and *The Iron Heel*: His Observations on the Famous Novel." *The New International* 11–12 (April 1945): 95.

Tsuji, Eiji. "Jack London and the Yellow Peril." *Jack London Newsletter* 9, no. 2 (May–August 1976): 96–99.

Tuchman, Barbara. *Stillwell and the American Experience in China 1911–45.* New York: Macmillan, 1970.

Turner, Fredrick Jackson. "The Significance of the Frontier in American History." In *The Early Writings of Frederick Jackson Turner,* 185–229. 1893. Reprint, Madison: University of Wisconsin Press, 1938.

Van Horne, Winston A., ed. *Ethnicity and War.* Milwaukee: University of Wisconsin System American Ethnic Studies Coordinating Committee, 1984.

Van Nuys, Frank W. "A Progressive Confronts the Race Question: Chester Rowell, the California Alien Land Act of 1913, and the Contradictions of Early-Twentieth-Century Racial Thought." *California History* 73 (Spring 1994): 2–13.

Von Eschen, Penny. *Race Against Empire: Black Americans and Anticolonialism, 1937–1957.* Ithaca, N.Y.: Cornell University Press, 1997.

Wald, Priscilla. *Constituting Americans: Cultural Anxiety and Narrative Form.* Durham, N.C.: Duke University Press, 1995.

Walker, Francis. "Immigration and Degradation." *Forum* 11 (August 1891): 634–44.

Walker, Franklin. *Frank Norris: A Biography.* Garden City, N.Y.: Doubleday, Doran, 1932.

Wallace, Henry. *New Frontiers.* New York: Reynal & Hitchcock, 1934.

———. *Our Job in the Pacific.* IPR Pamphlet No. 12. New York and San Francisco: American Council Institute of Pacific Relations, 1944.

———. Weekly column, *Wallaces' Farmer* 51 (October 8, 1926): 1314.

Wallinger, Michael John. "Dispersal of the Japanese Americans: Rhetorical Strategies of the War Relocation Authority 1942–1945." PhD. diss., University of Oregon, 1975. Ann Arbor, Mich.: University Microfilms International, 1984.

Wang, L. Ling-chi. "The Structure of Dual Domination: Toward a Paradigm for the Study of the Chinese Diaspora in the United States." *Amerasia* 21, nos. 1–2 (1995): 149–69.

War Relocation Authority. Transcript of "Conference on Evacuation of Enemy Aliens." Salt Lake City, Utah, April 7, 1942. Japanese American Evacuation and Resettlement Records, 1930–1974 (MSS 67/14c), C1.03. Bancroft Library, University of California at Berkeley.

———. *A Story of Human Conservation.* Washington, D.C.: Department of Interior, 1946.

———. "The Western Growers Association and Japanese Evacuation." Japanese American Evacuation and Resettlement Records, 1930–1974 (MSS 67/14c), A16.201. Bancroft Library, University of California at Berkeley.

Ward, Susan. "Ideology for the Masses: Jack London's *The Iron Heel.*" In *Critical Essays on Jack London*, edited by Jacqueline Tavernier-Courbin, 166–79. Boston: G. K. Hall, 1983.

Warne, Frank Julian. *The Slav Invasion and the Mine Workers: A Study in Immigration.* Philadelphia: J. B. Lippincott, 1904.

Warren, Kenneth. *Black and White Strangers: Race and American Literary Realism.* Chicago: University of Chicago Press, 1993.

Weglyn, Michi. *Years of Infamy: The Untold Story of America's Concentration Camps.* Reprint, Seattle: University of Washington Press, 1996.

Wei, William. *The Asian American Movement.* Philadelphia: Temple University Press, 1993.

Weiss, Robert. "Ethnicity and Reform: Minorities and the Ambience of the Depression Years." *Journal of American History* 66, no. 3 (December 1979): 566–85.

Westwood, J. N. *Russia Against Japan 1904–1905.* Albany: State University of New York Press, 1986.

White, Hayden. "The Forms of Wildness: Archeology of an Idea." In *The Wild Man Within: An Image in Western Thought from the Renaissance to Romanticism,* edited by Edward Dudley and Maximillian E. Novak, 3–38. Pittsburgh, Pa.: University of Pittsburgh Press, 1972.

White, Stewart Edward. "My Ming Collection." *Saturday Evening Post* 206, no. 11 (September 9, 1933): 12–13, 38–41.

White, Walter. *A Rising Wind.* Garden City, N.Y.: Doubleday, Doran, 1945.

Wilkie, Wendell. *One World.* New York: Simon and Shuster, 1943.

Williams, William Appleman. *The Roots of the Modern American Empire: A Study of the Growth and Shaping of Social Consciousness in a Marketplace Society.* New York: Random House, 1969.

Wilson, Christopher. "American Naturalism and the Problem of Sincerity." *American Literature* 54 (December 1982): 511–27.

Wittfogel, Karl. *Oriental Despotism: A Comparative Study of Total Power.* 1957. Reprint, New York: Vintage, 1981.

Wong, Eugene. "Asian American Middleman Minority Theory: The Framework of an American Myth." *Journal of Ethnic Studies* 13 (Spring 1985): 51–88.

Wong, Sau-ling Cynthia. "Denationalization Reconsidered: Asian American Cultural Criticism at a Theoretical Crossroads." *Amerasia* 21, nos. 1–2 (1995): 1–27.

Woodside, Alexander. "The Rise and Fall of the South East Asia Obsession in Sino-American Relations." In *Dragon and Eagle: United States–China Relations, Past and Future,* edited by Michel Oksenberg and Robert Oxnam, 302–27. New York: Basic Books, 1978.

Worster, Donald. *Rivers of Empire: Water, Aridity and the Growth of the American West.* New York: Pantheon, 1985.

Wu, William. *The Yellow Peril: Chinese Americans in American Fiction, 1850–1940.* Hamden, Conn.: Archon Books, 1982.

Yamada, Mitsuye. "Looking Out." In *Camp Notes and Other Writings.* 1976. Reprint, New Brunswick, N.J.: Rutgers University Press, 1998.

Yang Murray, Alice. "Introduction: The Internment of Japanese Americans." In *What Did the Internment of Japanese Americans Mean?* edited by Alice Yang Murray, 3–26. Boston: Bedford/St. Martin's, 2000.

Yoneda, Karl. "One Hundred Years of Japanese Labor in the U.S.A." In *Roots: An Asian American Reader,* edited by Amy Tachiki, 150–58. Los Angeles: Regents of the University of California, 1971.

Yu, Henry. *Thinking Orientals: Migration, Contact, and Exoticism in Modern America.* New York: Oxford University Press, 2001.

Yü, Yüh-chao. "Chinese Influences on Pearl S. Buck." *Tamkang Review* 2 (Fall 1980): 23–41.

Index

AAA (Agricultural Adjustment Act), 163, 170, 173, 215, 295n.34

ACLU (American Civil Liberties Union), 141, 200, 282n.4

Adams, Ansel, 201–2, 291n.129, 292n.133

Adams, Brooks, 21, 268n.16

Adams, R. L., 131–32, 135, 147, 148

AFL (American Federation of Labor), 19, 55, 115; position on Asian exclusion of, 270n.38

African Americans: potential sympathy with Japan of, 238; opposition to internment of, 282n.3; as subjects of New Deal, 142, 283n.8; and "yellow peril" discourse, 238, 299n.91

"After Strange Gods" (Norris), 48–49, 52

"Again the Covered Wagon" (Taylor), 148

Agrarian Populism. *See under* Populism

agrarianism, 58, 213; critique of, 152, 168, 185; racial figure produced by, 130; symbolism of used by New Deal agencies, 164; transplanted to China, 212, 231–32, 240–41

agriculture, in California: Bracero program, 165; centralization of by Japanese American internment, 138, 166–67; collectivization of, 192, 195; and Dust Bowl refugees, 142–44, 147, 148; industrial nature of, 114, 147; labor importation cycles in, 151–52; and labor movement, 115–16, 144–48, 150–53, 190; mechanization of, 133–35; "Oriental" character of, 193–96; overseas expansion of, 298n.83; Progressive reforms and, 132–34; racial makeup of laborers in, 145–46, 147, 148–49, 151–52; shrinking profits of, 145; controlling surplus in, 170; and post–World War I changes in industry, 135. *See also* Alien Land Laws; irrigation; Japanese American farmers; New Deal agricultural reform

agriculture, in China: and ever normal granary, 215; production management methods of as precedent for New Deal programs, 215; low productivity labor and, 219–20; rising tenancy in, 294n.31; traditional Western depictions of, 215

Aiiieeeee! (Chin et al., eds.), 204–5, 292n.5

Alien Land Law fiction, 117–30, 169. See also *Pride of Palomar; Seed of the Sun*

Alien Land Laws, 102, 108–17, 181; conservationist arguments for, 131–33; as corrective to unsustainable development, 158; and dummy whites, 91, 92, 126; lack of economic justification for, 108–9; entrepreneurism and, 110; methods of evasion of, 126–27; contribution of to poor farming practices, 157; history of, 109–10; substandard housing of farm laborers as justification for, 144–45; impact on Japanese farmers of, 111–12; moral arguments for, 130; *Oyama* vs. *California,* 110; popularity of, 108; Progressive support for, 131–32; restrictions entailed by, 110; parallels with Russian legislation of, 262n.41; social basis for, 110–11; states enacting, 110; Webb-Heney Act (1913), 110, 115, 203, 262n.41. *See also* agriculture, in California; Japanese American farmers; New Deal agricultural reform

America's Asia (Friedman and Selden), 4

American Defender, 106

An American Exodus: A Record of Human Erosion (Lange and Taylor), 167, 201

Americans Betrayed (Grodzins), 99, 100–101

anarchism, 62–63, 270n.41, 271n.44

Anglo-Japanese Alliance, 22

Anglo-Saxonism: and Asian exclusionism, 61–62; and Asiatic racial form, 51–54, 60–61, 70–72, 87–91; and threat of coolie labor, 55–56; and physical confrontations with coolies, 87–91; fecundity and, 53, 183; in Jack London, 35–36, 70–72, 86–88, 91, 93–95, 274n.93; and masculinity, 82; and meat eating, 55–57, 82; and anti-European nativism, 61–62; and nerves, 54; in Norris, 82, 86,

Anglo-Saxonism (*cont.*)
  88–93; and physiological inelasticity, 54, 268n.15. *See also* whiteness
antimonopoly fiction, 63–86, 169; Asiatic racial form in, 86. See also *Caesar's Column; The Good Earth, The Grapes of Wrath; The Iron Heel; Moran of the Lady Letty, The Octopus; Pride of Palomar; Seed of the Sun*
anti-Semitism, 59, 70, 269n.26, 273n.81; absence of in London's fiction, 70; in naturalism, 86; in *The Octopus,* 73–75; in Populism, 64; Postone's analysis of applied to Asian exclusion, 57–58
Aoki, Keith, 102
architecture, Japanese and Russian contrasted, 28
"Arms for China's Democracy" (Pearl S. Buck), 241
"Asia and Democracy" (Pearl S. Buck), 238
Asia magazine, 226
"Asian American": historical meaning of term, 284n.26; status of term in minority discourse, 2
Asian American studies: Asian exemplification and field legitimation in, 60; criticism of Pearl S. Buck in, 204–5; and Chicago school of sociology, 270n.37; history and preoccupations of, 5–6; ideological nature of sources for, 112; need of for local community research, 117; materialism in, 99–102; post-Marxism in, 6, 257n.19, 277n.33; theorization of race in, 6–7, 57, 98, 257 nn. 17 and 20, 258 nn. 27 and 31, 270n.37, 277n.33, 282 nn. 4 and 7; rural dimension of still undeveloped, 288n.88
Asian Americans: and economic modernity, 3, 112–13, 213, 244; history of literary self-expression of, 3; legal status of, 5; problems with minority status of, 2; stereotypes of, 5, 7, 11 (*see also* coolies)
Asian exclusion, 19–20, 51–58, 60–63, 146; AFL position on, 270n.38; and anarchism, 62–63, 270n.41, 271n.44; and antimonopoly fiction, 67–68; and Asian border at U.S. West Coast, 200; and China's domination of world trade, 54, 267n.13; and Chinatown bachelor societies, 190; Chinese Exclusion Act

(1882), 6, 49, 55, 66–67, 88, 267n.13, 290n.118; Chinese/Japanese distinctions in, 109; and decline of the West, 53, 267n.12, 268n.16; British Dominion policy of, 19; as component of U.S. expansionism, 20–23; Filipinos and, 20–21, 145–46, 261n.32, 284n.21; historiography of, 6–7, 98, 110–14; inspection of Chinese by immigration bureau, 63, 270n.43; Immigration Act (1903), 271n.44; and Japanese American internment, 98–103, 202–3; Japanese-Korean exclusion League, 23; and labor movement, 17, 19–20, 52, 61–62, 67, 88–89, 100, 109, 269 nn. 26 and 27, 270 nn. 34, 38, and 42; and land reform discourse, 156–57; threat to American manhood and, 55–56; McCarren-Walter Act (1952), 6; National Origins Immigration Act (1924), 51, 61–62, 101, 109, 113, 145, 181, 270n.39; and naturalism, 269n.26; in Pacific settler societies, 19–20; Page Law (1875), 290n.118; in reform movements, 57–58; in Russia, 22, 262n.41; San Francisco school segregation, 23–24, 203, 260n.22; and slavery, 20, 261 nn. 28, 30, and 31; Tydings-McDuffie Act (1934), 145–46, 284n.21; and whiteness, 20, 61, 261n.31. *See also* Alien Land Laws; Japanese American internment
"Asian Tigers" (newly industrialized countries of East Asia), 2–3, 244
Asiatic mode of production (AMP), 63–72, 194–95, 290n.119. *See also* Oriental despotism
the Asiatic question, 21, 24, 42, 46, 53; Steinbeck and, 152–53
Asiatic racial form, 6–11; and anarchism, 62–63; Anglo-Saxonism and, 51–54, 60–61, 70–72, 87–91; in antimonopoly fiction, 86; in *Caesar's Column,* 64–67; and California water policy, 139, 282n.101; in *Cannery Row,* 251–53; and crowds or hordes, 55, 63, 120–21; and decline of the West, 54–56, 95; and degeneration, 55–56; economic logic of, 13, 15–17, 25, 28–29, 30–32, 52–54, 102, 113, 158, 259n.5; hunger and, 84–86; and industrialization, 56–57; in *The Iron Heel,* 70–72; morphology of

Japanese farmers, 134–35; opposition of to nature, 93–95, 274n.96; neocoloniality of, 38; and the New Deal, 146; and Okies, 142–44, 151–53, 174, 185, 188–90; and social reform movements, 58–63; and "willing slavery," 67; Slavs said to be phenotypically Asian, 181; and Steinbeck's grotesques, 178; and Taylorism, 66; in "Thoroughbred," 49–51, 61; and unassimilability, 52; whiteness and, 35–37, 60–61, 174–78. *See also* coolies; "yellow peril" discourse

atavism, 47

Auerbach, Jonathan, 35

"The Autobiography of Mao Tse-tung, As Told to Edgar Snow" (Snow), 226, 229

Azuma, Eiichiro, 116–17

Baldwin, Roger, 200

Bankhead-Jones Farm Tenant Act (1937), 164

Bendiner, Robert, 137, 166–67

Bertillon system, 270n.43

Bertram, James, 232

Bonacich, Edna, 101

"Bonin Islands: An Incident of the Sealing Fleet of '93" (London), 12–13

Born Free and Equal (Ansel Adams), 201–2

Bracero program, 165

Buck, John Lossing, 217–20; biases in data of, 295n.45; differences of with Pearl S. Buck, 220; *Chinese Farm Economy,* 218, 234; *Land Utilization in China,* 218–19, 295n.45; on relationship of population size to living standards, 219; on productivity of Chinese farms, 220; research interests of, 217–18

Buck, Pearl S., 204–17, 232–43; accuracy of depiction of Chinese by, 205–7; on military alliance with China, 236–41; Asian American Studies' criticism of, 204–5; self-caricature of in fiction, 234–35; and CCP (Chinese Communist Party), 222–23, 241; and colonial discourse, 223; in debate with Chinese critic, 206–7; FBI investigation of, 243; personal history of, 217; and HUAC, 243; literary influences on, 207–8, 293n.19; and KMT (Kuomintang), 222–23, 296n.52; criticism of missionary enterprise by, 221–22; and Nanking uprising, 223; and Nobel Prize, 206, 207, 293n.12; as anti-Orientalist, 206; on race policy, 238–39; reputation of, 204–9; on scientific aid to China, 220; on farm technology, 240; on trade with China, 236–37; and "yellow peril" discourse, 239. *Works:* "Arms for China's Democracy," 241; "Asia and Democracy," 238; "Is There a Case for Foreign Missions?" 221; *My Several Worlds,* 222, 223, 235, 240; "Tinder for Tomorrow," 238–39; "Western Weapons in the Hands of the Reckless East," 239; "What Are We Fighting for in the Orient?" 236–37. See also *The Good Earth*

Bunje, Emil, 157, 158

Bureau of Agricultural Economics (BAE), 164

Caesar's Column (Donnelly), 63–71, 75, 86

California and the Fictions of Capital (Henderson), 135, 139

California and the Oriental (State Board of Control of California), 128, 130–32, 135, 139

California Commission of Immigration and Housing (CCIH), 114–15, 144–45, 289n.102

California Land Settlement Board, 130–31

Cannery Row (Steinbeck), 174; as first serious work with Asian character, 244; and Asiatic racial form, 251–53; representation of Chinese grocer in, 247–48, 251–52, 253–54; alternative community in, 244–45; Dust Bowl metaphors in, 249; as ecological text, 246–47, 250–54; economic crisis and magic in, 248–50; exchange in, 245, 246–49; and globalization, 253–54; property in, 245–46; Taoism in, 250–51

Carlson, Evans, 232

"The Causes of Race Superiority" (Ross), 52–54, 56

CCC (Civilian Conservation Corps), 160

CCP (Chinese Communist Party), 224, 228; on Pearl S. Buck, 222; and Comintern, 229; and presumed foreignness of communism in China, 228–29; positive impressions of by Western observers,

CCP (Chinese Communist Party) (*cont.*) 232, 241; soldiers of likened to American Revolutionary War farmer-soldiers, 240, 241. *See also* Mao Tse-tung; *Red Star over China*
Cecil, William, 137
Charlie Chan Is Dead, 3
Cheng, Lucie, 101
Chiang Kai-shek, 231, 242
Chiba, Toyoji, 114
China: "amateur phase" of writing about, 218; antiforeignism in, 237; communism presumed foreign to, 228–29; as extension of U.S. frontier, 212, 241–42; fantasy of as U.S. territory, 241–42; premodern history of viewed as cyclical, 212, 294n.30; as Western imperial goal, 20–22; in London's fiction, 40–41; Marx's analysis of as hastening European revolution, 21, 261n.35; pace of modernization of, 211; Open Door policy toward, 21–22, 262 nn. 37–38, 269n.26; as destination for political pilgrims, 233–34; postwar U.S. military interest in, 232–33; pro-nationalism of lobby for, 231–32; self-sufficiency of and possibility for foreign trade, 236; as "sleeping giant," 15–16; as a symbol of urban density, 30; relationship of to Japan in "yellow peril" discourse, 16–18, 23, 30–32, 37–38. *See also* Chinese
China Lobby, 231–32
"The Chinago" (London), 95
Chinatown (Polansky), as example of Orientalization of California water policy, 139, 196, 282n.101
Chinese: as indefatigable workers, 38; classification of, 54; cleanliness of, 30; as cooks, 80–81; difficulty in distinguishing, 63, 270n.43; fecundity of, 40; gender of, 50, 89–90, 190; nervelessness of, 54, 57; unassimilability of, 52–53. *See also* coolies
Chinese Characteristics (Smith), 54, 218
"The Chinese Communist Revolution and the Chinese Communist Party" (Mao), 228
Chinese Exclusion Act (1882), 6, 49, 55, 66–67, 88, 267n.13, 290n.118. *See also* Asian exclusion

Chinese Farm Economy (John Lossing Buck), 218, 234
Chinese Immigration and the Physiological Causes of the Decay of a Nation (Stout), 55–56
CIO (Congress of Industrial Organizations), 115
Clark, Chase, 162
Clark, Grover, 228
Cold War, 243
"Colonization and Rural Development in California" (conference, 1922), 131
Comintern, criticism of *Red Star over China* by, 229
Commission on Wartime Relocation and Internment of Civilians, 96–97
Committee of Concerned Asian Scholars, 4
Committee of One Thousand, 106
Communist Party, 141, 145
Concentration Camps (Daniels), 98, 102, 201, 291n.128
La Condition Humaine (Malraux), 222
Conn, Peter, 207
conservationist movement, 158; overlap of agencies for with internment agencies, 159. *See also* soil conservation
"Contemporary Background of California Labor" (Taylor), 147
"Cool Heads or Martial Law" (Bendiner), 137
coolies, 49–51, 54–58, 66, 67, 71, 91–95, 119, 129; as monstrous abstraction, 56–57; and anarchism, 62–63; temporal character of distinguished from "darky," 67; odd gendering of, 89–90, 266n.8; threat to American manhood of, 55–56; mass nature of, 45–46, 54–55; as symbol of dehumanizing modernism, 95; in Norris, 54–55, 89–90; in physical confrontation with Anglo-Saxons, 87–91; rice diet of, 55–57; and slavery, 20, 261 nn. 28, 30, and 31; Steinbeck on relationship of to organized labor, 151. *See also* Asiatic racial form; "yellow peril" discourse
The Corporate Reconstruction of American Capitalism (Sklar), 9, 269n.26
counterrevolution, in *The Iron Heel*, 41
Cowley, Malcolm, 205
criminal anthropology, 47, 270n.43. *See also* degeneration; miscegenation

Daniel, Cletus, 116, 144
Daniels, Roger, 98, 100, 102, 155–56, 285n.44
Dark Princess (Du Bois), 238
Darwin, Charles, theories of applied to economics, 268n.16
degeneration, 47, 50, 189, 267n.12; and "yellow peril" discourse, 55–56; in *Of Mice and Men* (Steinbeck), 175; and naturalism, 175; in Norris, 52
DeWitt, John L., 96, 97–98, 99, 103–5, 165
Dies, Martin, 172
diet: of Chinese, 64–65; of coolies, 55–57; of Japanese soldiers, 25, 29, 35
"Dr. Moffet" (London), 33–35, 42
Donnelly, Ignatius, 63–71, 75, 86
Donovan, William, 184
Drinnon, Richard, 100, 159
Drummond, David, 99, 101–2, 111, 138
Du Bois, W.E.B., 238
In Dubious Battle (Steinbeck), 143, 146, 150–51
"Dubious Battle in California" (Steinbeck), 150, 151–53, 190, 192
dummy whites, 91, 92, 126. *See also* Alien Land Laws
Dust Bowl, 142
Dust Bowl narratives, 169. See also *The Grapes of Wrath*
Dust Bowl refugees. *See* Okies
dystopian fiction, 63; by London, 14–15. See also *Caesar's Column;* "Goliah"; *The Iron Heel;* "The Unparalleled Invasion"

East of Eden (Steinbeck), 174, 253–54
Edwards, Percy, 127
Eisenhower, Milton, 159, 160, 170, 173
Engels, Frederick, 68
Eperjesi, John, 84
ethnic identity: addressing students on topic of, 1–2; in "Looking Out," 1
Executive Order 9066, 96, 102, 159, 201, 275n.1. *See also* Japanese American internment

Factories in the Field (McWilliams), 191–97
Fairbank, John, 224–25, 230
"Farm Labor" (R. L. Adams), 148

Farmers of Forty Centuries (King), 217
Farnsworth, Harley, 228
FBI: and Japanese Americans, 97; ranking by of Japanese American suspects, 106
FERA (Federal Emergency Relief Administration), 164
Final Report: Japanese Evacuation from the West Coast, 1942 (DeWitt), 103–5
"Fingers of a Cloud" (Steinbeck), 146
First International (International Workingman's Association), 67
food. *See* diet
Food for Freedom program, 106–7, 165
Friedman, Edward, 4
frontier, 18–24, 52–54, 82, 268n.16; displacement of to Chinese countryside, 212, 233; extension of to East Asia, 16–17, 241–44; Jack London on shrinking of, 268n.16; Norris on, 77, 82; and "savage war," 267n.14; elusiveness of U.S.-Asian, 53–54
"The Frontier Gone at Last" (Norris), 77, 82
FSA (Farm Security Administration), 138, 144, 159, 160, 162, 164, 165–66, 173

George, Henry, 66–67, 68, 267n.13
"Give Battle to Retard Enemy" (London), 35, 43–44
gold rush, 19
"Goliah" (London), 39–41
Gompers, Samuel, 55–56, 61; *Meat versus Rice,* 55–56, 57, 82, 88–89, 89 fig. 1
The Good Earth (Pearl S. Buck), 204–17, 224–32, 234–37, 239–41, 242; accumulation in, 214, 294n.32; as Horatio Alger story, 205, 211, 294n.28; instrumentality of to U.S.-China alliance, 237; anti-technology in, 240; as authority for Buck's Sino-Japanese war texts, 237; Chinese critics on, 206; class-conflict cyclical in, 211–12; communist movement depicted in, 226–28; conservationism in, 215; film adaptation of, 233, 294n.32; foreign woman in, 234–35; freedom in, 235–36; labor as antidote to sexual desire in, 212–13; protagonist of compared to Mao Tse-tung, 225–26, 229; representation of missionaries in, 221, 295n.47; noble savage in, 216; political economy of, 209–17; popularity

The Good Earth (*cont.*)
of, 204, 208, 224, 226; and
production/consumption balance,
214–15; and proletarian literature,
208–9, 293n.26; sentimentality of, 207;
skin color in, 216; as source of stereotype, 205
granary, ever normal, 215
The Grapes of Wrath (Steinbeck), 143,
146, 174, 186–87, 190; ancestral Asian
presence in, 153; counterhegemonic sub-
plots in, 152; machines as monsters in,
240–41; physical description in, 149;
sales success of, 283n.13; fall of the yeoman farmer in, 168–69
Greater East Asian Co-Prosperity Sphere,
239
Gregory, James, 143,
Grodzins, Morton, 99, 100–101, 113–14
Grower-Shipper Association, 99
Gulliver, Uncle Sam as, 89 fig. 1
Gunfighter Nation (Slotkin), 267n.14
Gunreibu, 97

Hays, John, 22
Head, Wade, 173
Henderson, George, 128, 135, 139
Higgs, Robert, 111
Higham, John, 60
Hindess, Barry, 69
Hirabayashi, James, 98, 99–100
Hirabayashi, Lane, 98, 99–100
Hirst, Paul, 69
Hobson, J. A., 57
Hofstader, Richard, 58–59, 88
homoeroticism, in "The Story of Port
Arthur," 26
How the Other Half Lives (Riis), 29,
59–60
HUAC (House Un-American Activities
Committee), 172, 232, 297n.69
Huk guerrillas, 224
Hunt, Michael, 206

Ignatius Donnelly, 213
Immigration Act (1903), 271n.44. *See also*
anarchism; Asian exclusion
imperialism, American, 53–54; and China,
20–22; implications of for late
nineteenth-century racial formation, 9;
nonterritorial nature of, 10

imperialism, Western: struggle for Asia of,
23
indispensable enemy: the Asiatic as labor's,
152
INS (Immigration and Naturalization Service), 145, 284n.21
Intercollegiate Socialist Society, 42
internment. *See* Japanese American
internment
The Iron Heel (London), 14–15, 38–39,
41–44, 51, 62, 64, 68–72, 86, 95,
266n.92
irrigation, 121, 131, 139; and Asiatic
racial form, 139, 282n.101; Wheeler-
Case program, 160
Irwin, Wallace, 117, 124–30, 133, 157,
279 nn. 65–66; labor movement portrayed by, 129; *Seed of the Sun*, 117,
124–30, 133–34, 135, 157, 169, 176
"Is There a Case for Foreign Missions?"
(Pearl S. Buck), 221
Isaacs, Harold, 204, 224
Iwata, Masakazu, 111
IWW (Industrial Workers of the World),
115, 116, 128, 129, 145

James, Thomas, 160–61
Japan: as alternatively figured by Progressivism and socialism, 37–38; architecture
of contrasted with Russia, 28; cleanliness of Japanese, 30; in Kennan's Port
Arthur reports, 24–32, 37–38; in London's fiction, 12–13, 33–35, 37–40, 42;
militarism of, 16–17, 38, 263n.52; in
discourses of modernity, 30–32; U.S.
racism and support for, 238–39; rice diet
of Japanese, 35; cultural differences of
with Russia, 23; ambivalence of United
States toward, 23, 263n.49; relationship
of to China in "yellow peril" discourse,
16–18, 23, 30–32, 37–38
"Japan Puts an End to the Usefulness of
Correspondents" (London), 32–33, 37
Japan–United States war scare (1907), 19,
24, 103
"If Japan Wakens China" (London), 15–16
Japanese American Evacuation and Resettlement Project (JERS), 99
Japanese American farmers: agricultural
practices of, 140, 157–58, 161, 167;
concentration of land of after intern-

ment, 138, 166–67; unreliability of statistical data on, 112; socially indeterminate status of in fiction, 129; history of, 109; poor quality housing of, 144–45; and hygiene, 106; and stoop labor, 134–35, 147–48, 157–58; and luxury foods, 107; replacement of by Okies, 166–67; and Populism, 130; in *Pride of Palomar,* 117–24; racial form of, 135–36; potential for sabotage of, 96–97, 102, 103–8, 113–14, 275n.7; and land speculators, 128; Steinbeck on, 151; apparent upward mobility of, 112–13, 116, 129–30; and wartime agricultural production, 137–38. *See also* Japanese American internment

Japanese American fishermen, 106, 276n.25

Japanese American internment, 96–108; and agricultural policy, 103–8, 113, 137–38; and corporate consolidation of agriculture, 138, 166–67; and Asian exclusion movement, 98–103, 202–3; and belief internees would want to stay, 156, 173; debates over causes of, 7; production of model citizens by, 200–201; Commission on Wartime Relocation and Internment of Civilians, 96–97; camps compared to concentration camps, 197–98, 291n.124; and conservation policy, 158, 159–63; economic motives behind, 99–101, 102; and demystification of efficiency of Asian labor, 171; Executive Order 9066, 96, 102, 159, 201, 275n.1; and FBI ranking of suspects, 106; delayed federal responsibility for management of, 159–60; work furlough program, 160; historiography of, 98–99, 102; internees as replacement labor for New Deal programs, 161; source of camp land for, 160; liberal position on, 141, 153–56, 282n.1, 282 nn. 3–4; and loyalty of Japanese Americans, 107–8, 200, 288n.88, 289n.100; Manzanar, 201; Carey McWilliams on, 153–56; and national minority question, 199; and New Deal, 141–42; and creation of Pacific Rim, 200–203; rumored pampering in camps, 172–73; photography of internees, 201–2, 291–92 nn. 129–30, 292n.133; Poston, 288n.87; productivity

of camps, 170–71; and promotion of second-generation Japanese, 185; as protective custody from racial terrorism, 161–62; as racial integration strategy, 155–56, 162, 199, 201, 284n.45; rationality of, 101; as federal reconstruction of California, 202; and Franklin Roosevelt, 97, 98; and source of rumors of Japanese espionage, 285n.44; and threat of sabotage, 96–97, 102, 103–8, 113–14, 275n.7; Steinbeck on, 183–85; strategic installations argument for, 103–6, 139; Tolan Committee, 139, 143; transfer of evacuated farms, 165–66, 278n.48; low wages paid to internees, 171–72; War Relocation Authority (WRA), 141, 159–62, 170, 171–72, 173, 185, 200–201; Western Growers and Shippers Association stand on, 136. *See also* Japanese American farmers

Japanese Americans (Petersen), 153–54, 282n.1

Japanese Americans: portrayal of as individuals in photography, 201–2; utility of for U.S. Pacific Rim interests, 200; prehistory of racialization of, 174–203. *See also* Japanese American farmers; Japanese American internment

"Japanese in Invisible War" (London), 33, 43

"Japanese Officers Consider Everything a Military Secret" (London), 32–33

"Japanese Supplies Rushed to Front by Man and Beast" (London), 45–46

Jeffersonian agrarianism. *See* agrarianism

Joad family, 149; discussed as if living, 143

"Johnny Bear" (Steinbeck), 176–78, 186, 253

Johnson, Hiram, 115

Judd, Walter, 231

The Jungle (Sinclair), 273n.76

Kaplan, Amy, 267n.14

Keeper of Concentration Camps (Drinnon), 159

Kennan, George, 18, 24–38; homoeroticism in, 26; differences of with London on characterization of Japanese, 36–38; "The Story of Port Arthur," 24–38

Kiang Kang-Hu, 206–7

Kiangsi, 224

King, F. H., 217
"King of the Greeks" (London), 94
Kingston, Maxine Hong, 204
Kittredge, Charmian, 36–37
KMT (Kuomintang), 222, 224, 231, 241
Knox, Frank, 97
Korea, as setting for London's Russo-Japanese War coverage, 32, 34–35, 45–46
Koshy, Susan, 60
Kyne, Peter, 117–24, 125, 127, 128, 133; *Pride of Palomar*, 117–24, 125, 127, 128, 133, 169, 279n.65

labor movement: AFL (American Federation of Labor), 19, 55, 115, 270n.38; antiracism in, 115, 116, 270n.42; foundational status of Asian exclusion to, 19; position of toward Asian immigration, 17, 19–20, 52, 61–62, 67, 88–89, 100, 109, 269 nn. 26 and 27, 270 nn. 34, 38, and 42; and California agriculture, 115–16, 144–48, 190; CIO (Congress of Industrial Organizations), 115; IWW (Industrial Workers of the World), 115, 116, 128, 129, 145; Jack London and, 17, 39; relationship of to naturalism in shaping Asian exclusion, 269n.26; negative portrayal of in *Seed of the Sun*, 129; Socialist Labor Party of California, 15; Steinbeck on, 150–53; suppression of, 151, 283n.13; Tagus ranch peach pickers' strike, 146; unpatriotic implications of support for, 150–51; Wheatland hop picker's strike, 114, 144
Laclau, Ernesto, 6
Land Utilization in China (John Lossing Buck), 218–19; biases in data of, 295n.45
Lange, Dorothea, 167, 201, 289n.103, 291n.129, 292n.130
Lao Tze, 251–52
The Law of Civilization and Decay (Brooks Adams), 268n.16
Lea, Homer, 24
Lenin, V. I., 57, 269n.24
Lewis, Cliff, 184
liberalism: complicity of in Alien Land Law legislation, 115, 139, 156–58; complicity of in Japanese American internment, 141, 156; totalitarian, 141,

153–54, 282n.3. *See also* Petersen, William
Liberals and the War Crisis (McWilliams), 198–99
Lippman, Walter, 141
The Log from the Sea of Cortez (Steinbeck), 250–51, 253, 254
Lombroso, Cesare, 47
London, Jack, 12–18; Anglo-Saxonism and, 35–36, 70–72, 86–88, 91, 93–95, 274n.93; and Pearl S. Buck on race policy, 238–39; representations of China by, 40–41; counterrevolution in fiction of, 15, 259n.7, 266n.92; critical reception of, 13, 259 nn. 3 and 7; dystopian fiction of, 14–15, 38–44, 265n.91; on shrinking frontier, 268n.16; as hyper-professionalized writer, 35–36, 265n.87; representations of Japan by, 36–40, 42; Japanese censors and, 32–33, 37, 42, 43, 44, 46, 264n.67; letters by to Charmian Kittredge, 36–37; and labor movement, 17, 39; and the critique of modernism, 36–37; noble savage in, 13, 259 nn. 4 and 5; and overpopulation, 268n.16; physique in, 51; and Polynesian effect, 274n.98; primitivism in, 35–36; and "red-blooded" school of literature, 82, 273n.76; race war with Asia in, 38–41; and the Russo-Japanese War, 17–18, 32–37, 42–44; socialism of, 15, 37–39, 42, 70–72, 259 nn. 7, 8, and 10, 260n.11, 266n.96, 271n.61; trends in scholarship about, 15, 260n.11; destabilized whiteness in, 36–37, 43–44, 46; symbolic wildernesses in, 35–36, 93–94, 265n.80; writing career of, 12; and "yellow peril" discourse, 15–18, 30, 36–46, 71–72. Works: "Bonin Islands: An Incident of the Sealing Fleet of '93," 12–13; "The Chinago," 95; "Dr. Moffet," 33–35, 42; "Give Battle to Retard Enemy," 35, 43–44; "Goliah," 39–41; "If Japan Wakens China," 15–16; *The Iron Heel*, 14–15, 38–39, 41–44, 51, 62, 64, 68–72, 86, 95, 266n.92; "Japan Puts an End to the Usefulness of Correspondents," 32–33, 37; "Japanese in Invisible War," 33, 43; "Japanese Officers Consider Everything a Military Secret," 32–33; "Japanese Supplies Rushed to Front by

Man and Beast," 45–46; "King of the Greeks," 94; "The Monkey Cage," 33, 35; *The People of the Abyss,* 72; "The Plague Ship," 87; "The Run Across," 12; *The Sea Wolf,* 51; "Story of a Typhoon off the Coast of Japan," 12; *Tales of the Fish Patrol,* 51, 93–94; "The Unparalleled Invasion," 40–41, 265n.91; "The Yellow Peril," 15–18, 38, 239, 266n.99
Long March, 224, 233
"Looking Out" (Yamada), 1
Loti, Pierre, 48
Luce, Henry, 231
Lukács, Georg, 8, 86–87

Mackinder, Halford, 23
Madama Butterfly (Puccini), 48
Madame Chrysanthemum (Loti), 48
Mahan, Alfred T., 21, 22, 23, 263 nn. 45–46
Malraux, André, 222
Manchuria. *See* Russo-Japanese War
Manzanar, 201
Mao Tse-tung, 224–26, 228, 229; "autobiography" of, 225–26; compared to protagonist of *The Good Earth,* 225–26, 229. See also *Red Star over China*
Marx, Karl, 21, 68; on China, 21
masculinity: in Norris, 81–82; as racializing trope, 50
Matthews, Blayney, 106
McCarren-Walter Act (1952), 6. *See also* Asian exclusion
McCarthyism, 231–32, 242
McClure's Magazine, 72
McKinley, William, assassination of, 62
McTeague (Norris), 51, 90, 175, 288n.91
McWilliams, Carey, 108, 110, 127, 153–56, 167, 173, 190–99, 200, 202, 203; changing position on Japanese American internment, 154–55. *Works: Factories in the Field,* 191–97; *Liberals and the War Crisis,* 198–99; "Moving the West Coast Japanese," 155–56, 197, 197, 199; *Prejudice,* 154, 199, 200, 203; "Yellow Peril," 127
Mead, Elwood, 130–31, 156
Mears, Elliot, 134–35
Meat versus Rice (Gompers), 55–56, 57, 82, 88–89, 89 fig. 1

Michaels, Walter Benn, 8
Mink, Gwendolyn, 61
"minority," student perceptions of term, 1–2
miscegenation: in "After Strange Gods," 48; in "Johnny Bear," 176–77; in London's fiction, 35–36
missionaries, in China, 237
Mitchell, Don, 144, 146
"model minority" myth: difficulties in dispelling, 4; origins of, 2, 112, 172, 244, 277n.40, 255n.6, 257n.16; relationship of to "yellow peril" discourse, 5, 38, 258n.31
"The Monkey Cage" (London) 33, 35
Monroe, Paul, 228
Moore, Chester, 136, 137
Moran of the Lady Letty (Norris), 51, 89–93
Mouffe, Chantal, 6
Mount Weather Agreement, 159
"Moving the West Coast Japanese" (McWilliams), 155–56, 197, 199
Mowry, George, 115
multiculturalism, relationship of race scholarship to, 5–6
Munson, Curtis B., 97
My Several Worlds (Pearl S. Buck), 222, 223, 235, 240
Myer, Dillon, 159, 161
Myths and Facts about Japanese Americans (War Relocation Authority), 161

NAACP (National Association for the Advancement of Colored People), 204, 238
Nanking uprising, 222–23
National Life and Character (Pearson), 268n.15
National Origins Immigration Act (1924), 51, 61–62, 101, 109, 113, 145, 181, 270n.39. *See also* Asian exclusion
National Program of Rural Rehabilitation, 164
National Review, 141
National Security Council (NSC), 243
naturalism, 7–9, 47, 57, 246; anti-Semitism in, 86; and labor movement in shaping of Asian exclusion, 269n.26; Asiatic in, 86; and autonomy of the subject, 86–87; as failed critique of capitalism, 8; coolies symbolic of dehumanizing

naturalism (*cont.*)
modernism in, 95; critical approaches to, 269n.25; and degeneration, 175; and the grotesque, 208; Lukács's critique of, 86–87; representations of monopoly capitalism in, 57, 269n.26; and Orientalization of modernity, 69; preoccupation of with physique, 7, 51, 56–57, 70–71; primitive in, 51, 56; relationship of to Progressivism, 7–8; relationship of to proletarian literature, 208–9; distinguished from realism, 86, 273n.83; and Steinbeck, 149–50, 175; taxonomic slipperiness of, 87

New Deal, 141, 153; African American subjects of, 142, 283n.8; few Asian Americans served by, 142, 283n.9; conservation and, 169–70; national defense rhetoric of, 191; problem of surplus for, 170

New Deal agricultural reform, 163–67; agrarian symbolism used in, 164; precedent for in Chinese agricultural management methods, 215; and Japanese American internment, 153–56, 165–66; migrant labor camps built by, 165; price and surplus control schemes of, 163, 295n.34; and rural rehabilitation, 163–65

noble savage: in *The Good Earth*, 216; in Jack London, 13, 259 nn. 4 and 5; in Norris, 81; in Steinbeck, 146, 284n.24

Norris, Frank 47–55, 58, 62, 72–86; Anglo-Saxonism and, 82, 86, 88–93; representation of coolies by, 54–55, 89–90; on the frontier, 77, 82; masculinity in, 49–51, 82–83, 89–90; nativism in, 73–74; Orientalism in, 47–51; physique in, 51, 175; and "red-blooded" school of literature, 82, 273n.76; reputation of, 72. *Works*: "After Strange Gods," 48–49, 52; "The Frontier Gone at Last," 77, 82; *McTeague* (Norris), 51, 90, 175, 288n.91; *Moran of the* Lady Letty, 51, 89–93; "Outward and Visible Signs," 47, 48; *The Pit*, 77; "She and the Other Fellow," 47–48; "Thoroughbred," 49–51, 54–55, 62, 90, 93. See also *The Octopus*

Norton, Henry Kittredge, 228

The Octopus, 51, 64, 72–86, 88, 122; anti-Semitic representations in, 74–75; commodity exchange and trade in, 75–77; consumption and hunger in, 78–86, 273n.75; critical interpretations of, 73, 272 nn. 65–66; beset masculine body in, 82–83; nativism in, 73–74; popularity of, 72; wheat as inspiration for, 72, 272n.74

Of Mice and Men (Steinbeck), 143, 174–76, 178, 186, 245, 251; degeneration in, 175

Okies, 142–44, 147–49, 191–92, 283n.13; Americanness of, 150, 152, 153; anthropomorphized as frogs in *Cannery Row*, 249; complex relationship to the Asiatic of, 153; compared to Chinese immigrants, 143, 151–52; coolie ancestry of, 189–90; in Dust Bowl narratives, 167–69; not exploitable like minority labor, 191; and genetic superiority, 187–88; as recipients of Japanese internee land, 166; association of with Japanese internees, 166–67; Joad family 143, 149; labor camp suggested for, 143; dismal living conditions of, 188–89; morphology of, 148; relationship of name to racial slurs, 284n.14; Steinbeck on, 151–52; uncertain whiteness of, 148–49. See also *The Grapes of Wrath*

Okihiro, Gary, 99, 101–2, 111, 138
Olsen, Culbert, 154, 190, 191
One World (Wilkie), 243, 300n.102
"Open Door Notes" (Hays), 22, 223
Open Door policy, 21–22, 262 nn. 37–38, 269n.26
Opium Wars, 21, 261n.35
organized labor. *See* labor movement
"Oriental agriculture," 193–96
Oriental despotism, 22, 34, 36, 68–69, 215–16, 233; California water policy and, 139–40; Russia as example of, 23; totalitarianism derived from, 216; unwitting U.S. support for, 242. *See also* Asiatic mode of production
Orientalism (Said), 3
Orientalism: American, 3; in Pearl S. Buck, 204–5, Californian, 51, 86, 90, 194–97; in McWilliams, 193–96; in Norris, 47–48; in Populist movement, 64–65; in Steinbeck, 174, 250–54

"Our Stakes in the Japanese Exodus" (Lange and Taylor), 201
The Outlook, 18, 24
"Outward and Visible Signs" (Norris), 47, 48
Overland Monthly, 47
Oyama vs. California, 110. See also Alien Land Laws
Takao Ozawa vs. United States, 62, 127

The Pacific Cruise, 19, 260n.22
Pacific Rim, 19, 243, 254; role of Japanese American internment in creating, 200–203
Page Law (1875), 290n.118. See also Asian exclusion
Pastures of Heaven (Steinbeck), 179–86, 250
Pearl Harbor, 96–97, 101, 107, 184, 276n.21; and rumors of secret signals from farmers, 106
Pearson, Charles, 268n.15
Peffer, Nathaniel, 228
The People of the Abyss (London), 72
Personal Justice Denied (Commission on Wartime Relocation and Internment of Civilians), 96–97
Petersen, William, 141, 153–54, 282 nn. 1 and 3
physique: in Jack London, 51; in naturalism, 7, 51, 56–57, 70–71; in Norris, 51, 175
Pick, Daniel, 50, 56
The Pit (Norris), 77
"The Plague Ship" (London), 87
political pilgrims, 233–34
The Politics of Prejudice (Daniels), 100
Popular Front, 141, 197, 232, 241–43
Populism, 58–59, 63–64; agrarian, 58; anti-Semitism and, 64; Asian exclusionism in, 57–58, 61–63; and Asiatic racial form, 58–63; and fictions of ordinary lived experience, 208; and Japanese farmers, 130; Orientalism in, 64–65;
Port Arthur siege, 24–32. See also Russo-Japanese War; "The Story of Port Arthur"
Poston, 173, 288n.87. See also Japanese American internment
Postone, Moishe, 57–58
Powderly, Terence, 62–63

Prejudice (McWilliams), 154, 199, 200, 203
Prejudice, War, and the Constitution (ten-Broek et al.), 99, 100
Preston, William, 59
Pride of Palomar (Kyne), 117–24, 125, 127, 128, 133, 169, 279n.65
primitive: in Jack London, 35–36; in naturalism, 51, 56; in Steinbeck, 178. See also noble savage
Progress and Poverty (George), 68
Progressivism, 57, 115, 189; and support for Alien Land Laws, 131–32; Asian exclusionism in, 57–58; and conservationist movement, 158; difference between efforts of on behalf of Asian and Mexican farm workers, 145; relationship of to literary naturalism, 7–8, 72; and racial taxonomy, 134. See also Simon J. Lubin Society
proletarian literature, 72, 208–9, 293n.26
Proposition 209, 2
Puccini, 48

Quach, Gianna, 223

RA (Resettlement Administration), 162, 163–64. See also FSA (Farm Security Administration)
race. See Anglo-Saxonism; anti-Semitism; Asian exclusion; Asiatic racial form; coolies; whiteness; "yellow peril" discourse
racial rent premium, 101, 102, 111
realism: American tradition of 46; in Pearl S. Buck, 205–9; California rural, 128; distinguished from naturalism, 86, 273n.83; and control of urban space, 264n.65. See also naturalism
Red Star over China (Snow), 224–31, 242–43; Comintern criticism of, 229; as critique of U.S. pro-nationalist policy, 242; Chinese communism as indigenous movement in, 229–30; cultural influence of, 224–25; as American frontier tale, 230–31, 233; exposure of Kuomintang corruption in, 242; Long March as adventure story in, 233; popularity of, 224–25, 226, 296n.55; used as training manual, 224
Reed, Ernest, 170–71

Ricketts, Edward F., 250
Riis, Jacob, 29, 59–60, 63, 264n.65
The Rising Tide of Color (Stoddard), 238
Roberts, Owen J., 97
Robinson, Greg, 98
Roediger, David, 20, 61
Roosevelt, Franklin Delano, 142, 143,
    153, 163, 169, 184, 232; and Japanese
    American internment, 97, 98; and sym-
    pathy to aliens, 291n.123
Roosevelt, Theodore, 24, 52, 103,
    263n.50; and Nobel Prize, 260n.18
Ross, Edward A., 52–54, 56
Rowell, Chester, 189
"The Run Across" (London), 12
Russia: Asian exclusion in, 22, 262n.41;
    relations of with Great Britain, 22–23; in
    Kennan's Port Arthur reports, 24–32; as
    Oriental despotic power, 23; semi-Asi-
    atic conditions of development of, 228;
    in U.S. popular culture, 23, 263n.48
Russo-Japanese War, 18, 22–24, 239;
    Great Britain's interests in, 22–23, 43;
    Kennan's reporting on, 24–32; London's
    reporting on, 17–18, 32–37, 42–44; and
    Port Arthur seige, 24; and seapower vs.
    landpower debate, 23, 263n.46; U.S. in-
    terests in, 23; and "yellow peril" dis-
    course, 22–24, 239

Said, Edward, 3
Salvage, William, 132–33
San Francisco Examiner, 17, 36
Saxton, Alexander, 19, 61, 66, 100
Sea of Cortez (Steinbeck and Ricketts),
    250. See also *The Log from the Sea of
    Cortez*
The Sea Wolf (London), 51
Seed of the Sun (Irwin), 117, 124–30,
    133–34, 135, 157, 169, 176; labor
    movement portrayed in, 129
Selden, Mark, 4
"She and the Other Fellow" (Norris),
    47–48
Shima, George: criticized for reclaiming
    wetlands, 157; short legs of said to allow
    him to work faster, 148
Simon J. Lubin Society, 187, 289n.102
Sinclair, Upton, 42, 273n.76
Sino-Japanese War, 232, 236, 237, 239,
    240

Sklar, Martin J., 9, 269n.26
slavery: and Asian exclusion, 20, 51, 261
    nn. 28, 30, and 31; as defining object of
    working class, 61
Slotkin, Richard, 267n.14
smallpox, 49
Smith, Arthur, 54, 218
Snow, Edgar, 224–25; "The Autobiography
    of Mao Tse-tung, As Told to Edgar
    Snow," 226, 229; pioneer origins of,
    230. See also *Red Star over China*
Snow, Helen, 208
socialism: and China trade, 267n.13; First
    International (International Working-
    man's Association), 67; Intercollegiate
    Socialist Society, 42; and Jack London,
    15, 37–39, 42, 70–72, 259 nn. 7, 8, and
    10, 260n.11, 266n.96; Orientalization of
    corporate oligarchy in, 42–44; pervasive-
    ness in of Asian exclusionism, 57–58;
    Socialist Labor Party of California, 15;
    Socialist Party, 141
Socialist Labor Party of California, 15
Socialist Party, 141
soil conservation, 156–61; and tenant
    farming, 132–33; practices of repre-
    sented in fiction, 133–34; Soil Conserva-
    tion and Domestic Allotment Adminis-
    tration, 132–33; Soil Conservation
    Service (SCS), 159
Spanish Civil War, 233–34
The Spectre of Sabotage (Matthews), 106
Starr, Kevin, 146
Steinbeck, John, 142, 143, 144; people as
    animals in, 149–50, 175–78; and indige-
    nous status of Asian Americans, 192–93,
    253; Asian characters in, 146, 183, 244–
    54; and Asiatic question, 152–53; on
    coolies and organized labor, 151; cri-
    tique of colonial capitalism by, 241; and
    Eastern philosophy, 250–51; and govern-
    ment reform, 192, 197; grotesque in,
    178, 182–83; intelligence report by on
    Japanese Americans, 184–85; anti-
    Japanese spying parodied by, 183–85; on
    Japanese American farmers, 151; and
    labor movement, 150–53; machines as
    monsters in, 240–41; and naturalism,
    149–50, 175; and the noble savage, 146,
    182–84, 284n.24; on Okie and Asian
    farmers, 151–52; Oriental themes in,

174; primitivism in, 178; racial views of, 192; and regional literature, 178–79. *Works*: "Dubious Battle in California," 150, 151–53, 190, 192; *East of Eden,* 174, 253–54; "Fingers of a Cloud," 146; *In Dubious Battle,* 143, 146, 150–51; "Johnny Bear," 176–78, 186, 253; *The Log from the Sea of Cortez,* 250–51, 253, 254; *Of Mice and Men,* 143, 174–76, 178, 186, 245, 251; —, degeneration in, 175; *Pastures of Heaven,* 179–86, 250; *Sea of Cortez,* 250; *Their Blood Is Strong,* 187–89. See also *Cannery Row*; *The Grapes of Wrath*

Stillwell, Joseph, 231
Stimson, Henry L., 96; doctrine of, 233
Stoddard, Lothrop, 238
"Story of a Typhoon off the Coast of Japan" (London), 12
A Story of Human Conservation (War Relocation Authority), 159, 160, 161–62, 167
The Story of Japanese Farming (Bunje), 111, 157, 158
"The Story of Port Arthur" (Kennan), 24–38; homoeroticism in, 26
Stout, Arthur, 55–56, 268n.19
Sun Yat-sen, 211, 231

Tagus ranch peach-pickers' strike, 146
Tales of the Fish Patrol (London), 51, 93–94
Tao Teh Ching, 250
Taro, Katsura, 24
Taylor, Paul, 147–48, 167, 201
Taylorism, 66
tenBroek, Jacobus, 99, 100
tenements, 59; characterized as Asian, 29–30
Their Blood Is Strong (Steinbeck), 187–89
"Their Blood Is Strong" photograph (Lange), 188
Thomas, Dorothy Swaine, 141
Thomas, Norman, 141
Thompson, James, 222
"Thoroughbred" (Norris), 49–51, 54–55, 62, 90, 93
"Tinder for Tomorrow" (Pearl S. Buck), 238–39
Tolan Committee, 139, 143. See also Japanese American internment

Trachtenberg, Alan, 90
trade unions. See labor movement
Trotsky, 228–29; on *The Iron Heel,* 43, 266n.92
Turner, Fredrick Jackson, 52, 77
Tydings-McDuffie Act (1934), 145–46, 284n.21. See also Asian exclusion

Uncle Sam, as Gulliver, 89 fig. 1
unions. See labor movement
United States vs. *Baghat Singh Thind,* 62
"The Unparalleled Invasion" (London), 40–41, 265n.91
"Uprisings on the Farms" (Taylor and Kerr), 148
utopian fiction. See dystopian fiction

Vietnam War, and America's Asia, 4

Wallace, Henry, 215, 243
Wallace's Farmer, 215
Walsh, Richard, 226
War Relocation Authority (WRA), 141, 159–62, 170, 171–72, 173, 185, 200–201. See also Japanese American internment
Warren, Earl, 96, 141
Warren, Kenneth, 67
Webb-Heney Act (1913), 110, 115, 203, 262n.41. See also Alien Land Laws
Weglyn, Michi, 98
Welles, Sumner, 238
Western Growers and Shippers Association, 113, 136
Western Growers Protective Association, 108
"Western Weapons in the Hands of the Reckless East" (Pearl S. Buck), 239
"What Are We Fighting for in the Orient?" (Pearl S. Buck), 236–37
wheat, California economy of, 273n.79. See also *The Octopus*
Wheatland hop picker's strike, 114, 144
Wheeler-Case program, 160
white slavery, 20
whiteness: constituted through Asian exclusion, 20, 61, 127, 261n.31; and Asiatic racial form, 60–61; of iconic Great Depression figures, 142; instability of as category, 61–62; destabilized form of in Jack London, 36–37, 39, 43–44, 46; of

whiteness (*cont.*)
   migrant workers in literature, 146; and
   racial uncertainty of Okies, 148–49;
   wages of, 109. *See also* Anglo-
   Saxonism
Wilhelm II, Kaiser, 22
Wilkie, Wendell, 243, 300n.102
Wilson, Woodrow, 203
Wittfogel, Karl, 140, 215
Wobblies. *See* IWW (Industrial Workers of
   the World)
World's Fair, Chicago (World's Columbian
   Exposition, 1893), as setting for Norris,
   48–49, 52
WPA (Works Progress Administration),
   160

Yamada, Mitsuye, 1
Years of Infamy (Weglyn), 98
"The Yellow Peril" (London), 15–18, 38,
   239, 266n.99
"Yellow Peril" (McWilliams), 127

The Yellow Peril (painting), 22, 262n.42
"yellow peril" discourse, 12–46, 55–56,
   67, 89, 108, 121–22, 151, 184; and
   African Americans, 238, 299n.91;
   Anglo-American formulation of, 19, 23;
   beginnings of, 18–19; as anticolonial nationalism, 10; and Pearl S. Buck, 239; relationship of China and Japan in, 16–18,
   23, 30–32, 38; and degeneration, 55–
   56; in Germany, 22, 262n.42; and
   nineteenth-century immigration, 18–19;
   and invisibility of Asiatics, 55; as means
   of labor suppression, 152; and Jack London, 15–18, 30, 36–46, 71–72; and
   "model minority" discourse, 5, 38; in
   rural setting, 114; in Russia, 22–23; relationship of Russia and Japan in, 23; and
   the Russo-Japanese War, 22–24, 239;
   and American socialism, 15; parody of
   by Steinbeck, 183–85. *See also* Asian exclusion; Asiatic racial form; coolies
yeoman farmer, 58, 212